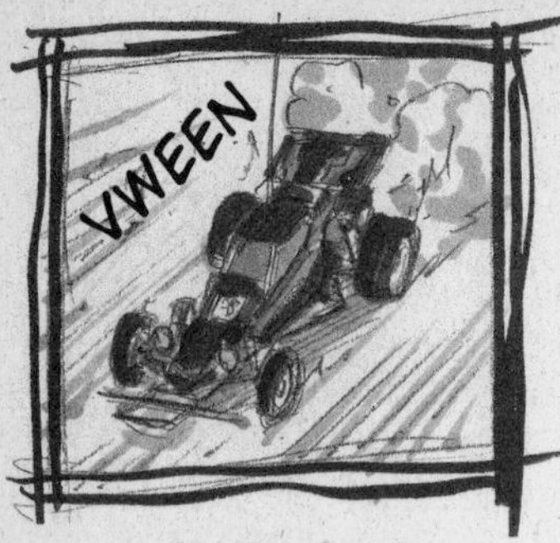
VWEEN

Nostalgic radio-controlled plastic model vehicles have recently made a comeback, just a bit smaller and easier to operate! So cool, I can't stand it!! The most popular models are, as before, buggy types like the Hornet and Mighty Frog! ...Please bring back my previous favorite, Pajero, too, Mr. Tamiya!

—*Masashi Kishimoto, 2007*

岸本斉史

Author/artist Masashi Kishimoto was born in 1974 in rural Okayama Prefecture, Japan. After spending time in art college, he won the Hop Step Award for new manga artists with his manga **Karakuri** (Mechanism). Kishimoto decided to base his next story on traditional Japanese culture. His first version of **Naruto**, drawn in 1997, was a one-shot story about fox spirits; his final version, which debuted in **Weekly Shonen Jump** in 1999, quickly became the most popular ninja manga in Japan.

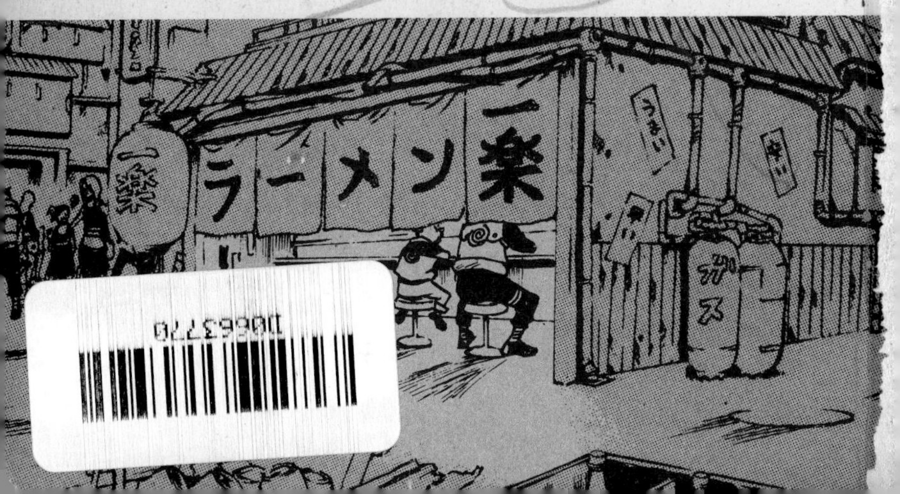
ラーメン一楽

NARUTO VOL. 40
The SHONEN JUMP Manga Edition

STORY AND ART BY MASASHI KISHIMOTO

Translation/Mari Morimoto
English Adaptation/Deric A. Hughes & Benjamin Raab
Touch-up Art & Lettering/Inori Fukuda Trant
Design/Gerry Serrano
Editor/Joel Enos

Editor in Chief, Books/Alvin Lu
Editor in Chief, Magazines/Marc Weidenbaum
VP, Publishing Licensing/Rika Inouye
VP, Sales & Product Marketing/Gonzalo Ferreyra
VP, Creative/Linda Espinosa
Publisher/Hyoe Narita

Printed in the U.S.A.

Published by VIZ Media, LLC
P.O. Box 77010
San Francisco, CA 94107

SHONEN JUMP Manga Edition

10 9 8 7 6 5 4 3 2 1
First printing, March 2009

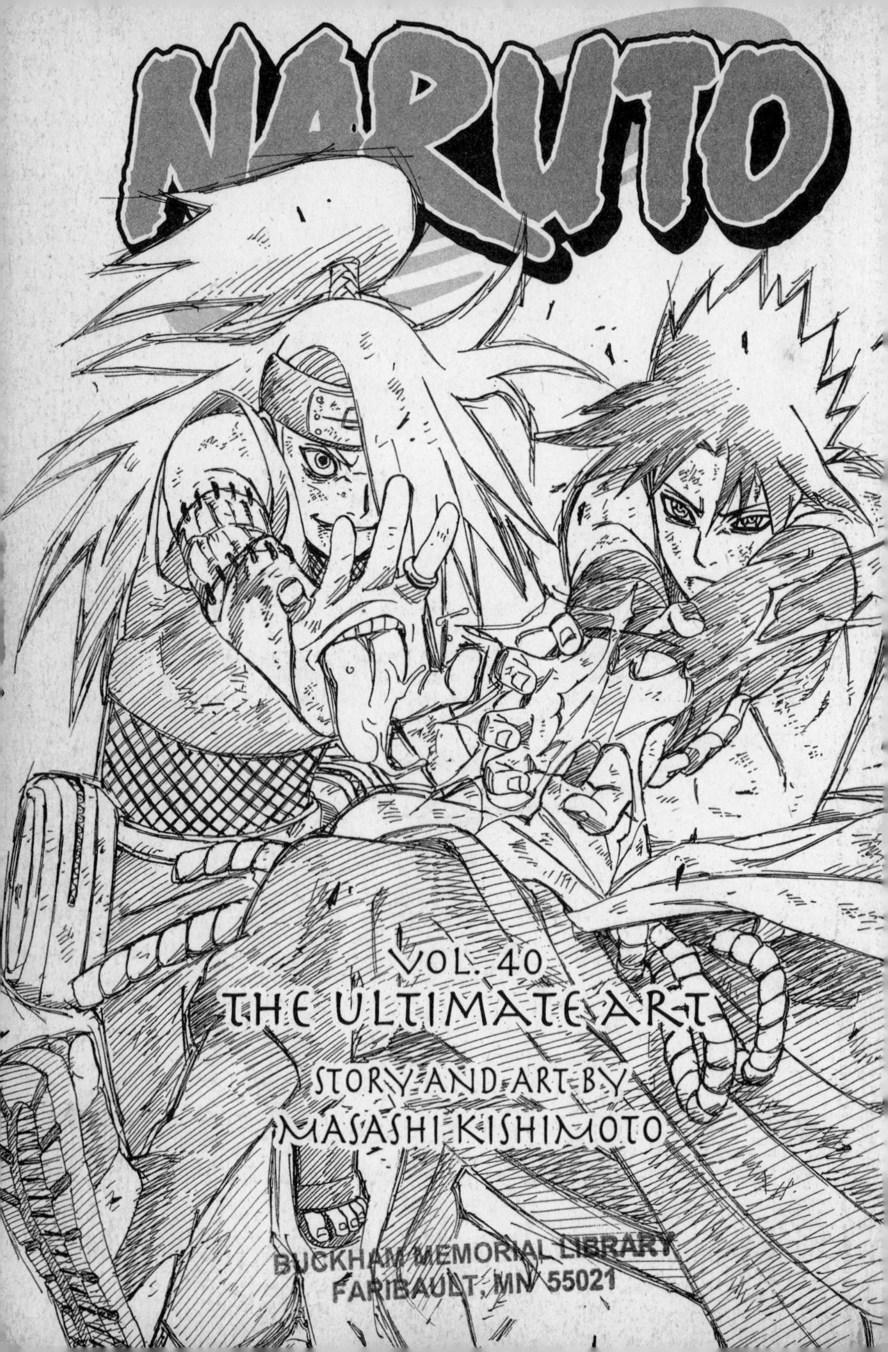
NARUTO
VOL. 40
THE ULTIMATE ART
STORY AND ART BY
MASASHI KISHIMOTO

CHARACTERS

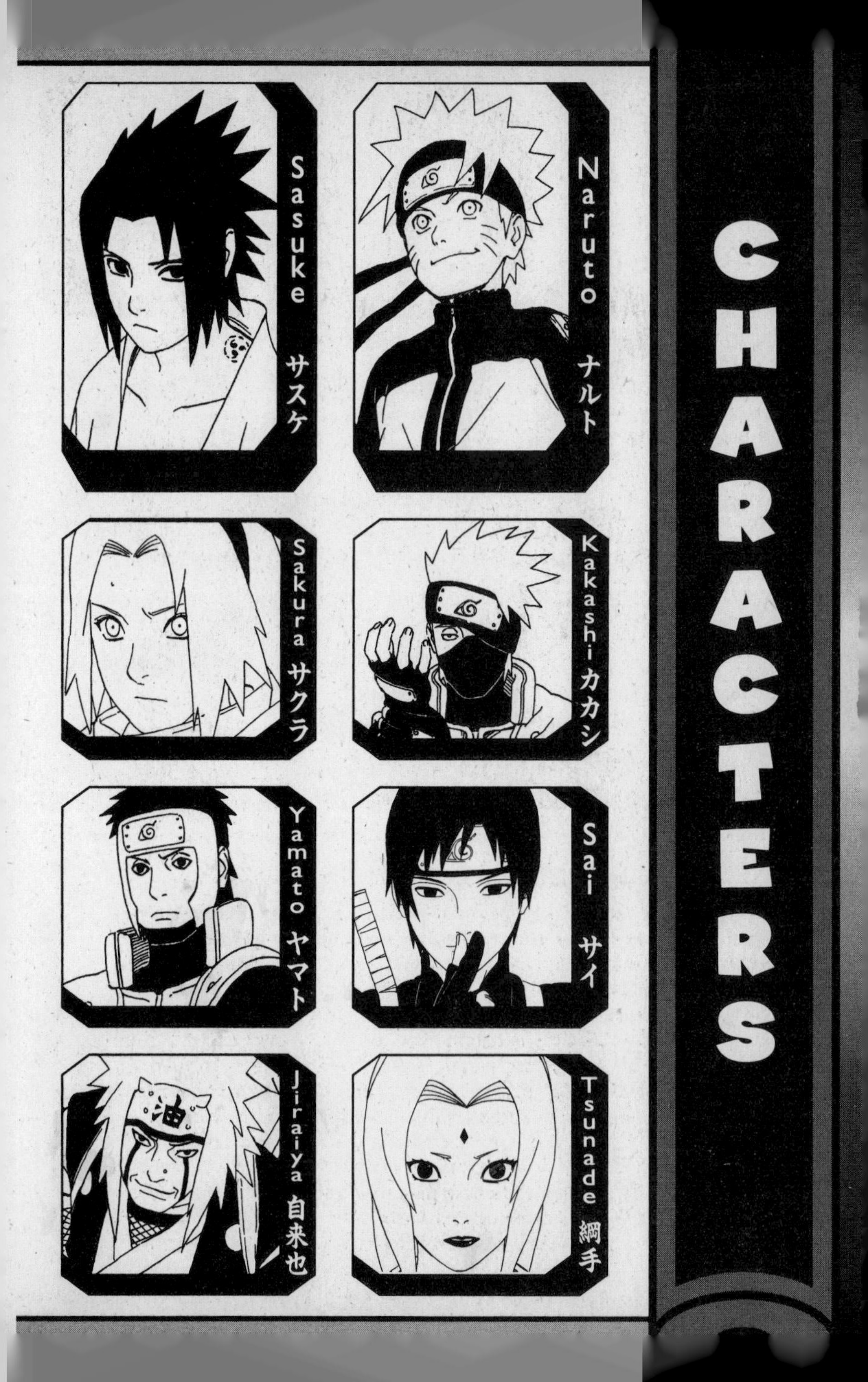
Naruto ナルト
Sasuke サスケ
Kakashi カカシ
Sakura サクラ
Sai サイ
Yamato ヤマト
Tsunade 綱手
Jiraiya 自来也

Jugo 重吾

Karin 香燐

Suigetsu 水月

Tobi トビ

Deidara デイダラ

Kisame 鬼鮫

Itachi イタチ

THE STORY SO FAR...

Once the bane of the Konohagakure Ninja Academy, Uzumaki Naruto now serves dutifully among the ranks of the Konoha shinobi—an illustrious group of ninja sworn to protect their village from the forces of evil seeking to destroy it from without and within...

After his former classmate, Uchiha Sasuke, is seduced by the evil Orochimaru, Naruto makes it his personal mission to find and save his friend from the darkness growing inside him. Unfortunately, Sasuke doesn't want to be saved. All he wants is revenge on the one person he hates most in the world... the person he blames for the murder of his parents... his older brother, Uchiha Itachi.

Assembling his shinobi cell, The Hebi, Sasuke sets out to find and kill his brother. But his quest for vengeance soon brings him into conflict with Deidara and Tobi—members of the insidious organization known as the Akatsuki. Though Sasuke quickly gains the upper hand with the formidable power of his Sharingan, Deidara tips the scales by unveiling his latest masterpiece of destruction...

NARUTO

VOL. 40
THE ULTIMATE ART

CONTENTS

Number 360: The C4 Karura

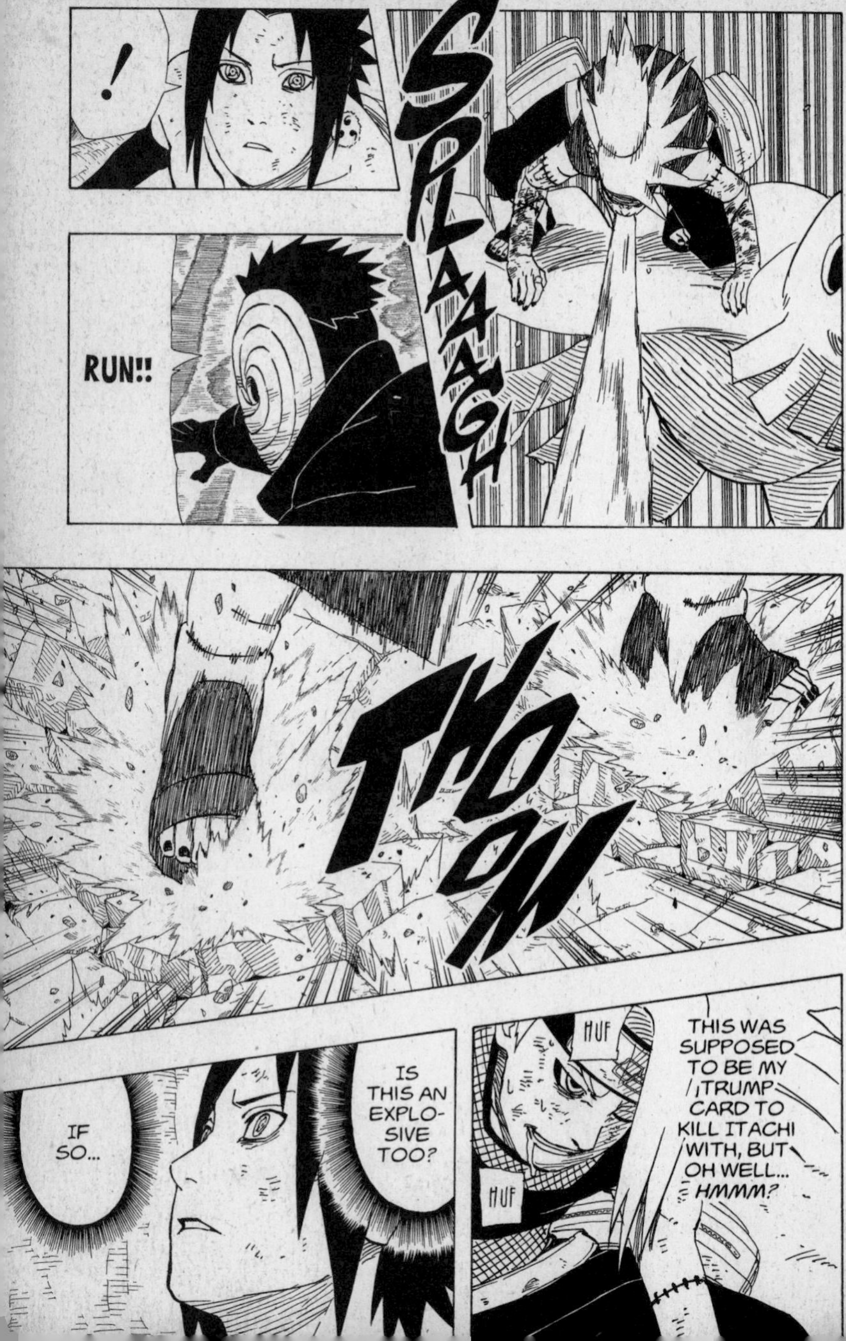
SPLAAGH
!
RUN!!
THOOM
HUF
THIS WAS SUPPOSED TO BE MY TRUMP CARD TO KILL ITACHI WITH, BUT OH WELL... HMMM?
HUF
IS THIS AN EXPLOSIVE TOO?
IF SO...

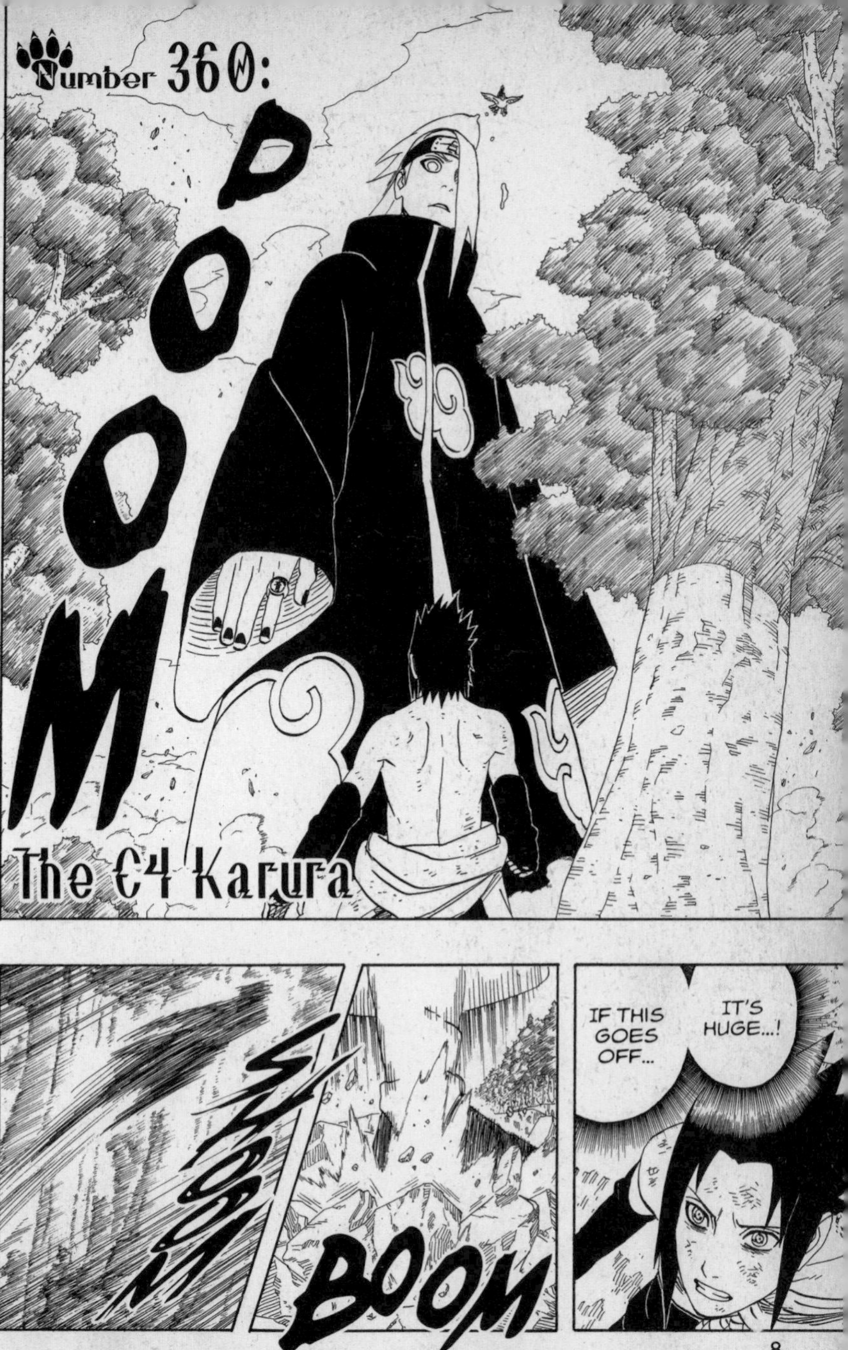
Number 360:
DOOM
The C4 Karura
IT'S HUGE...!
IF THIS GOES OFF...
BOOM
SHWOOM

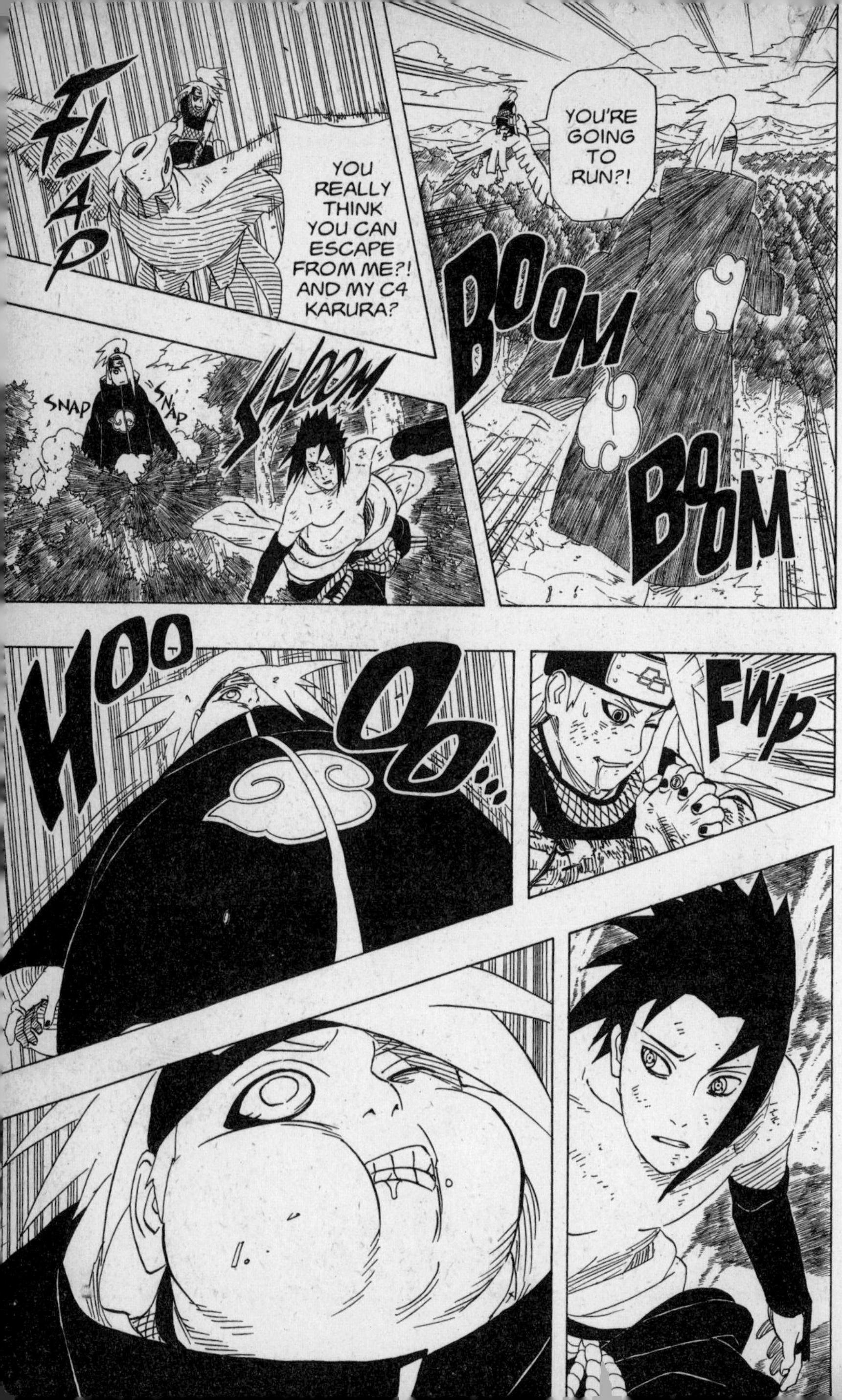
YOU'RE GOING TO RUN?!
BOOM
BOOM
FLAP
YOU REALLY THINK YOU CAN ESCAPE FROM ME?! AND MY C4 KARURA?
SHOOM
SNAP
SNAP
FWP
HOOOOO...

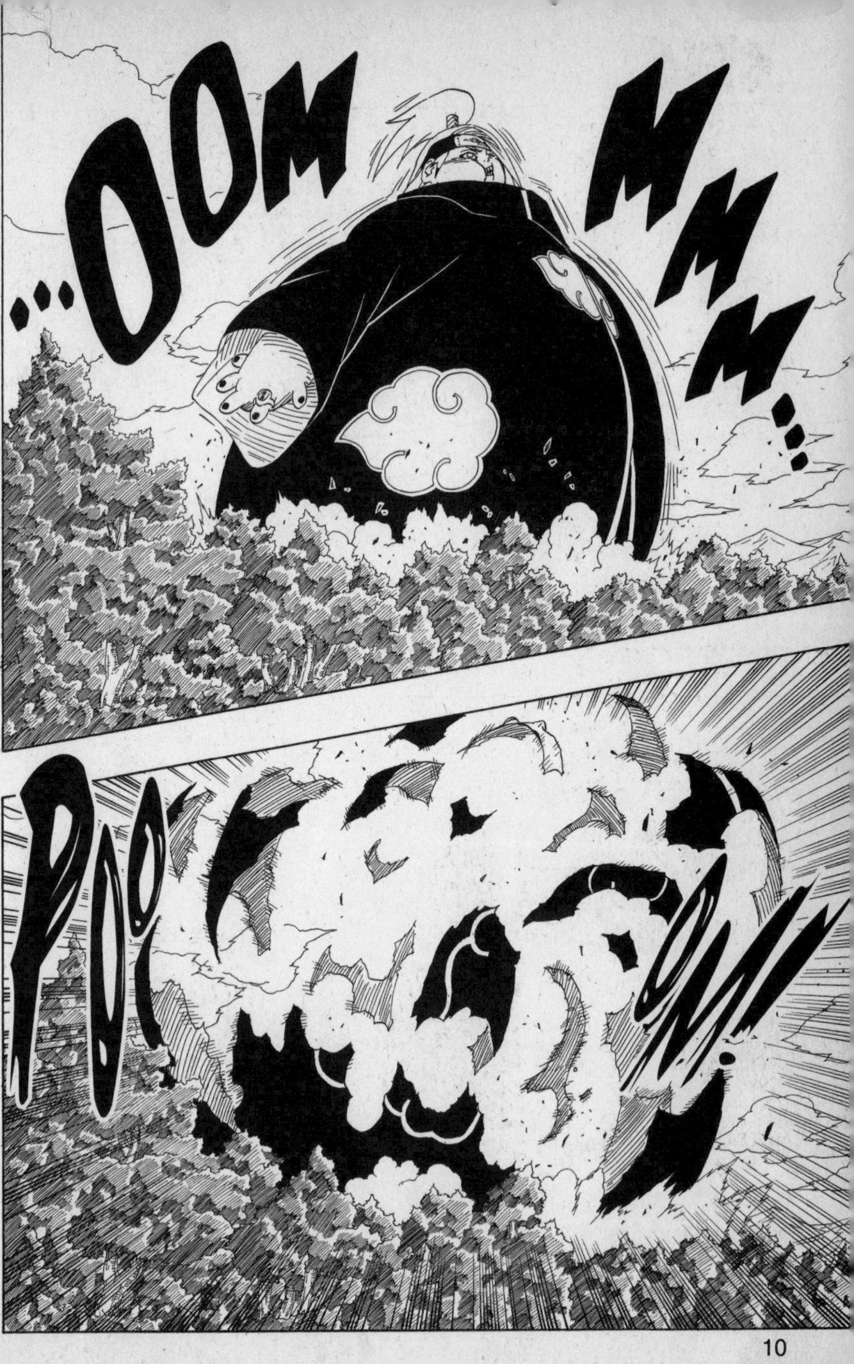
...OOM MMM...
POOOOM!

READ THIS WAY

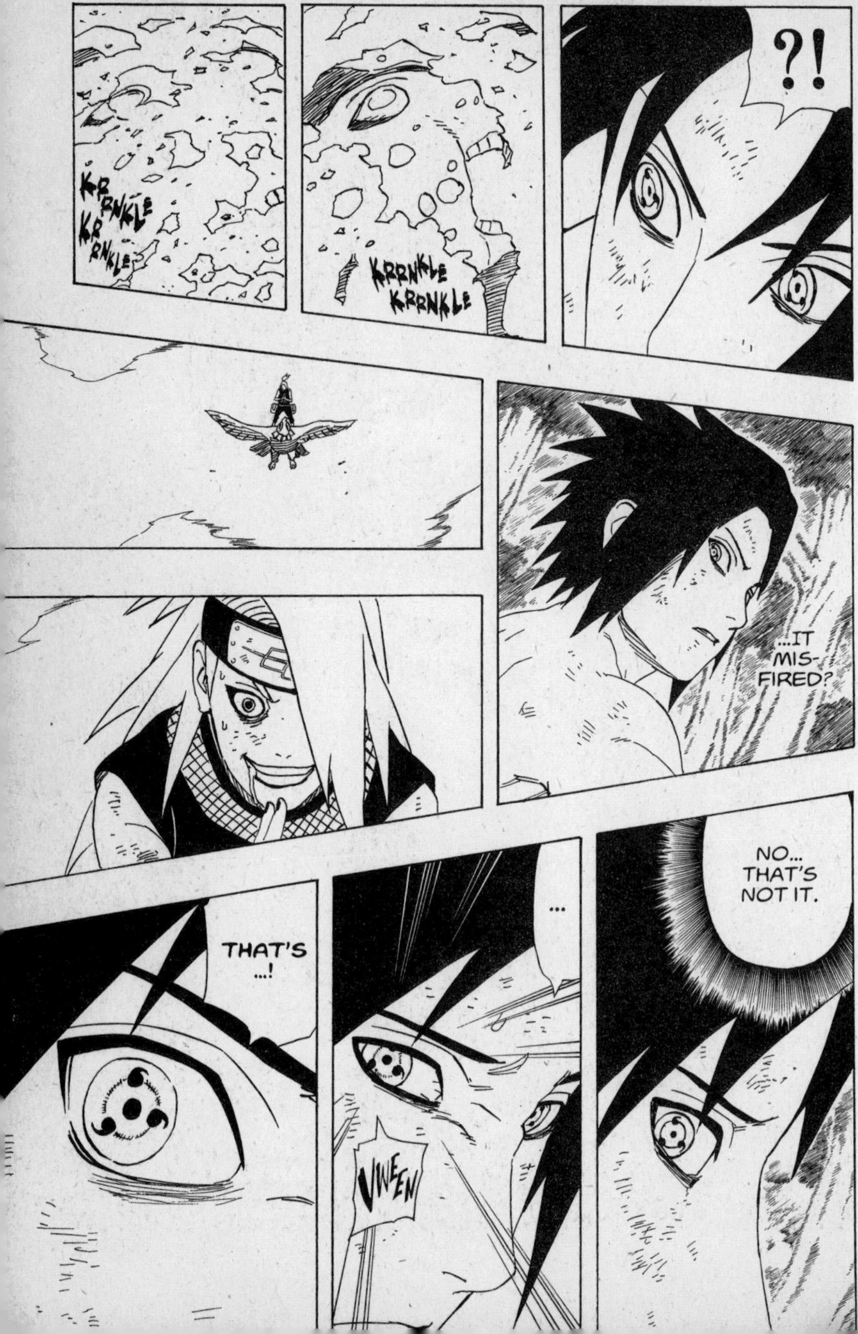
?!
KRRNKLE KRRNKLE
KRRNKLE KRRNKLE
...IT MIS-FIRED?
NO... THAT'S NOT IT.
...
VWEEN
THAT'S ...!

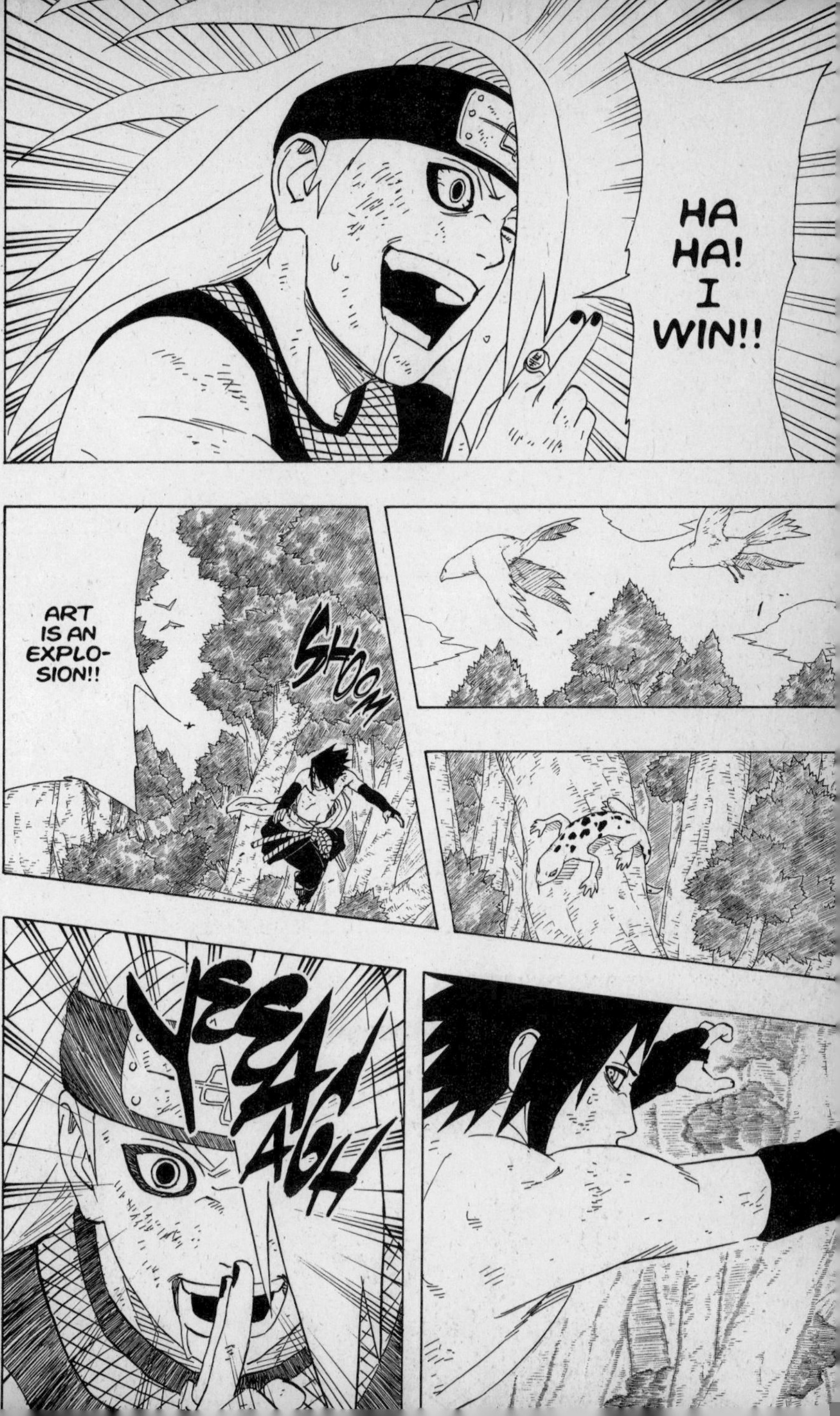
HA HA! I WIN!!
ART IS AN EXPLOSION!!
SHOOM
YEEAAAGH

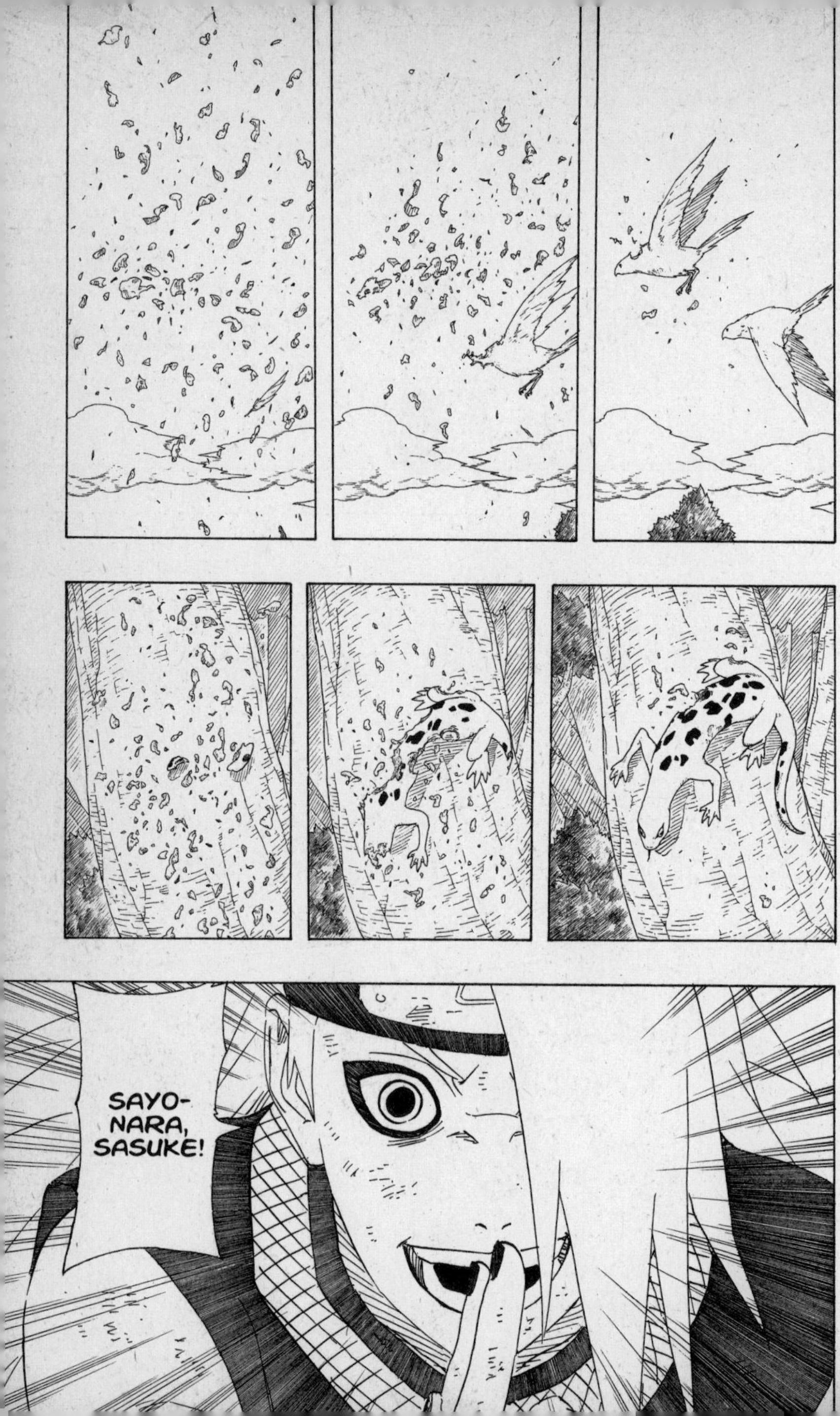
SAYO-NARA, SASUKE!

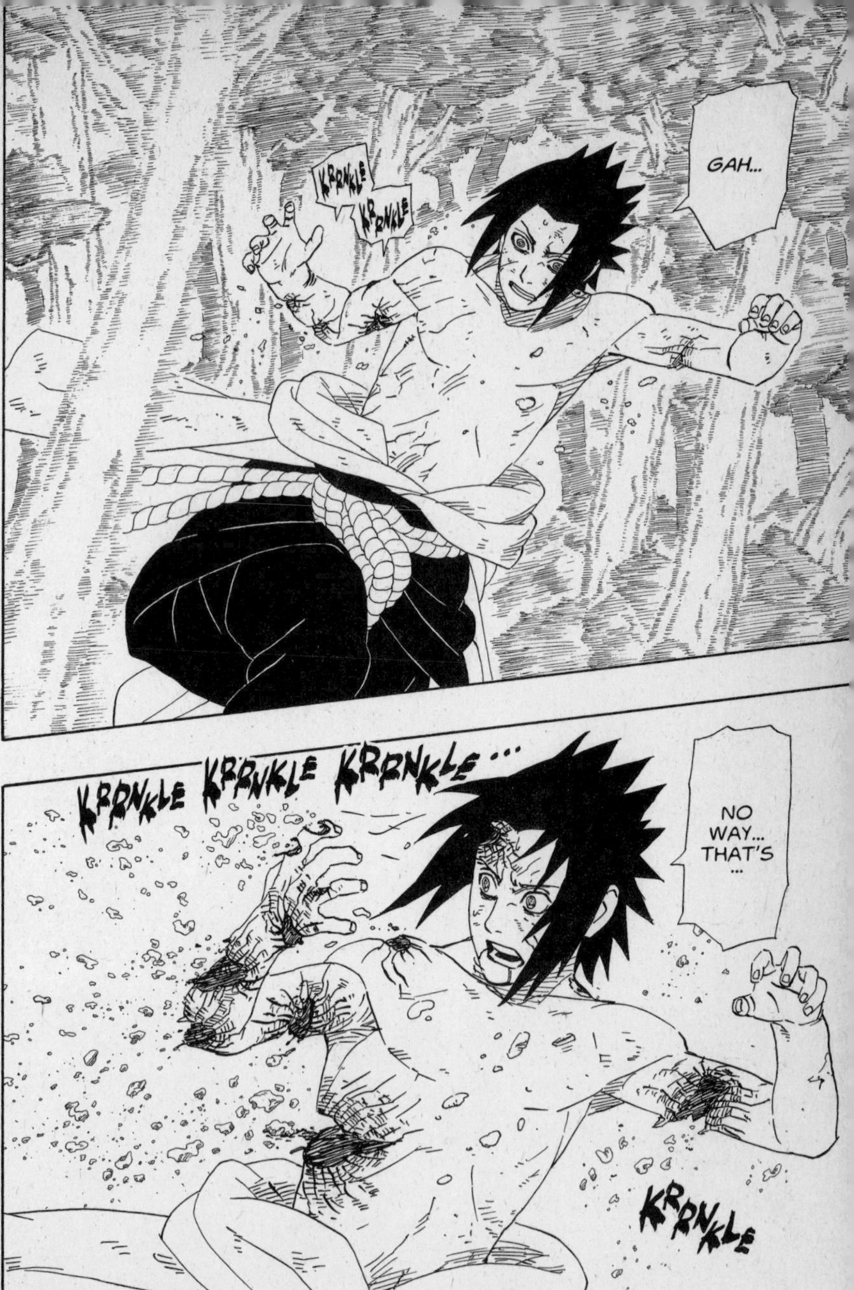
GAH...
KRONKLE
KRONKLE
NO WAY... THAT'S ...
KRONKLE KRONKLE KRONKLE...
KRONKLE

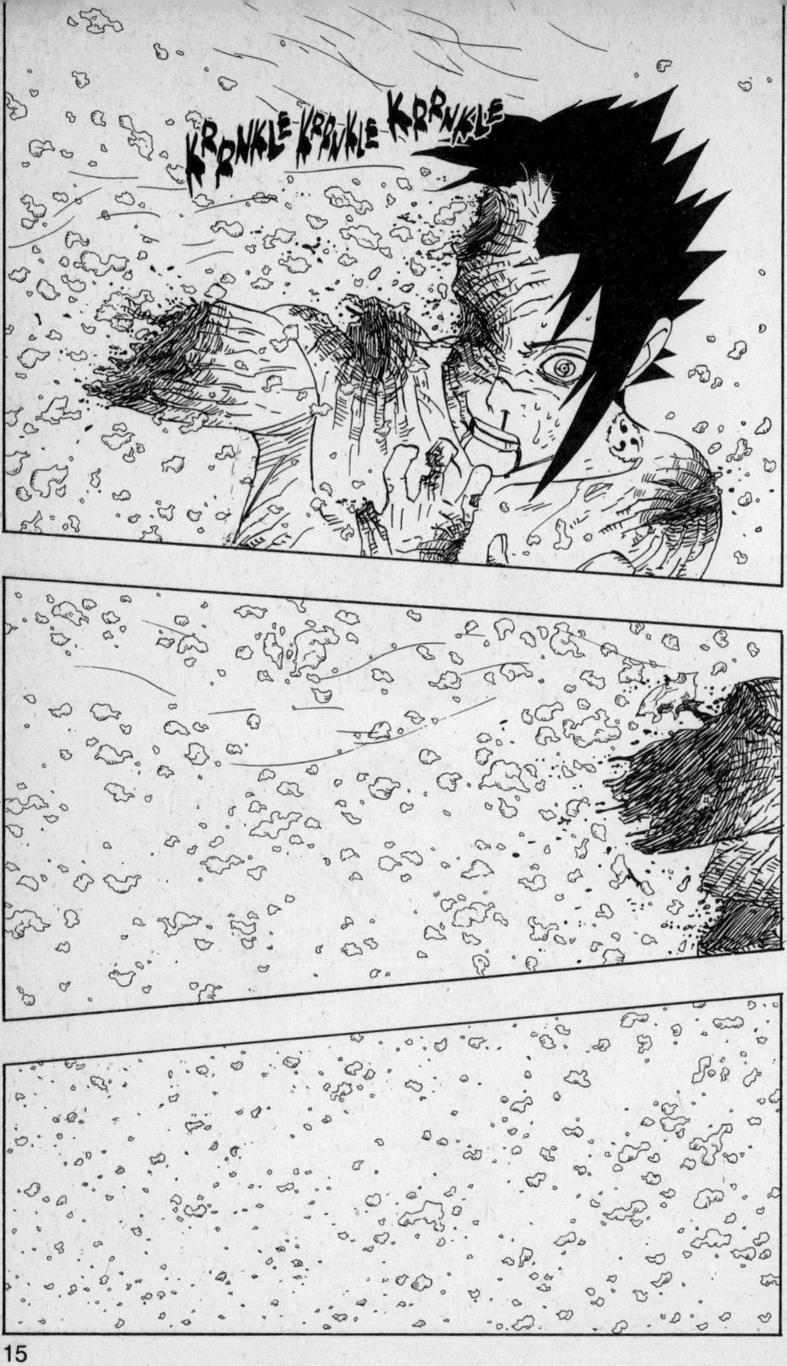
KRRNKLE KRRNKLE KRRNKLE

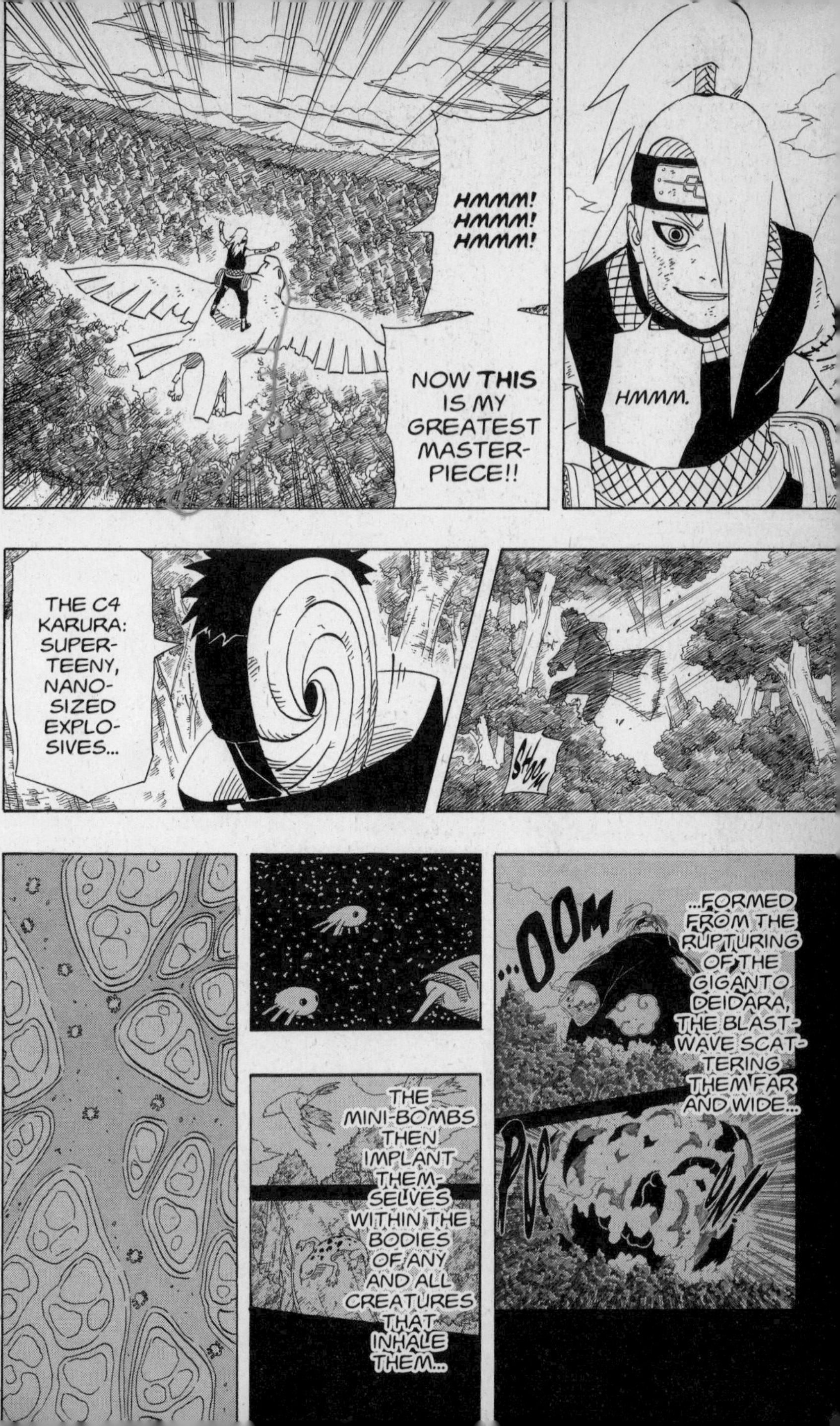
HMMM.
HMMM! HMMM! HMMM!
NOW THIS IS MY GREATEST MASTER-PIECE!!
SHOOM
THE C4 KARURA: SUPER-TEENY, NANO-SIZED EXPLOSIVES...
...FORMED FROM THE RUPTURING OF THE GIGANTO DEIDARA, THE BLAST-WAVE SCATTERING THEM FAR AND WIDE...
...OOM
THE MINI-BOMBS THEN IMPLANT THEMSELVES WITHIN THE BODIES OF ANY AND ALL CREATURES THAT INHALE THEM...

READ THIS WAY

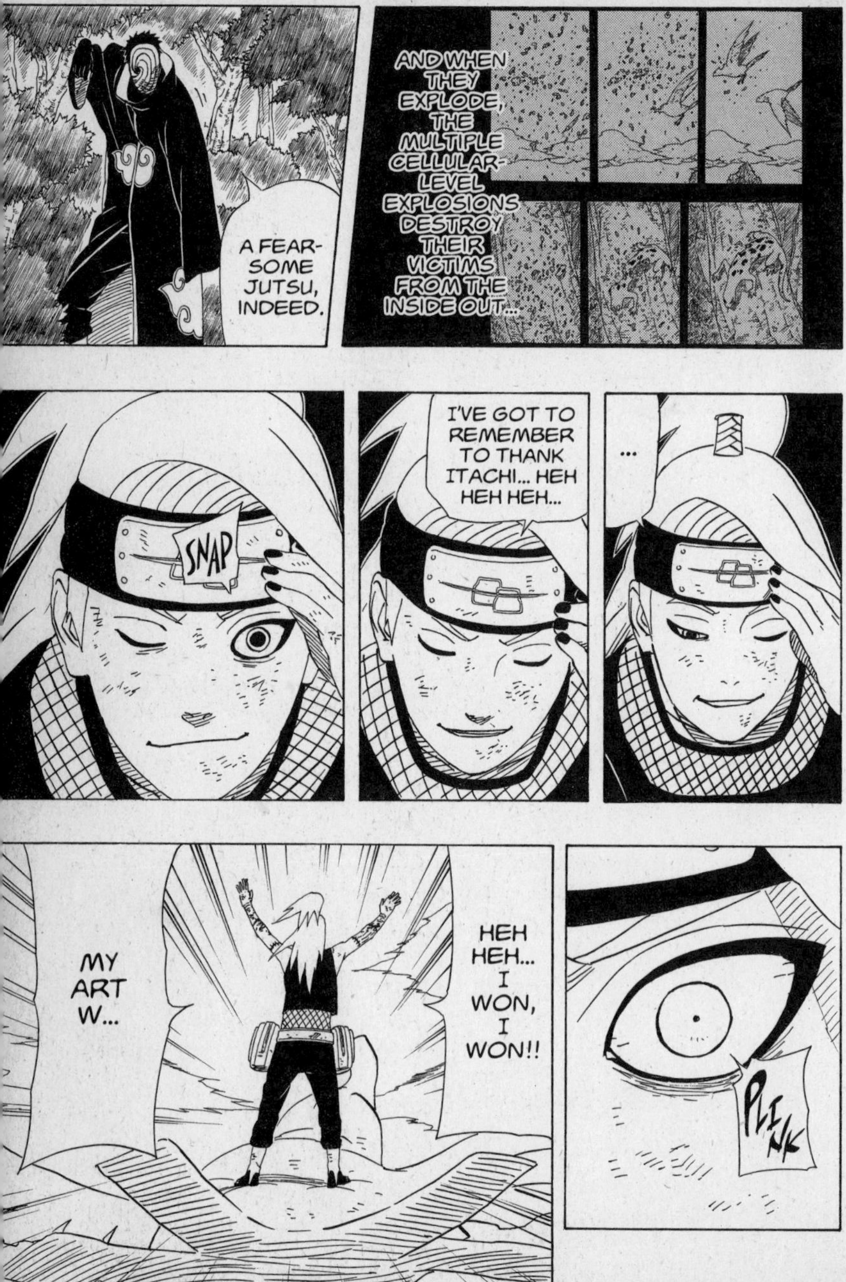
AND WHEN THEY EXPLODE, THE MULTIPLE CELLULAR-LEVEL EXPLOSIONS DESTROY THEIR VICTIMS FROM THE INSIDE OUT...
A FEAR-SOME JUTSU, INDEED.
...
I'VE GOT TO REMEMBER TO THANK ITACHI... HEH HEH HEH...
SNAP
PLINK
HEH HEH... I WON, I WON!!
MY ART W...

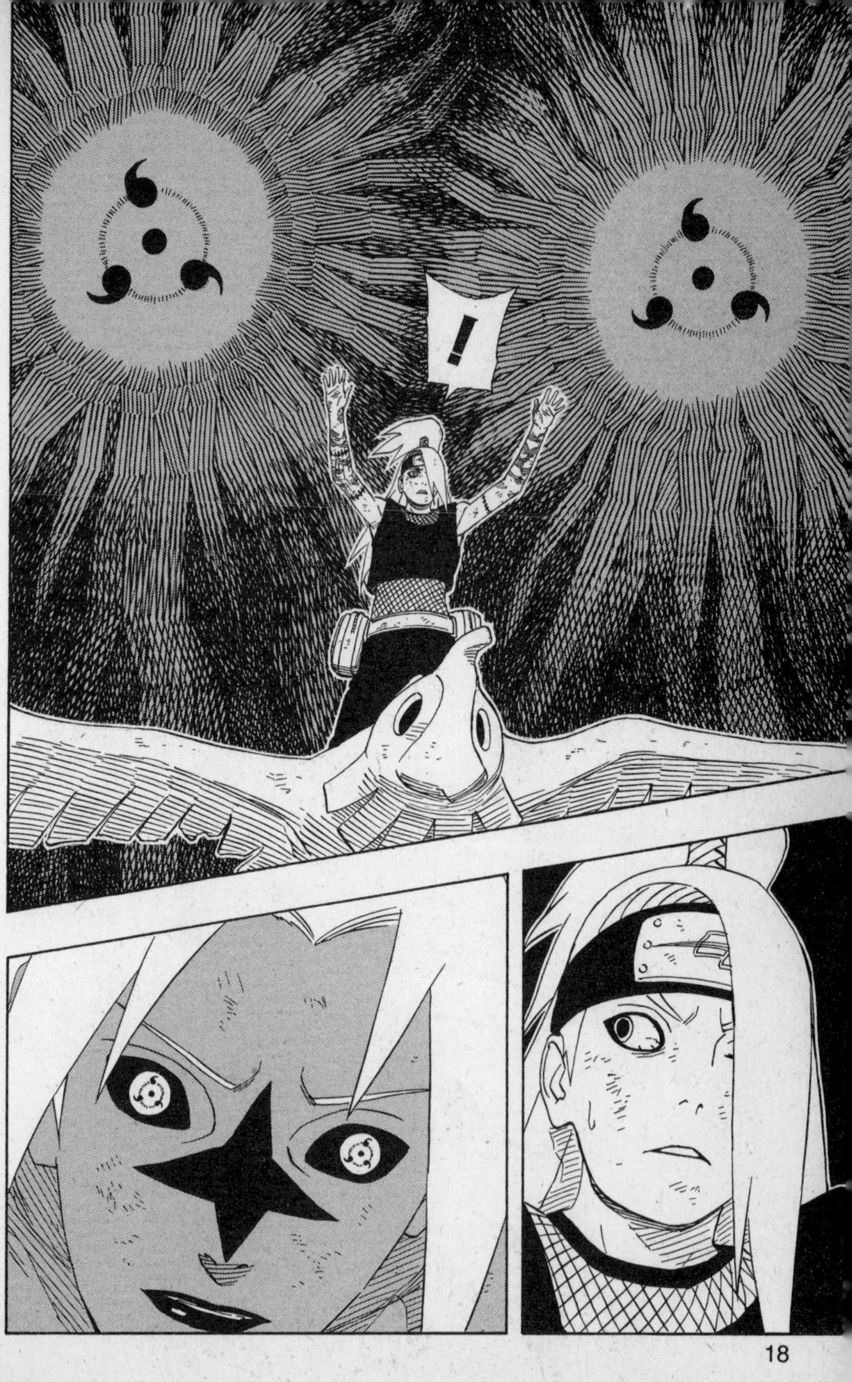
!

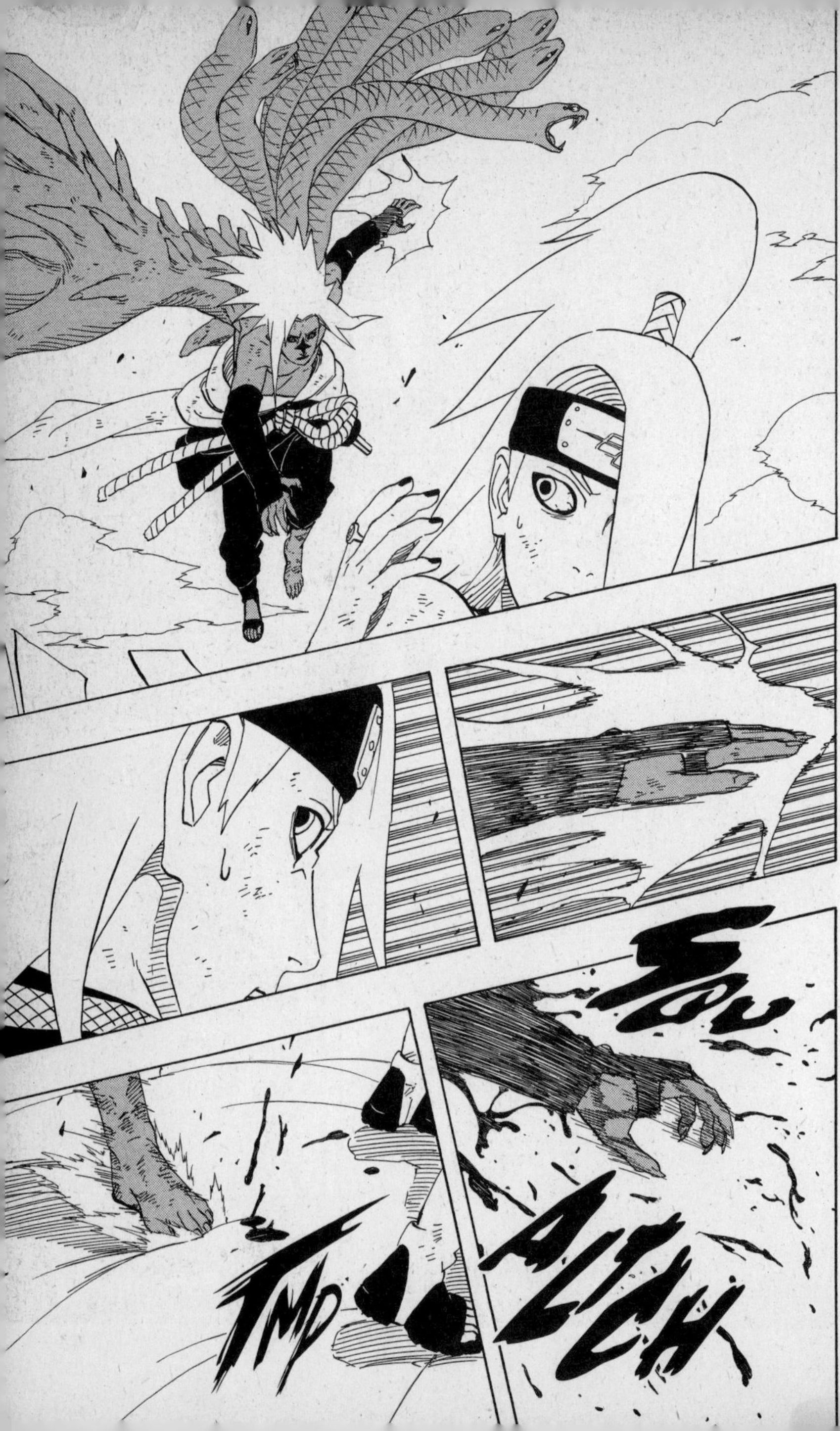

YOU
TMP
AITCH

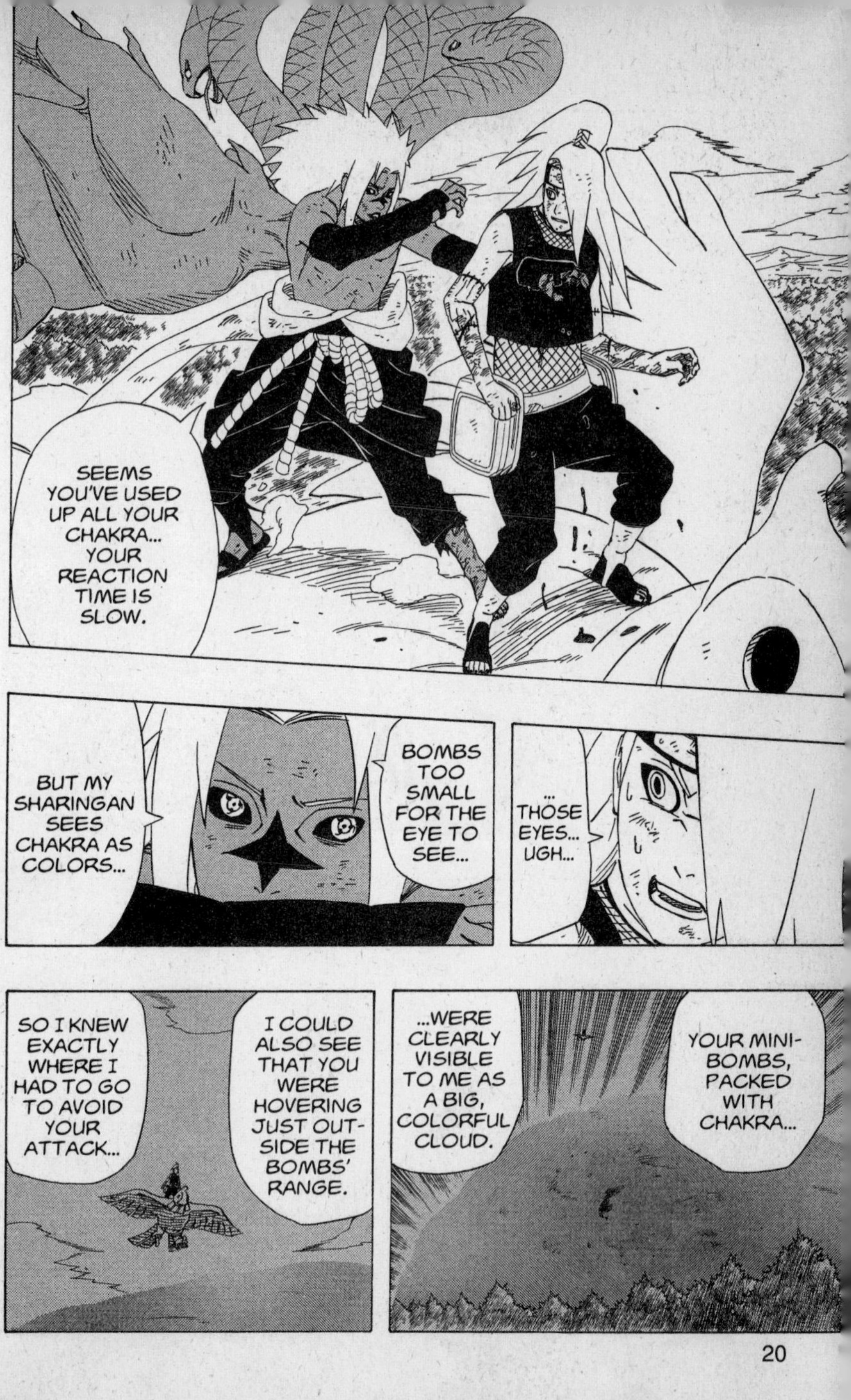
SEEMS YOU'VE USED UP ALL YOUR CHAKRA... YOUR REACTION TIME IS SLOW.
... THOSE EYES... UGH...
BOMBS TOO SMALL FOR THE EYE TO SEE...
BUT MY SHARINGAN SEES CHAKRA AS COLORS...
YOUR MINI-BOMBS, PACKED WITH CHAKRA...
...WERE CLEARLY VISIBLE TO ME AS A BIG, COLORFUL CLOUD.
I COULD ALSO SEE THAT YOU WERE HOVERING JUST OUT-SIDE THE BOMBS' RANGE.
SO I KNEW EXACTLY WHERE I HAD TO GO TO AVOID YOUR ATTACK...

READ THIS WAY

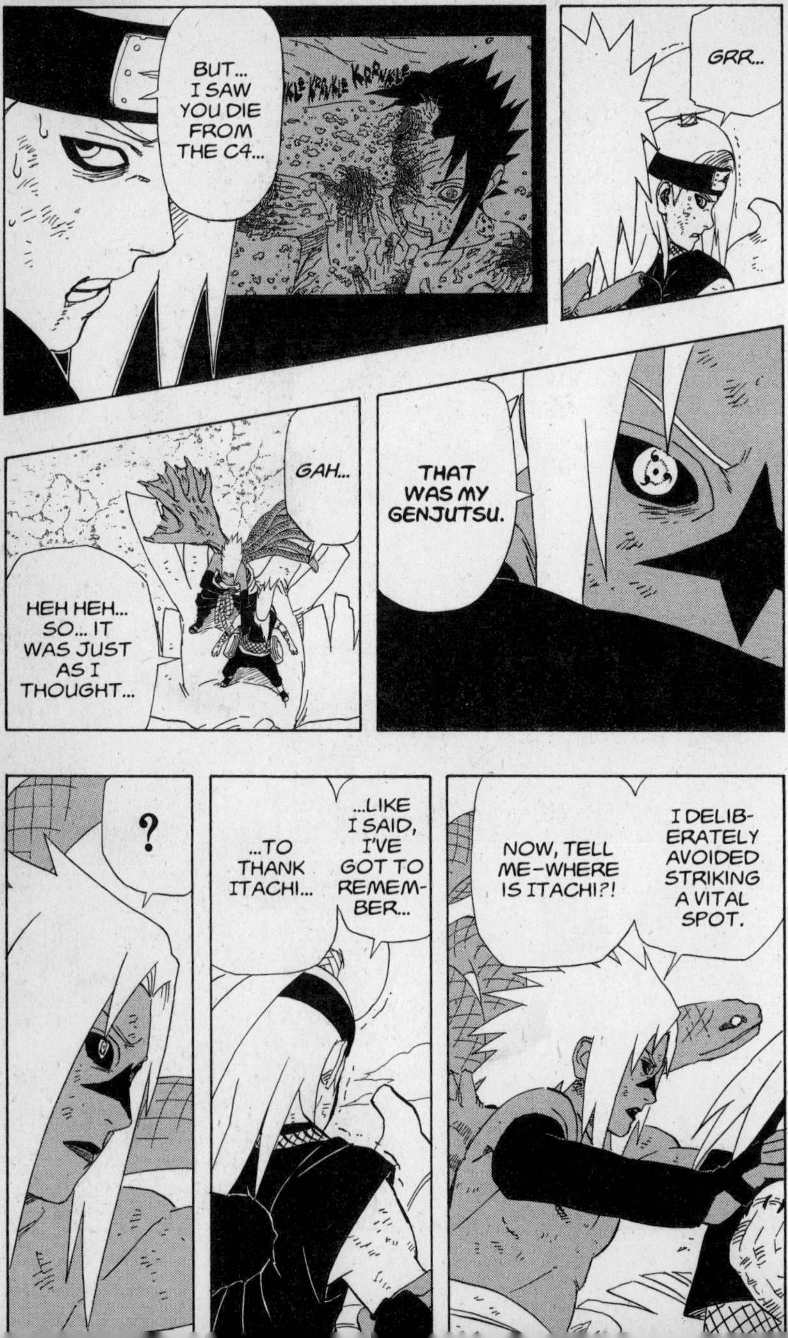
GRR...
BUT... I SAW YOU DIE FROM THE C4...
KRAKKLE KRAKKLE
THAT WAS MY GENJUTSU.
GAH...
HEH HEH... SO... IT WAS JUST AS I THOUGHT...
I DELIB-ERATELY AVOIDED STRIKING A VITAL SPOT.
NOW, TELL ME—WHERE IS ITACHI?!
...LIKE I SAID, I'VE GOT TO REMEM-BER...
...TO THANK ITACHI...
?

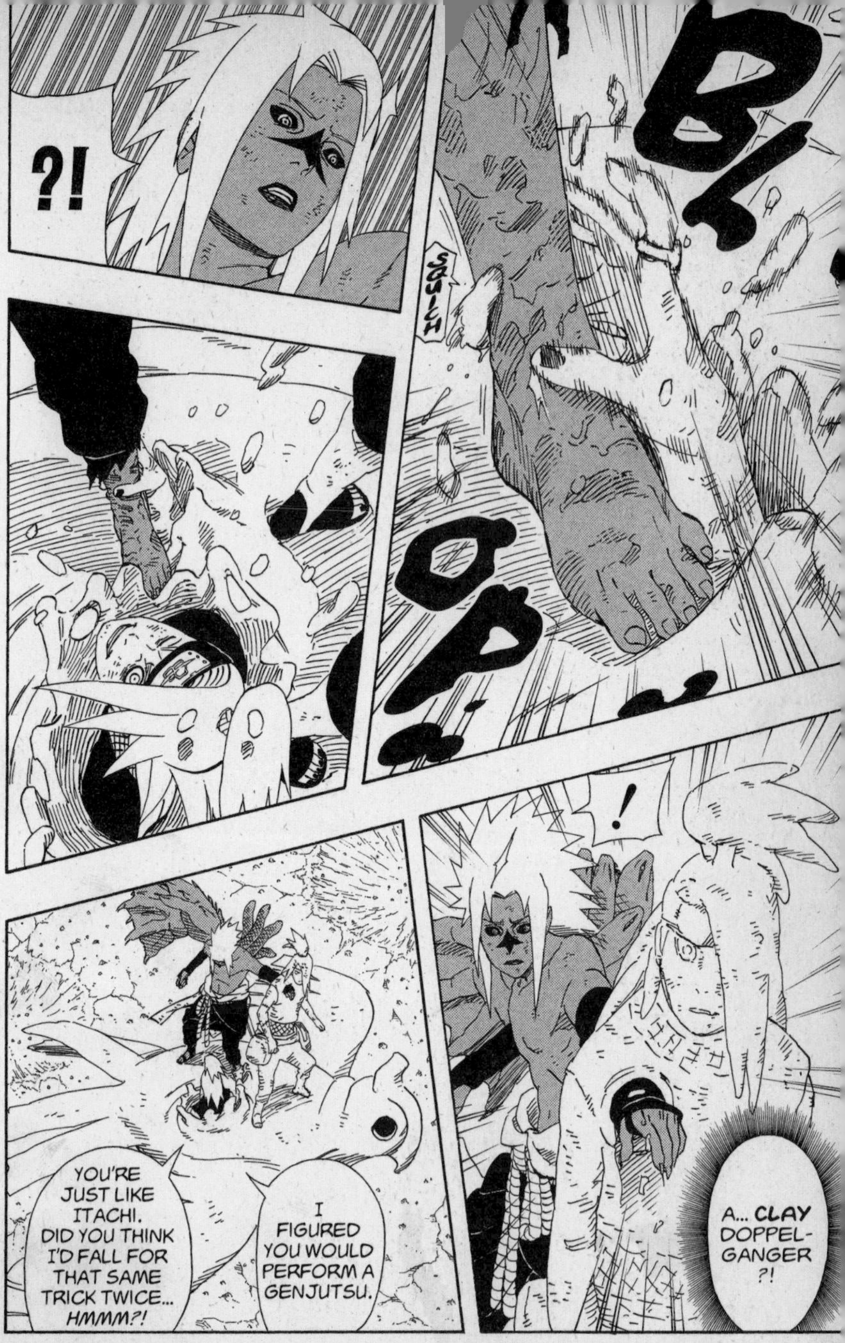
SQUICH
BLOOP
?!
!
A... CLAY DOPPEL-GANGER ?!
I FIGURED YOU WOULD PERFORM A GENJUTSU.
YOU'RE JUST LIKE ITACHI. DID YOU THINK I'D FALL FOR THAT SAME TRICK TWICE... HMMM?!

READ THIS WAY

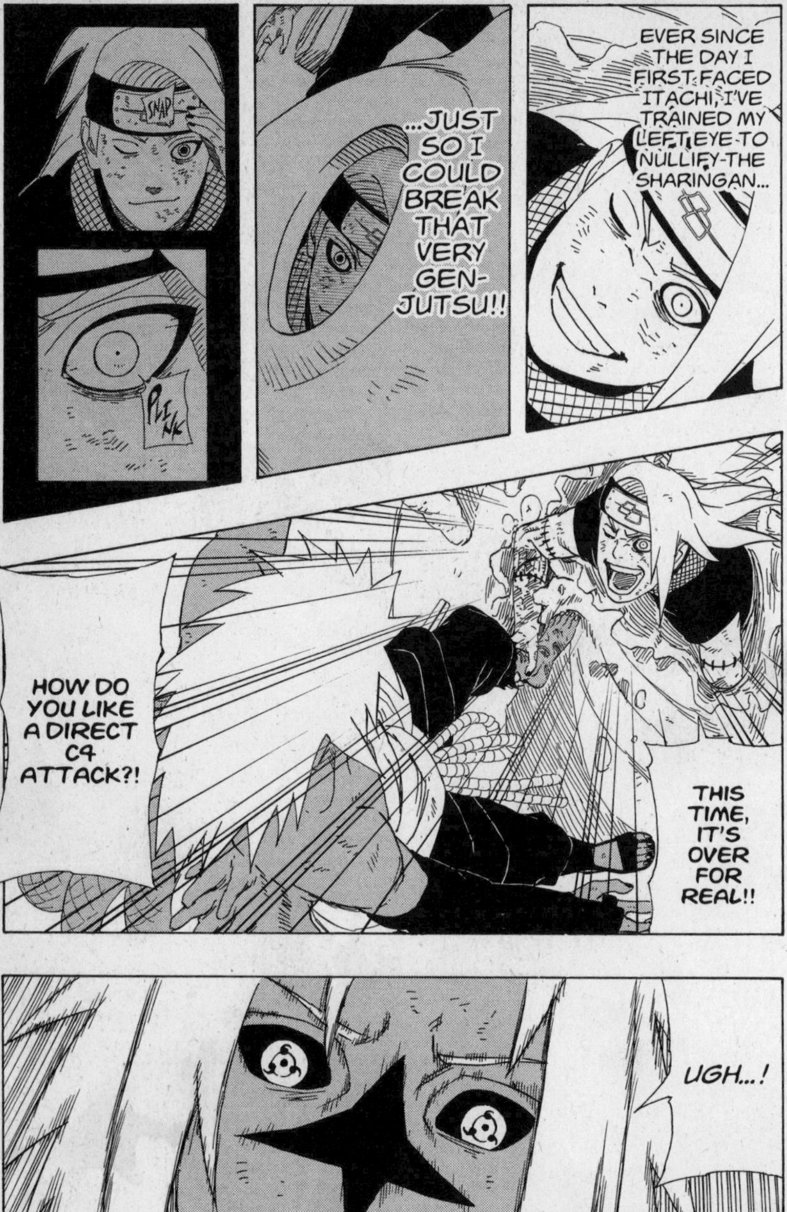
EVER SINCE THE DAY I FIRST FACED ITACHI, I'VE TRAINED MY LEFT EYE TO NULLIFY THE SHARINGAN...
...JUST SO I COULD BREAK THAT VERY GEN-JUTSU!!
SNAP
PLENK
THIS TIME, IT'S OVER FOR REAL!!
HOW DO YOU LIKE A DIRECT C4 ATTACK?!
UGH...!

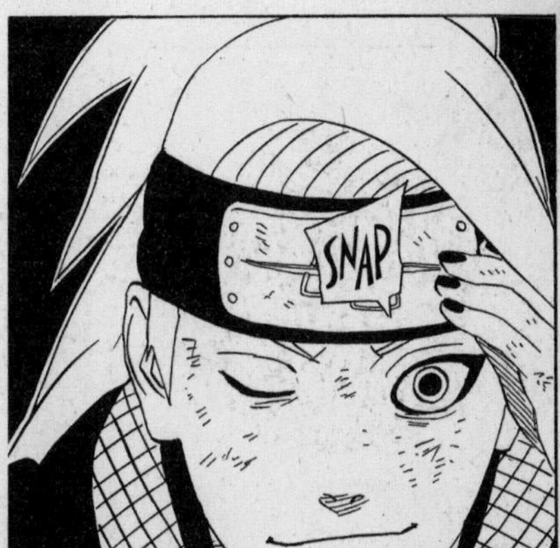
SNAP

Number 361: Achilles' Heel...!!

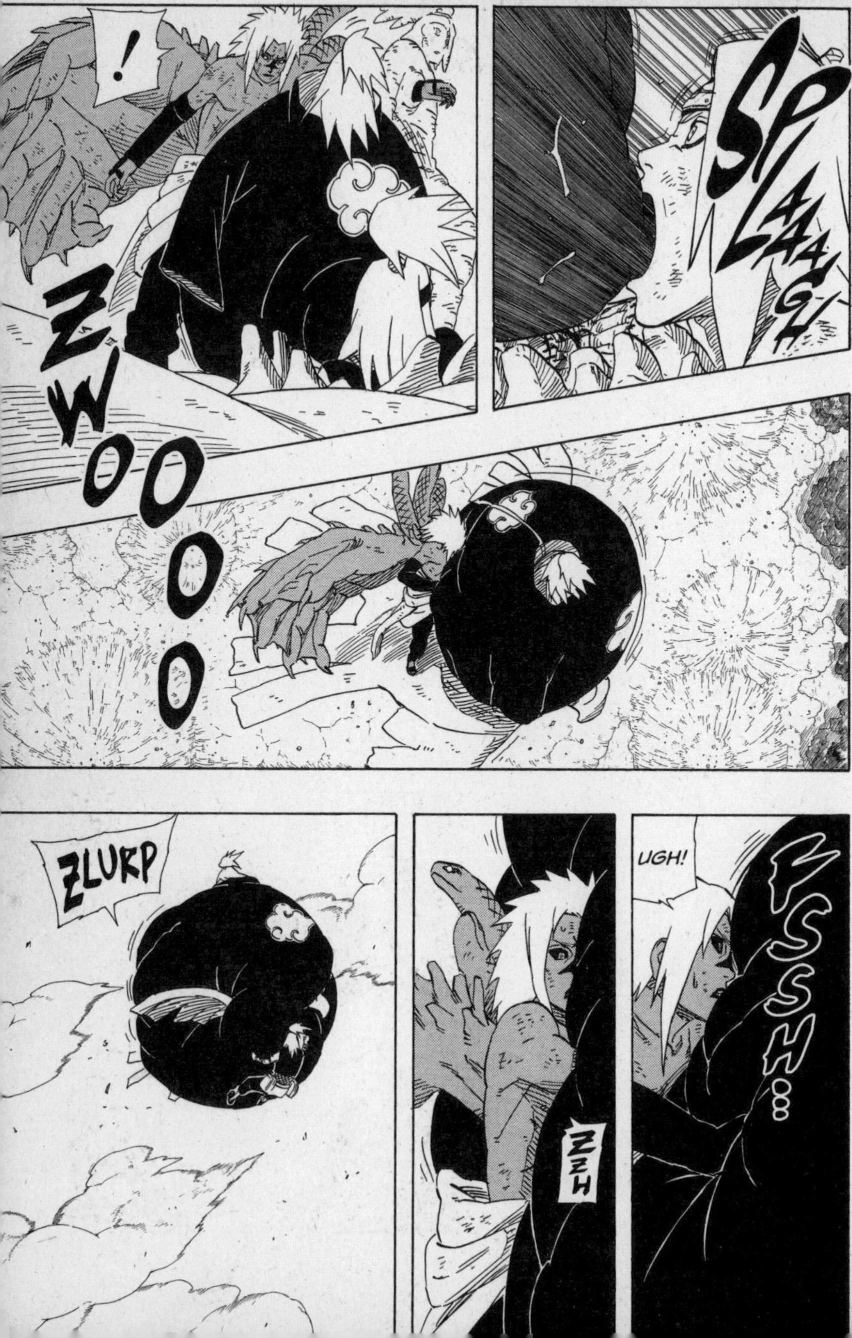
SPLAAGH
!
ZWOOOO
UGH!
FSSSH..
ZZZH
ZLURP

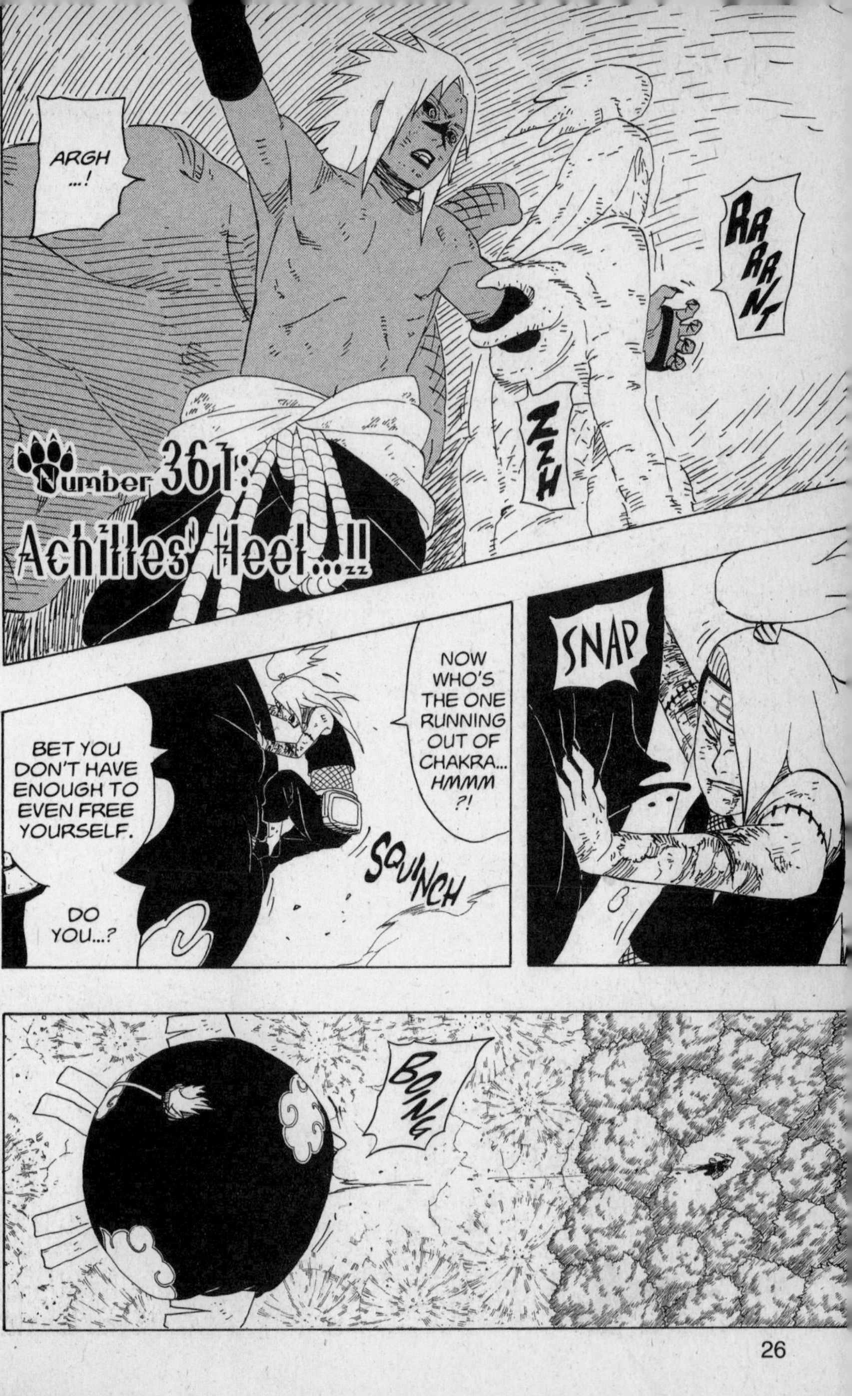
RRRRNT
ZZH
ARGH ...!
Number 361: Achilles' Heel...!!
SNAP
NOW WHO'S THE ONE RUNNING OUT OF CHAKRA... HMMM ?!
BET YOU DON'T HAVE ENOUGH TO EVEN FREE YOURSELF.
SQUINCH
DO YOU...?
BOING

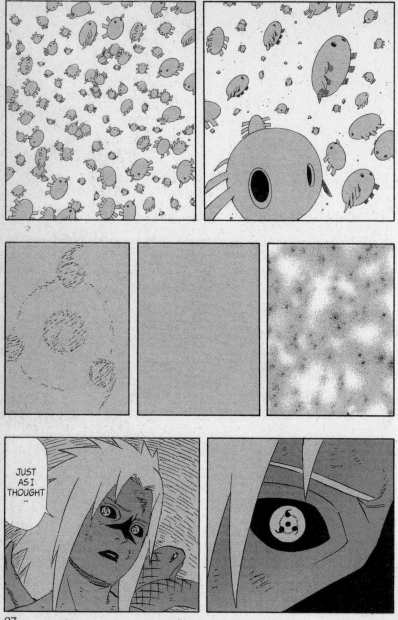

JUST
AS I
THOUGHT
...

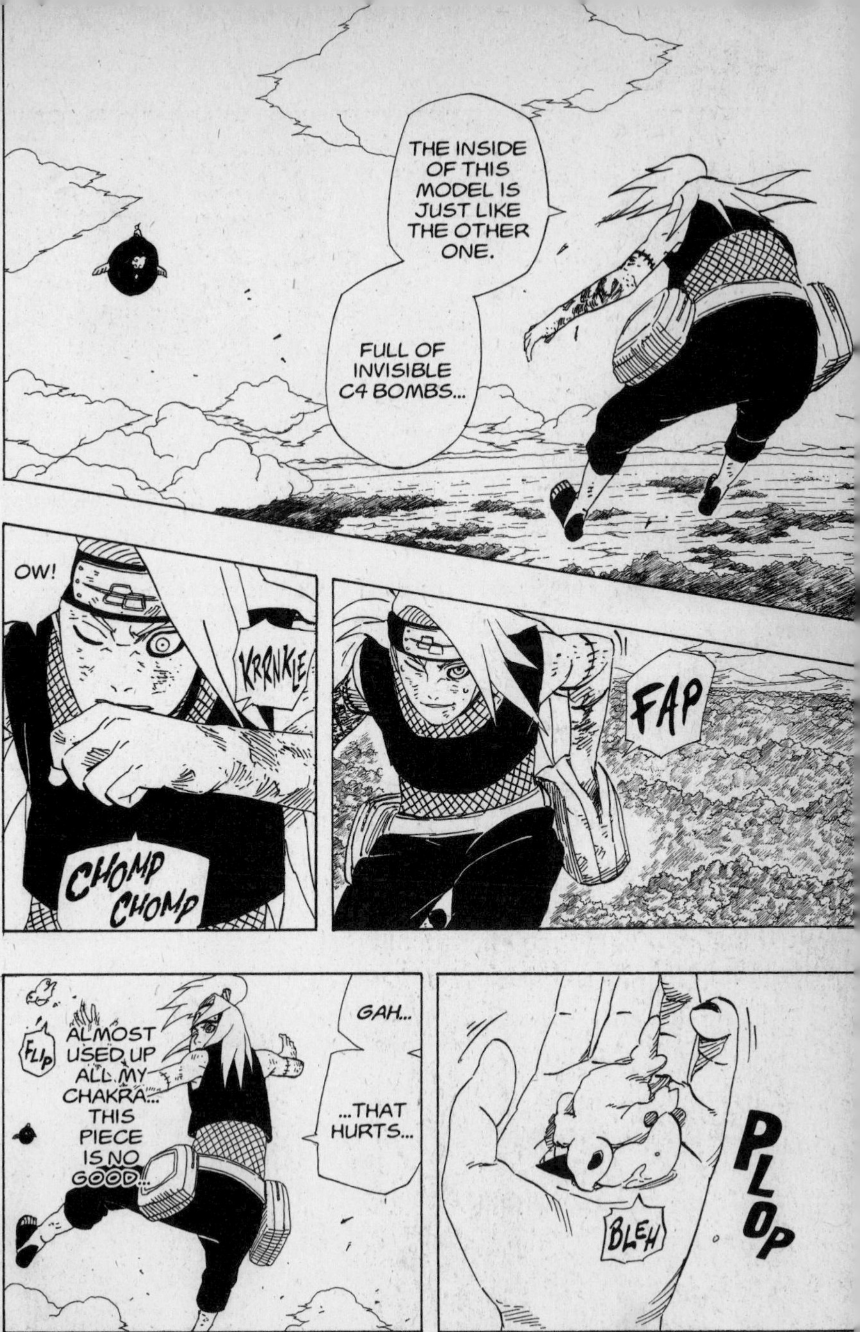
THE INSIDE OF THIS MODEL IS JUST LIKE THE OTHER ONE.
FULL OF INVISIBLE C4 BOMBS...
FAP
OW!
KRRNKLE
CHOMP CHOMP
PLOP
BLEH
GAH...
...THAT HURTS...
ALMOST USED UP ALL MY CHAKRA... THIS PIECE IS NO GOOD...
FLIP

READ THIS WAY

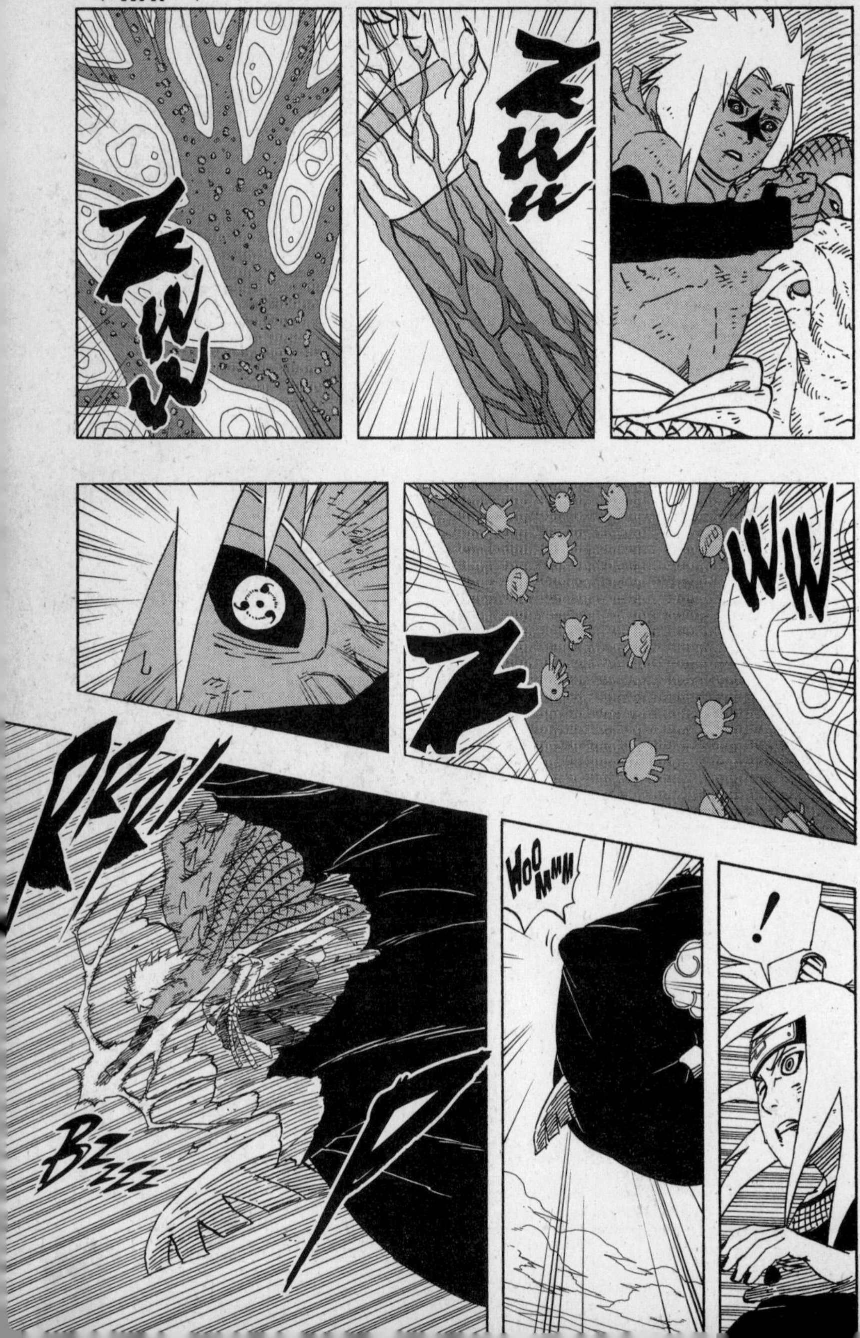
!
WHOOMMM
BZZZZ

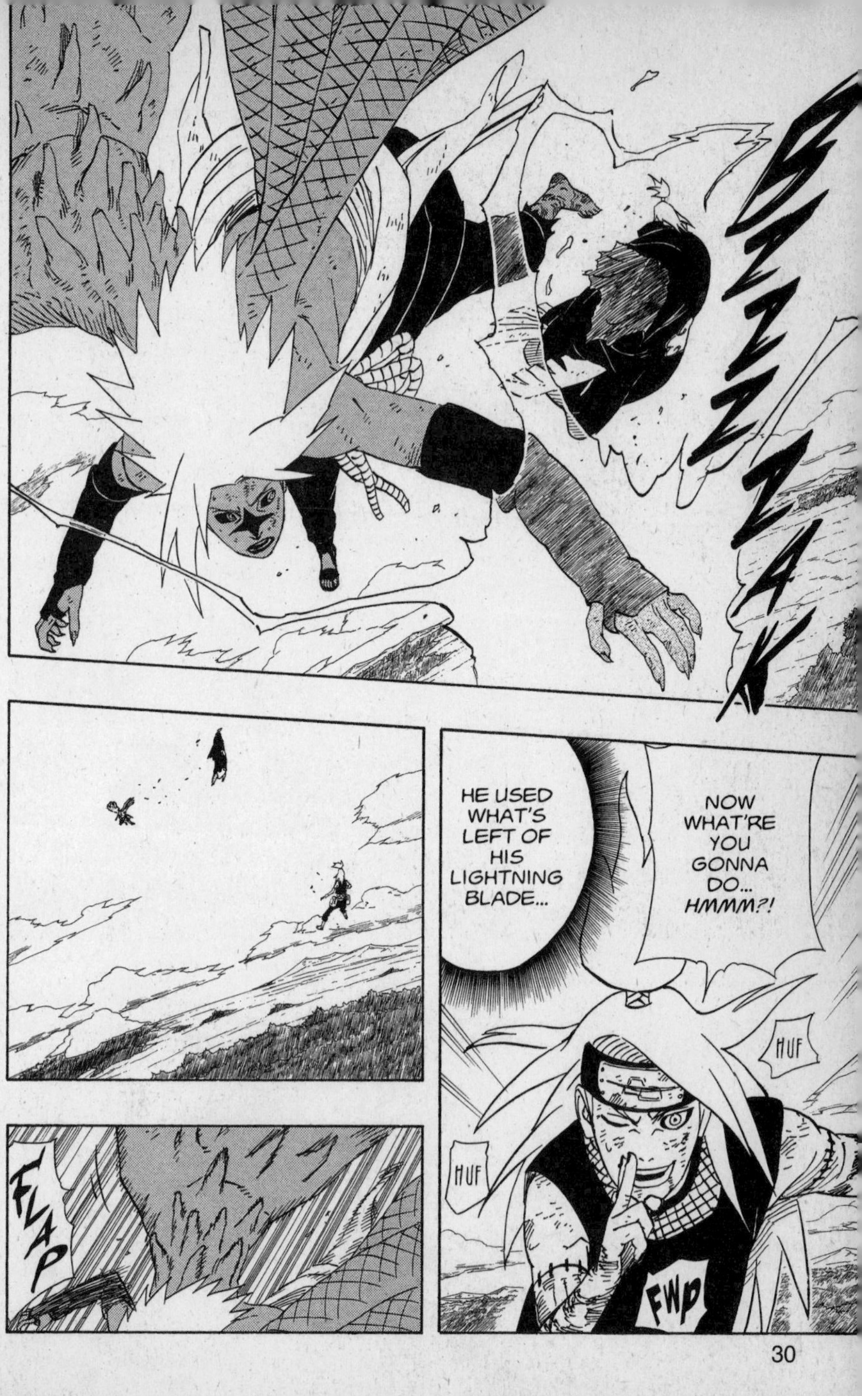
NOW WHAT'RE YOU GONNA DO... HMMM?!
HE USED WHAT'S LEFT OF HIS LIGHTNING BLADE...
HUF
HUF
FWP
FLAP

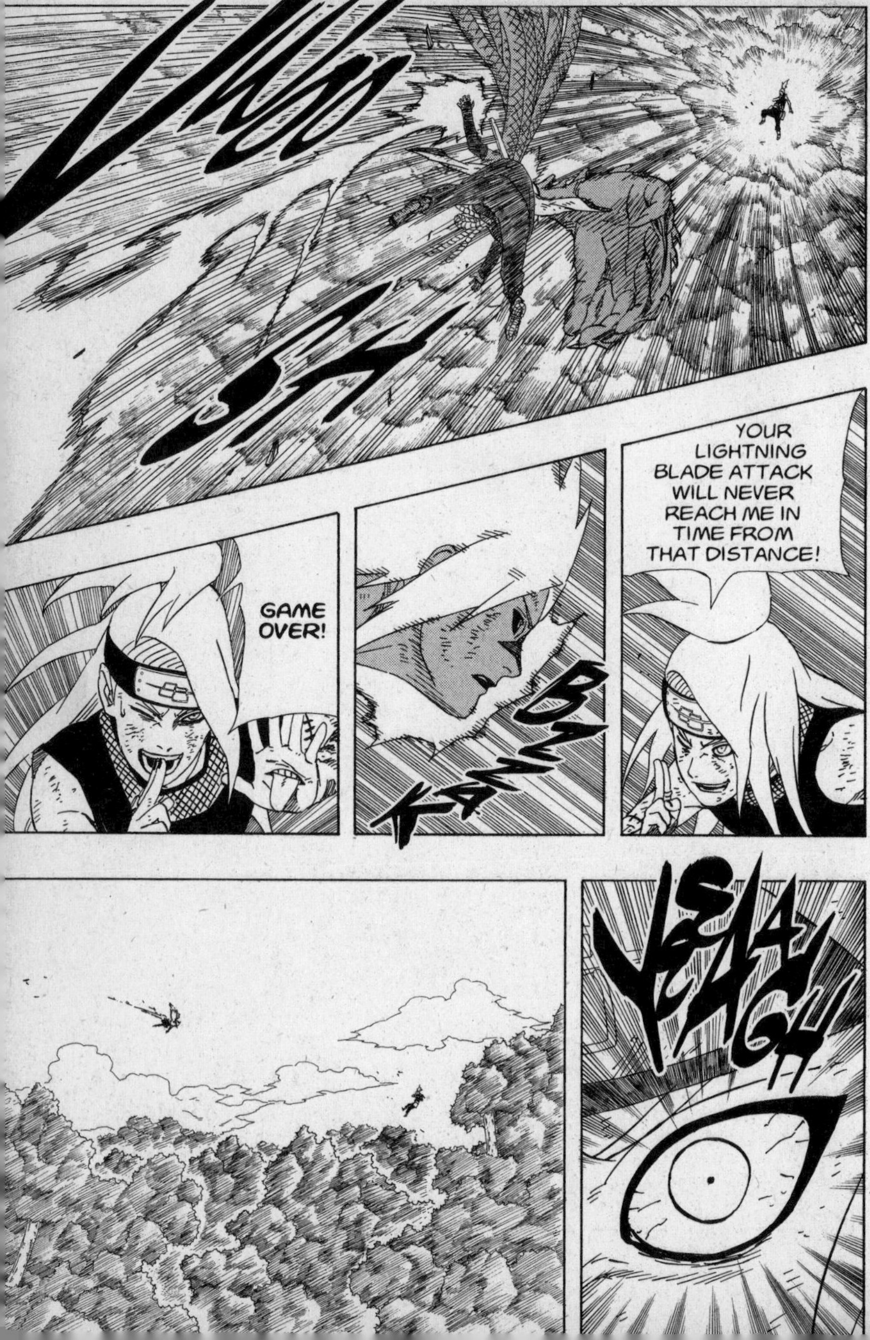
YOUR LIGHTNING BLADE ATTACK WILL NEVER REACH ME IN TIME FROM THAT DISTANCE!
BWAKA
GAME OVER!

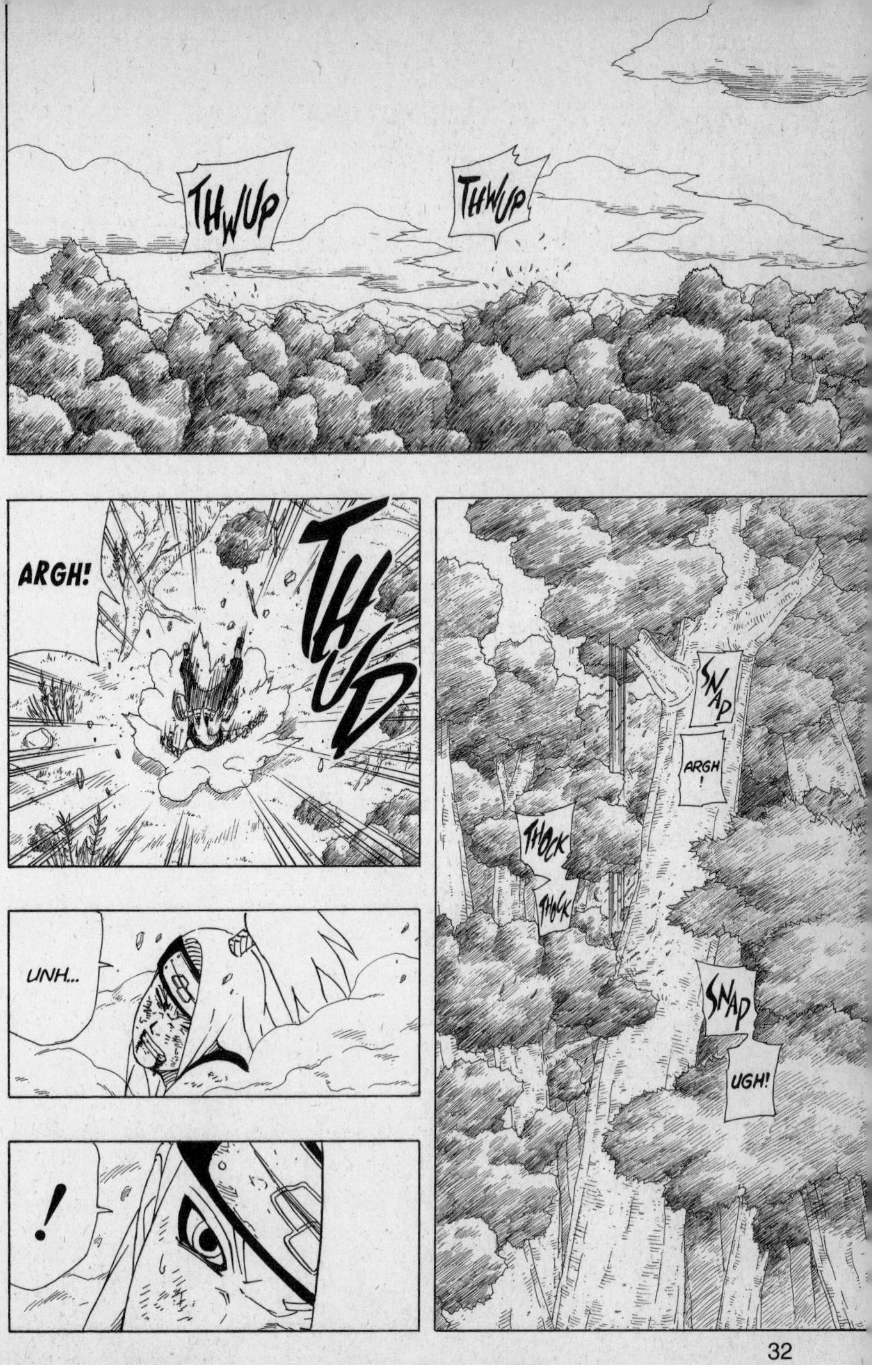
THWUP
THWUP
SNAP
ARGH!
THOCK
THOCK
SNAP
UGH!
ARGH!
THUD
UNH...
!

READ THIS WAY

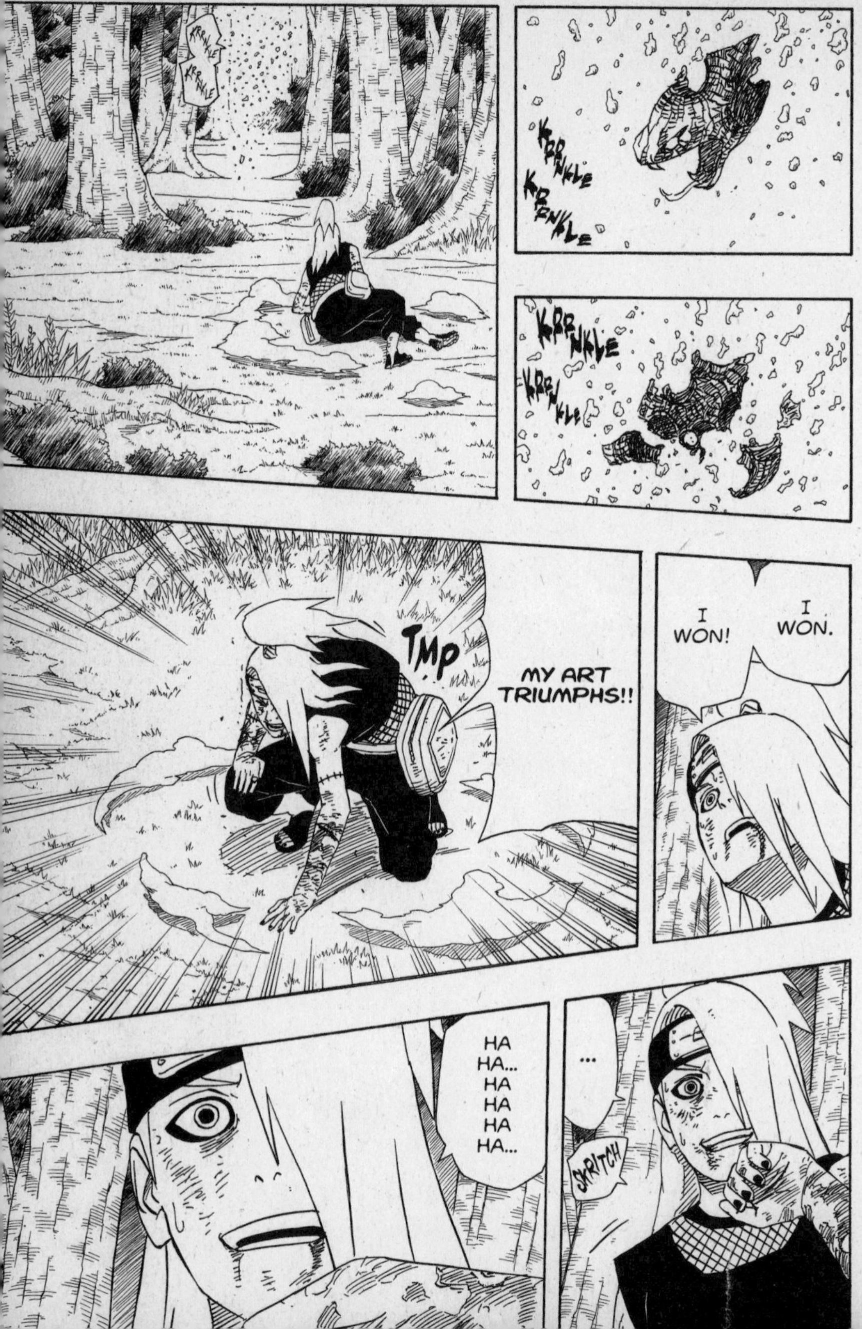
KRRNKLE
KRRNKLE
KRRNKLE
KRRNKLE
KRRNKLE
KRRNKLE
I WON.
I WON!
MY ART TRIUMPHS!!
TMP
...
SKRITCH
HA HA... HA HA HA HA...

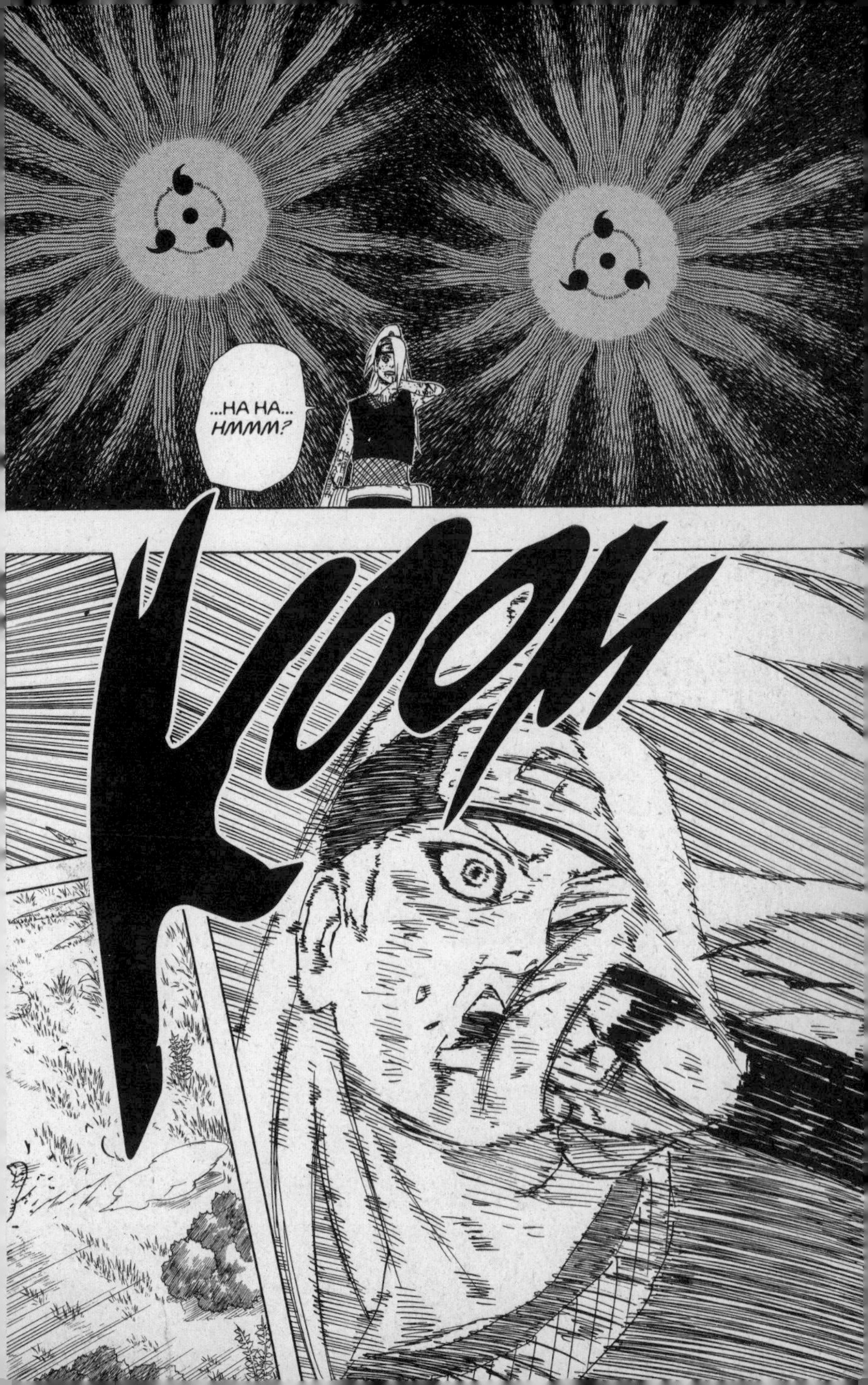
...HA HA...
HMMM?
VOOOM

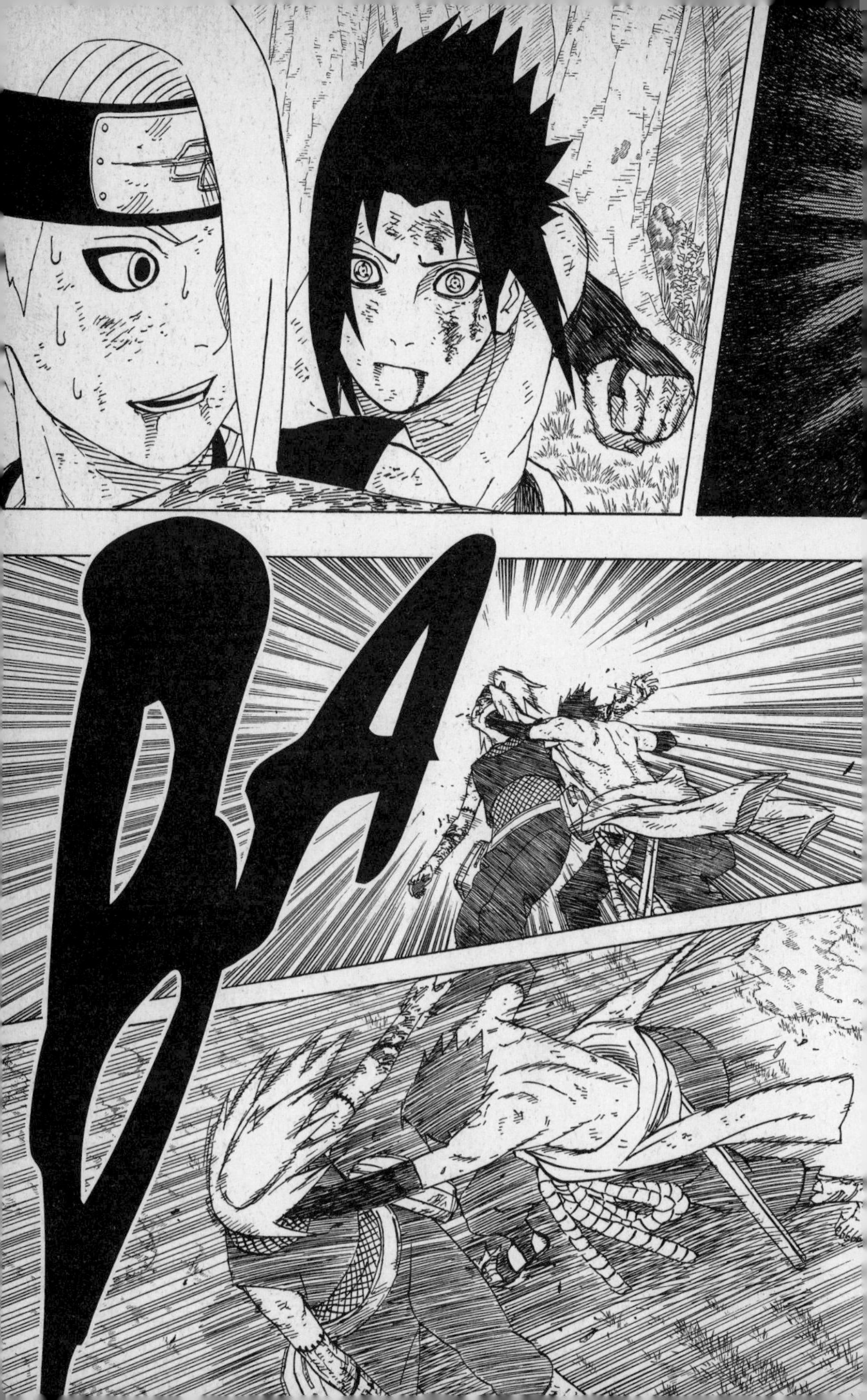
BAM

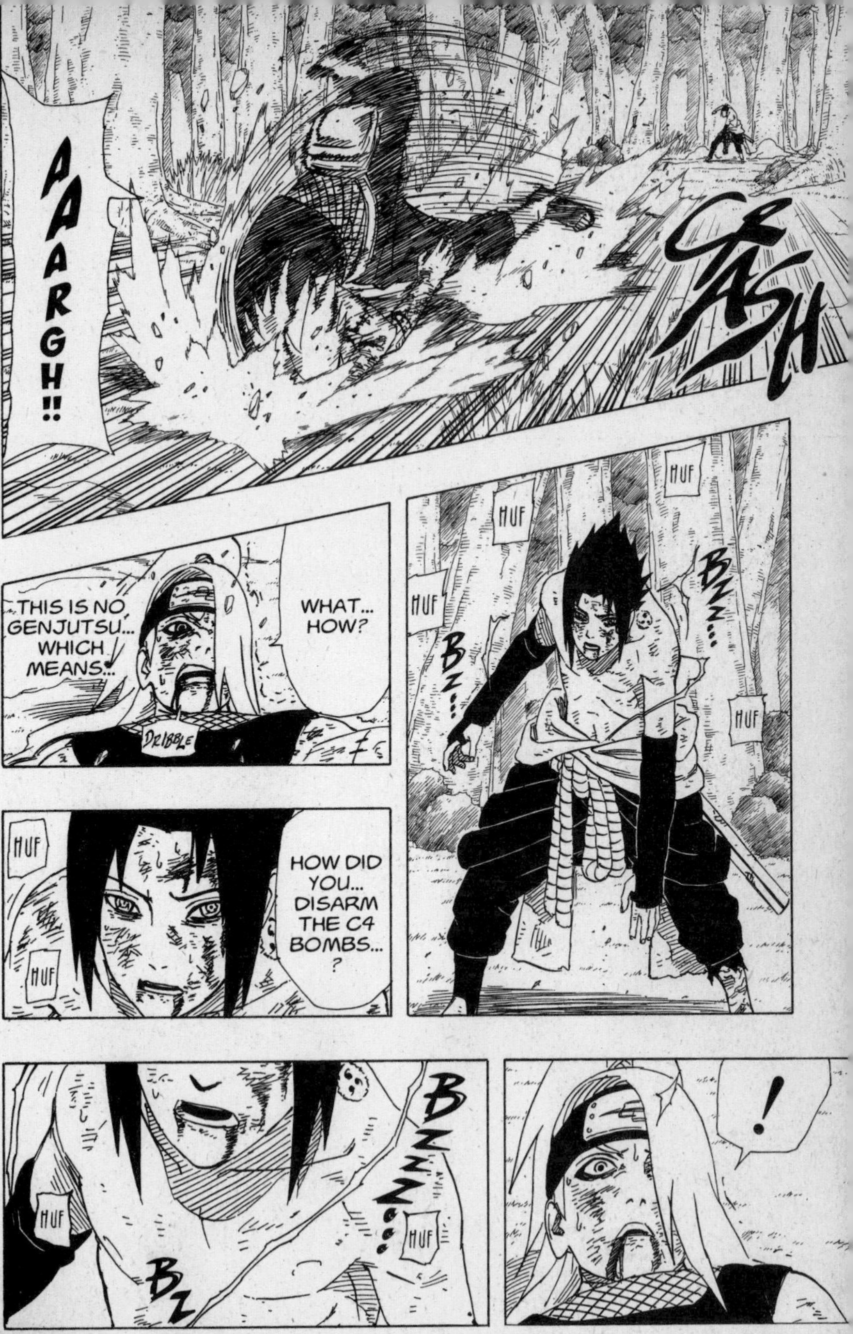
CRASH
AAARGH!!
HUF
HUF
BZZ...
BZ...
HUF
WHAT... HOW?
THIS IS NO GENJUTSU... WHICH MEANS...
DRIBBLE
HOW DID YOU... DISARM THE C4 BOMBS...?
HUF
HUF
!
BZZZZ...
HUF
HUF
BZ

READ THIS WAY

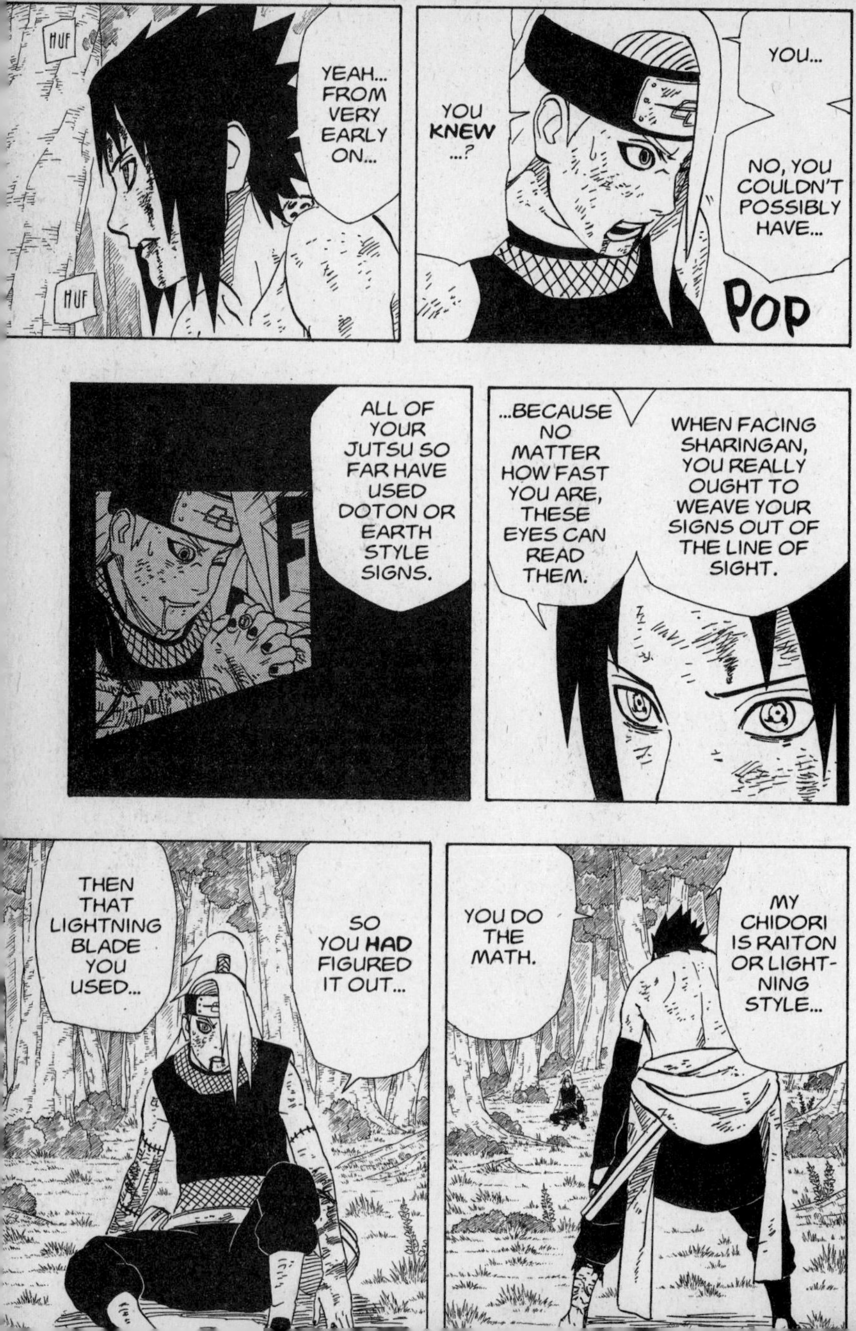
YOU...
YOU **KNEW** ...?
NO, YOU COULDN'T POSSIBLY HAVE...
POP
HUF
YEAH... FROM VERY EARLY ON...
HUF
WHEN FACING SHARINGAN, YOU REALLY OUGHT TO WEAVE YOUR SIGNS OUT OF THE LINE OF SIGHT.
...BECAUSE NO MATTER HOW FAST YOU ARE, THESE EYES CAN READ THEM.
ALL OF YOUR JUTSU SO FAR HAVE USED DOTON OR EARTH STYLE SIGNS.
MY CHIDORI IS RAITON OR LIGHT-NING STYLE...
YOU DO THE MATH.
SO YOU **HAD** FIGURED IT OUT...
THEN THAT LIGHTNING BLADE YOU USED...

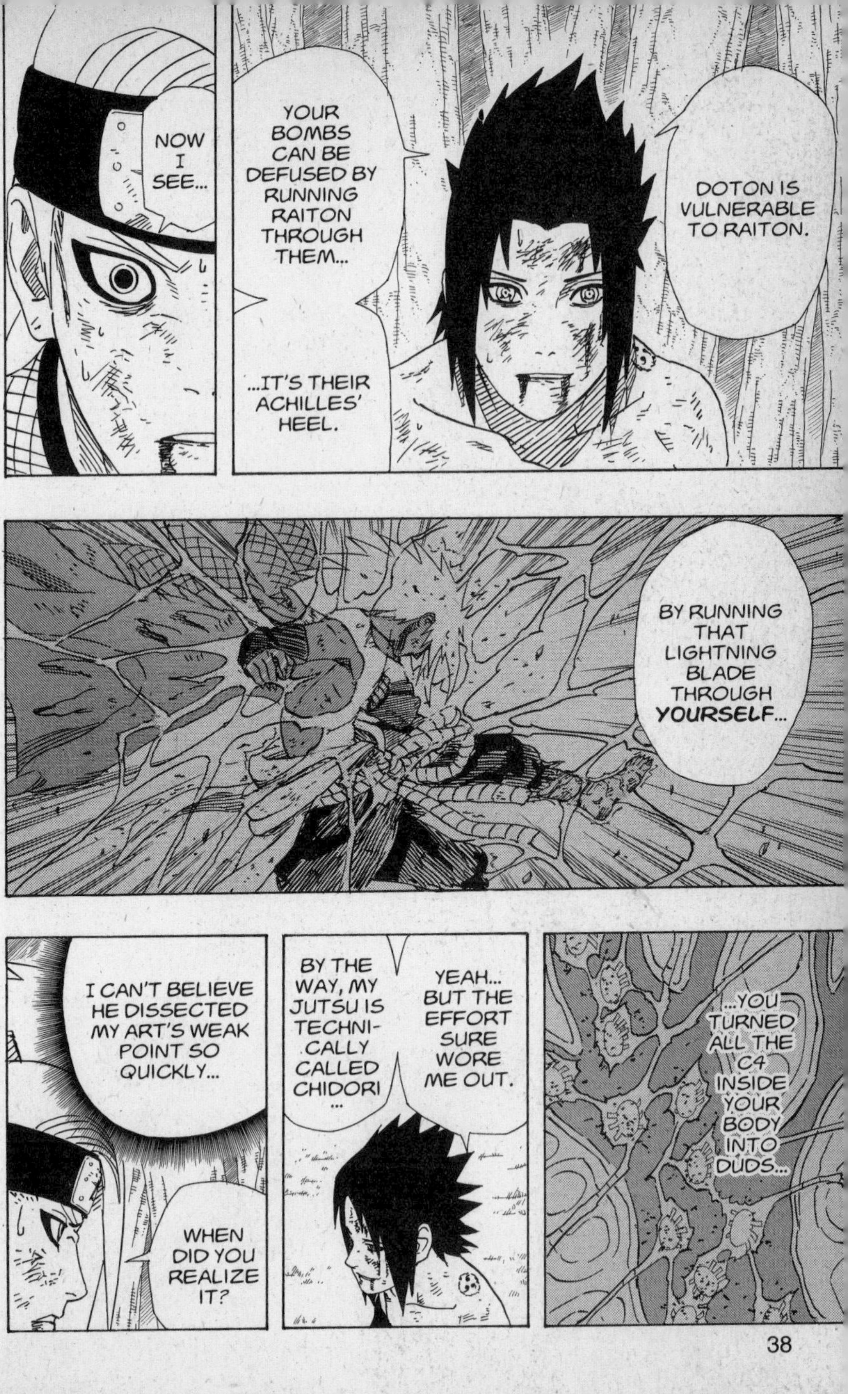
DOTON IS VULNERABLE TO RAITON.
YOUR BOMBS CAN BE DEFUSED BY RUNNING RAITON THROUGH THEM...
...IT'S THEIR ACHILLES' HEEL.
NOW I SEE...
BY RUNNING THAT LIGHTNING BLADE THROUGH **YOURSELF**...
...YOU TURNED ALL THE C4 INSIDE YOUR BODY INTO DUDS...
YEAH... BUT THE EFFORT SURE WORE ME OUT.
BY THE WAY, MY JUTSU IS TECHNI-CALLY CALLED CHIDORI...
I CAN'T BELIEVE HE DISSECTED MY ART'S WEAK POINT SO QUICKLY...
WHEN DID YOU REALIZE IT?

READ THIS WAY

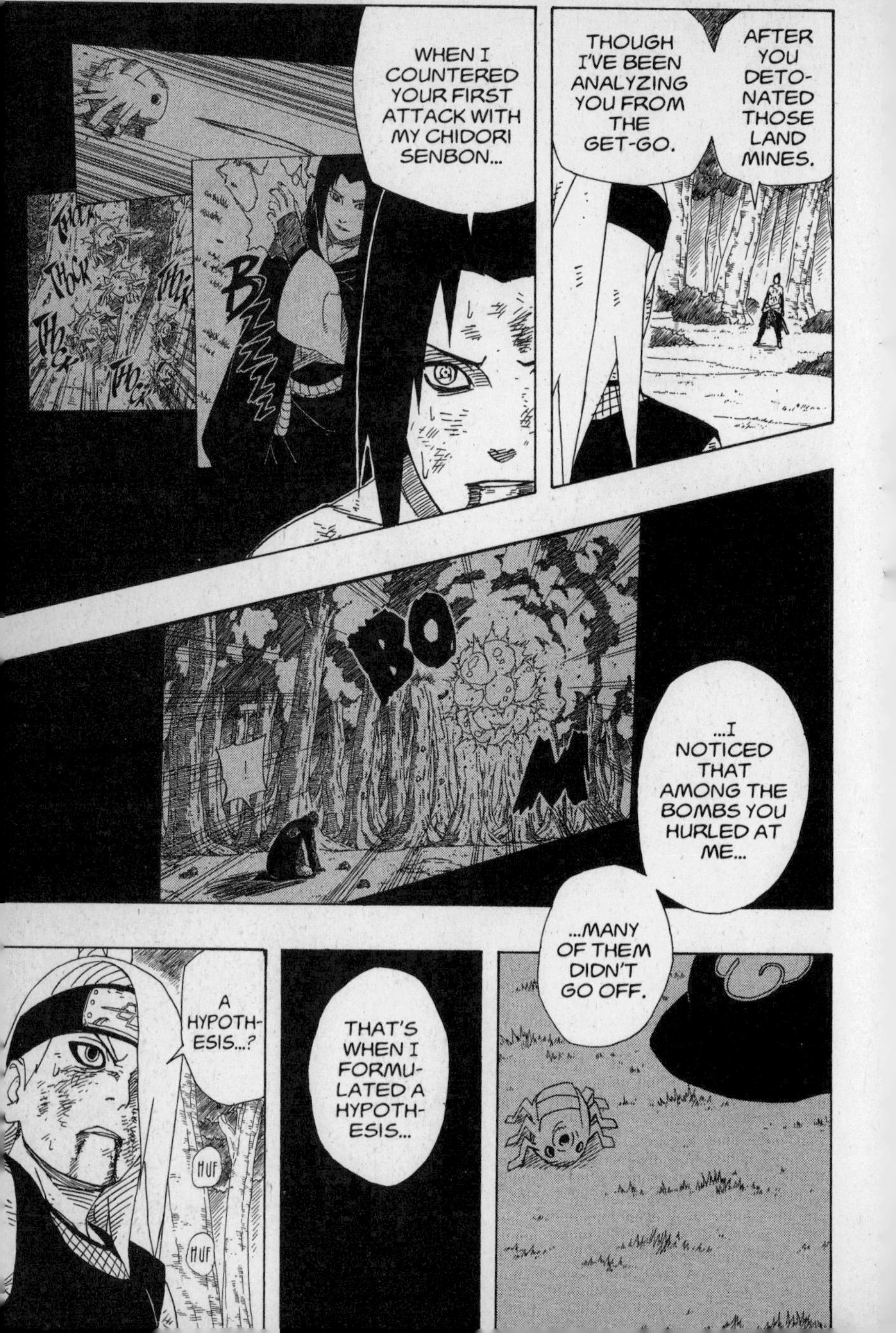
AFTER YOU DETO-NATED THOSE LAND MINES.
THOUGH I'VE BEEN ANALYZING YOU FROM THE GET-GO.
WHEN I COUNTERED YOUR FIRST ATTACK WITH MY CHIDORI SENBON...
THOCK
THOCK
THOCK
...I NOTICED THAT AMONG THE BOMBS YOU HURLED AT ME...
...MANY OF THEM DIDN'T GO OFF.
THAT'S WHEN I FORMULATED A HYPOTH-ESIS...
A HYPOTH-ESIS...?
HUF
HUF

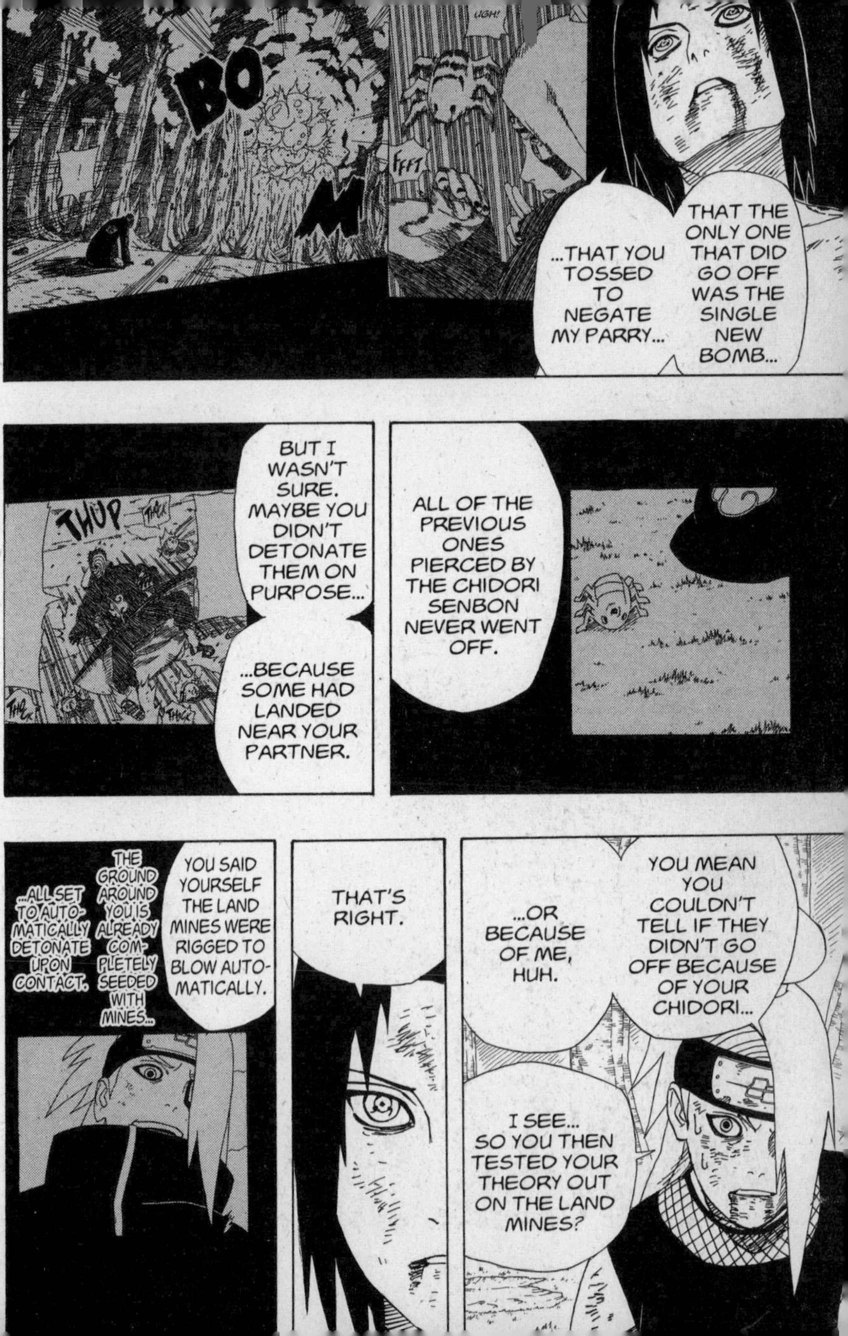
THAT THE ONLY ONE THAT DID GO OFF WAS THE SINGLE NEW BOMB...
...THAT YOU TOSSED TO NEGATE MY PARRY...
UGH!
FFFT
BOOM
ALL OF THE PREVIOUS ONES PIERCED BY THE CHIDORI SENBON NEVER WENT OFF.
BUT I WASN'T SURE. MAYBE YOU DIDN'T DETONATE THEM ON PURPOSE...
...BECAUSE SOME HAD LANDED NEAR YOUR PARTNER.
THUP
YOU MEAN YOU COULDN'T TELL IF THEY DIDN'T GO OFF BECAUSE OF YOUR CHIDORI...
...OR BECAUSE OF ME, HUH.
I SEE... SO YOU THEN TESTED YOUR THEORY OUT ON THE LAND MINES?
THAT'S RIGHT.
YOU SAID YOURSELF THE LAND MINES WERE RIGGED TO BLOW AUTOMATICALLY.
THE GROUND AROUND YOU IS ALREADY COMPLETELY SEEDED WITH MINES...
...ALL SET TO AUTOMATICALLY DETONATE UPON CONTACT.

READ THIS WAY

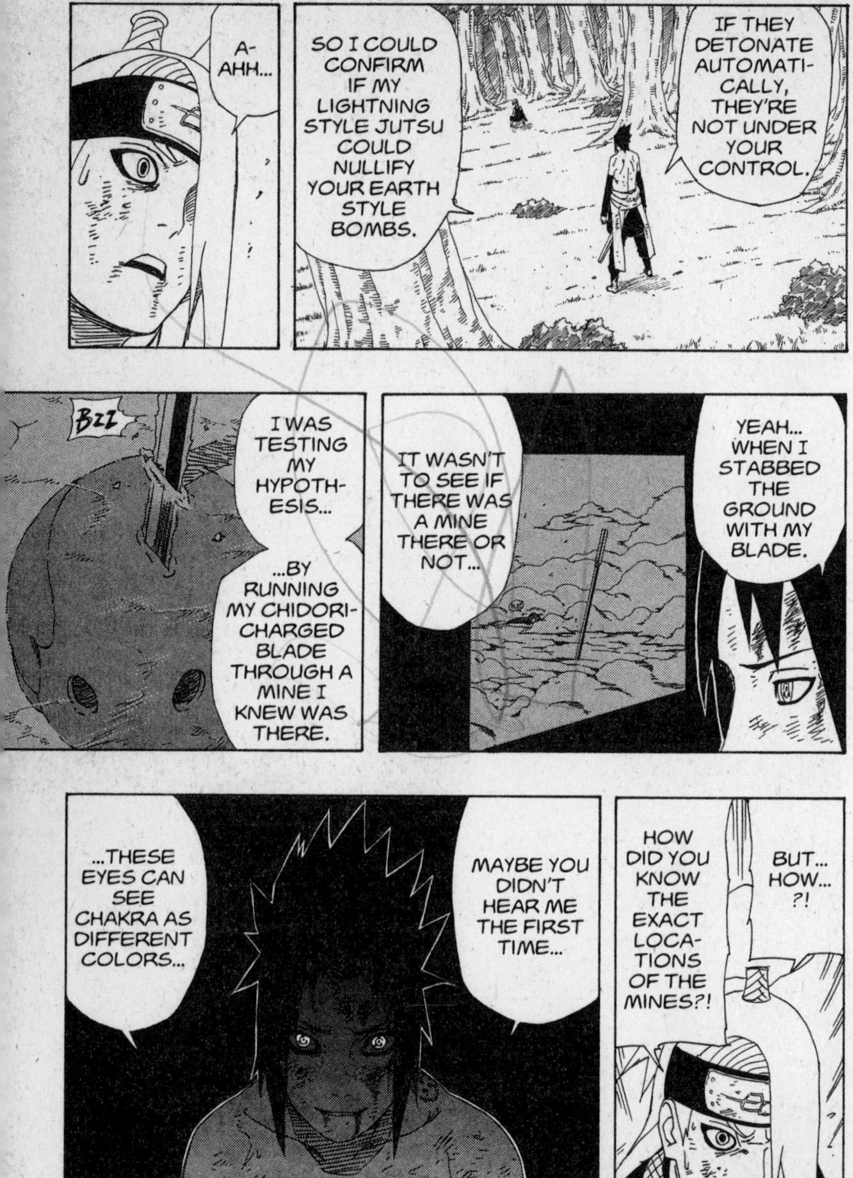
IF THEY DETONATE AUTOMATICALLY, THEY'RE NOT UNDER YOUR CONTROL.
SO I COULD CONFIRM IF MY LIGHTNING STYLE JUTSU COULD NULLIFY YOUR EARTH STYLE BOMBS.
A-AHH...
YEAH... WHEN I STABBED THE GROUND WITH MY BLADE.
IT WASN'T TO SEE IF THERE WAS A MINE THERE OR NOT...
I WAS TESTING MY HYPOTHESIS...
...BY RUNNING MY CHIDORI-CHARGED BLADE THROUGH A MINE I KNEW WAS THERE.
BZZ
BUT... HOW...?!
HOW DID YOU KNOW THE EXACT LOCATIONS OF THE MINES?!
MAYBE YOU DIDN'T HEAR ME THE FIRST TIME...
...THESE EYES CAN SEE CHAKRA AS DIFFERENT COLORS...

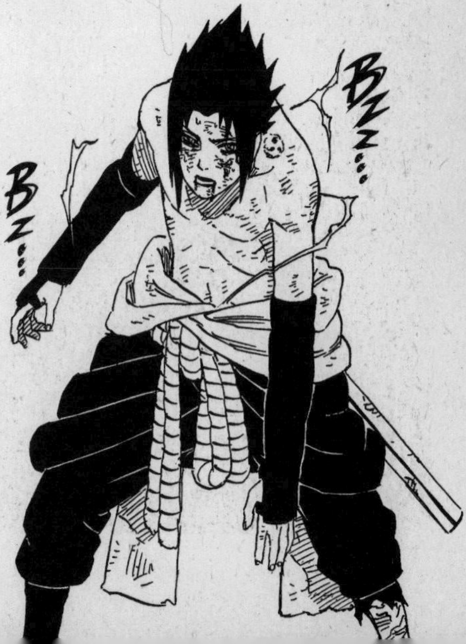
BZZ...
BZ...

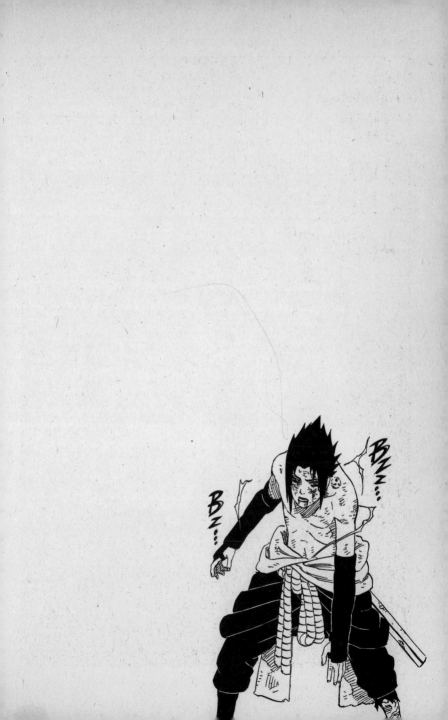

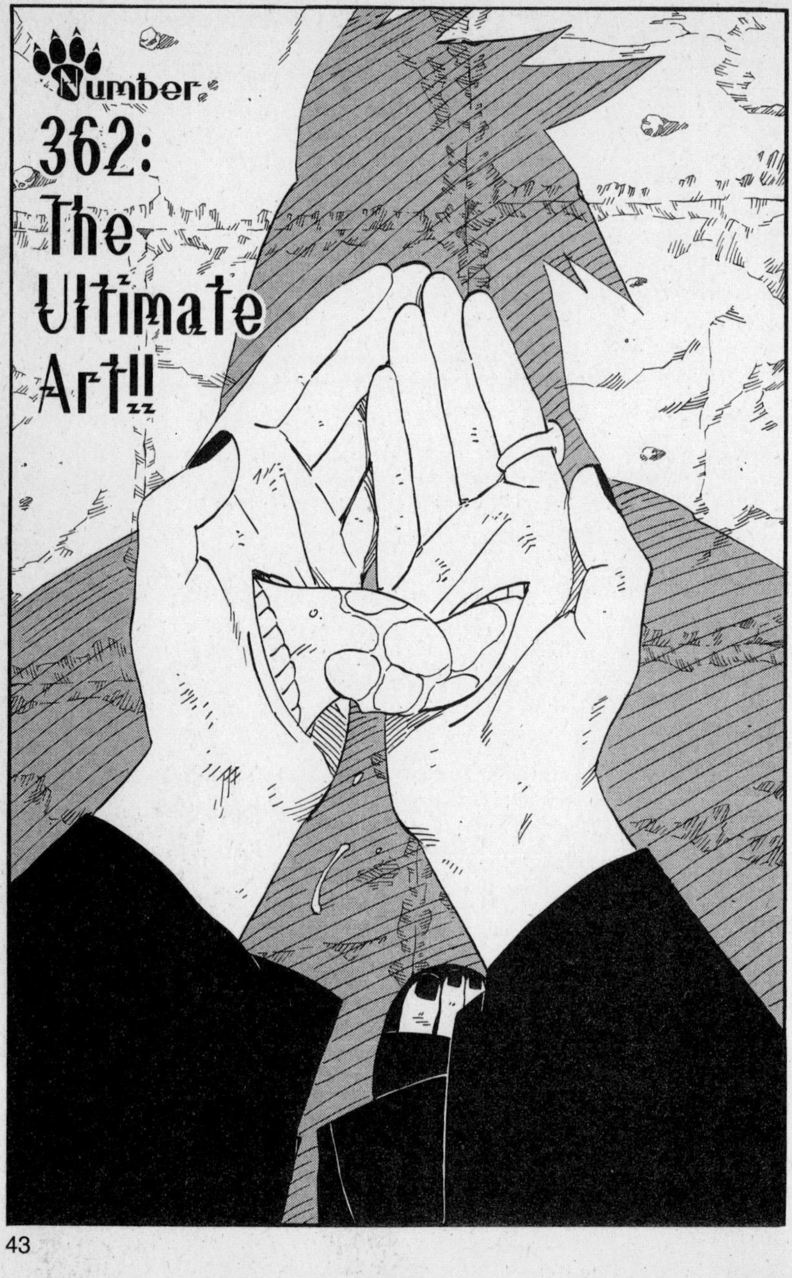
Number 362: The Ultimate Art!!

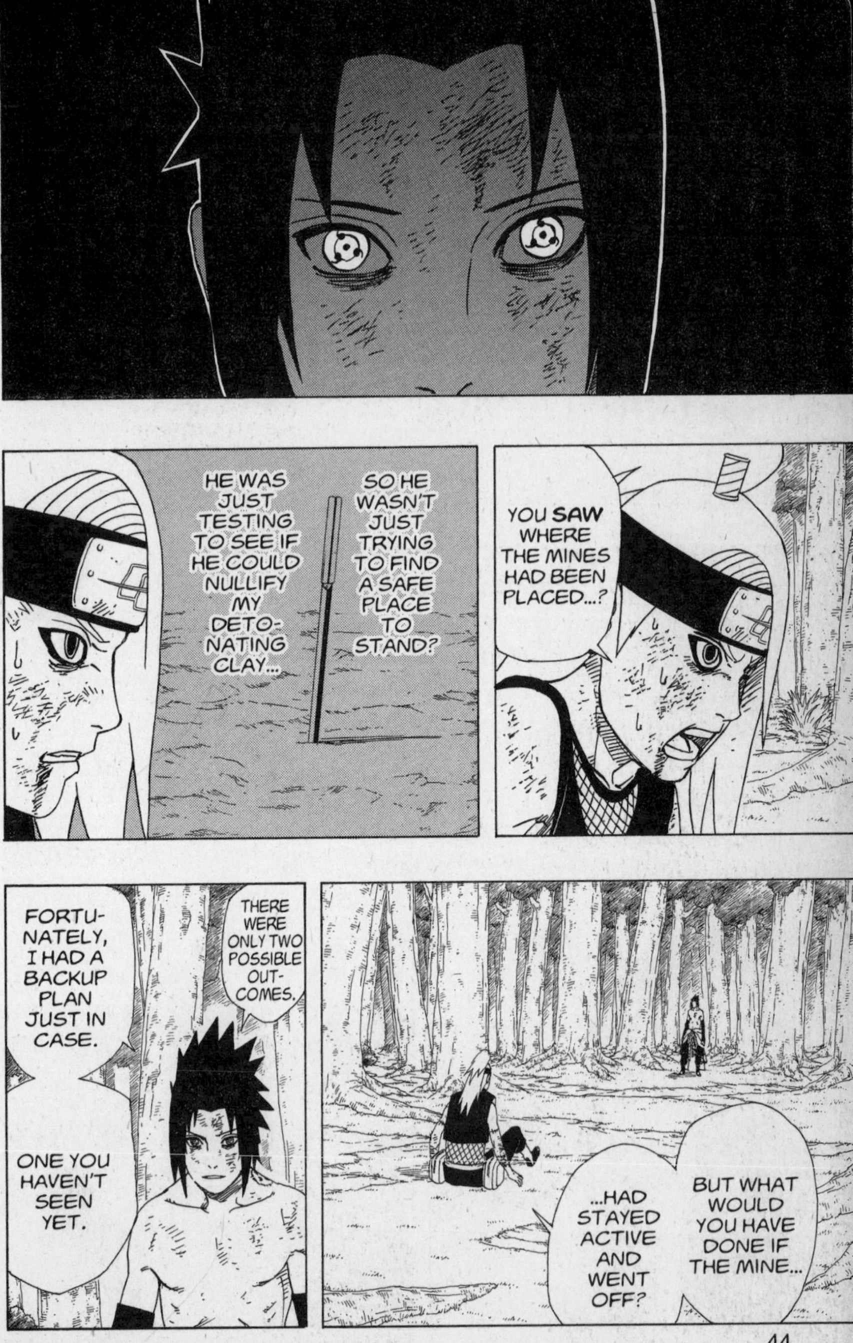
YOU **SAW** WHERE THE MINES HAD BEEN PLACED...?
SO HE WASN'T JUST TRYING TO FIND A SAFE PLACE TO STAND?
HE WAS JUST TESTING TO SEE IF HE COULD NULLIFY MY DETONATING CLAY...
BUT WHAT WOULD YOU HAVE DONE IF THE MINE...
...HAD STAYED ACTIVE AND WENT OFF?
THERE WERE ONLY TWO POSSIBLE OUTCOMES.
FORTUNATELY, I HAD A BACKUP PLAN JUST IN CASE.
ONE YOU HAVEN'T SEEN YET.

READ THIS WAY

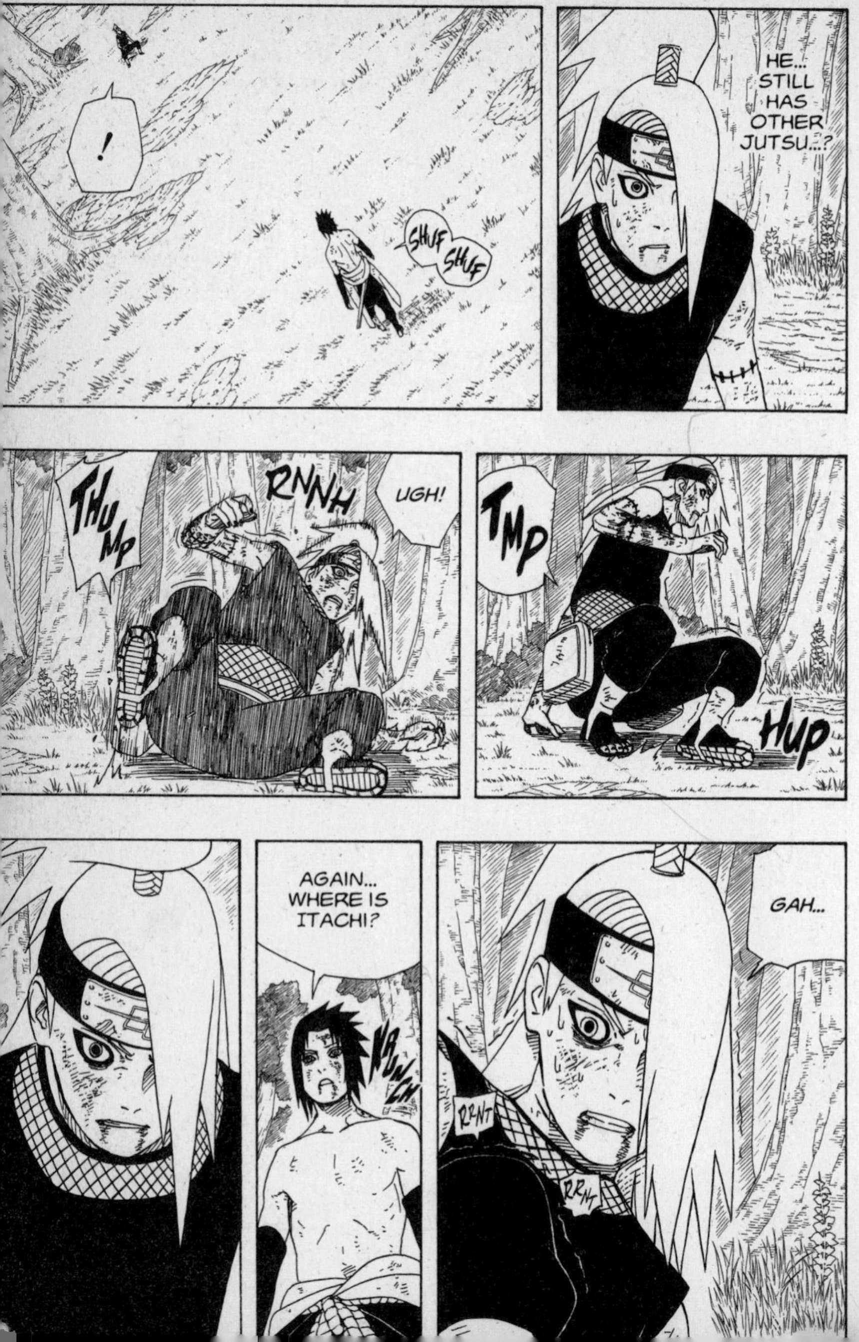
HE... STILL HAS OTHER JUTSU...?
!
SHUF SHUF
HUP
TMP
UGH!
RNNH
THUMP
GAH...
RRNT
RRNT
AGAIN... WHERE IS ITACHI?
KRUNCH

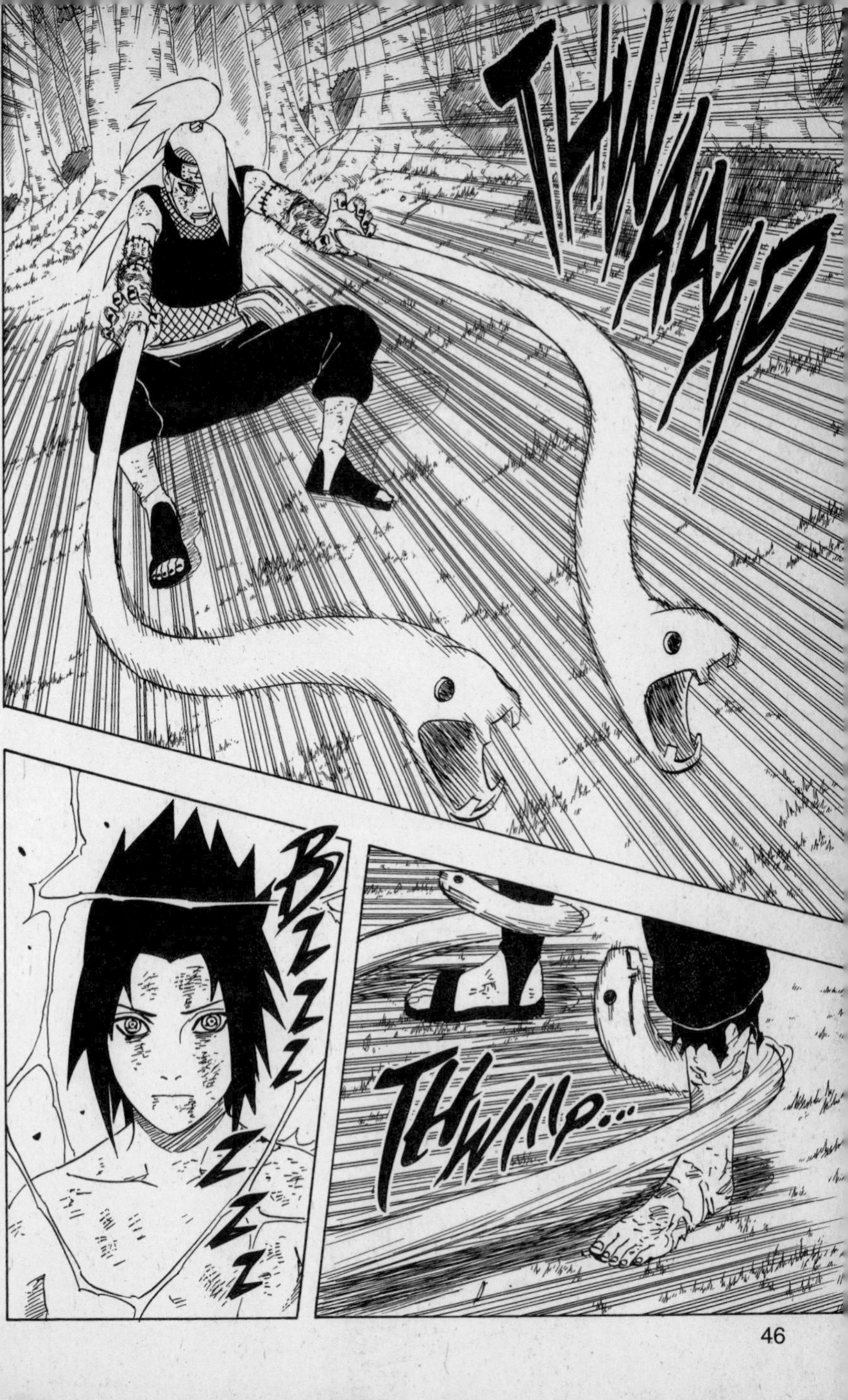
THWAAAP
THWIP...
BZZZZZZZ

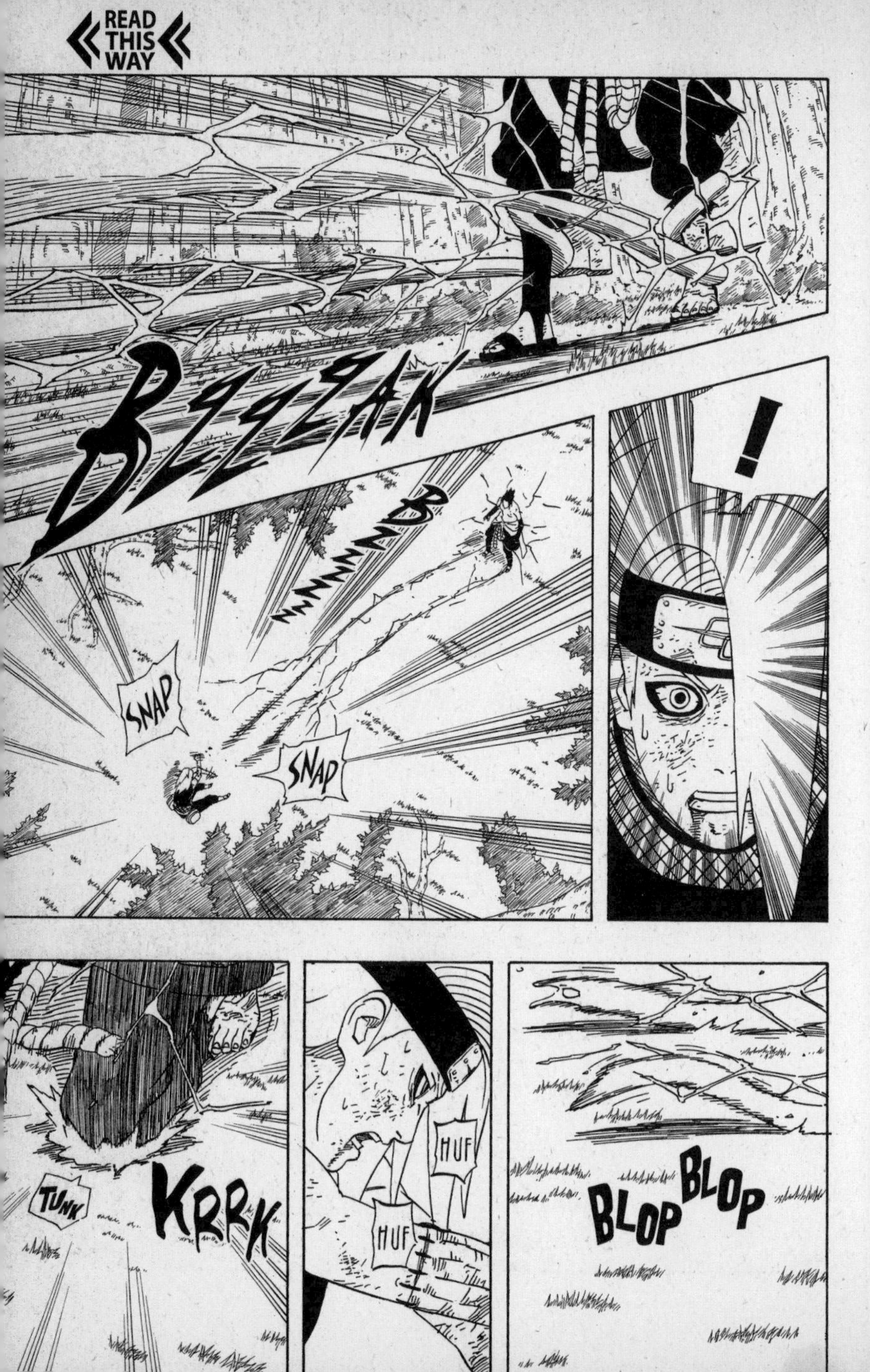
READ THIS WAY
BZZZAK
!
BZZZZ
SNAP
SNAP
BLOP BLOP
HUF
HUF
KRRK
TUNK

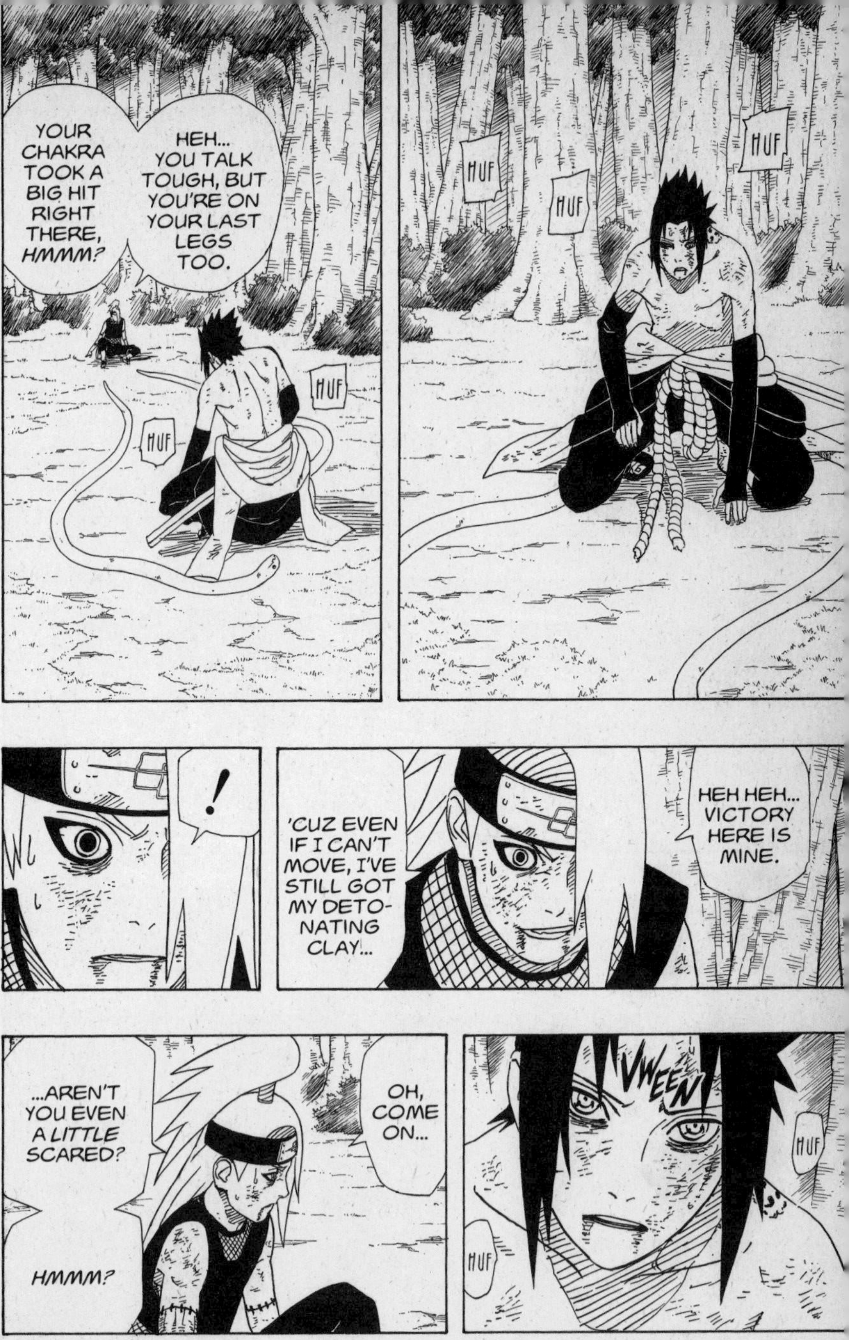
HUF
HUF
HUF
HEH... YOU TALK TOUGH, BUT YOU'RE ON YOUR LAST LEGS TOO.
YOUR CHAKRA TOOK A BIG HIT RIGHT THERE, HMMM?
HUF
HUF
HEH HEH... VICTORY HERE IS MINE.
'CUZ EVEN IF I CAN'T MOVE, I'VE STILL GOT MY DETO-NATING CLAY...
!
VWEEN
HUF
HUF
OH, COME ON...
...AREN'T YOU EVEN A LITTLE SCARED?
HMMM?

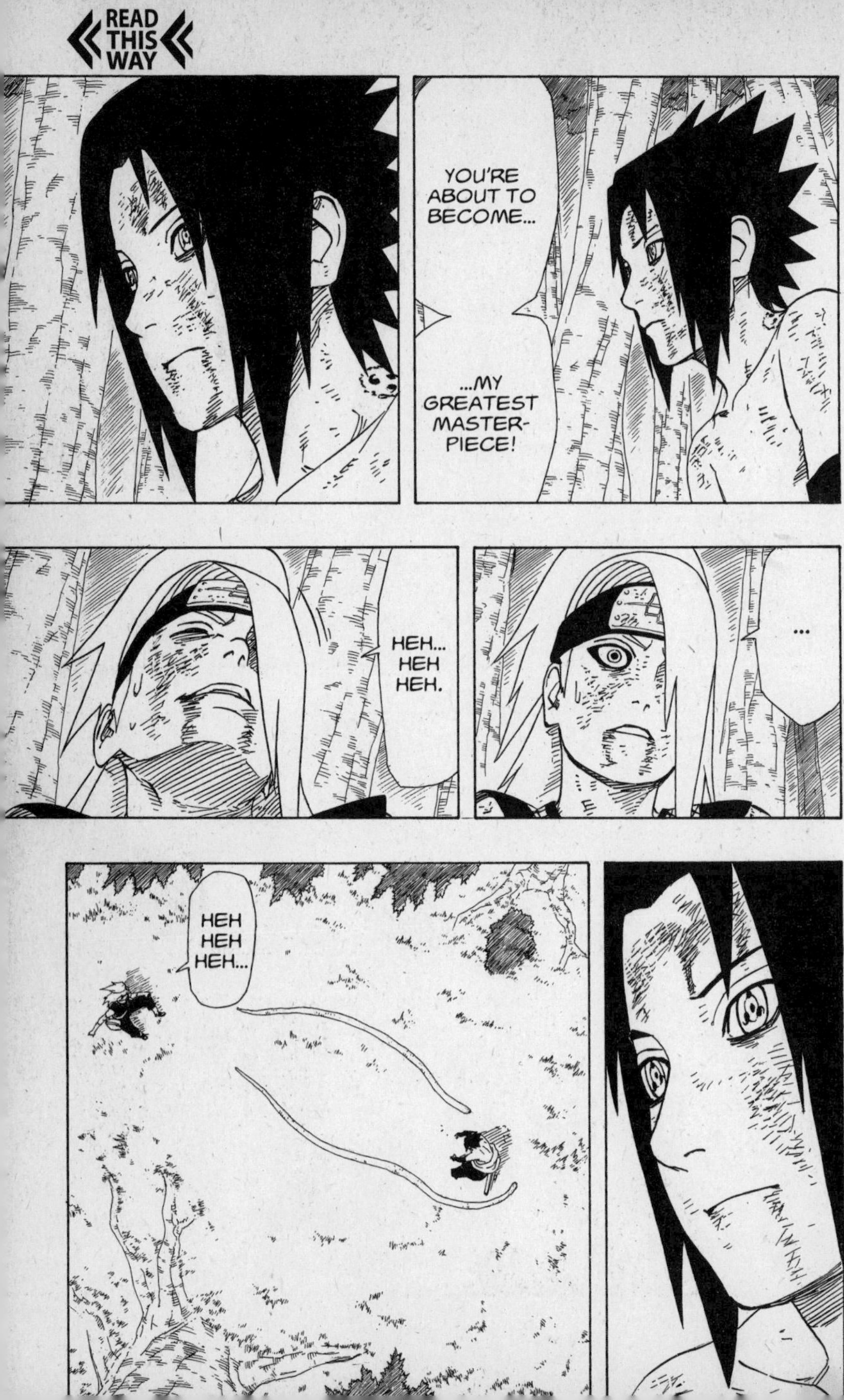
READ THIS WAY
YOU'RE ABOUT TO BECOME...
...MY GREATEST MASTER-PIECE!
...
HEH... HEH HEH.
HEH HEH HEH...

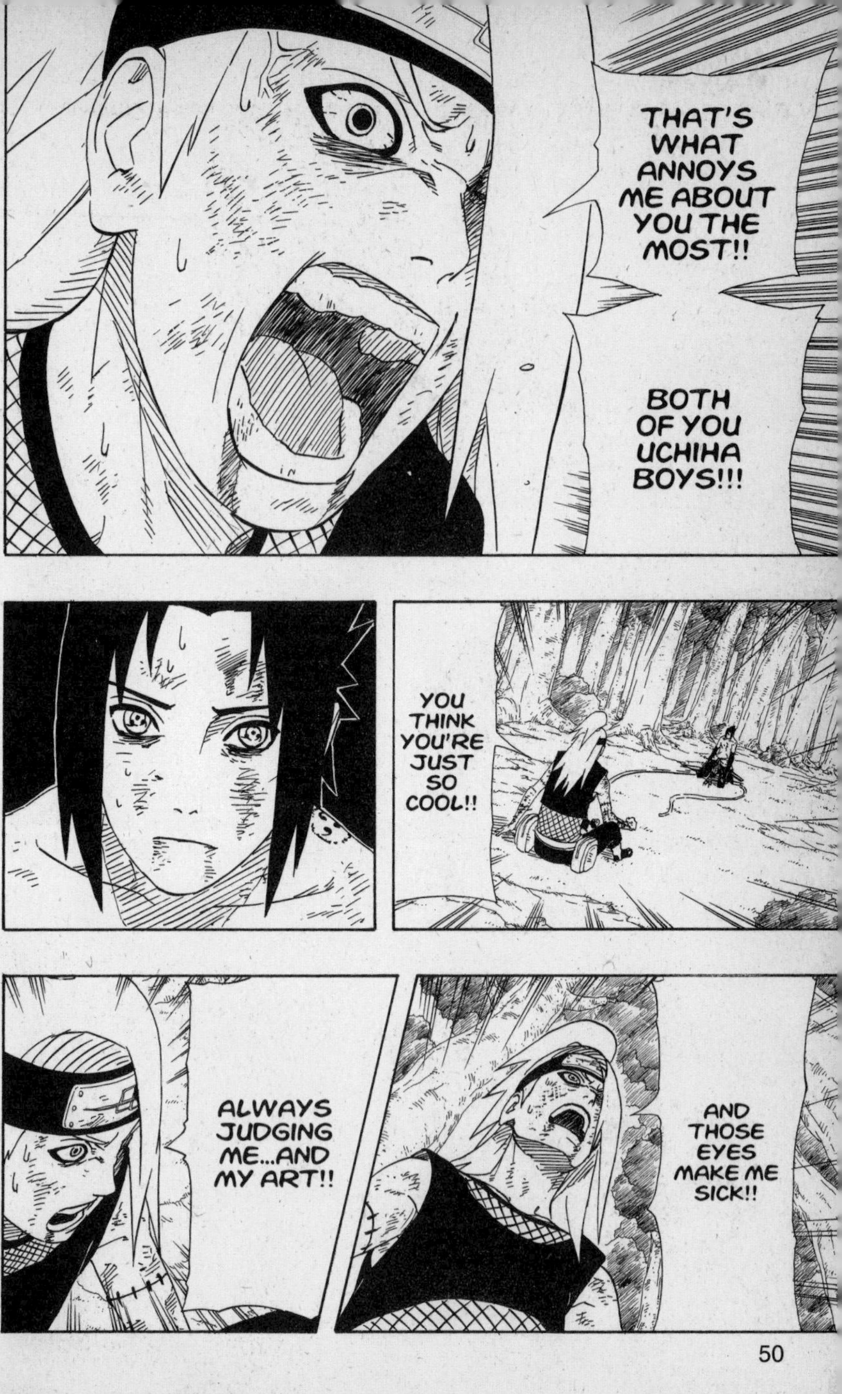
THAT'S WHAT ANNOYS ME ABOUT YOU THE MOST!!
BOTH OF YOU UCHIHA BOYS!!!
YOU THINK YOU'RE JUST SO COOL!!
AND THOSE EYES MAKE ME SICK!!
ALWAYS JUDGING ME...AND MY ART!!

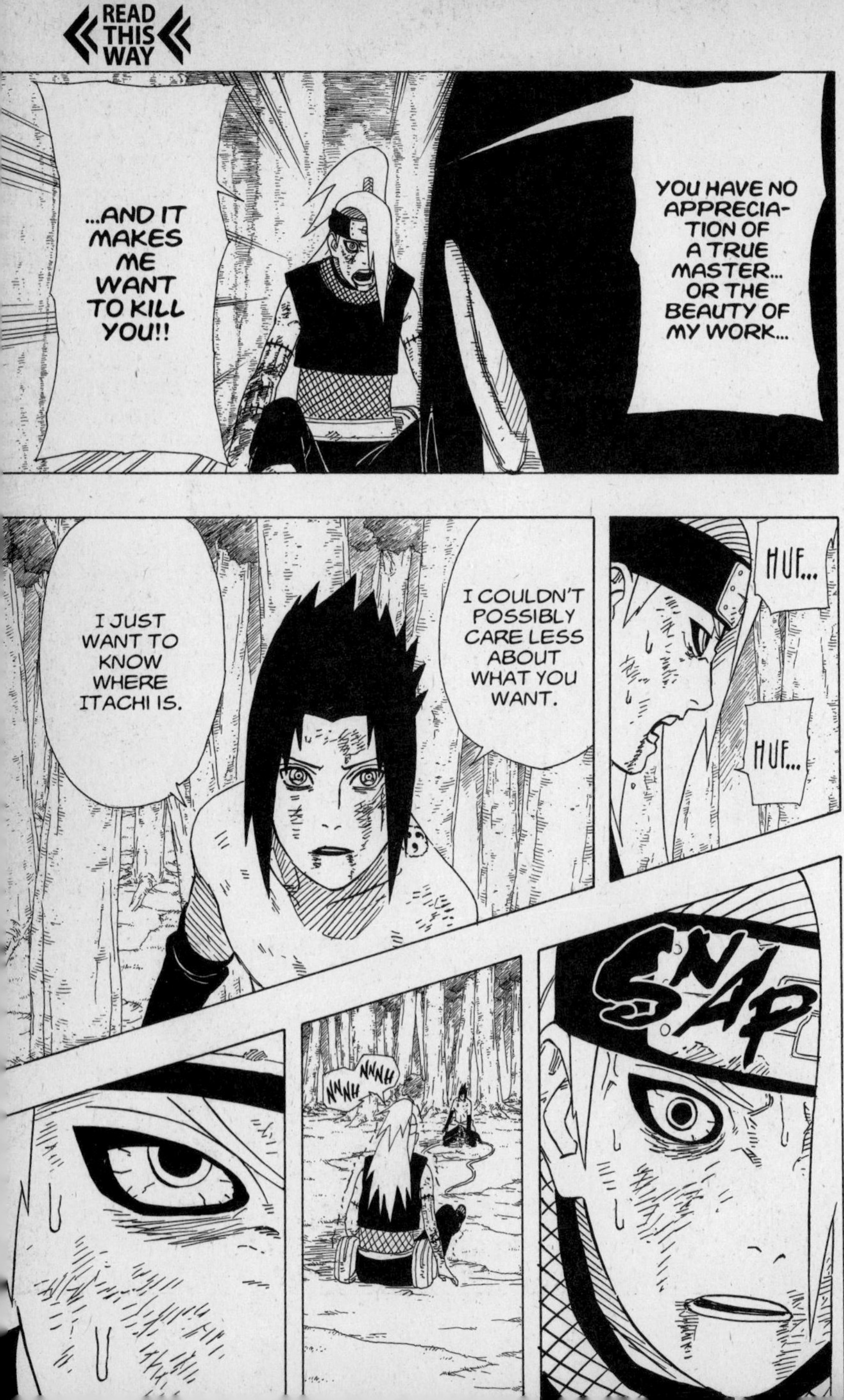
READ THIS WAY
YOU HAVE NO APPRECIA-TION OF A TRUE MASTER... OR THE BEAUTY OF MY WORK...
...AND IT MAKES ME WANT TO KILL YOU!!
HUF...
HUF...
I COULDN'T POSSIBLY CARE LESS ABOUT WHAT YOU WANT.
I JUST WANT TO KNOW WHERE ITACHI IS.
SNAP
NNNH
NNNH

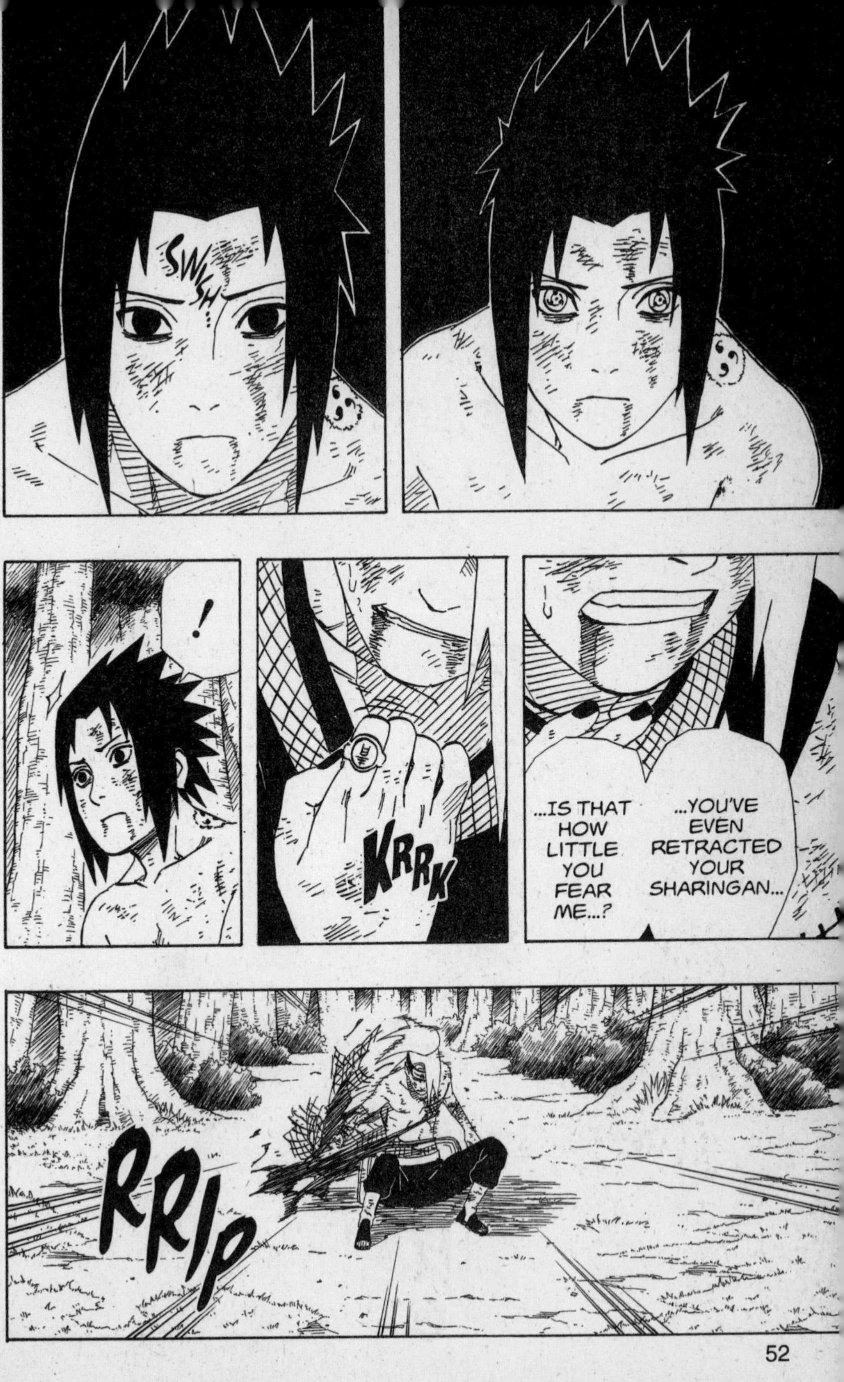
SWISH
...YOU'VE EVEN RETRACTED YOUR SHARINGAN...
...IS THAT HOW LITTLE YOU FEAR ME...?
KRRK
!
RRIP

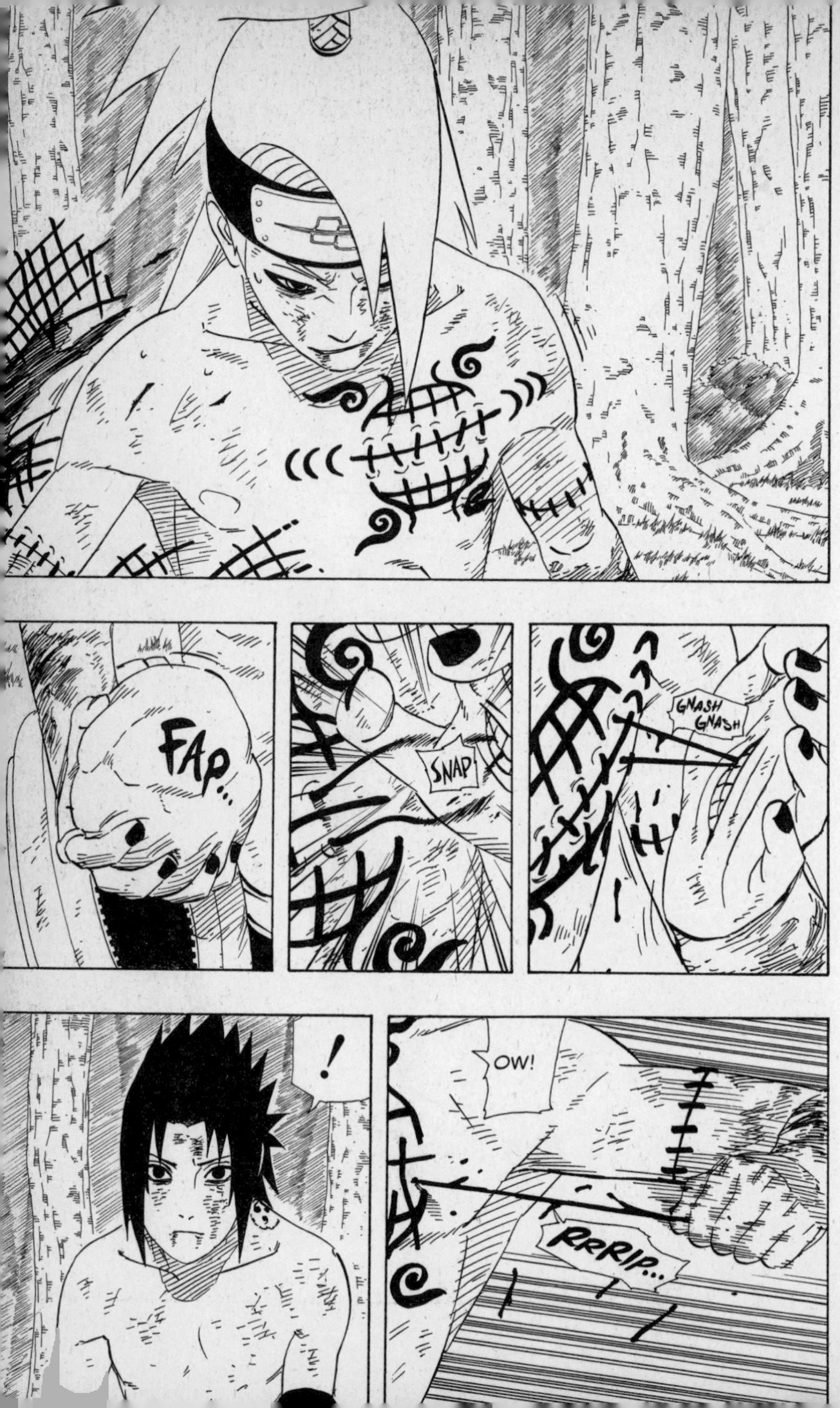
GNASH GNASH
SNAP
FAP...
OW!
RRRIP...
!

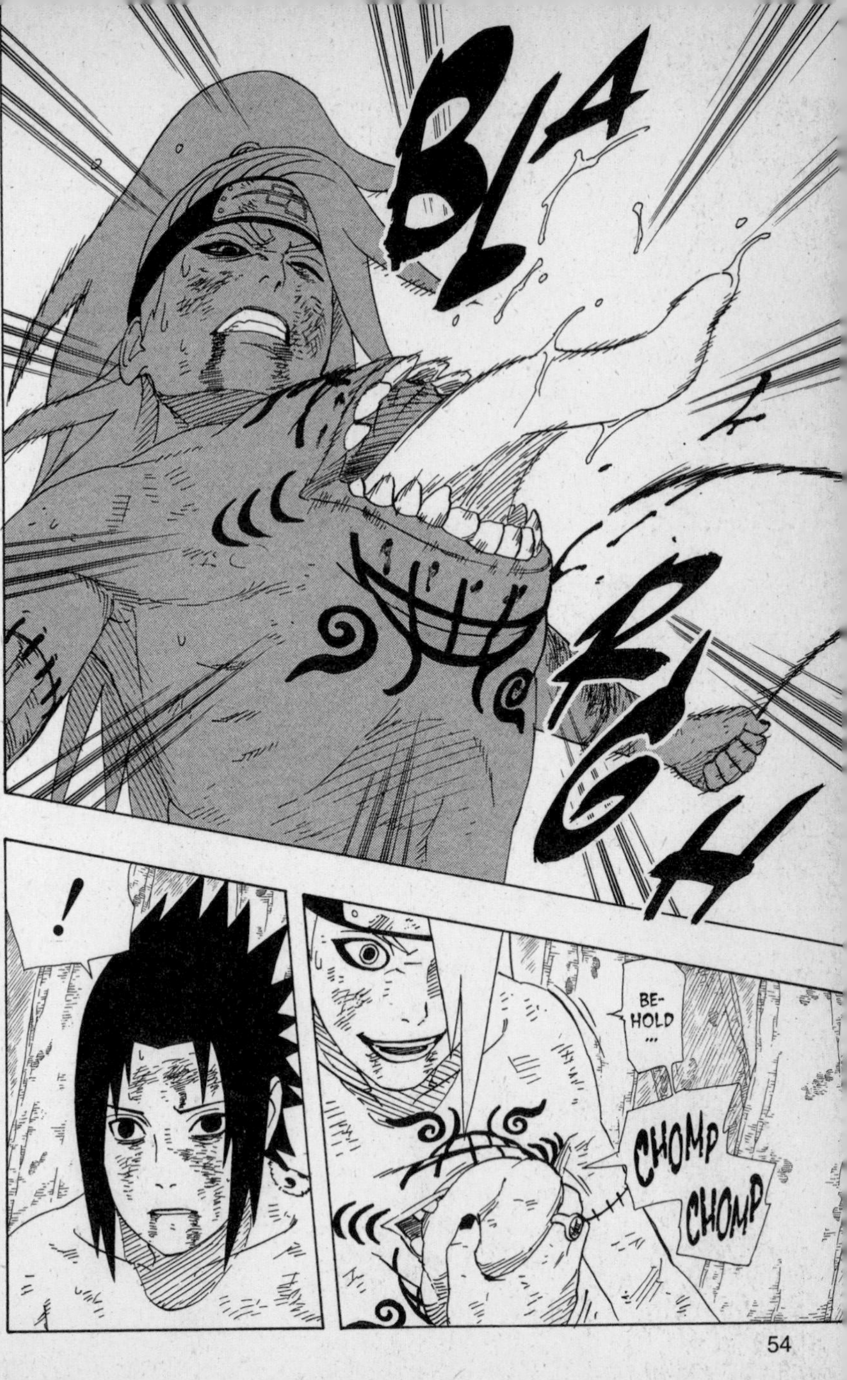
BLARGH
BE-HOLD ...
CHOMP CHOMP
!

READ THIS WAY

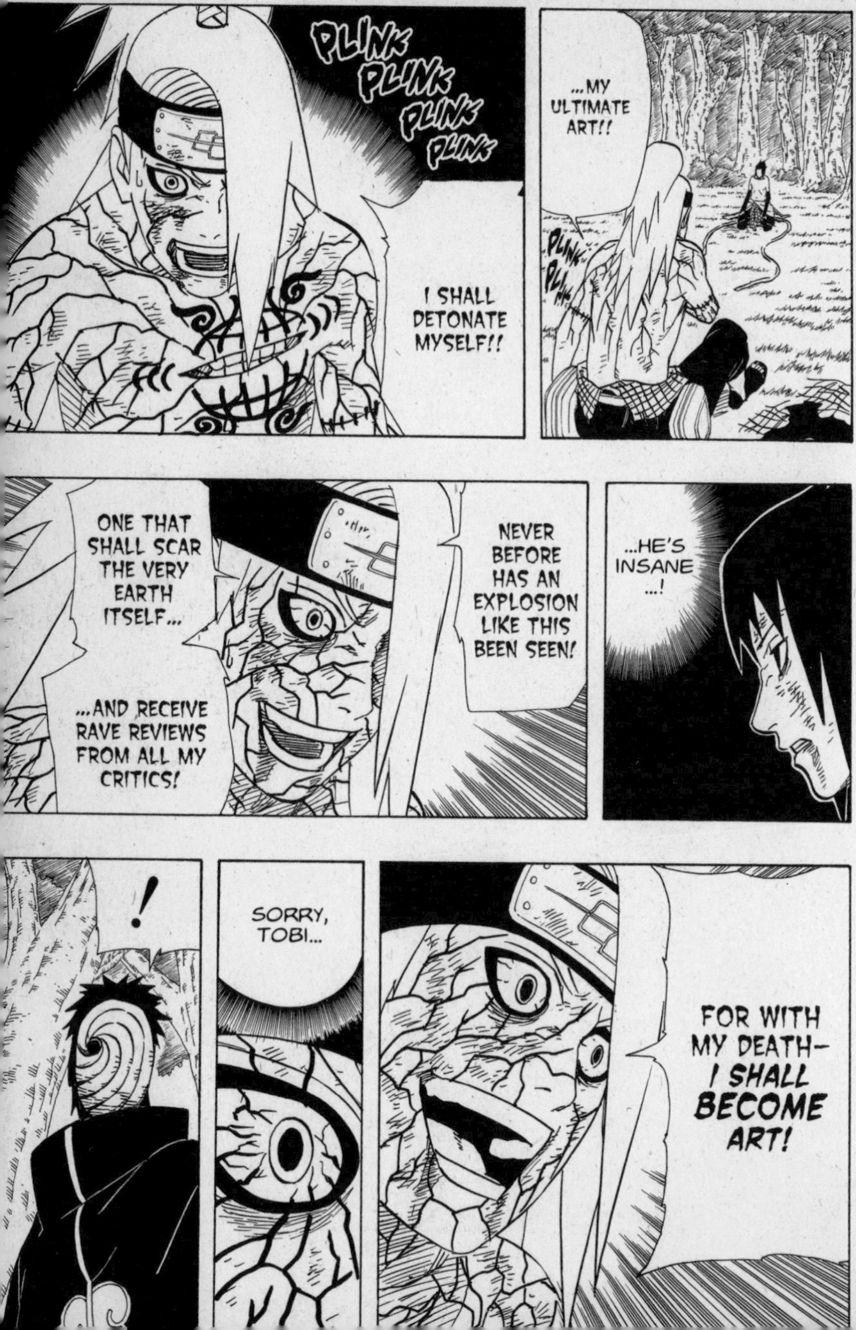
...MY ULTIMATE ART!!
PLINK PLINK
PLINK PLINK PLINK PLINK
I SHALL DETONATE MYSELF!!
...HE'S INSANE ...!
NEVER BEFORE HAS AN EXPLOSION LIKE THIS BEEN SEEN!
ONE THAT SHALL SCAR THE VERY EARTH ITSELF...
...AND RECEIVE RAVE REVIEWS FROM ALL MY CRITICS!
FOR WITH MY DEATH— I SHALL BECOME ART!
SORRY, TOBI...
!

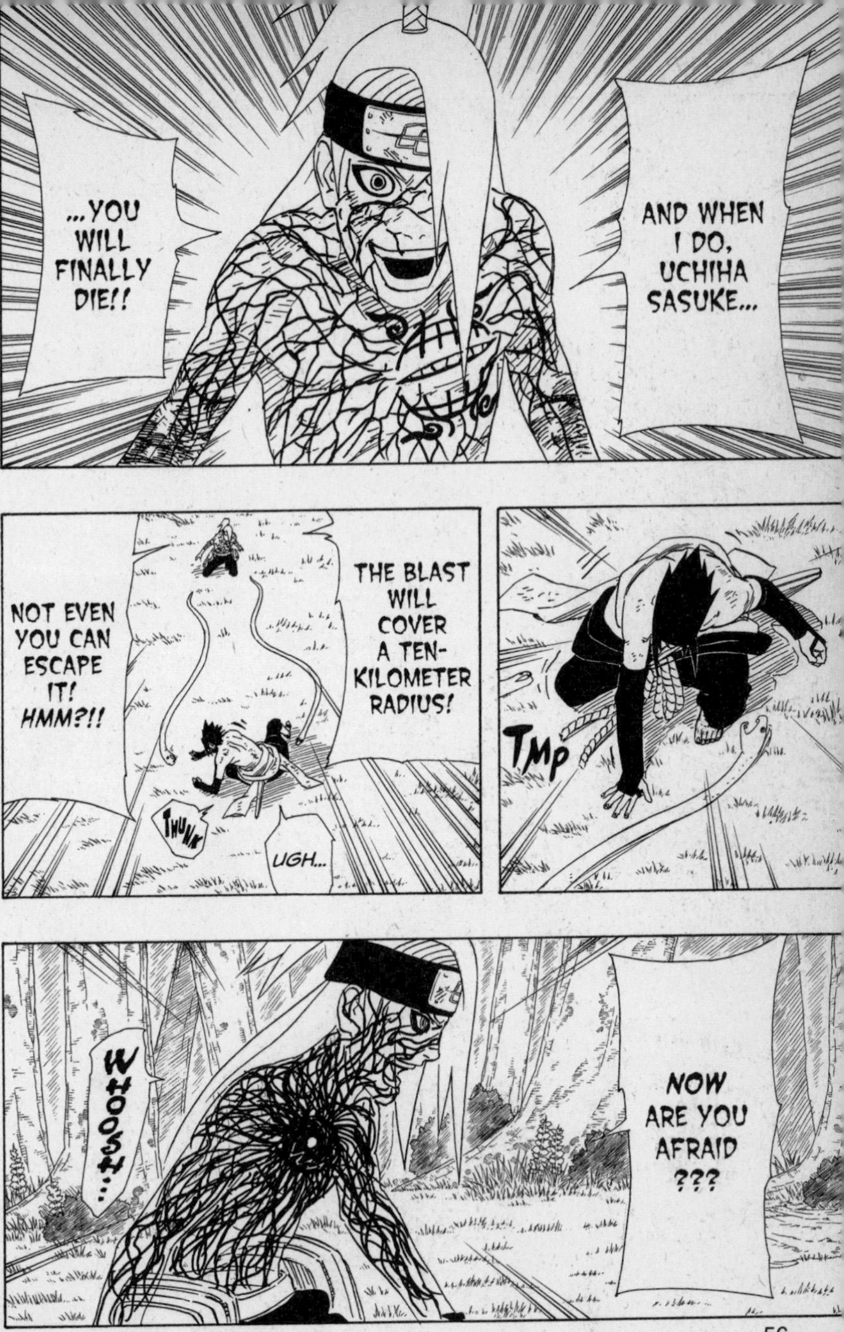
AND WHEN I DO, UCHIHA SASUKE...
...YOU WILL FINALLY DIE!!
TMP
THE BLAST WILL COVER A TEN-KILOMETER RADIUS!
NOT EVEN YOU CAN ESCAPE IT! HMM?!!
THUNK
UGH...
NOW ARE YOU AFRAID ???
WHOOSH...

READ THIS WAY

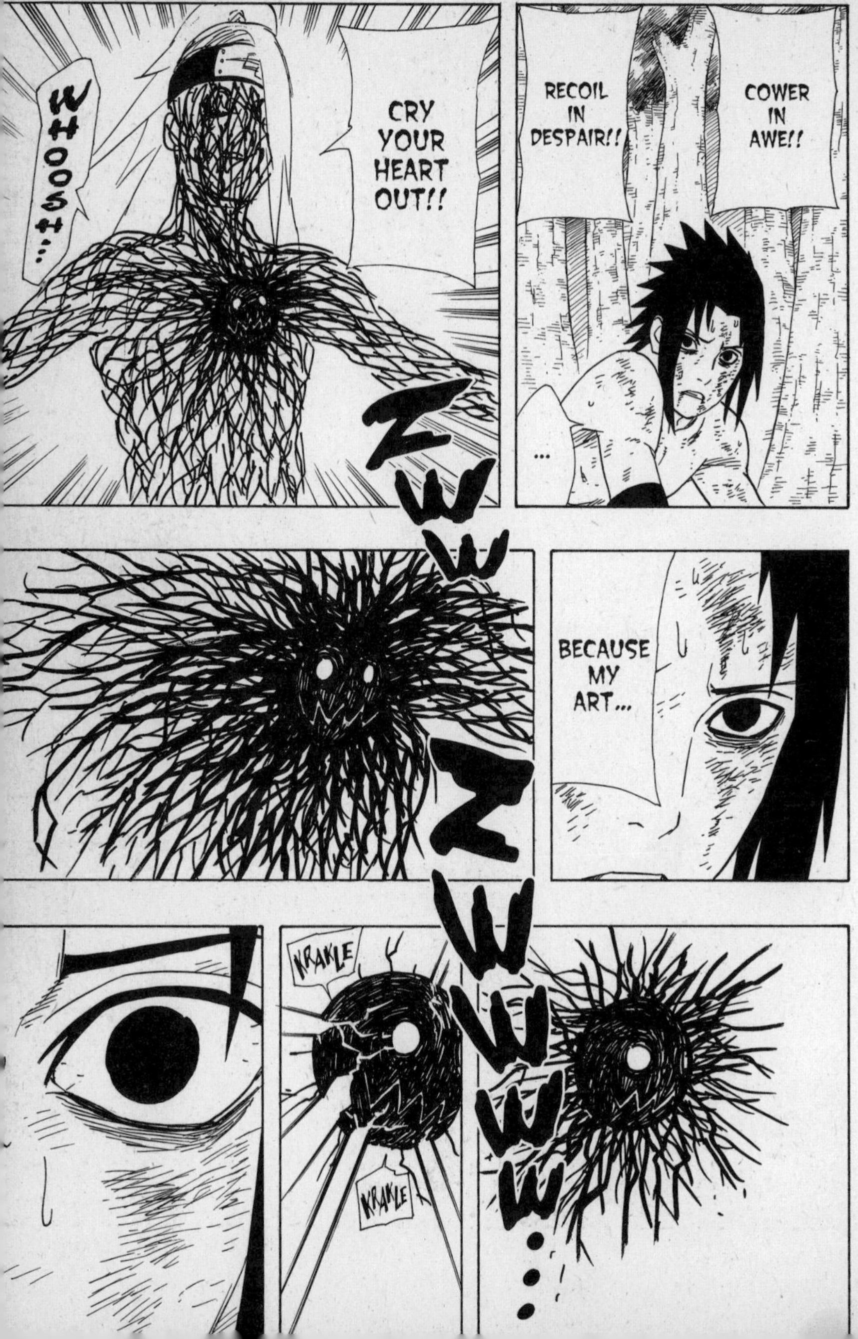
COWER IN AWE!!
RECOIL IN DESPAIR!!
...
CRY YOUR HEART OUT!!
WHOOSH...
BECAUSE MY ART...
KRAKLE
KRAKLE

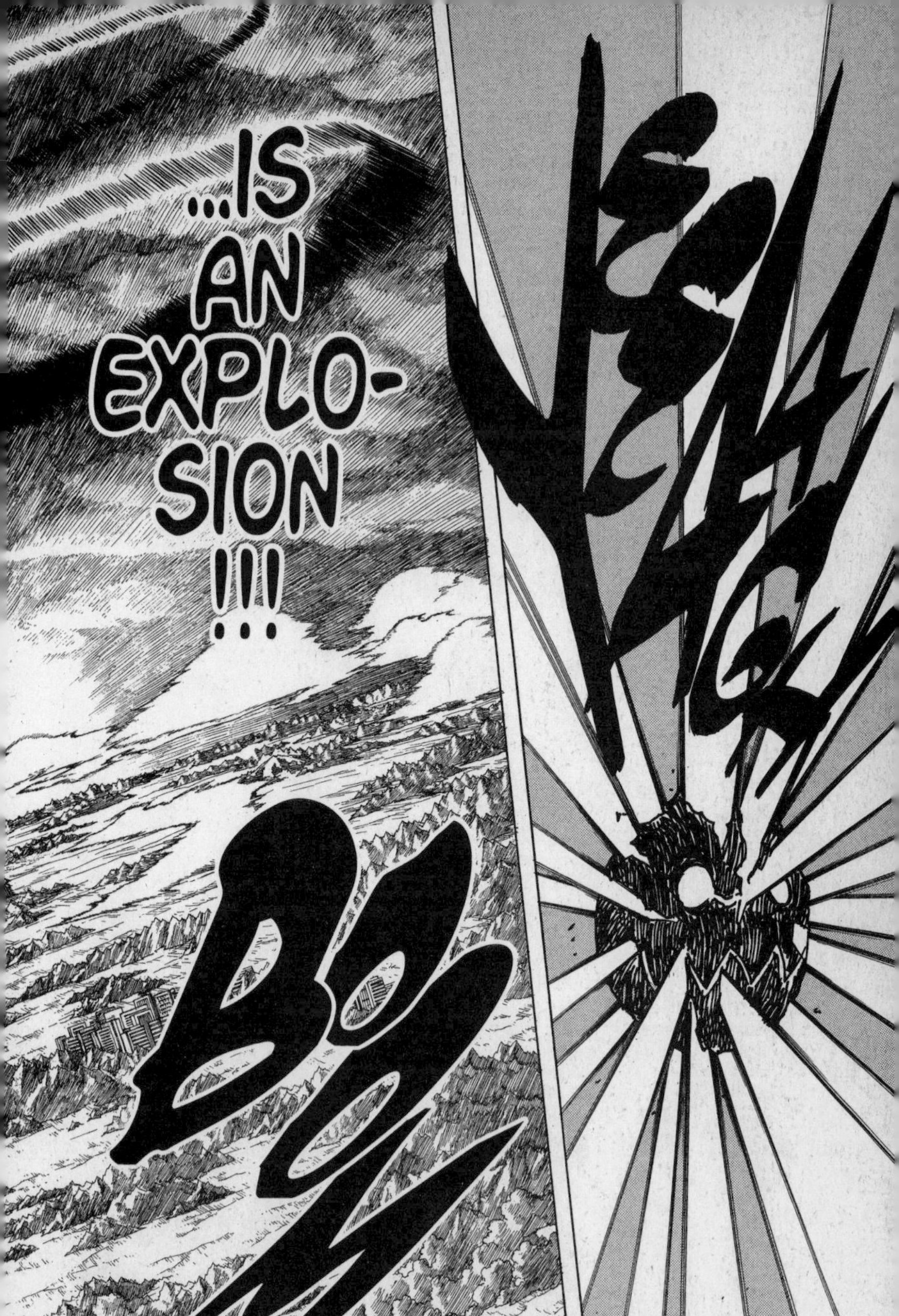
...IS AN EXPLOSION !!!...

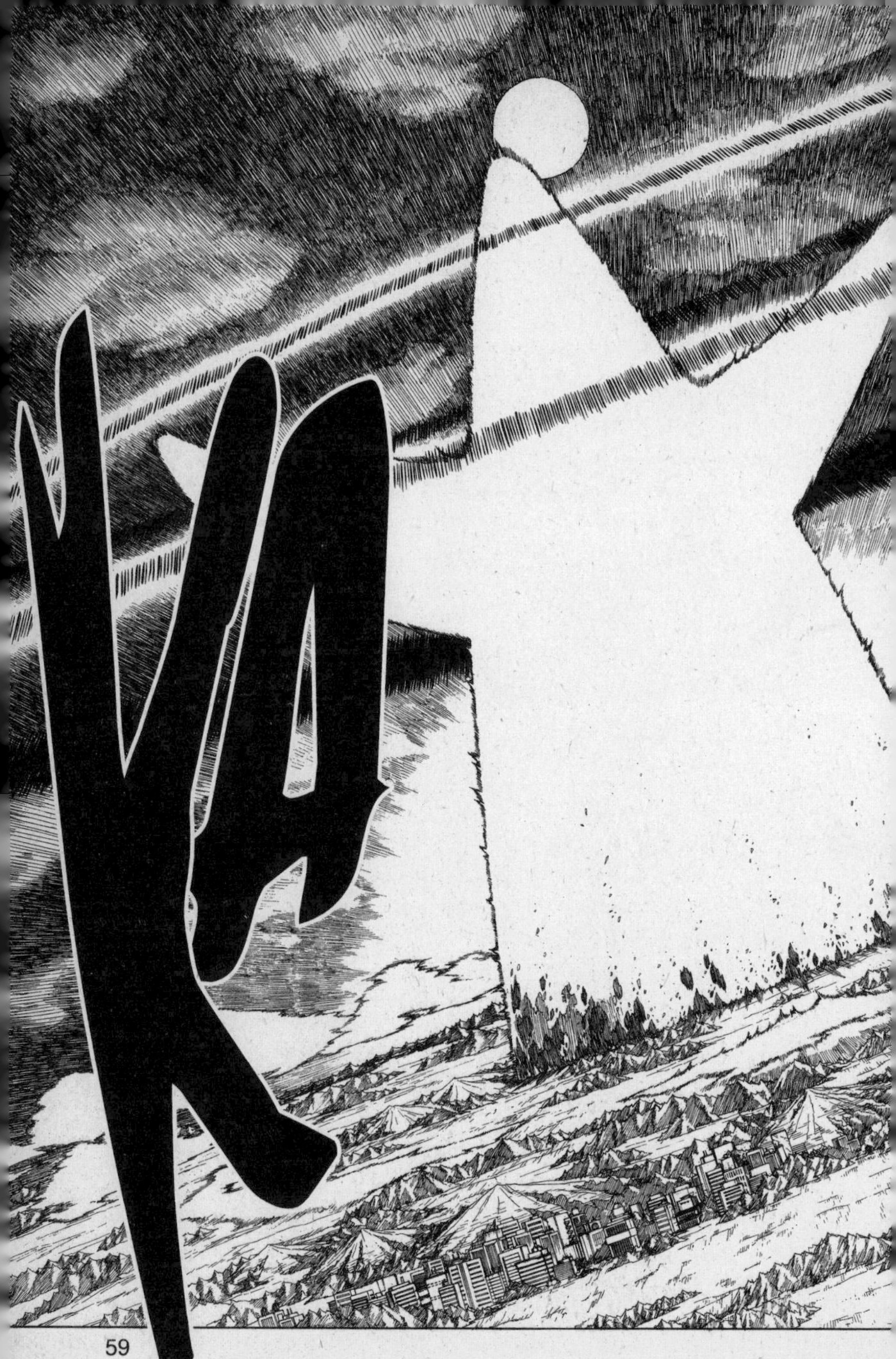
KA

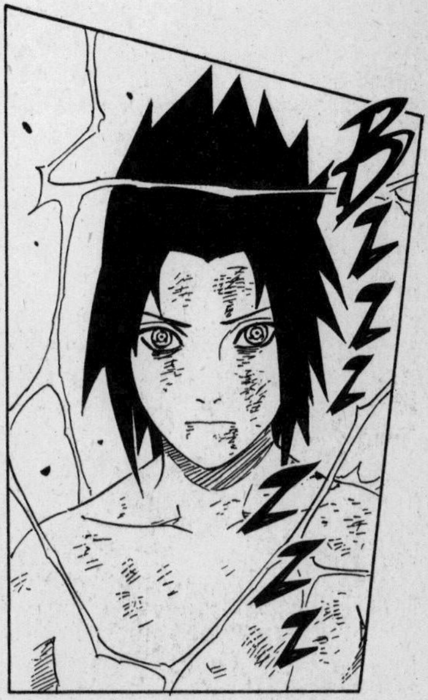
BZZZZZZZ

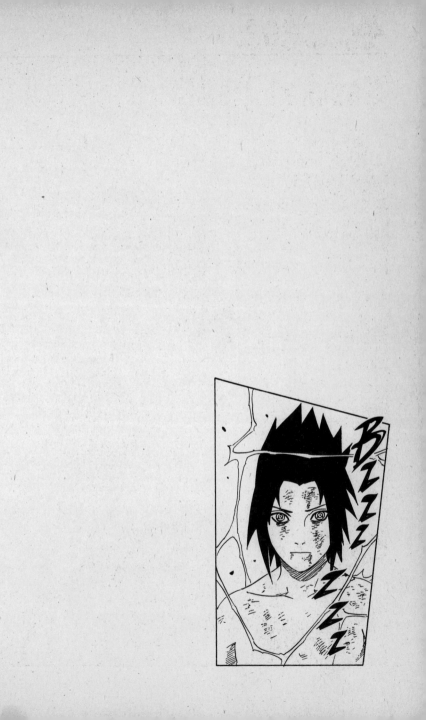

Number 363:

Sasuke's Death...!!

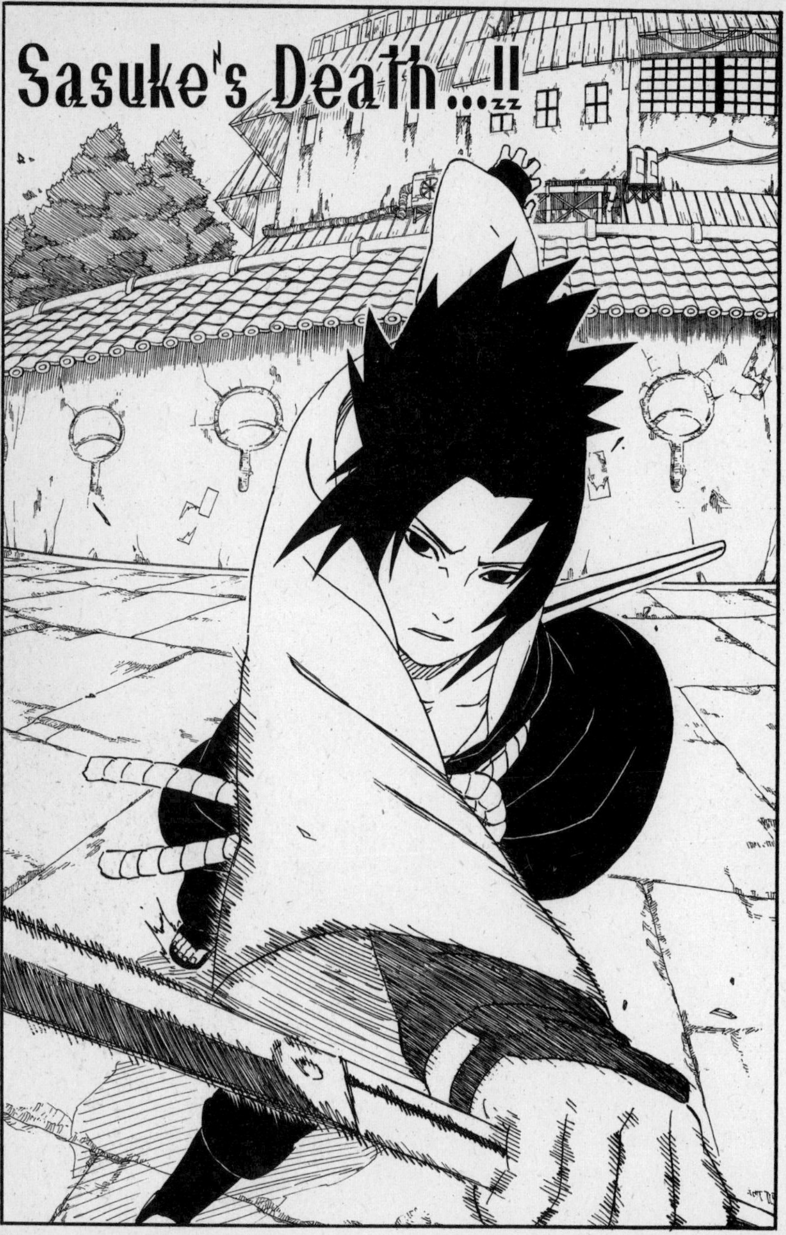

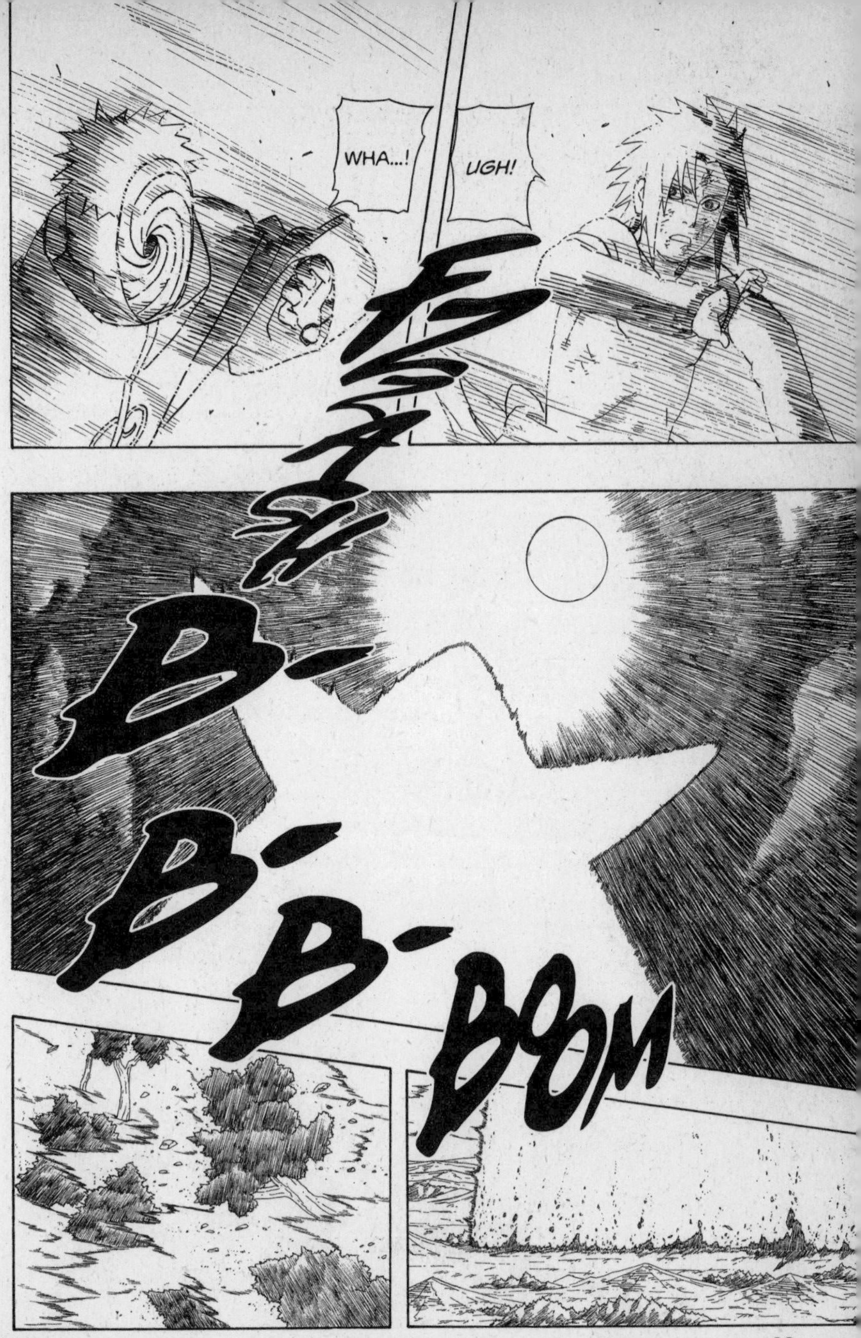
UGH!
WHA...!
B-B-B-BOOM

READ THIS WAY

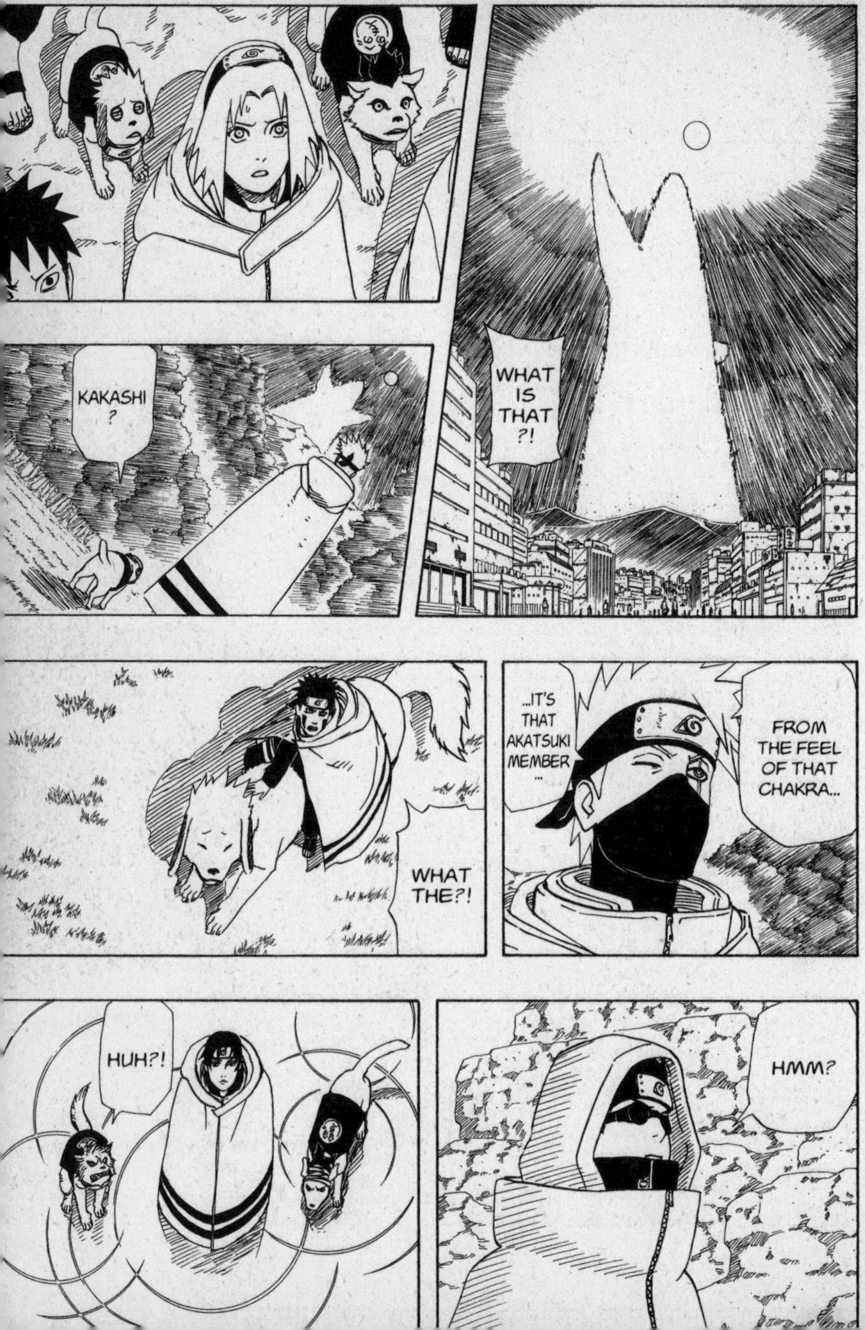
WHAT IS THAT?!
KAKASHI?
FROM THE FEEL OF THAT CHAKRA...
...IT'S THAT AKATSUKI MEMBER...
WHAT THE?!
HMM?
HUH?!

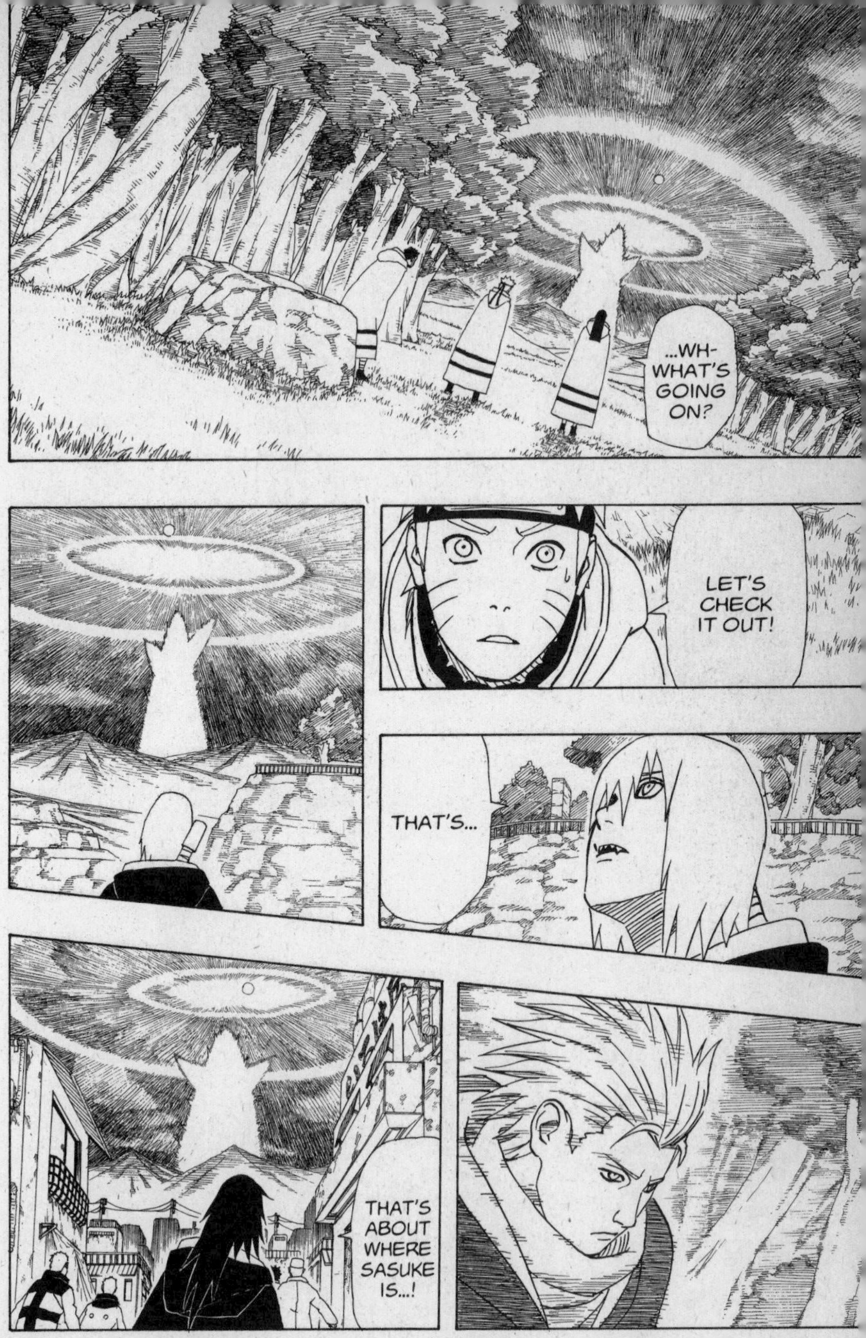
...WH- WHAT'S GOING ON?
LET'S CHECK IT OUT!
THAT'S...
THAT'S ABOUT WHERE SASUKE IS...!

READ THIS WAY

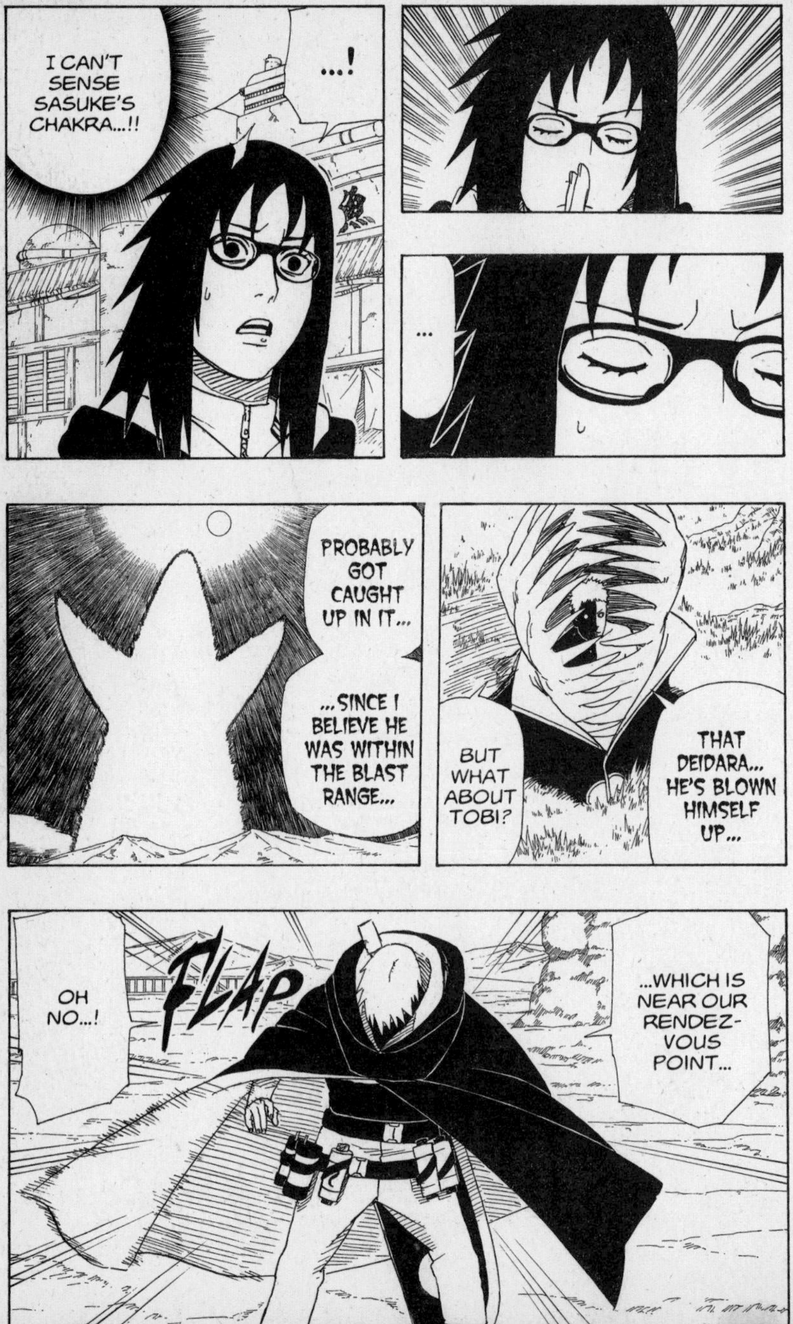
...
...!
I CAN'T SENSE SASUKE'S CHAKRA...!!
THAT DEIDARA... HE'S BLOWN HIMSELF UP...
BUT WHAT ABOUT TOBI?
PROBABLY GOT CAUGHT UP IN IT...
...SINCE I BELIEVE HE WAS WITHIN THE BLAST RANGE...
...WHICH IS NEAR OUR RENDEZ-VOUS POINT...
FLAP
OH NO...!

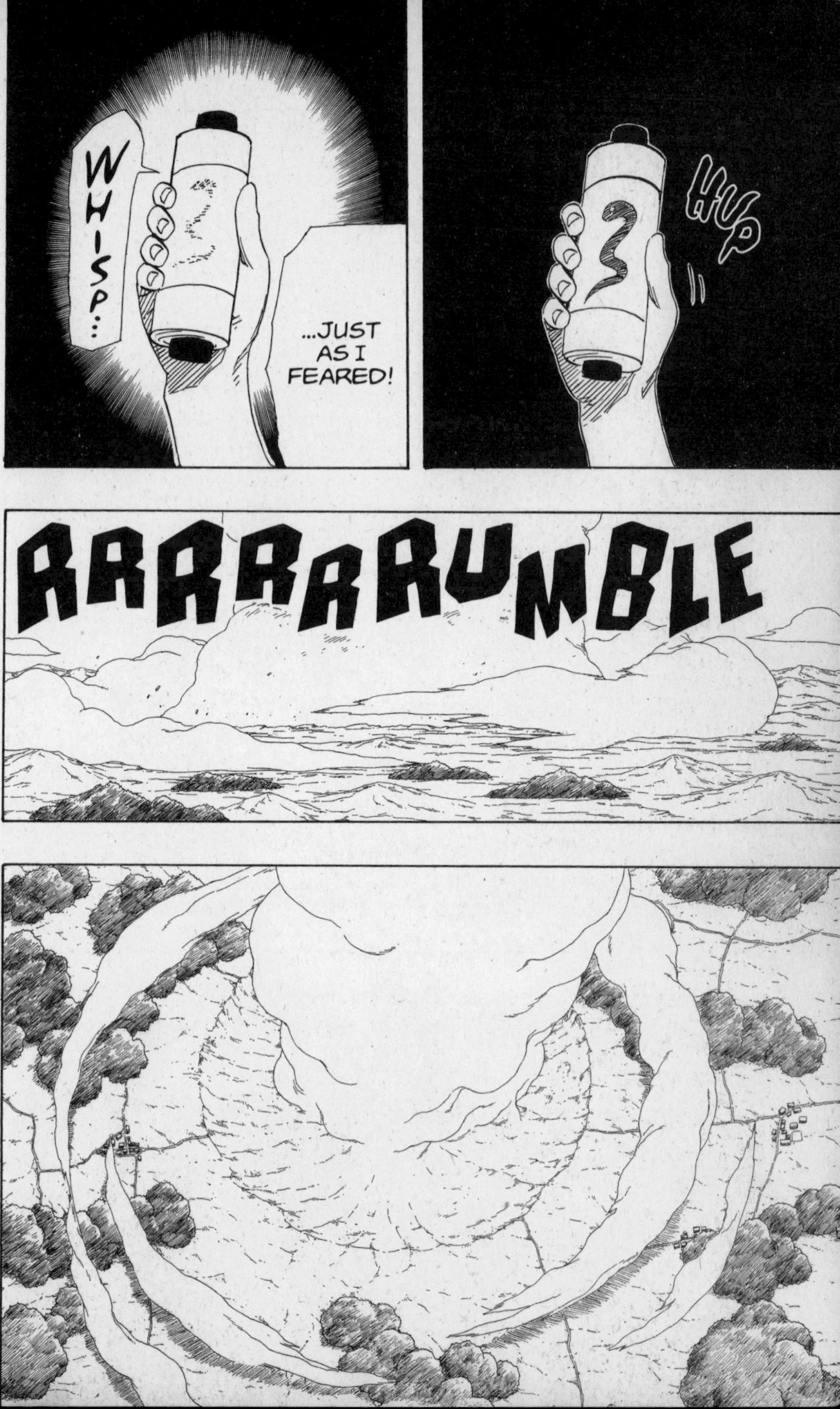
HUP
WHISP...
...JUST AS I FEARED!
RRRRRRUMBLE

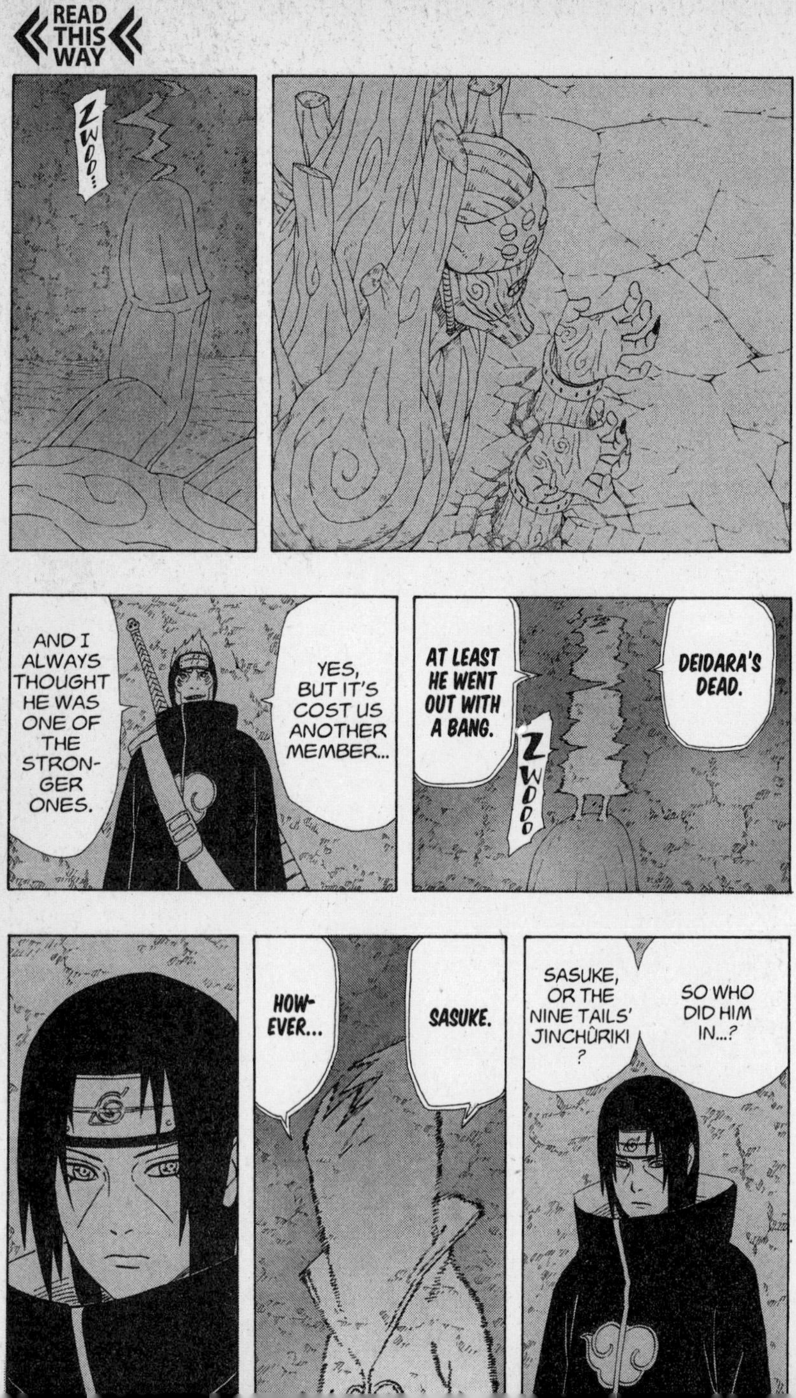
READ THIS WAY
ZWOO...
DEIDARA'S DEAD.
AT LEAST HE WENT OUT WITH A BANG.
ZWOOO
YES, BUT IT'S COST US ANOTHER MEMBER...
AND I ALWAYS THOUGHT HE WAS ONE OF THE STRONGER ONES.
SO WHO DID HIM IN...?
SASUKE, OR THE NINE TAILS' JINCHÛRIKI?
SASUKE.
HOWEVER...

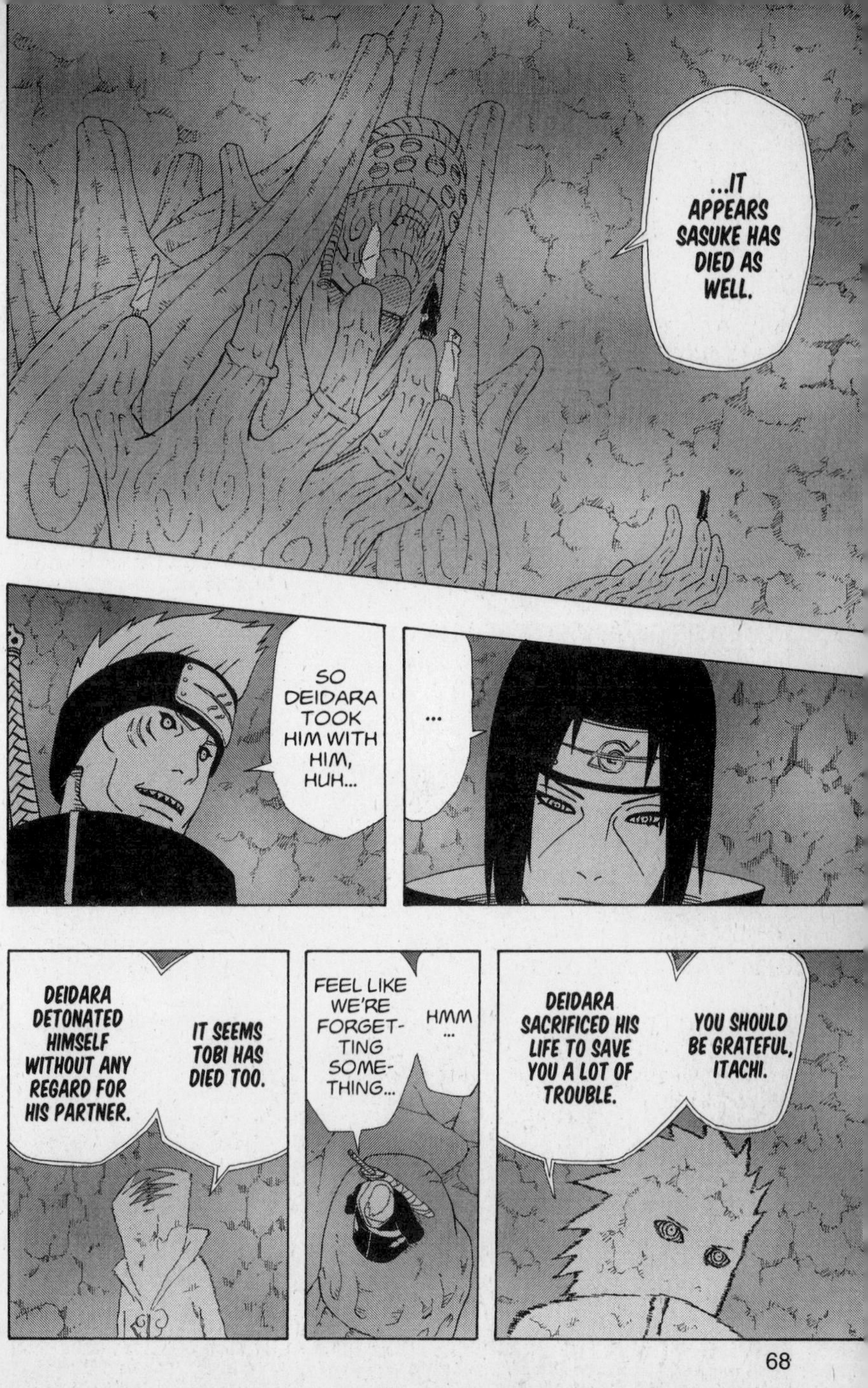
...IT APPEARS SASUKE HAS DIED AS WELL.
...
SO DEIDARA TOOK HIM WITH HIM, HUH...
YOU SHOULD BE GRATEFUL, ITACHI.
DEIDARA SACRIFICED HIS LIFE TO SAVE YOU A LOT OF TROUBLE.
HMM...
FEEL LIKE WE'RE FORGETTING SOMETHING...
IT SEEMS TOBI HAS DIED TOO.
DEIDARA DETONATED HIMSELF WITHOUT ANY REGARD FOR HIS PARTNER.

READ THIS WAY

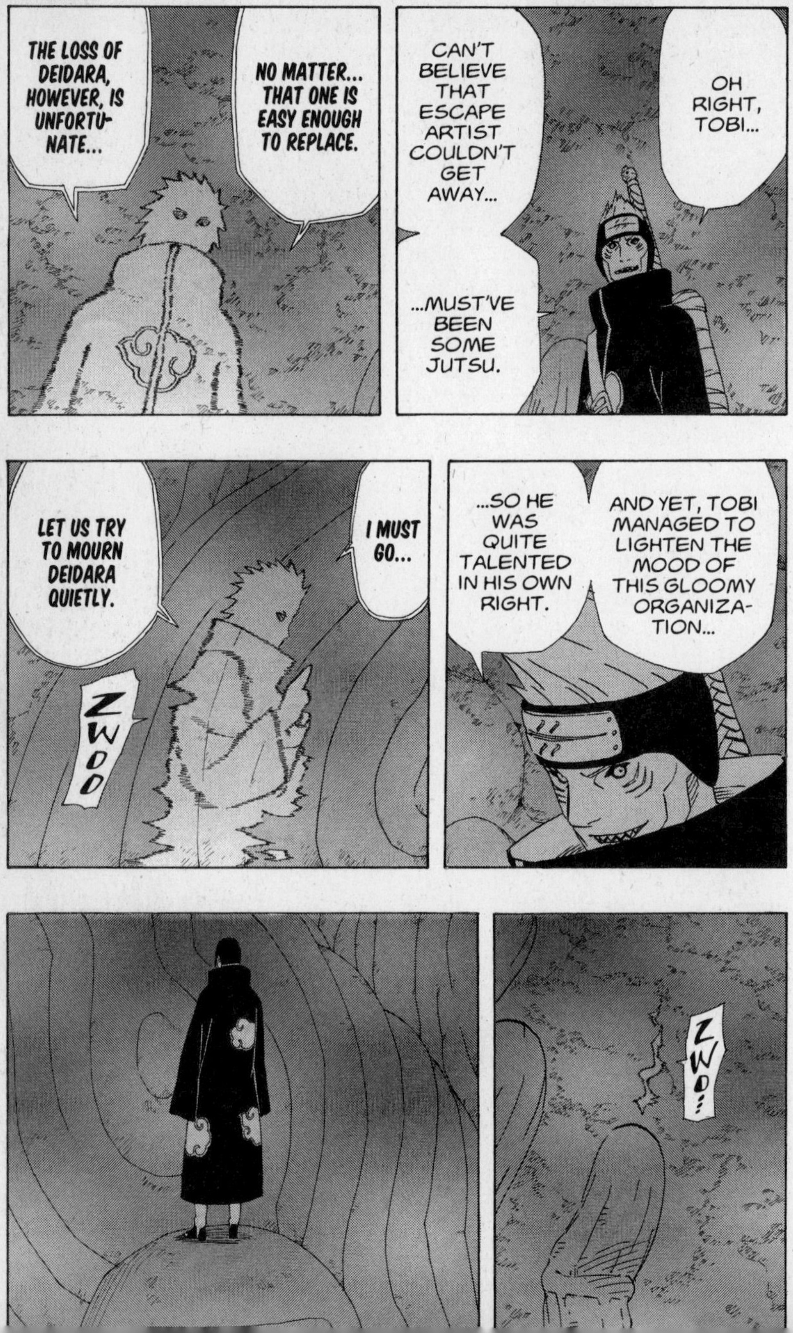
OH RIGHT, TOBI...
CAN'T BELIEVE THAT ESCAPE ARTIST COULDN'T GET AWAY...
...MUST'VE BEEN SOME JUTSU.
NO MATTER... THAT ONE IS EASY ENOUGH TO REPLACE.
THE LOSS OF DEIDARA, HOWEVER, IS UNFORTU-NATE...
AND YET, TOBI MANAGED TO LIGHTEN THE MOOD OF THIS GLOOMY ORGANIZA-TION...
...SO HE WAS QUITE TALENTED IN HIS OWN RIGHT.
I MUST GO...
LET US TRY TO MOURN DEIDARA QUIETLY.
ZWOO
ZWOO!

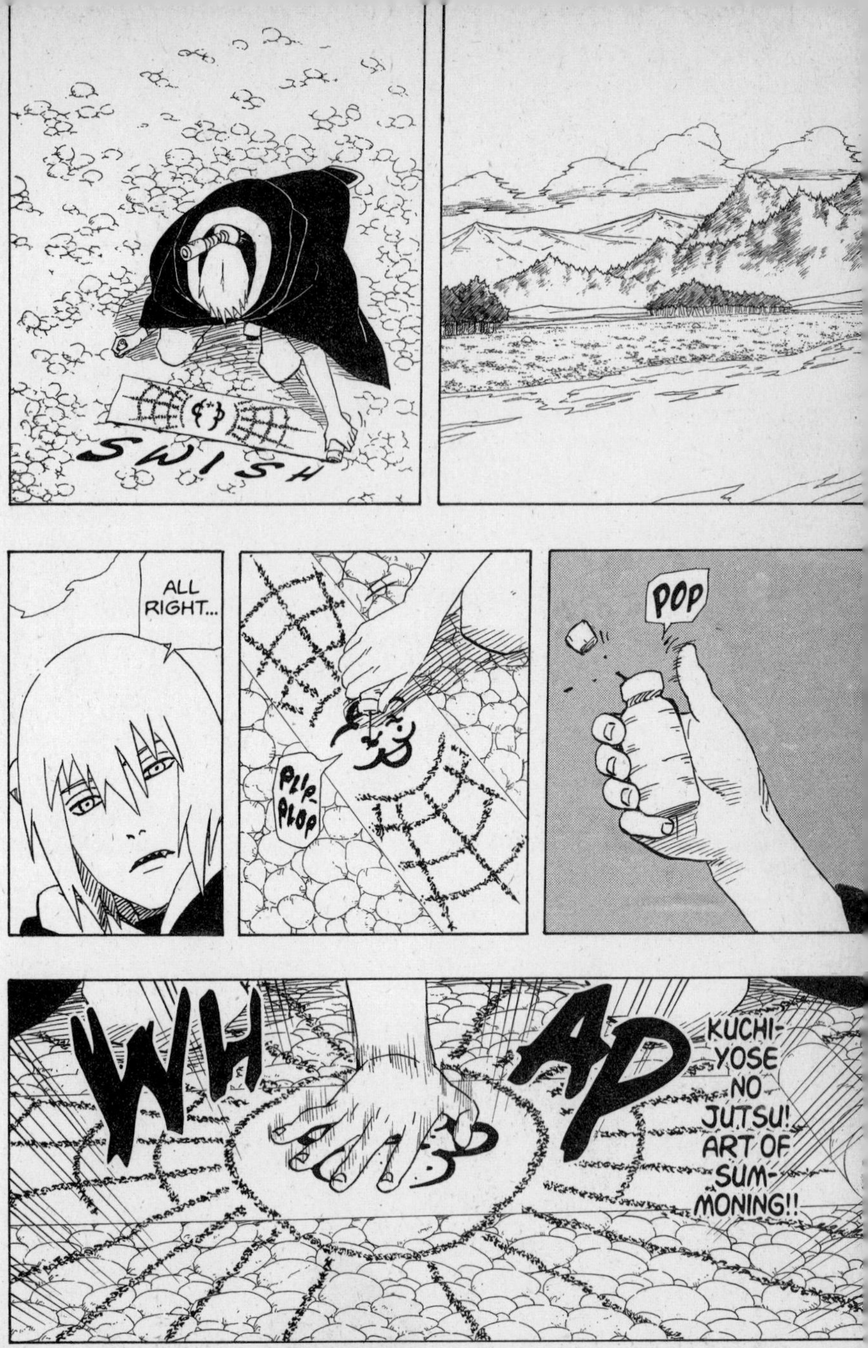
SWISH
POP
PLIP PLOP
ALL RIGHT...
KUCHI-YOSE NO JUTSU! ART OF SUM-MONING!!
WHAP

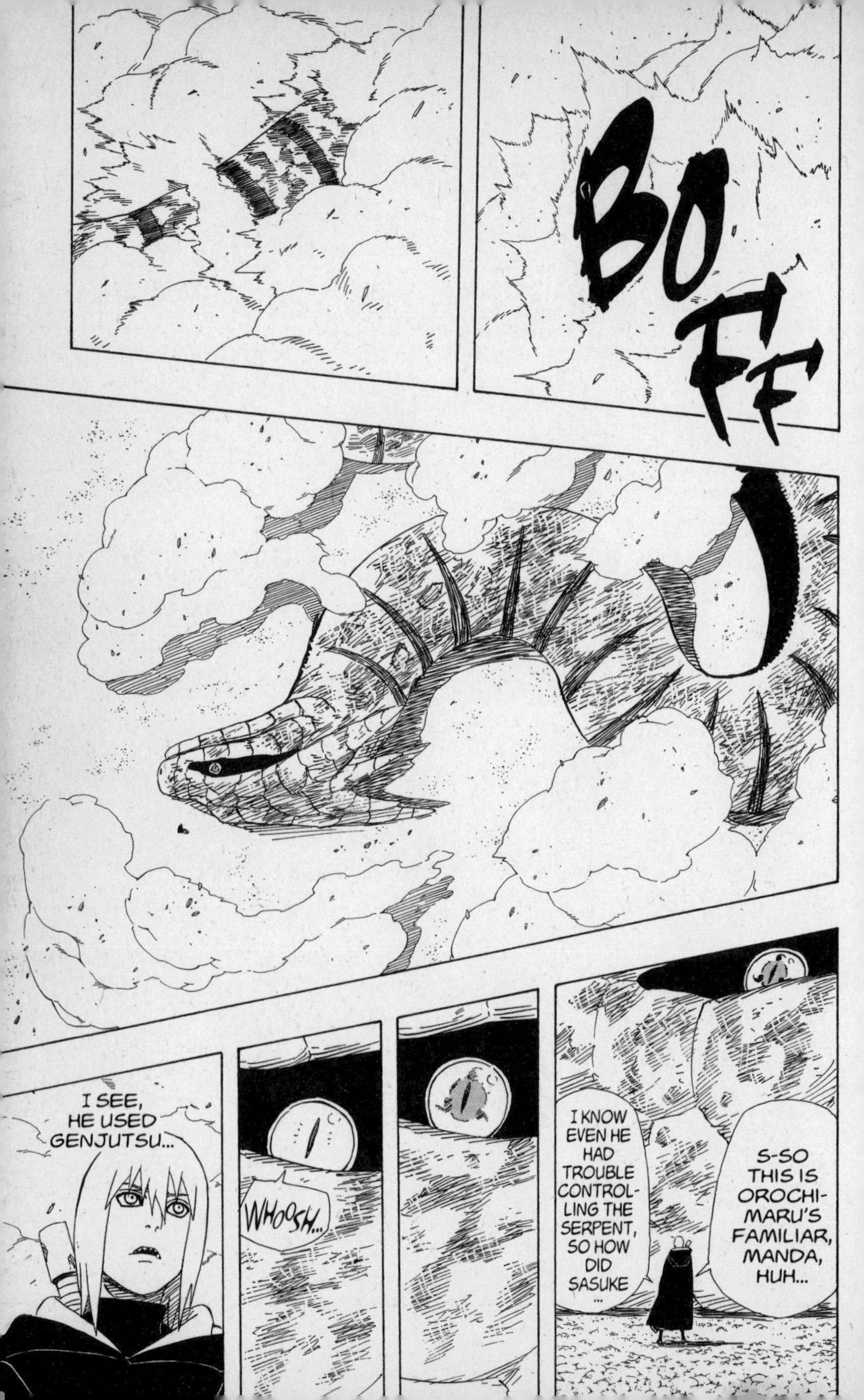
BOFF
S-SO THIS IS OROCHI-MARU'S FAMILIAR, MANDA, HUH...
I KNOW EVEN HE HAD TROUBLE CONTROL-LING THE SERPENT, SO HOW DID SASUKE ...
WHOOSH...
I SEE, HE USED GENJUTSU...

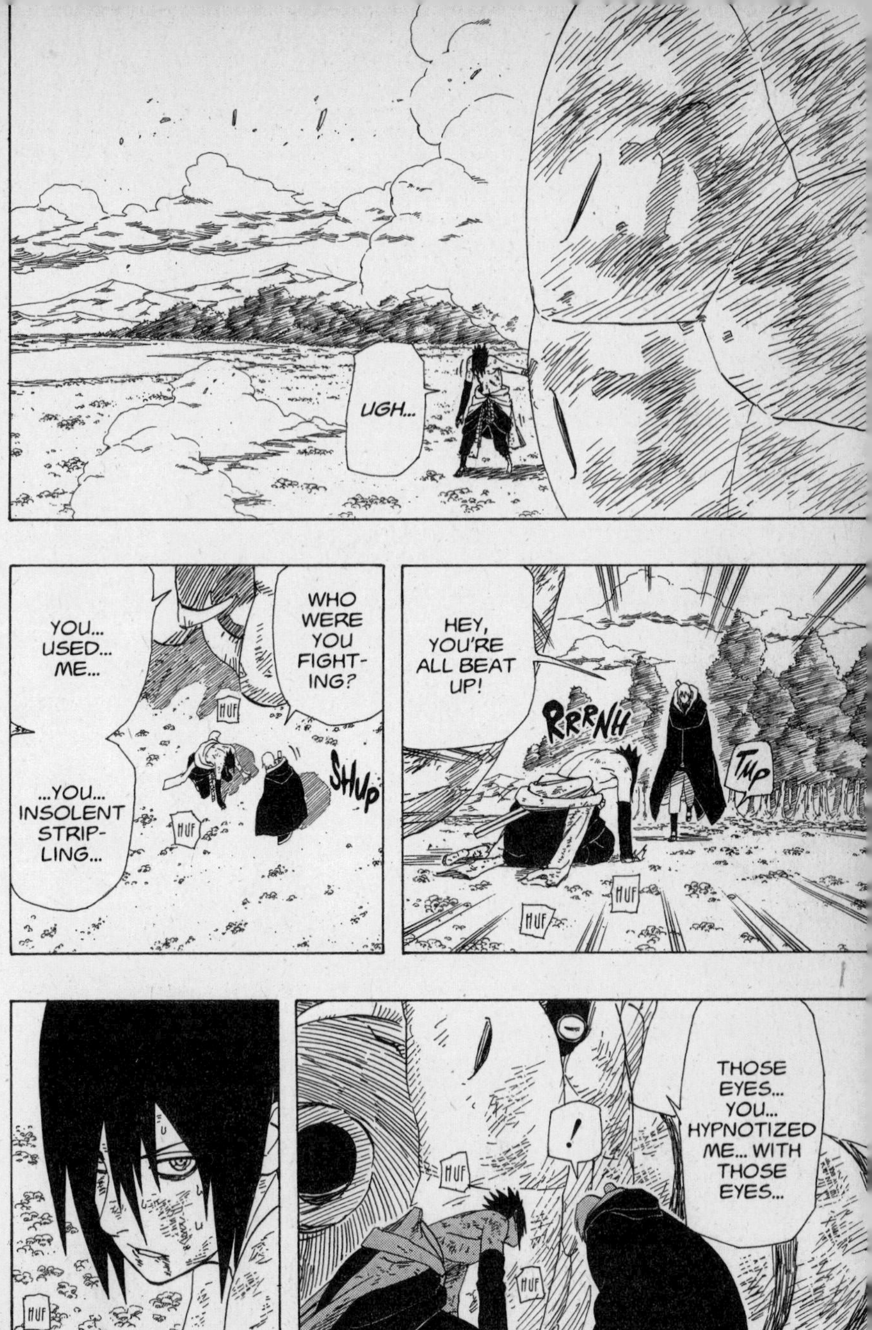
UGH...
HEY, YOU'RE ALL BEAT UP!
RRRNH
TMP
HUF
HUF
WHO WERE YOU FIGHTING?
SHUP
YOU... USED... ME...
HUF
...YOU... INSOLENT STRIPLING...
HUF
THOSE EYES... YOU... HYPNOTIZED ME... WITH THOSE EYES...
!
HUF
HUF
HUF

READ THIS WAY

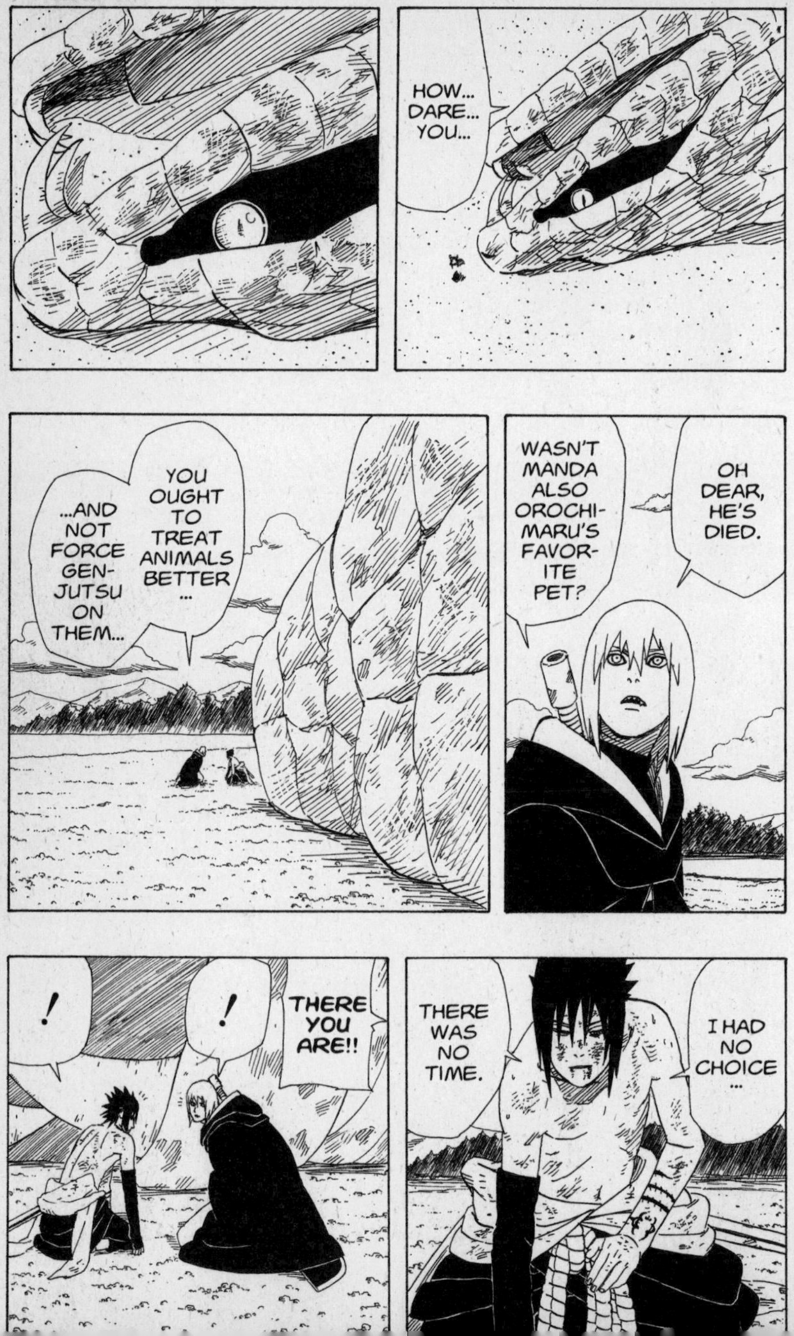
HOW... DARE... YOU...
OH DEAR, HE'S DIED.
WASN'T MANDA ALSO OROCHI-MARU'S FAVOR-ITE PET?
YOU OUGHT TO TREAT ANIMALS BETTER ...
...AND NOT FORCE GEN-JUTSU ON THEM...
I HAD NO CHOICE ...
THERE WAS NO TIME.
THERE YOU ARE!!
!
!

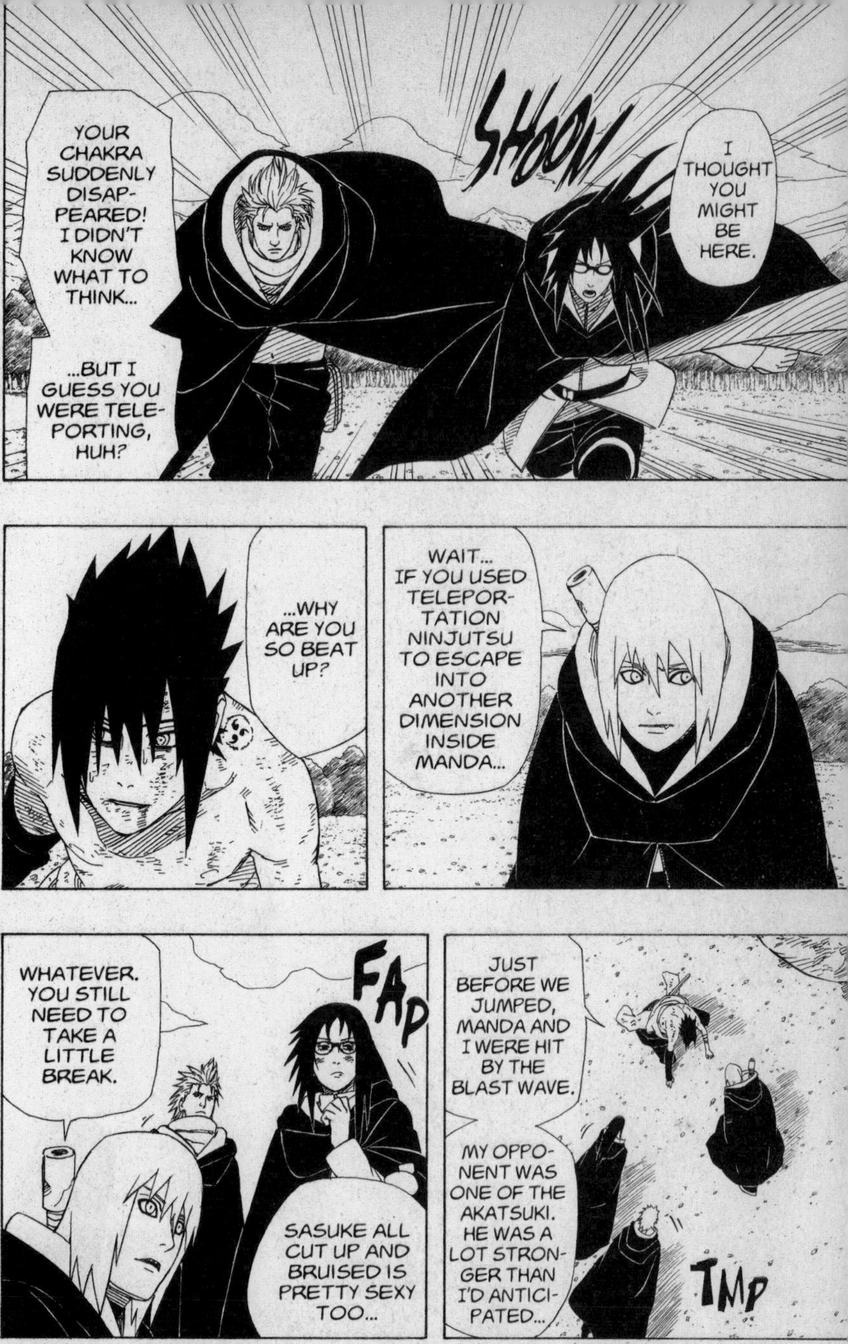
I THOUGHT YOU MIGHT BE HERE.
SHOOM
YOUR CHAKRA SUDDENLY DISAP-PEARED! I DIDN'T KNOW WHAT TO THINK...
...BUT I GUESS YOU WERE TELE-PORTING, HUH?
WAIT... IF YOU USED TELEPOR-TATION NINJUTSU TO ESCAPE INTO ANOTHER DIMENSION INSIDE MANDA...
...WHY ARE YOU SO BEAT UP?
JUST BEFORE WE JUMPED, MANDA AND I WERE HIT BY THE BLAST WAVE.
MY OPPO-NENT WAS ONE OF THE AKATSUKI. HE WAS A LOT STRON-GER THAN I'D ANTICI-PATED...
TMP
FAP
WHATEVER. YOU STILL NEED TO TAKE A LITTLE BREAK.
SASUKE ALL CUT UP AND BRUISED IS PRETTY SEXY TOO...

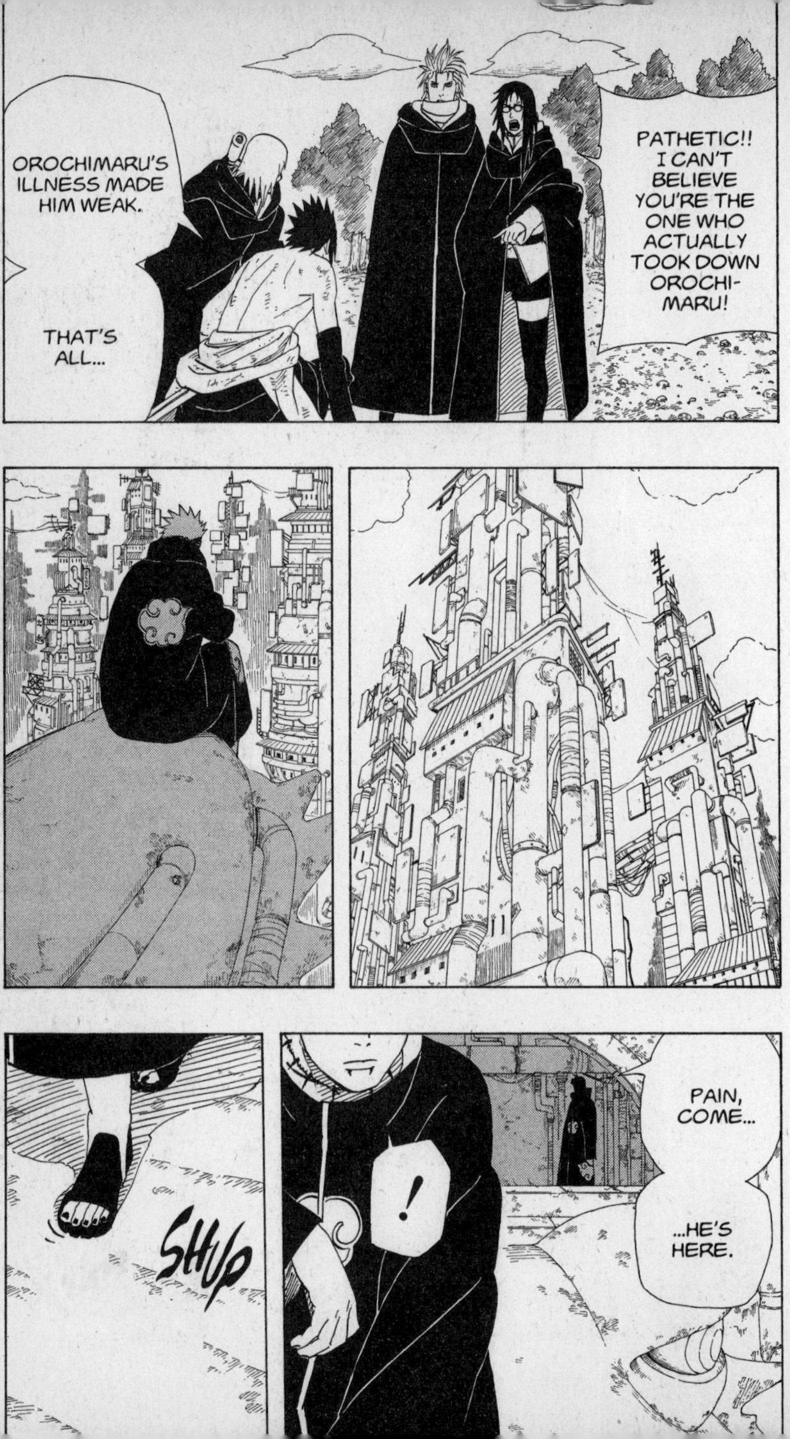
PATHETIC!! I CAN'T BELIEVE YOU'RE THE ONE WHO ACTUALLY TOOK DOWN OROCHI-MARU!
OROCHIMARU'S ILLNESS MADE HIM WEAK.
THAT'S ALL...
PAIN, COME...
...HE'S HERE.
!
SHUP

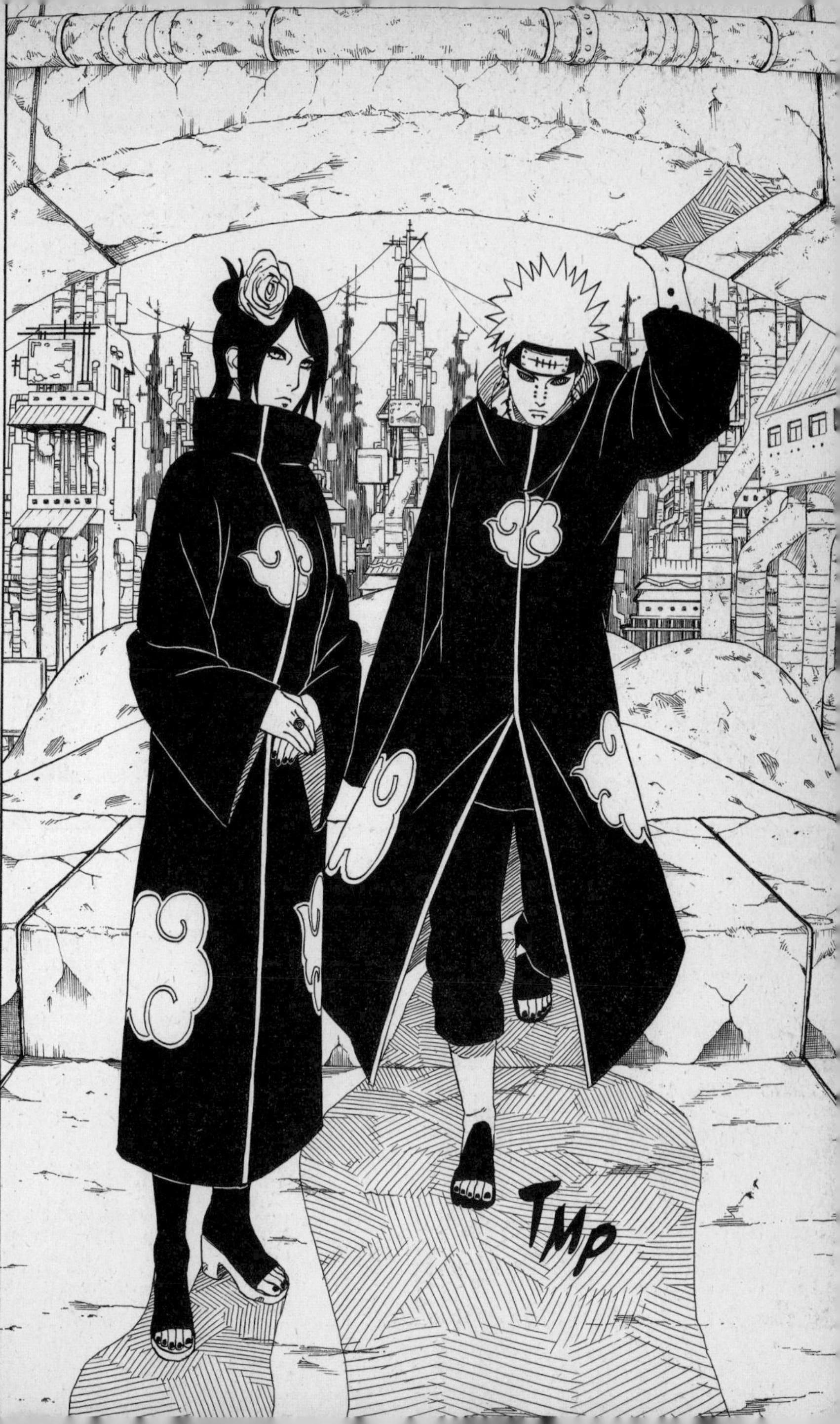
TMP

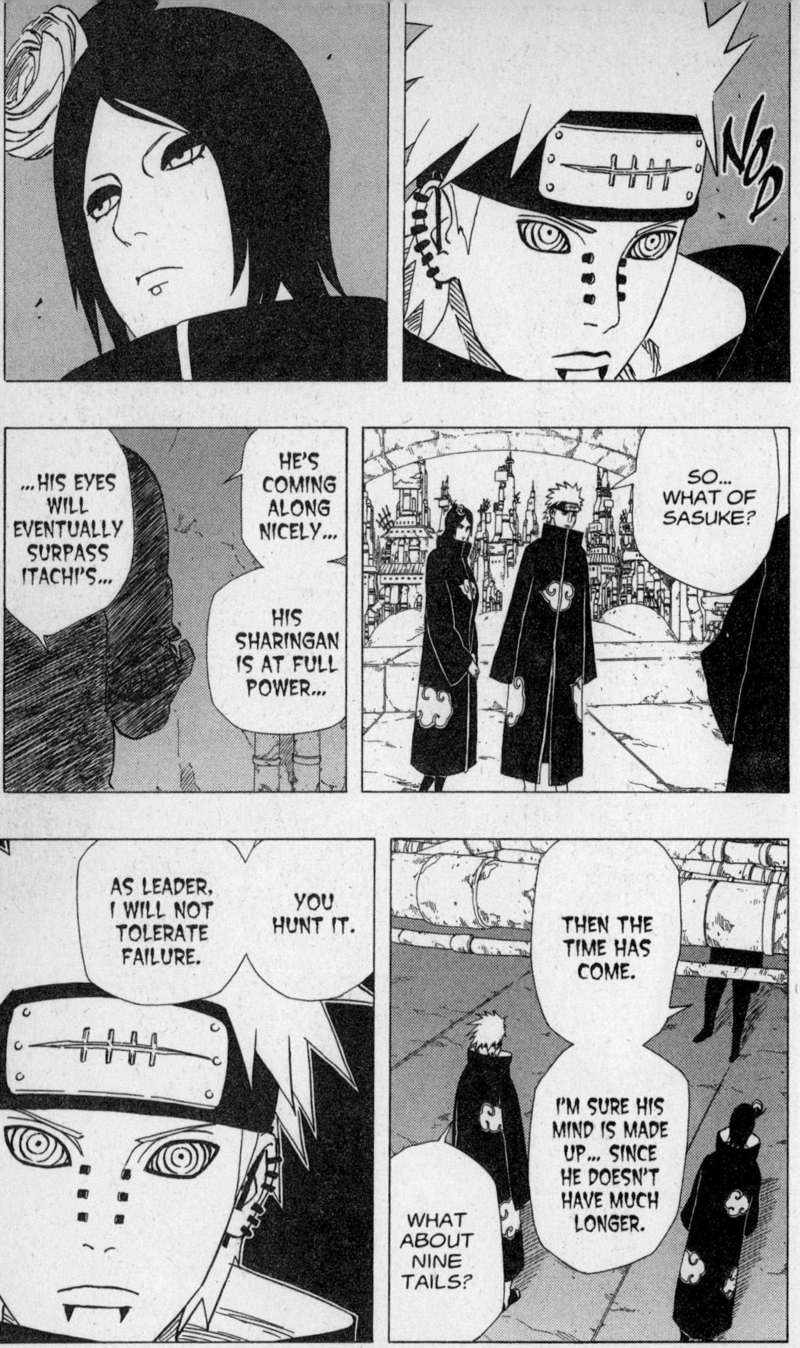
NOD
SO... WHAT OF SASUKE?
HE'S COMING ALONG NICELY...
HIS SHARINGAN IS AT FULL POWER...
...HIS EYES WILL EVENTUALLY SURPASS ITACHI'S...
THEN THE TIME HAS COME.
I'M SURE HIS MIND IS MADE UP... SINCE HE DOESN'T HAVE MUCH LONGER.
WHAT ABOUT NINE TAILS?
YOU HUNT IT.
AS LEADER, I WILL NOT TOLERATE FAILURE.

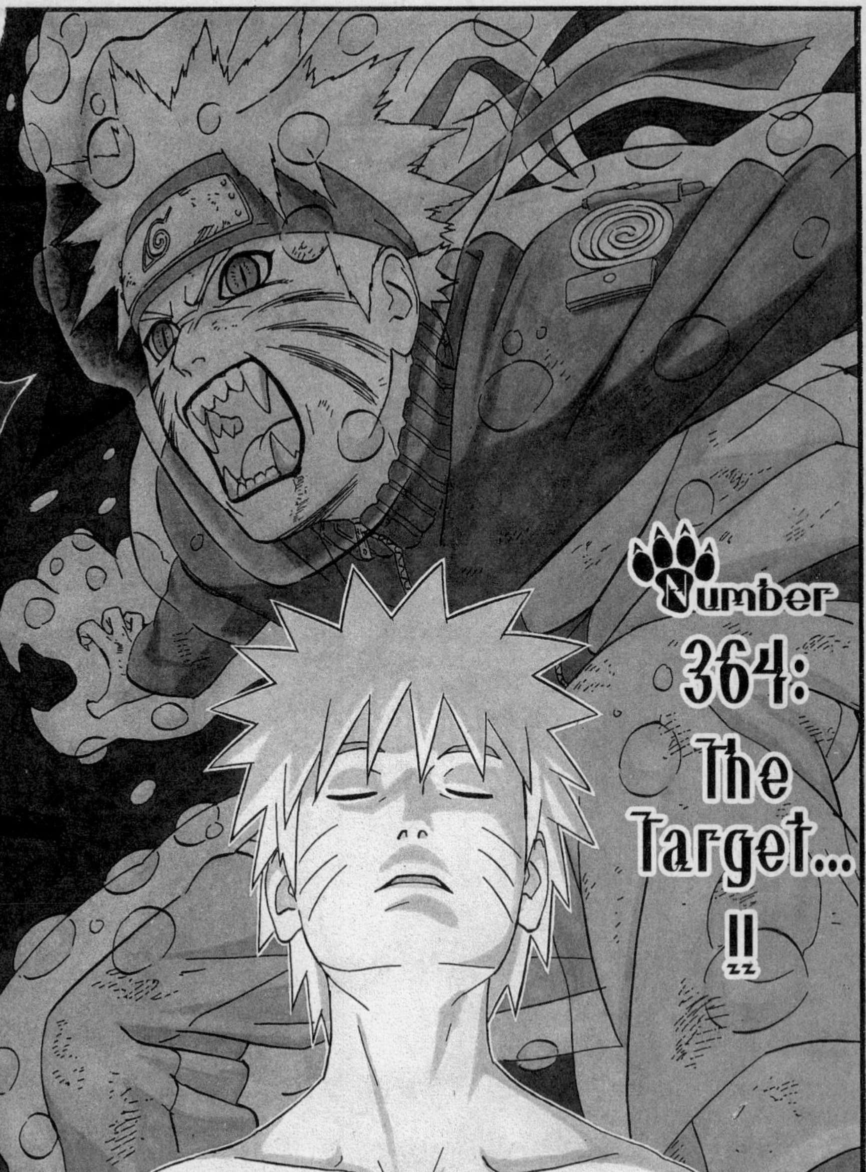
Number
364:
The
Target...
!!

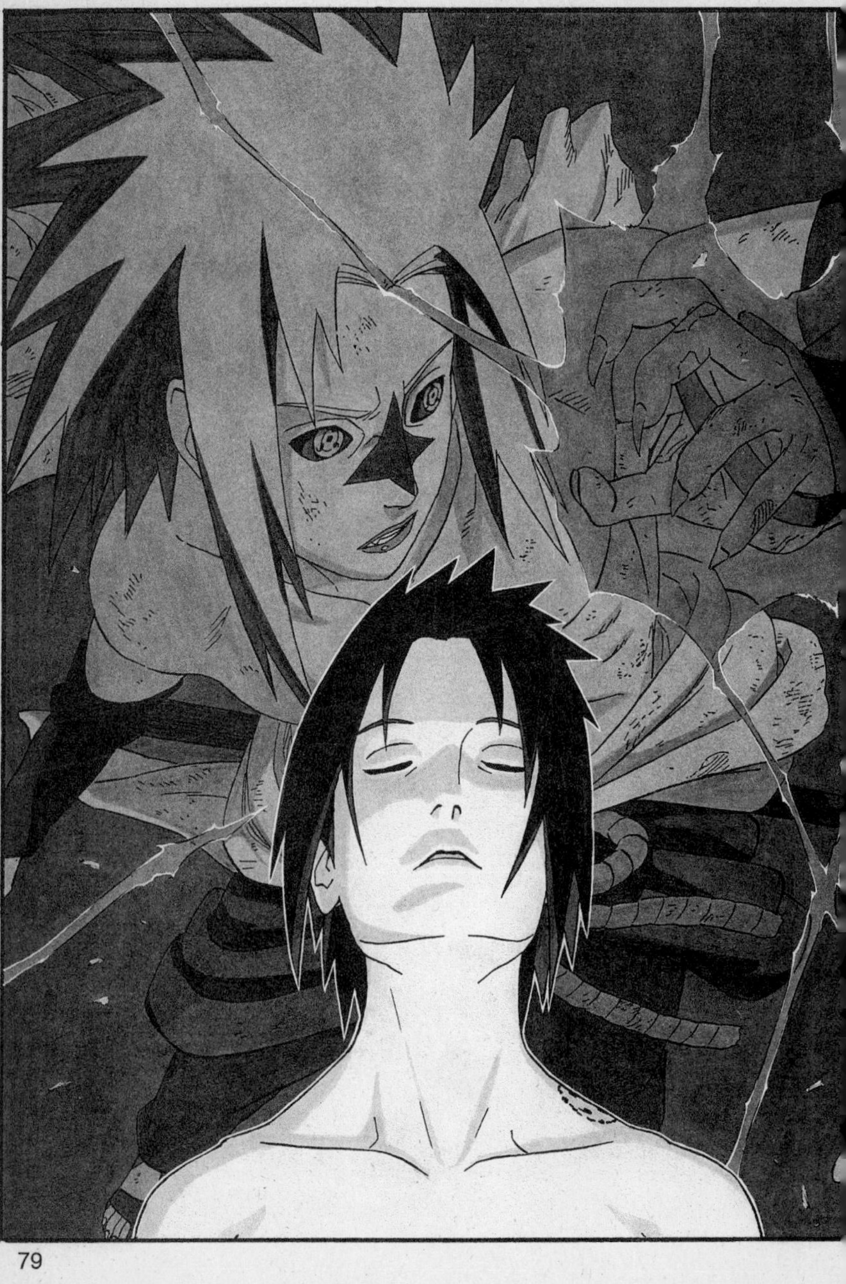

NARUTO

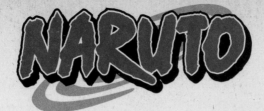

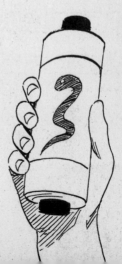

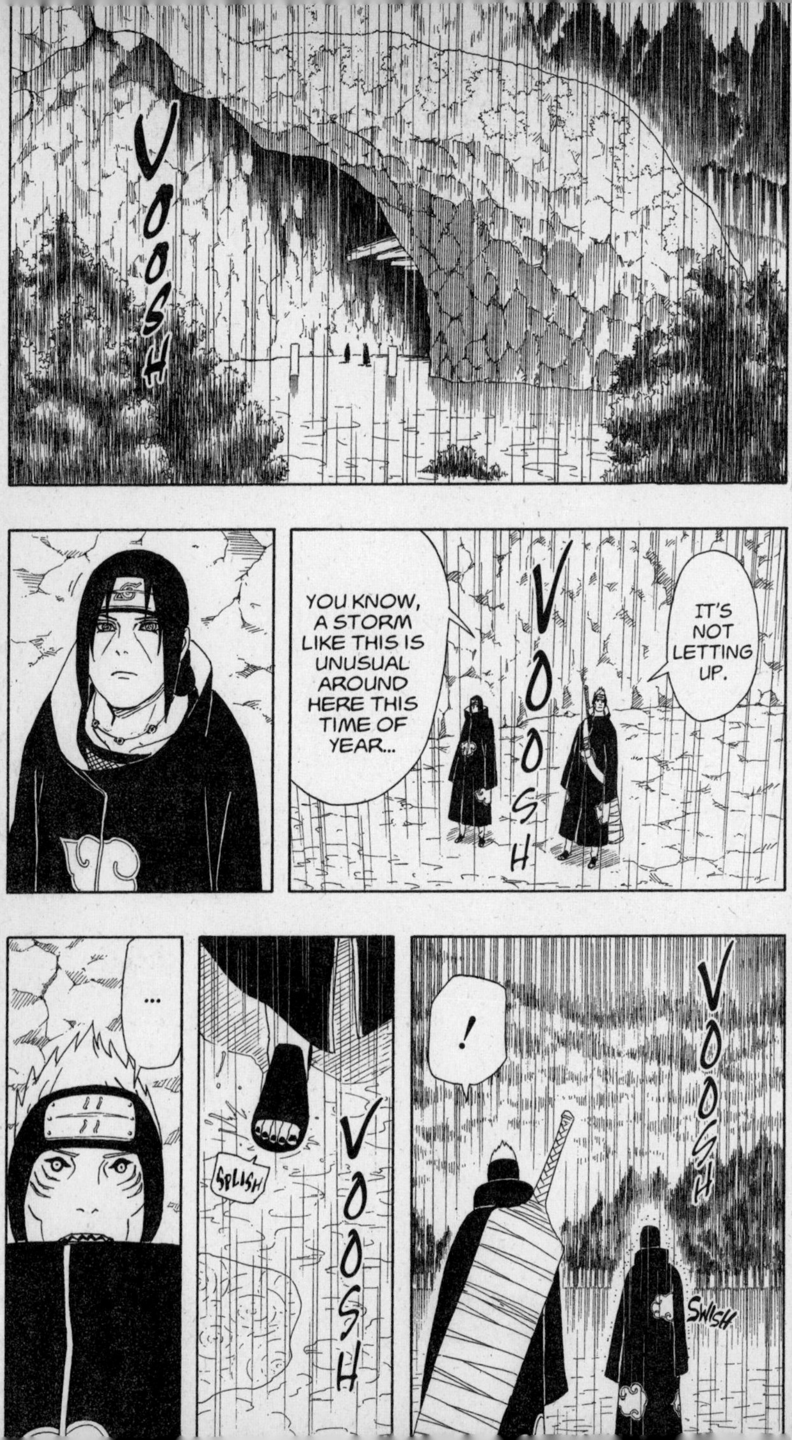
VOOSH
IT'S NOT LETTING UP.
VOOSH
YOU KNOW, A STORM LIKE THIS IS UNUSUAL AROUND HERE THIS TIME OF YEAR...
VOOSH
!
SWISH
VOOSH
SPLISH
...

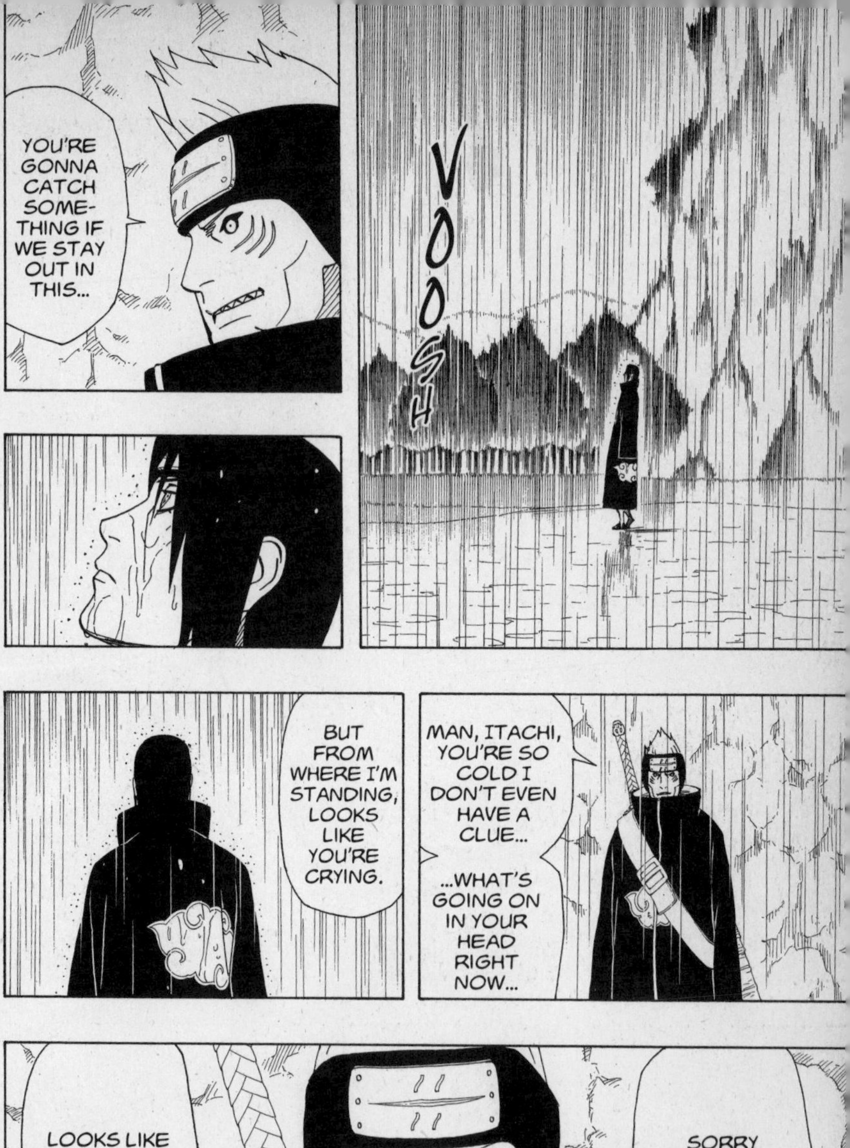
VOOSH
YOU'RE GONNA CATCH SOME-THING IF WE STAY OUT IN THIS...
MAN, ITACHI, YOU'RE SO COLD I DON'T EVEN HAVE A CLUE...
...WHAT'S GOING ON IN YOUR HEAD RIGHT NOW...
BUT FROM WHERE I'M STANDING, LOOKS LIKE YOU'RE CRYING.
SORRY ABOUT YOUR LITTLE BROTHER...
LOOKS LIKE YOU'RE ALL THAT'S LEFT OF THE UCHIHA CLAN...

READ THIS WAY

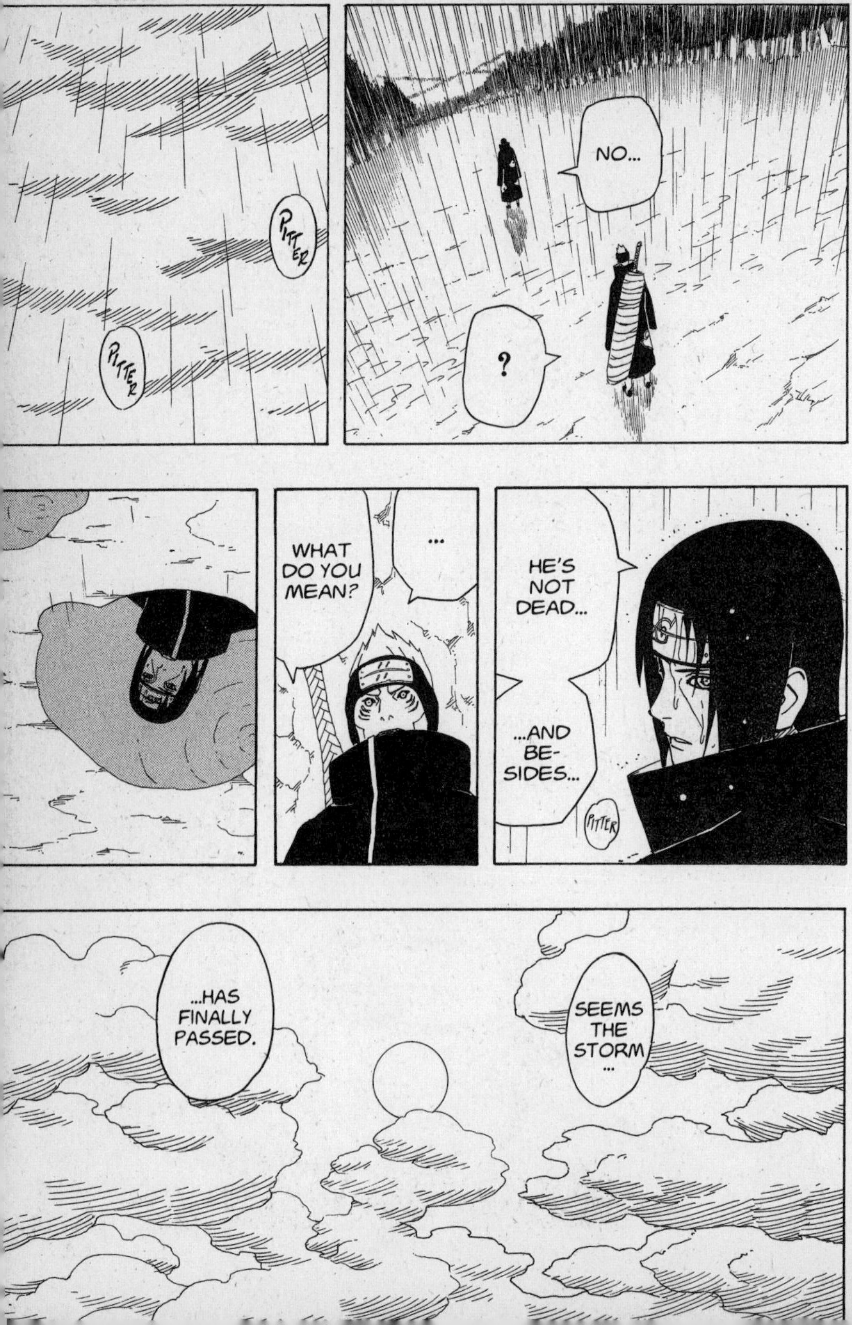

NO...
?
PITTER
PITTER
HE'S NOT DEAD...
...AND BE-SIDES...
PITTER
...
WHAT DO YOU MEAN?
SEEMS THE STORM ...
...HAS FINALLY PASSED.

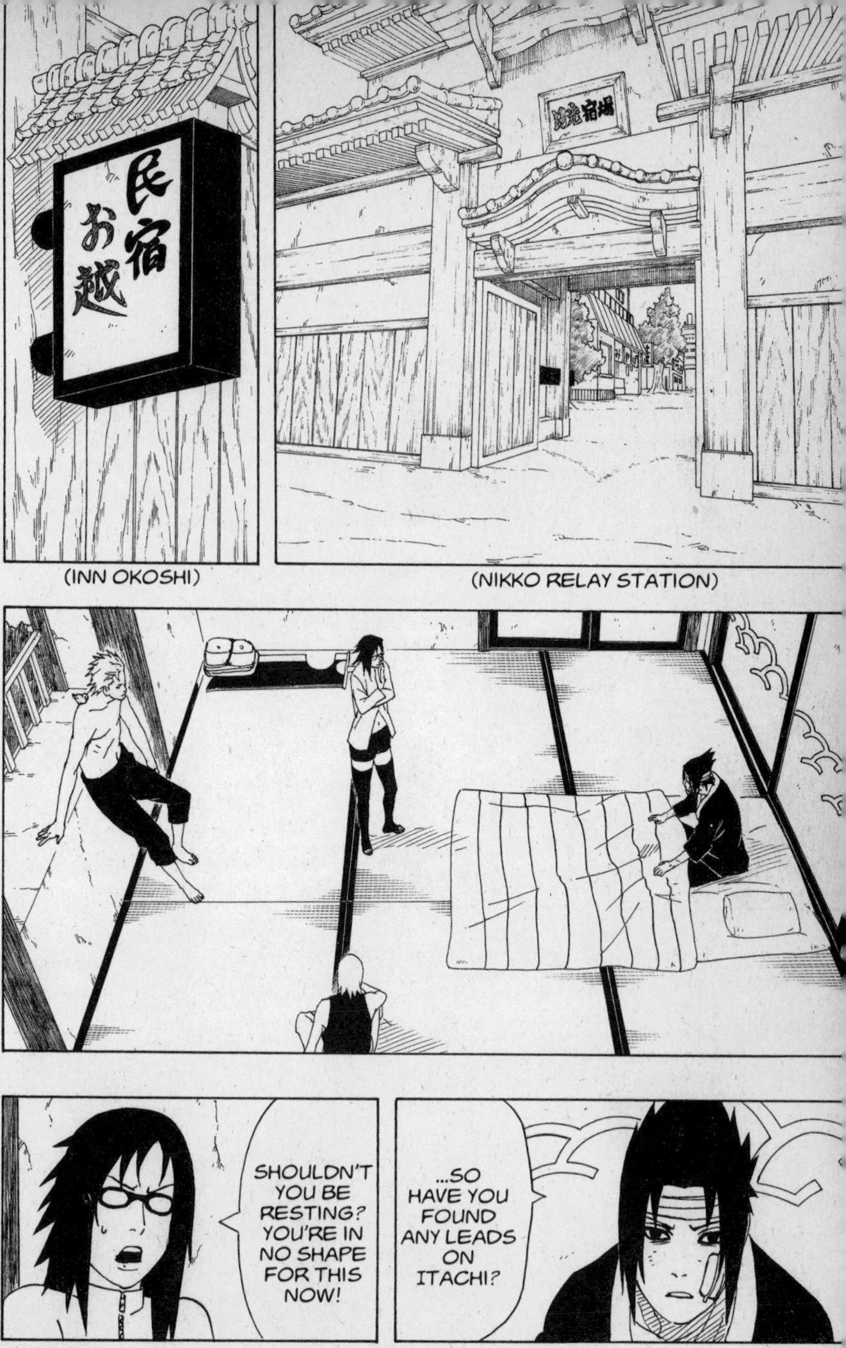
(NIKKO RELAY STATION)
民宿
お越
(INN OKOSHI)
...SO HAVE YOU FOUND ANY LEADS ON ITACHI?
SHOULDN'T YOU BE RESTING? YOU'RE IN NO SHAPE FOR THIS NOW!

READ THIS WAY

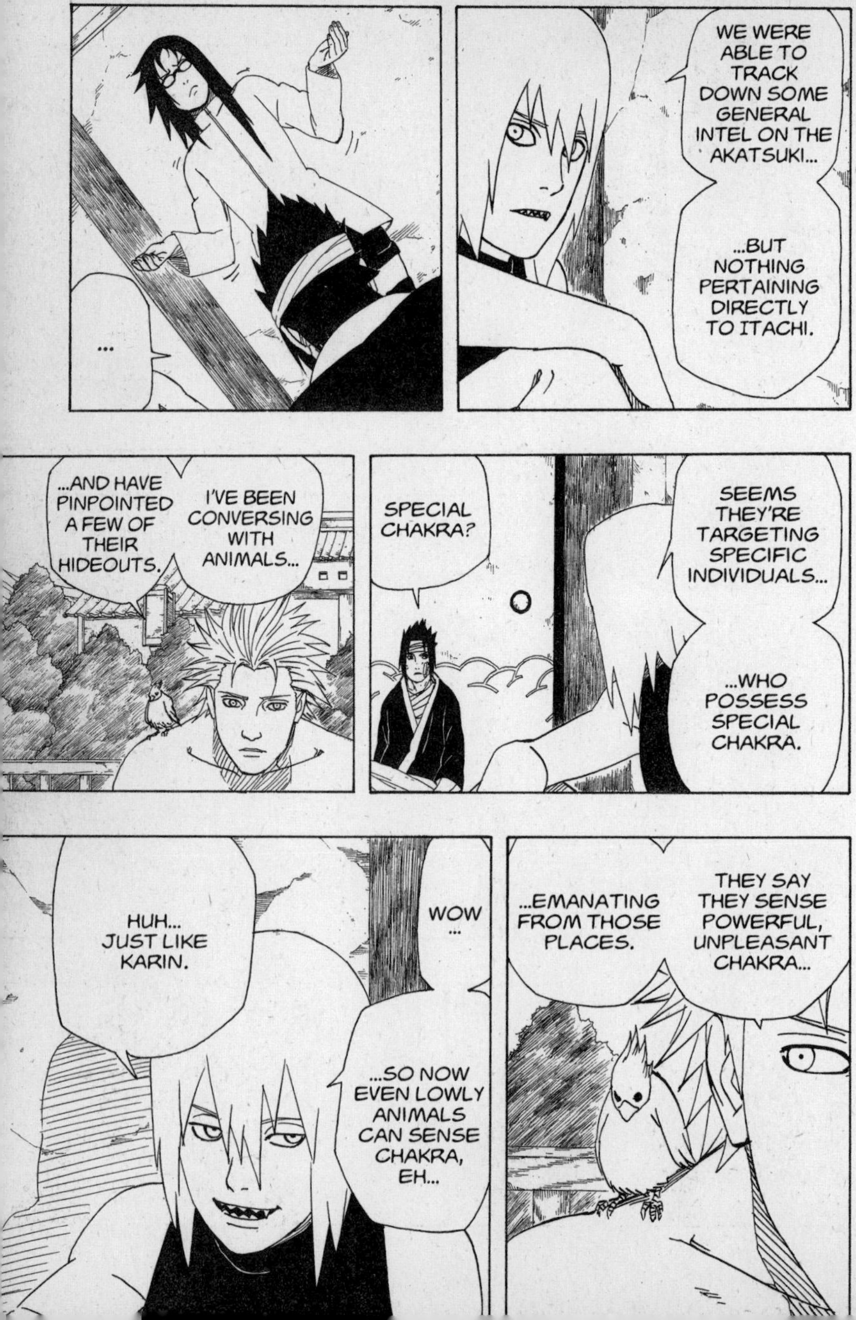
WE WERE ABLE TO TRACK DOWN SOME GENERAL INTEL ON THE AKATSUKI...
...BUT NOTHING PERTAINING DIRECTLY TO ITACHI.
...
SEEMS THEY'RE TARGETING SPECIFIC INDIVIDUALS...
...WHO POSSESS SPECIAL CHAKRA.
SPECIAL CHAKRA?
I'VE BEEN CONVERSING WITH ANIMALS...
...AND HAVE PINPOINTED A FEW OF THEIR HIDEOUTS.
THEY SAY THEY SENSE POWERFUL, UNPLEASANT CHAKRA...
...EMANATING FROM THOSE PLACES.
WOW...
HUH... JUST LIKE KARIN.
...SO NOW EVEN LOWLY ANIMALS CAN SENSE CHAKRA, EH...

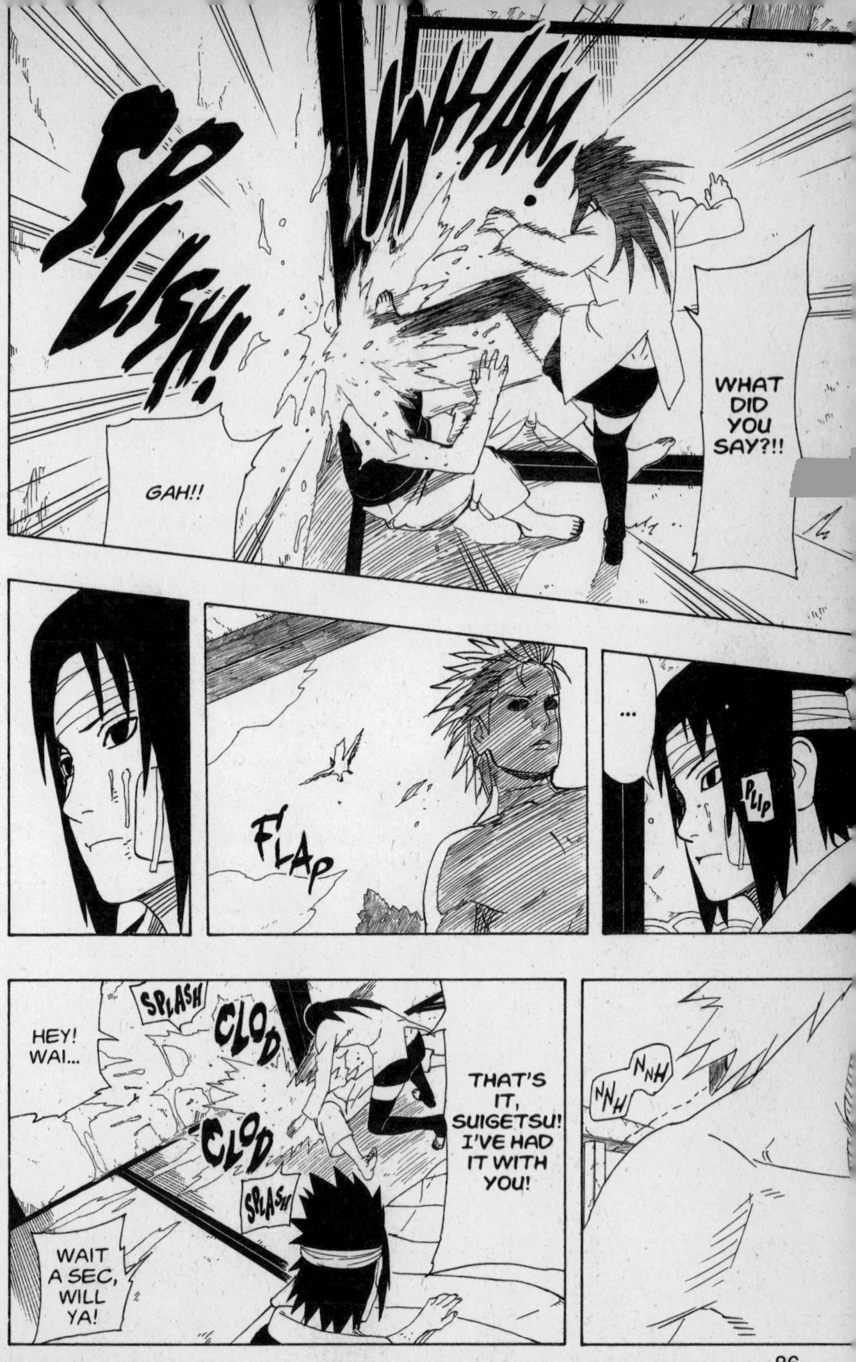
WHAT DID YOU SAY?!!
WHAM
SPLISH!
GAH!!
...
PLIP
FLAP
NNH
NNH
THAT'S IT, SUIGETSU! I'VE HAD IT WITH YOU!
CLOD
SPLASH
HEY! WAI...
CLOD
SPLASH
WAIT A SEC, WILL YA!

READ THIS WAY

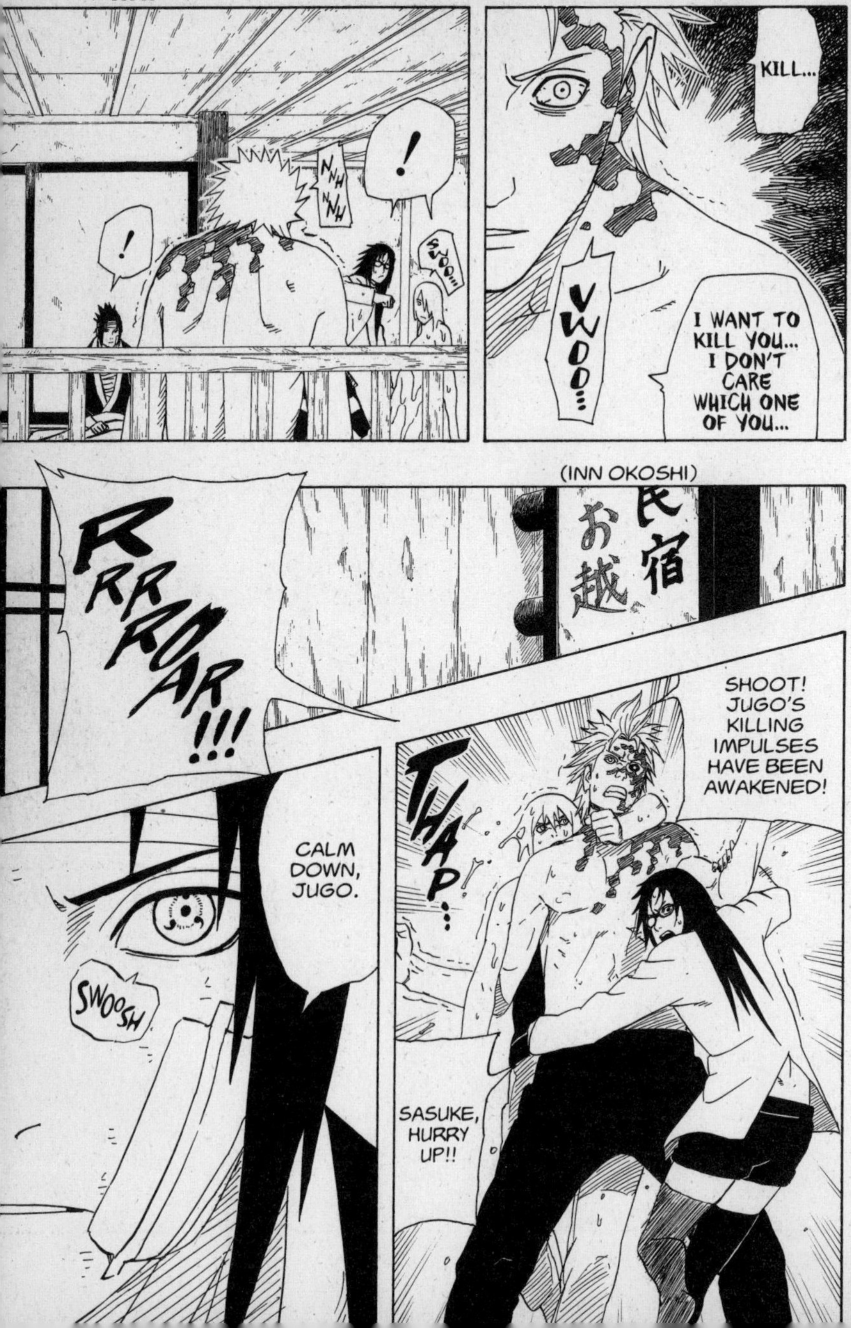

KILL...
VWOOO...
I WANT TO KILL YOU... I DON'T CARE WHICH ONE OF YOU...
!
NNH NNH
SWOO...
!
(INN OKOSHI)
民宿お越
RRROAR!!!
SHOOT! JUGO'S KILLING IMPULSES HAVE BEEN AWAKENED!
THAP...
SASUKE, HURRY UP!!
CALM DOWN, JUGO.
SWOOSH

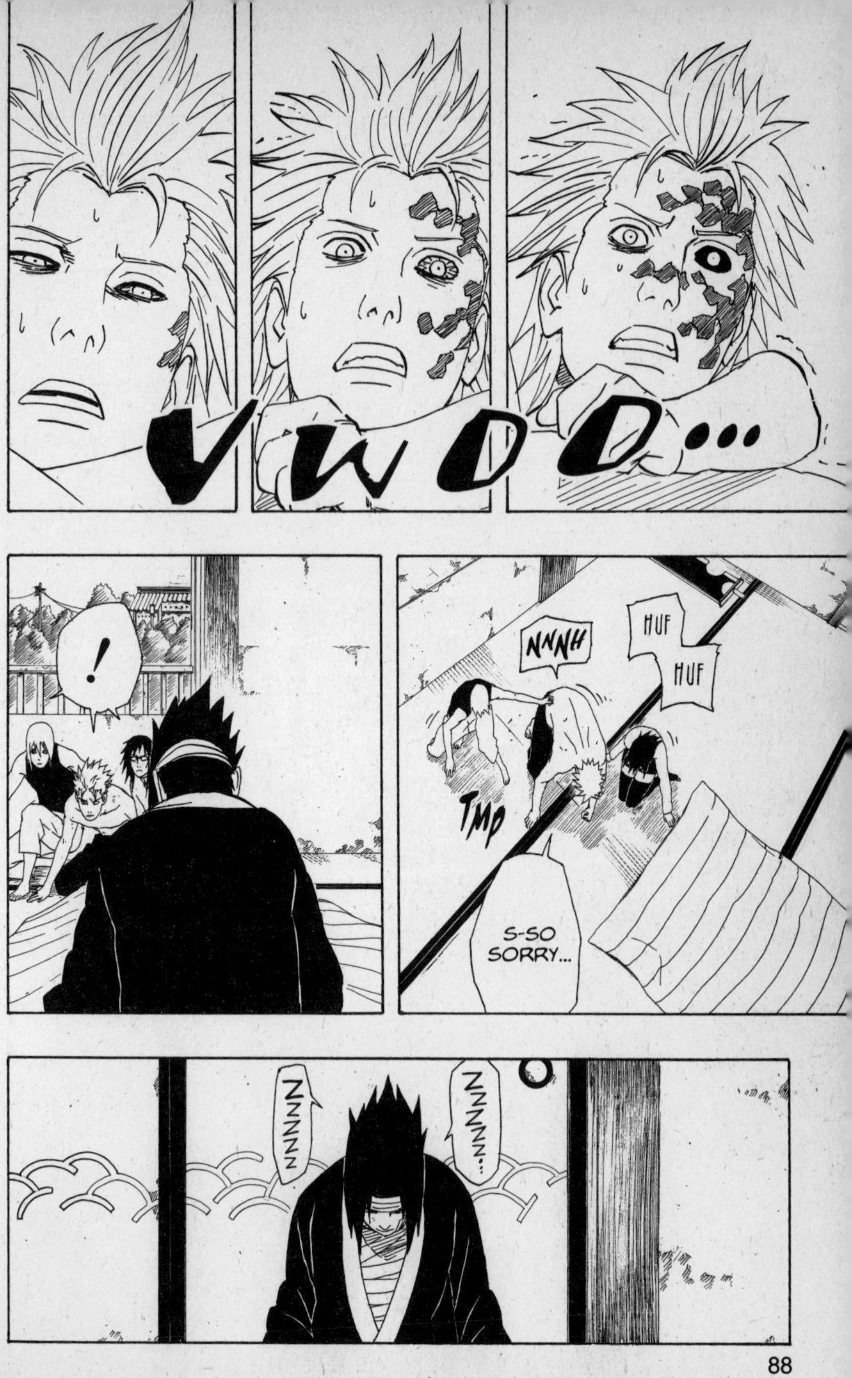
VWDD...
HUF
HUF
NNNH
TMP
S-SO SORRY...
!
ZZZZZ...
ZZZZZ

READ THIS WAY

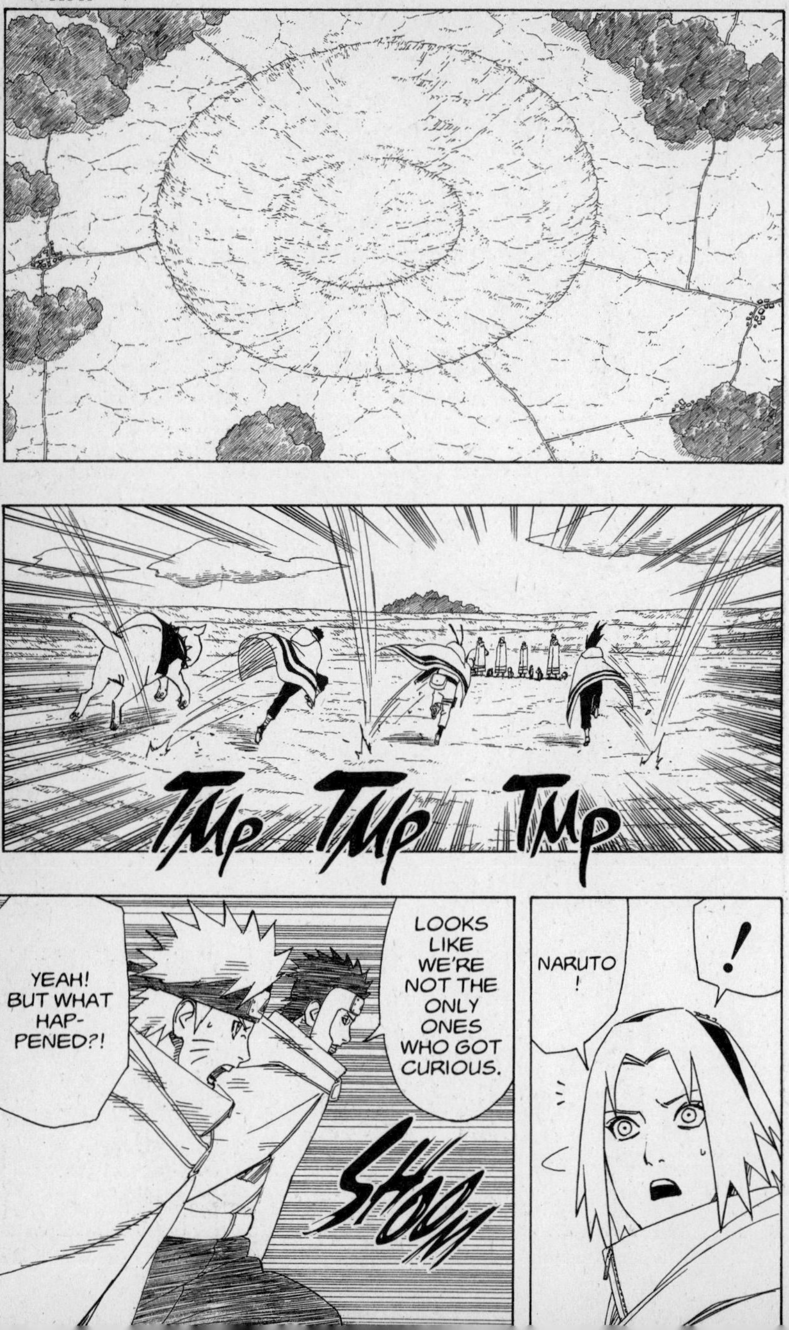
TMP TMP TMP
!
NARUTO!
LOOKS LIKE WE'RE NOT THE ONLY ONES WHO GOT CURIOUS.
YEAH! BUT WHAT HAP-PENED?!
SHOOM

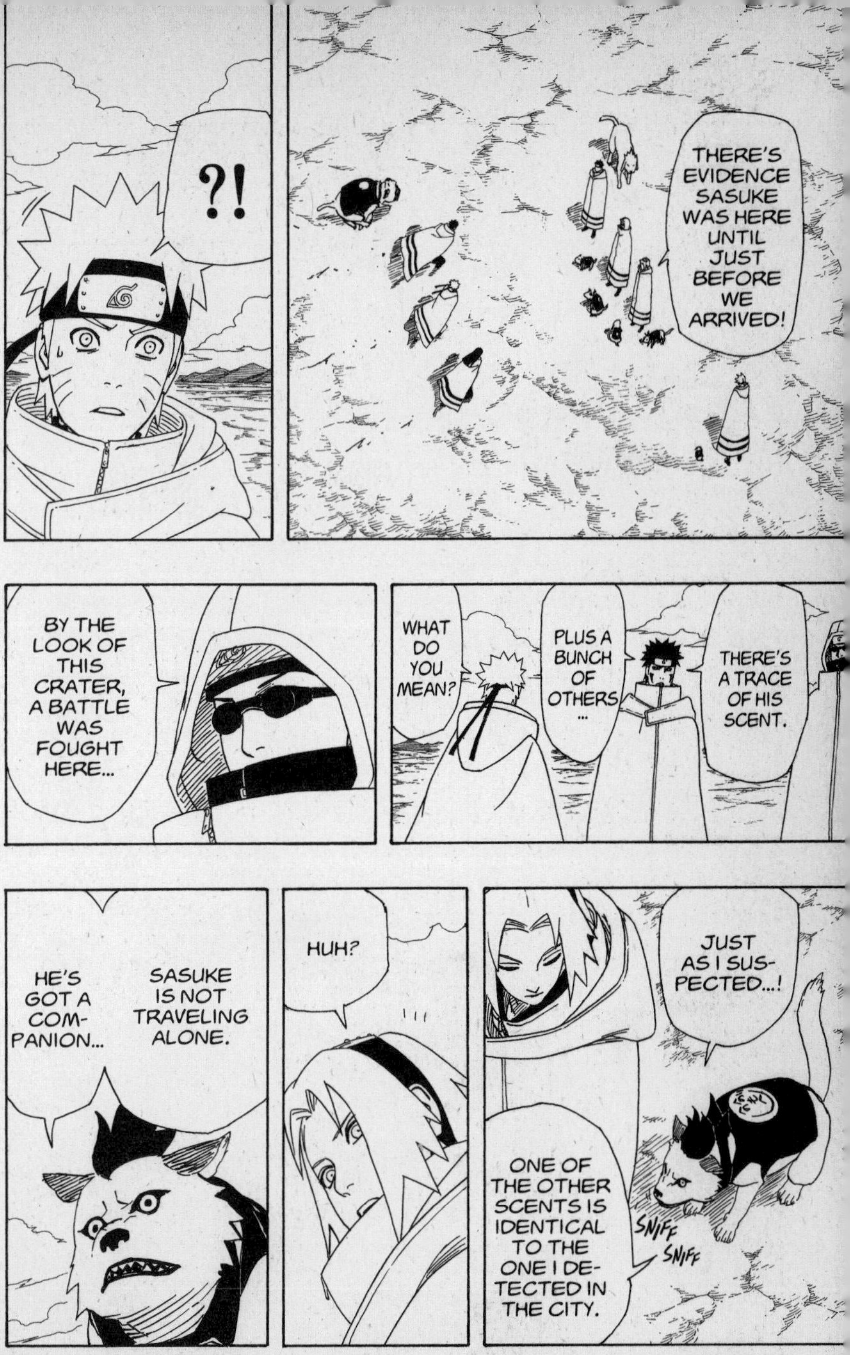
THERE'S EVIDENCE SASUKE WAS HERE UNTIL JUST BEFORE WE ARRIVED!
?!
THERE'S A TRACE OF HIS SCENT.
PLUS A BUNCH OF OTHERS...
WHAT DO YOU MEAN?
BY THE LOOK OF THIS CRATER, A BATTLE WAS FOUGHT HERE...
JUST AS I SUS-PECTED...!
ONE OF THE OTHER SCENTS IS IDENTICAL TO THE ONE I DE-TECTED IN THE CITY.
SNIFF
SNIFF
HUH?
SASUKE IS NOT TRAVELING ALONE.
HE'S GOT A COM-PANION...

READ THIS WAY

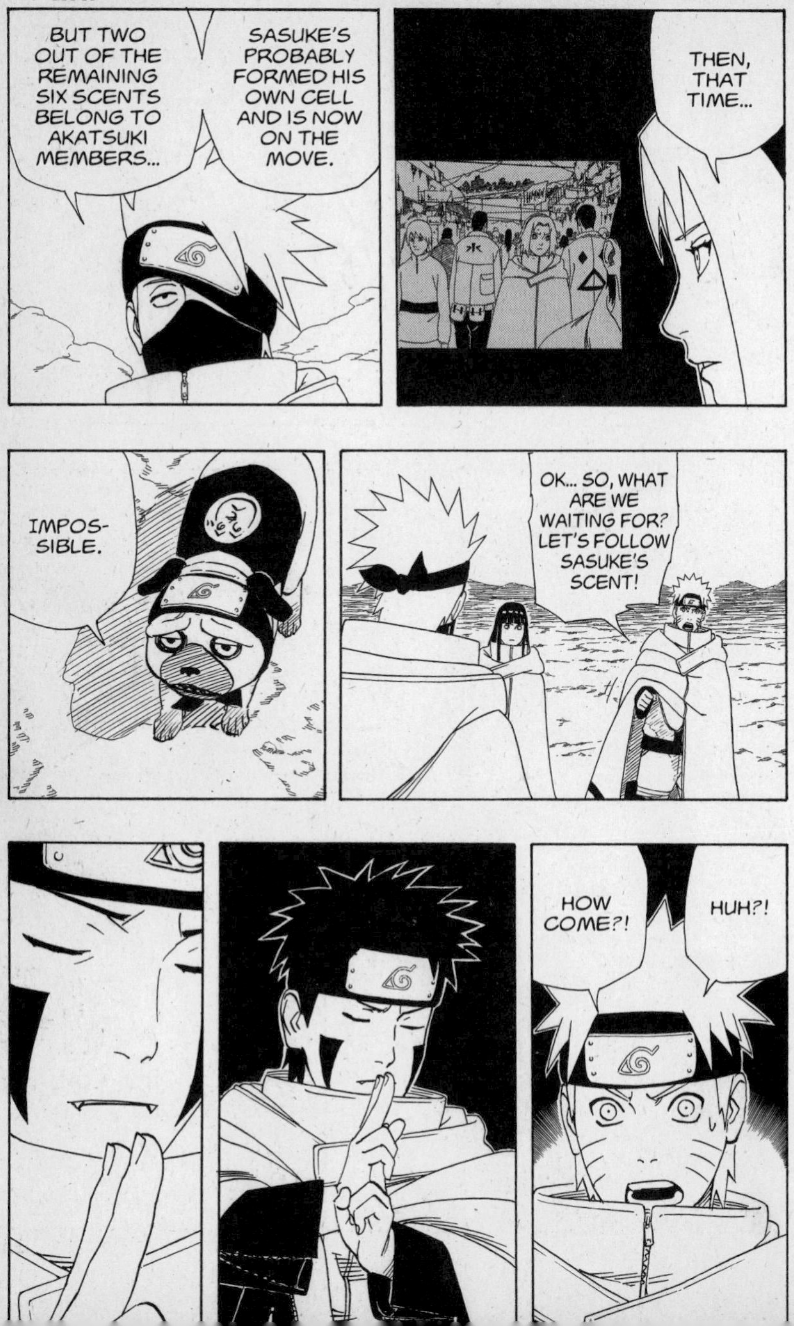
THEN, THAT TIME...
SASUKE'S PROBABLY FORMED HIS OWN CELL AND IS NOW ON THE MOVE.
BUT TWO OUT OF THE REMAINING SIX SCENTS BELONG TO AKATSUKI MEMBERS...
OK... SO, WHAT ARE WE WAITING FOR? LET'S FOLLOW SASUKE'S SCENT!
IMPOS-SIBLE.
HUH?!
HOW COME?!

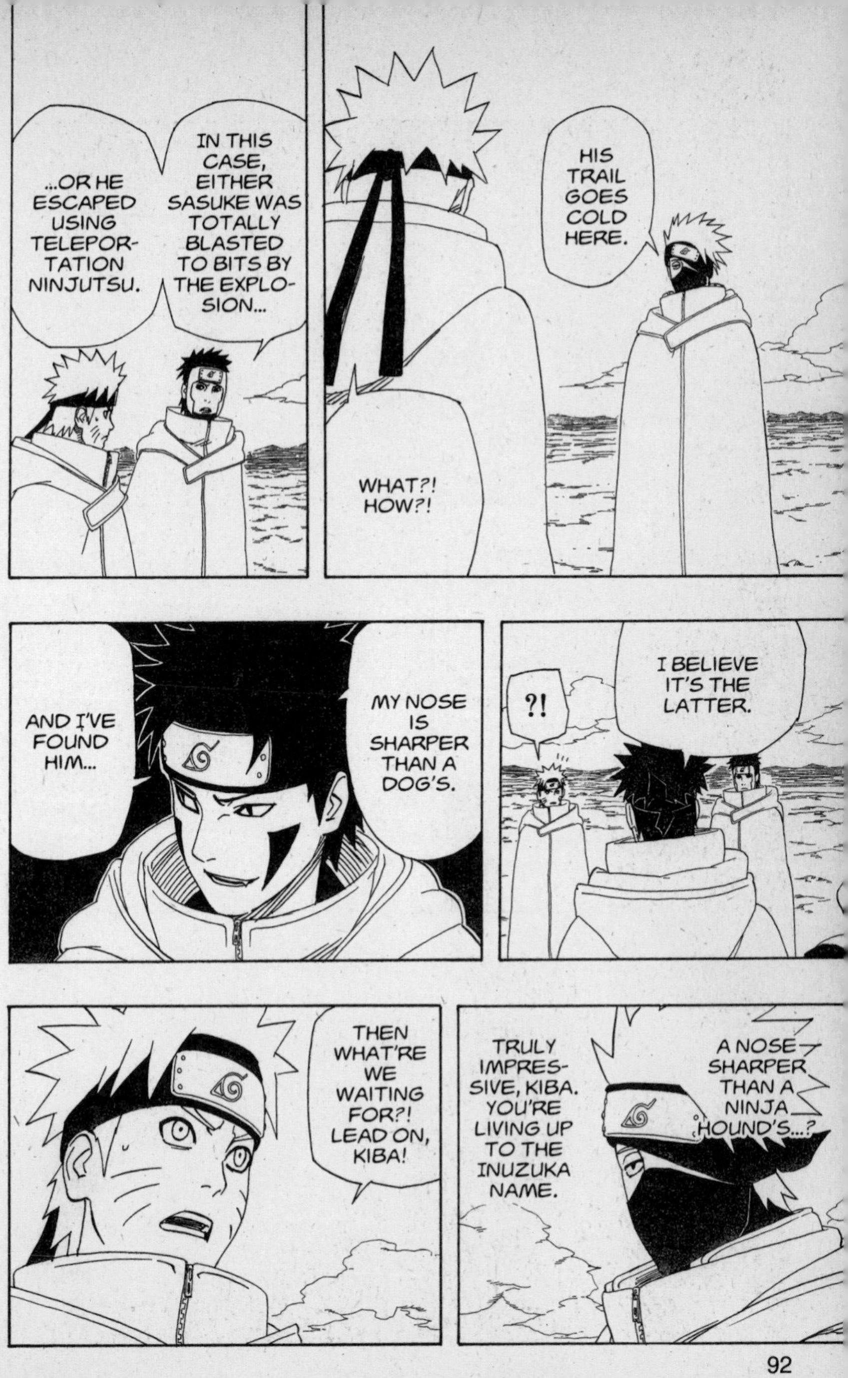
HIS TRAIL GOES COLD HERE.
WHAT?! HOW?!
IN THIS CASE, EITHER SASUKE WAS TOTALLY BLASTED TO BITS BY THE EXPLOSION...
...OR HE ESCAPED USING TELEPORTATION NINJUTSU.
I BELIEVE IT'S THE LATTER.
?!
MY NOSE IS SHARPER THAN A DOG'S.
AND I'VE FOUND HIM...
A NOSE SHARPER THAN A NINJA HOUND'S...?
TRULY IMPRESSIVE, KIBA. YOU'RE LIVING UP TO THE INUZUKA NAME.
THEN WHAT'RE WE WAITING FOR?! LEAD ON, KIBA!

READ THIS WAY

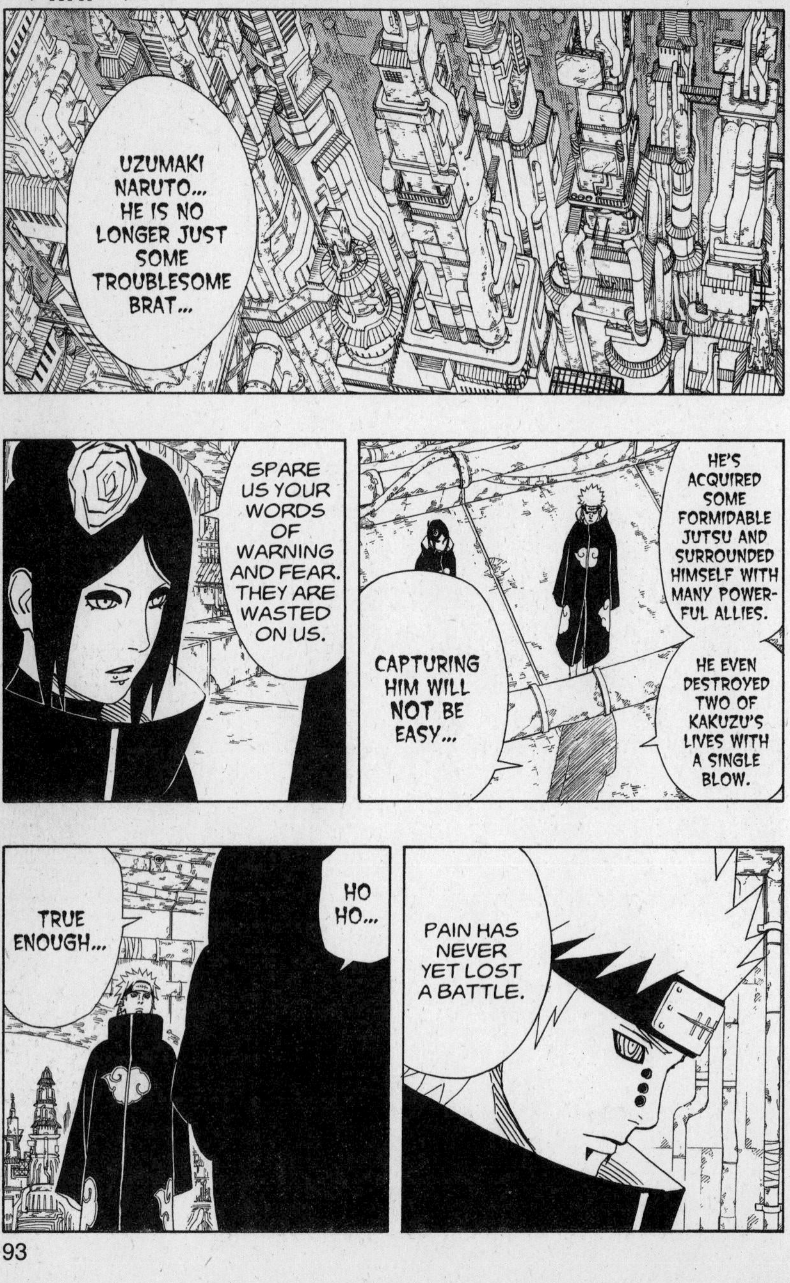
UZUMAKI NARUTO... HE IS NO LONGER JUST SOME TROUBLESOME BRAT...
HE'S ACQUIRED SOME FORMIDABLE JUTSU AND SURROUNDED HIMSELF WITH MANY POWER-FUL ALLIES.
HE EVEN DESTROYED TWO OF KAKUZU'S LIVES WITH A SINGLE BLOW.
CAPTURING HIM WILL NOT BE EASY...
SPARE US YOUR WORDS OF WARNING AND FEAR. THEY ARE WASTED ON US.
PAIN HAS NEVER YET LOST A BATTLE.
HO HO...
TRUE ENOUGH...

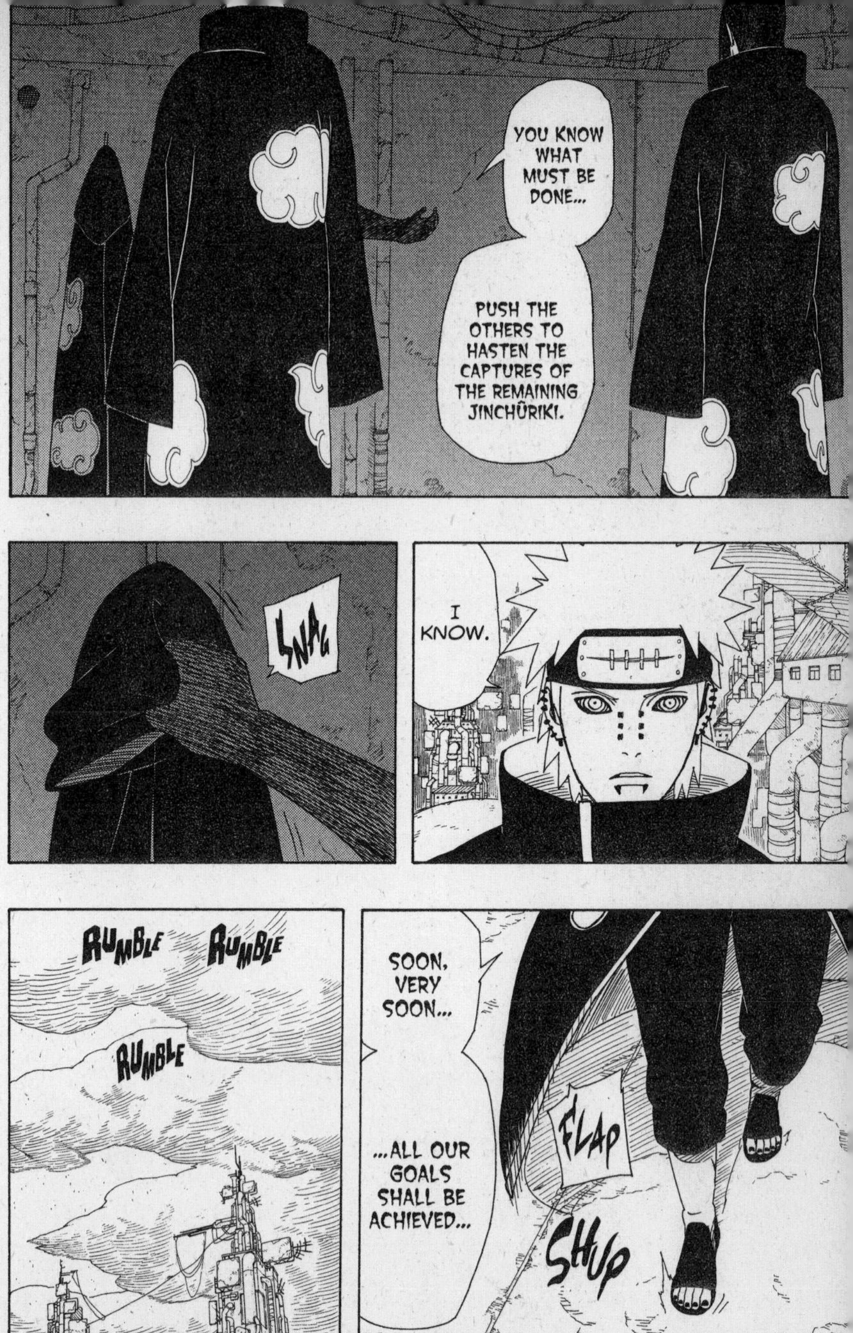
YOU KNOW WHAT MUST BE DONE...
PUSH THE OTHERS TO HASTEN THE CAPTURES OF THE REMAINING JINCHŪRIKI.
I KNOW.
SNAG
SOON, VERY SOON...
...ALL OUR GOALS SHALL BE ACHIEVED...
FLAP
SHUP
RUMBLE
RUMBLE
RUMBLE

READ THIS WAY

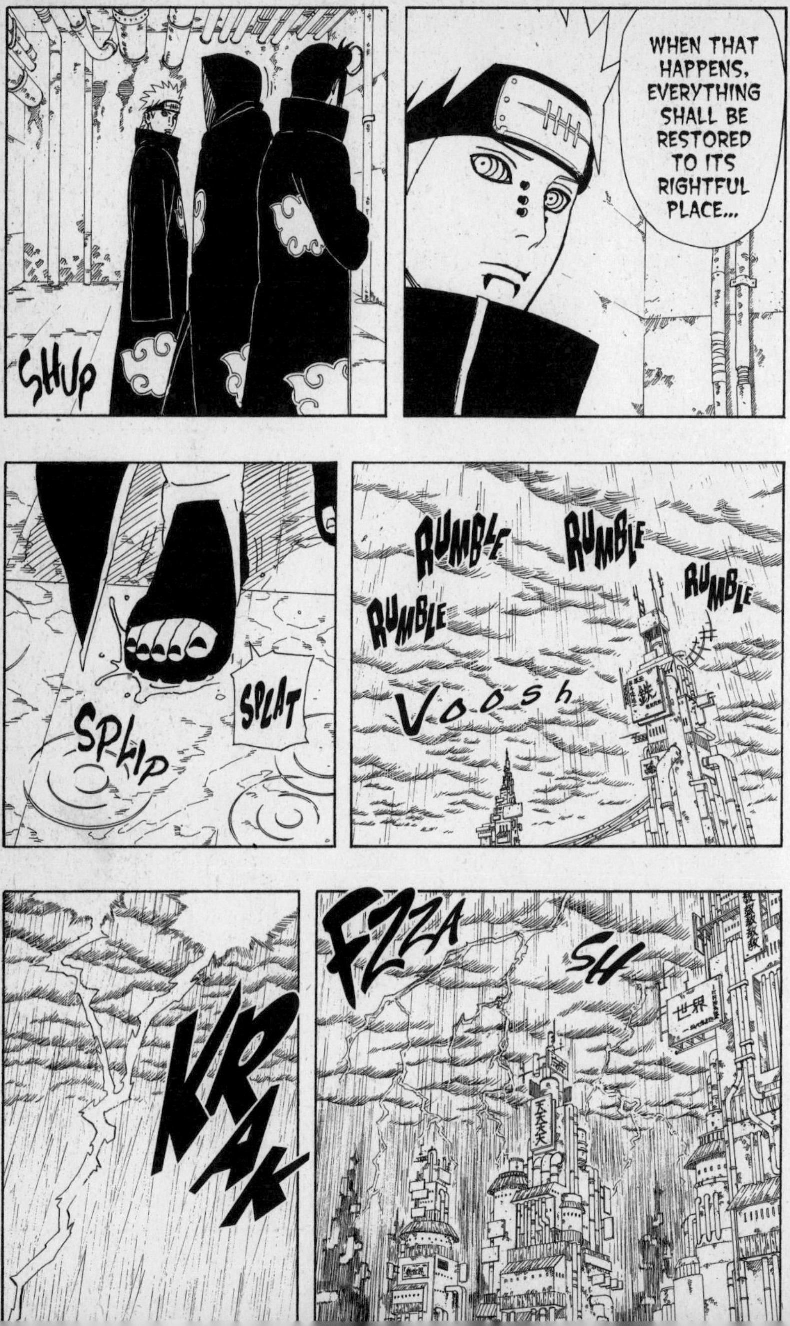
WHEN THAT HAPPENS, EVERYTHING SHALL BE RESTORED TO ITS RIGHTFUL PLACE...
SHUP
RUMBLE
RUMBLE
RUMBLE
RUMBLE
VOOSH
鉄
SPLAT
SPLIP
FZZASH
世界
KRAK

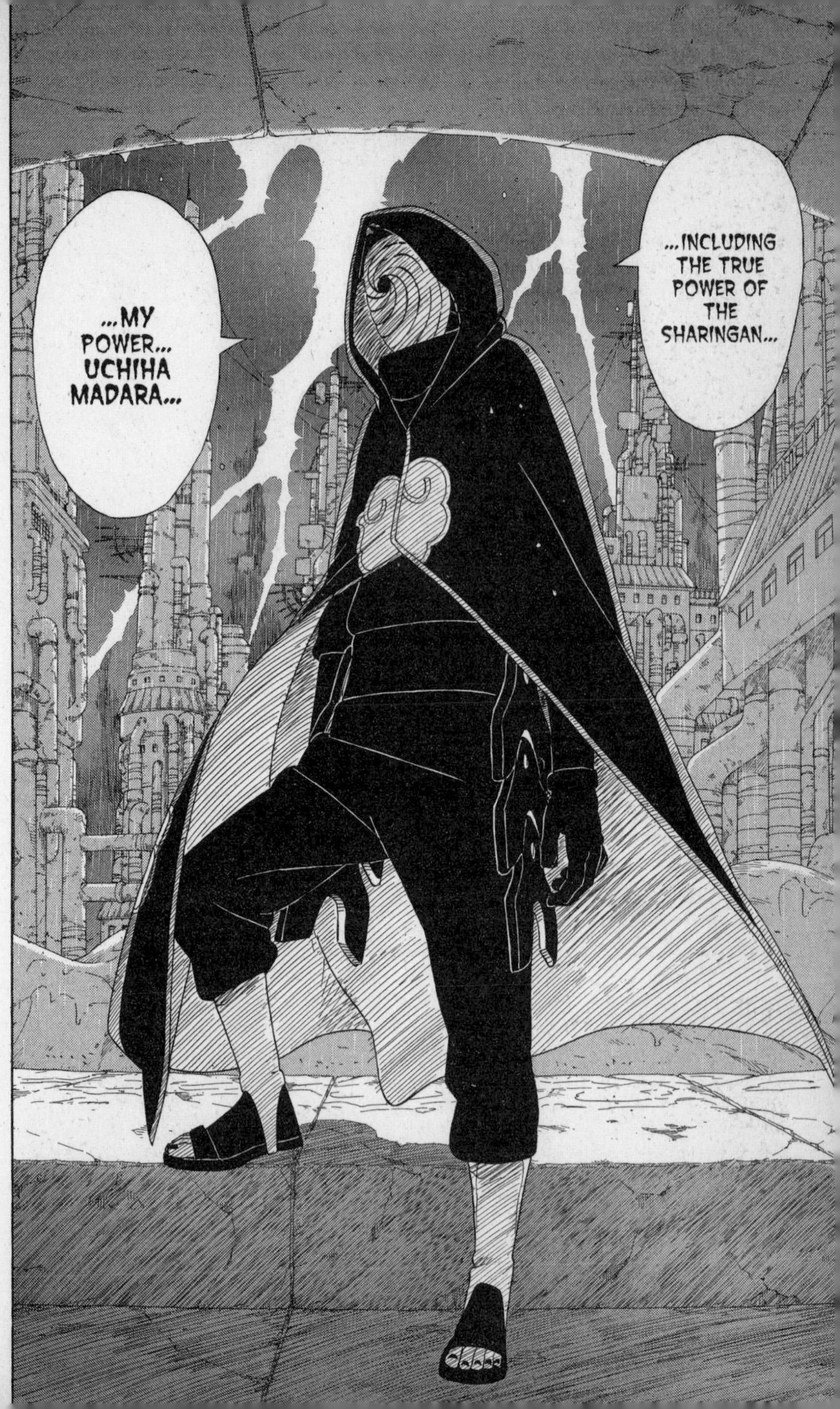
...INCLUDING THE TRUE POWER OF THE SHARINGAN...
...MY POWER... UCHIHA MADARA...

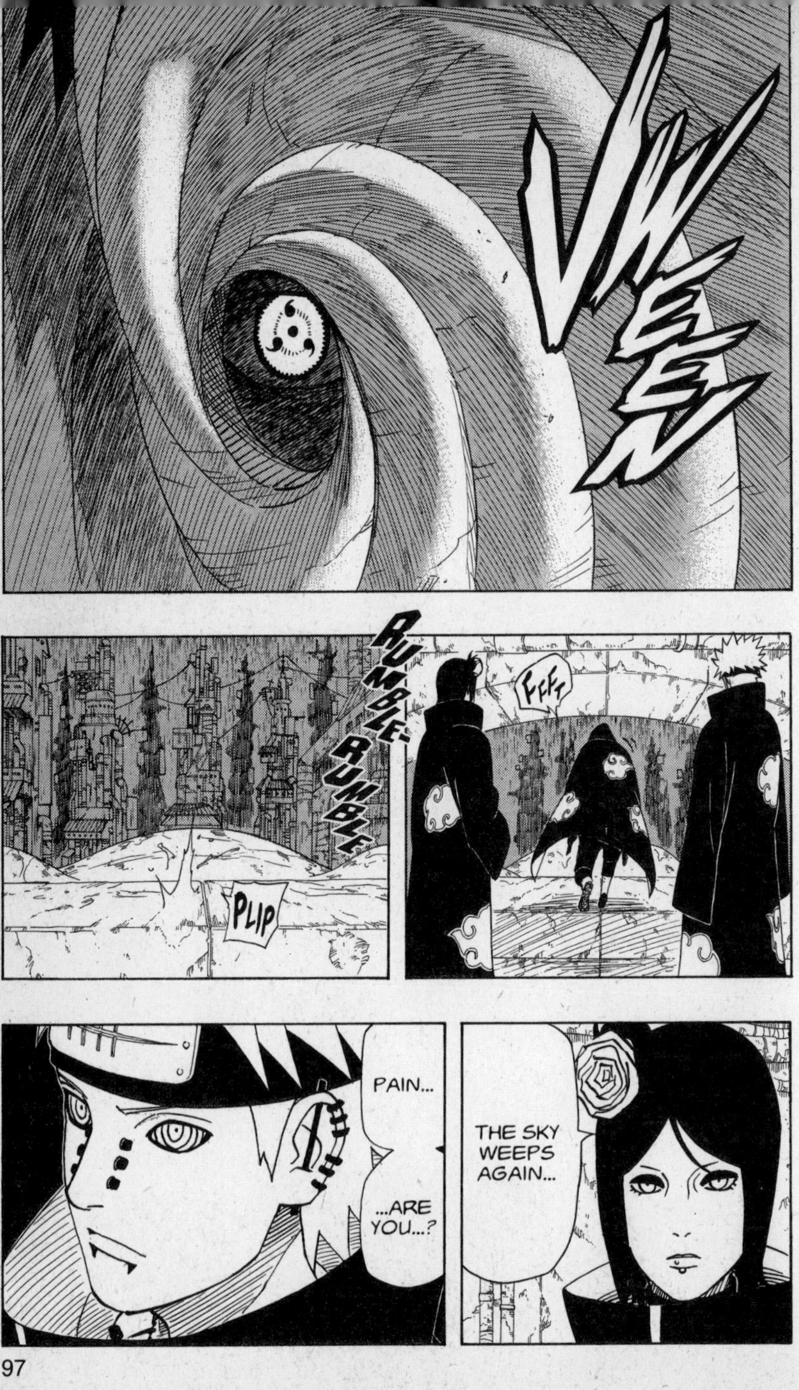
VWEEN
RUMBLE RUMBLE RUMBLE
FFFT
PLIP
THE SKY WEEPS AGAIN...
PAIN...
...ARE YOU...?

NARUTO

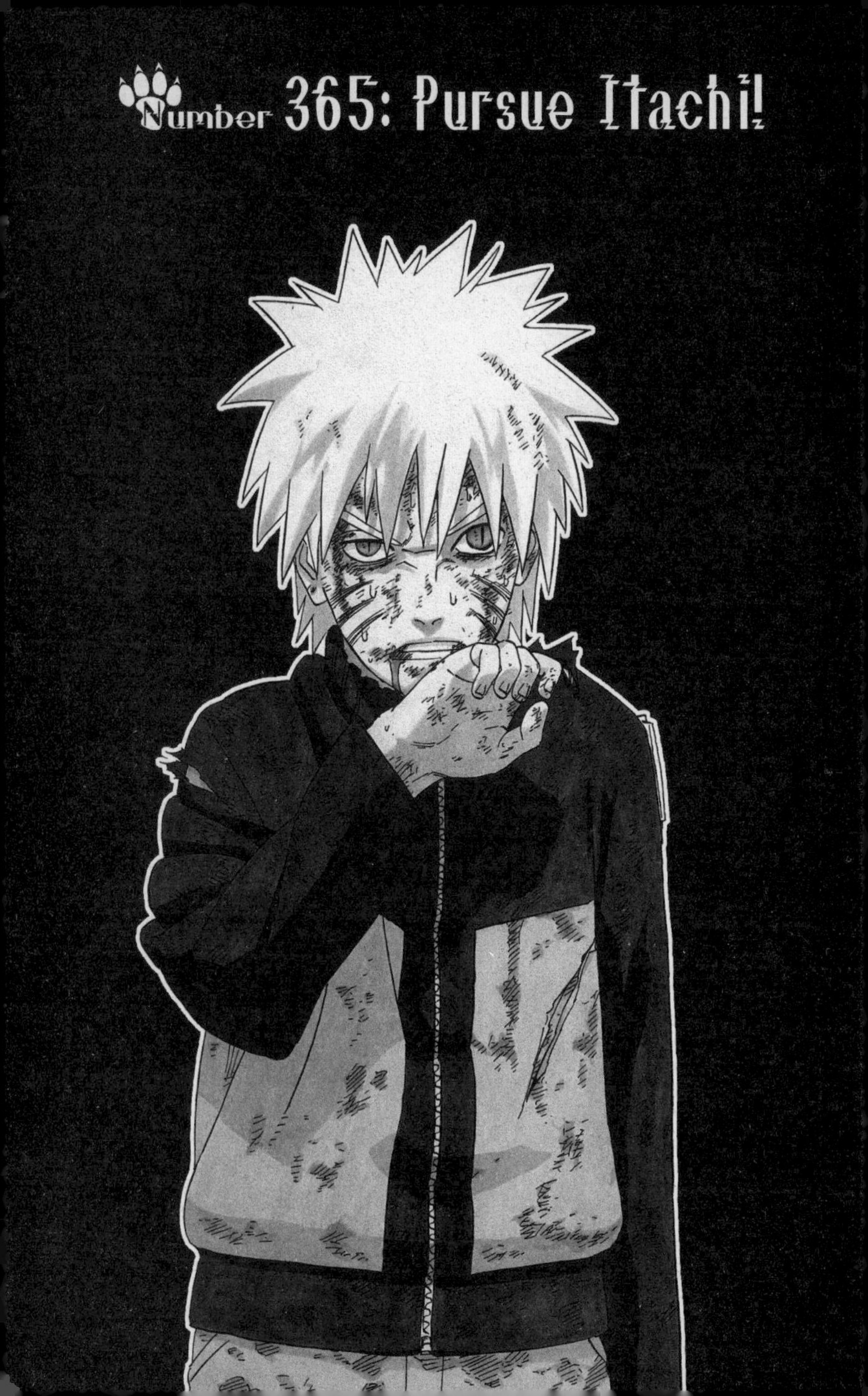
Number 365: Pursue Itachi!

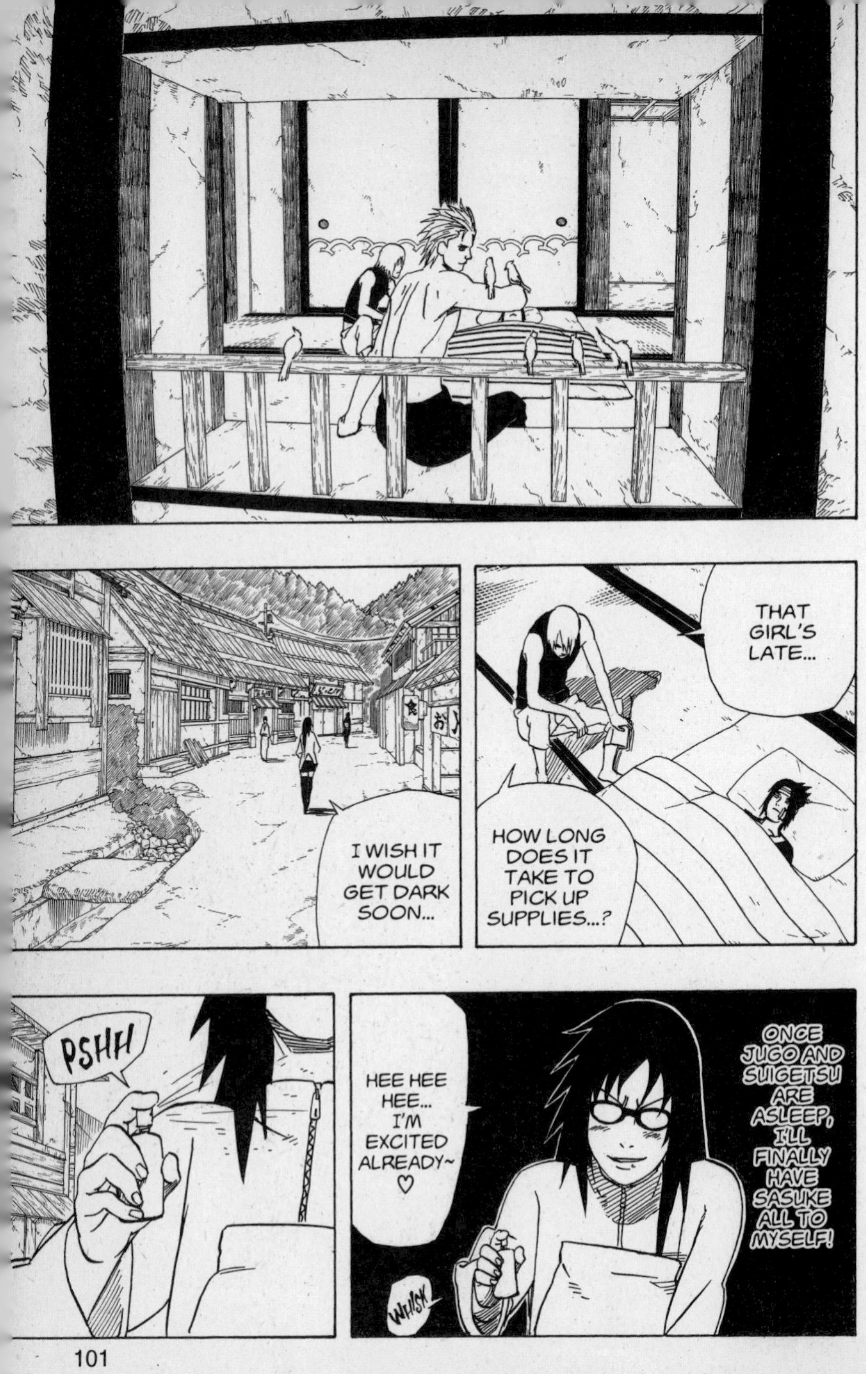
THAT GIRL'S LATE...
HOW LONG DOES IT TAKE TO PICK UP SUPPLIES...?
I WISH IT WOULD GET DARK SOON...
ONCE JUGO AND SUIGETSU ARE ASLEEP, I'LL FINALLY HAVE SASUKE ALL TO MYSELF!
HEE HEE HEE... I'M EXCITED ALREADY~ ♡
WHISK
PSHH

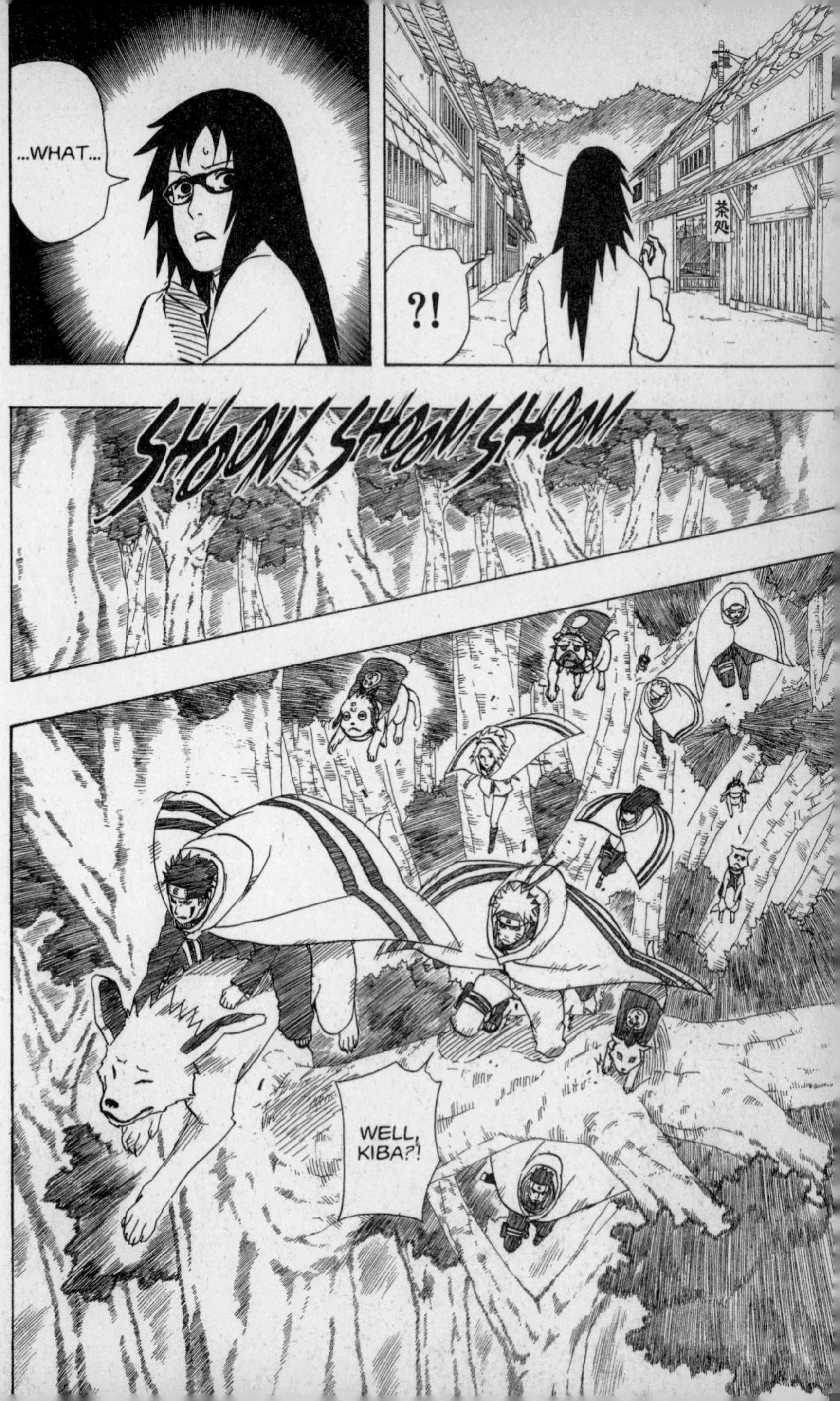
茶処
?!
...WHAT...
SHOOM SHOOM SHOOM
WELL, KIBA?!

READ THIS WAY

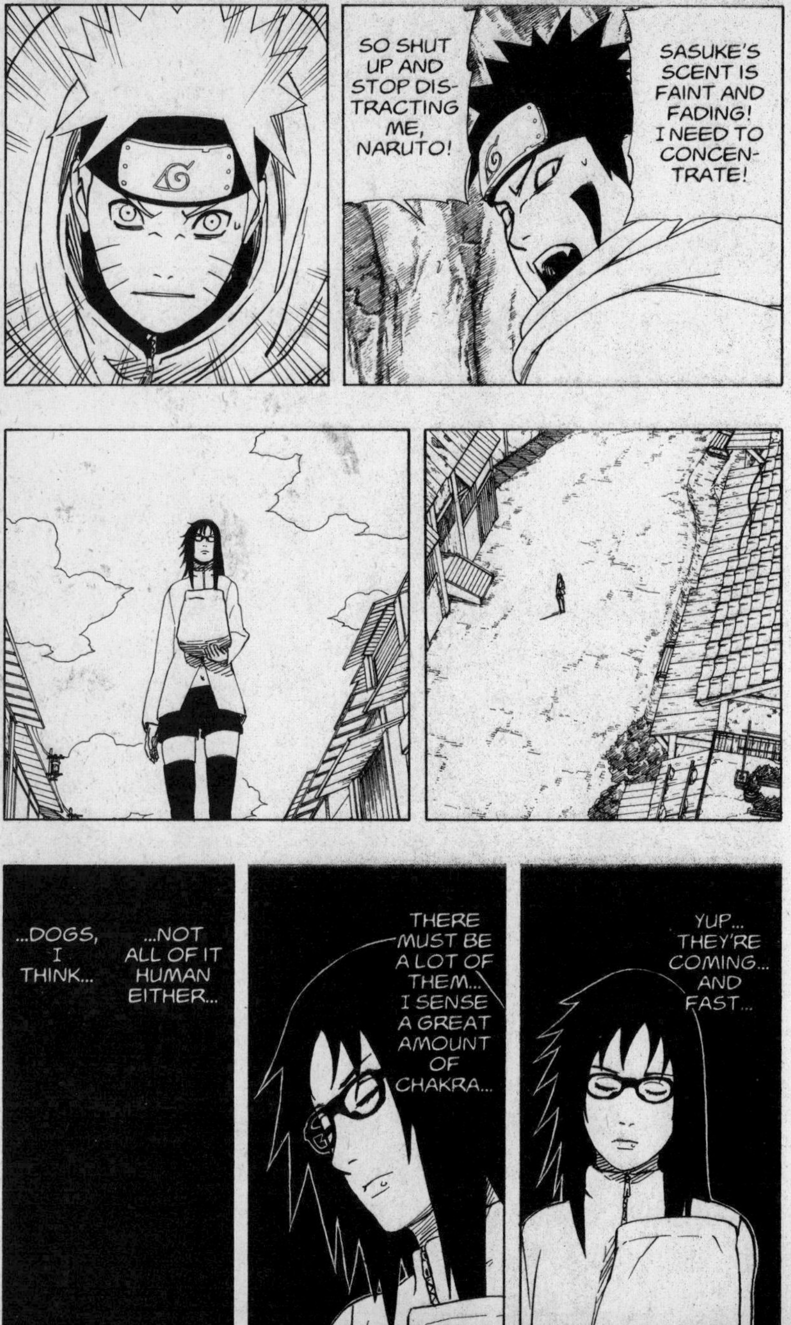
SASUKE'S SCENT IS FAINT AND FADING! I NEED TO CONCENTRATE!
SO SHUT UP AND STOP DISTRACTING ME, NARUTO!
YUP... THEY'RE COMING... AND FAST...
THERE MUST BE A LOT OF THEM... I SENSE A GREAT AMOUNT OF CHAKRA...
...NOT ALL OF IT HUMAN EITHER...
...DOGS, I THINK...

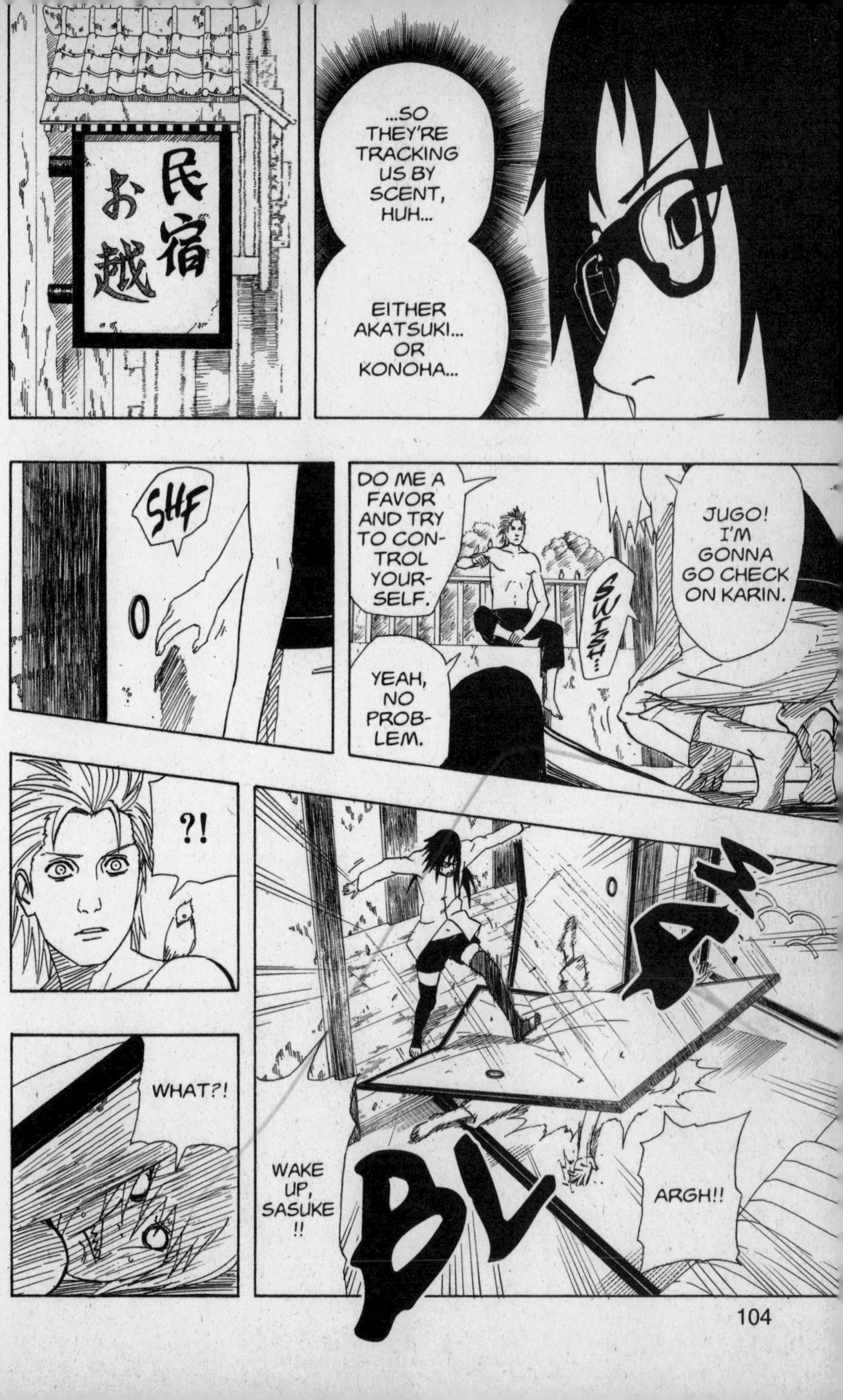
...SO THEY'RE TRACKING US BY SCENT, HUH...
EITHER AKATSUKI... OR KONOHA...
民宿
お越
JUGO! I'M GONNA GO CHECK ON KARIN.
DO ME A FAVOR AND TRY TO CONTROL YOURSELF.
SWISH...
YEAH, NO PROBLEM.
SHF
ARGH!!
WAKE UP, SASUKE!!
?!
WHAT?!

READ THIS WAY

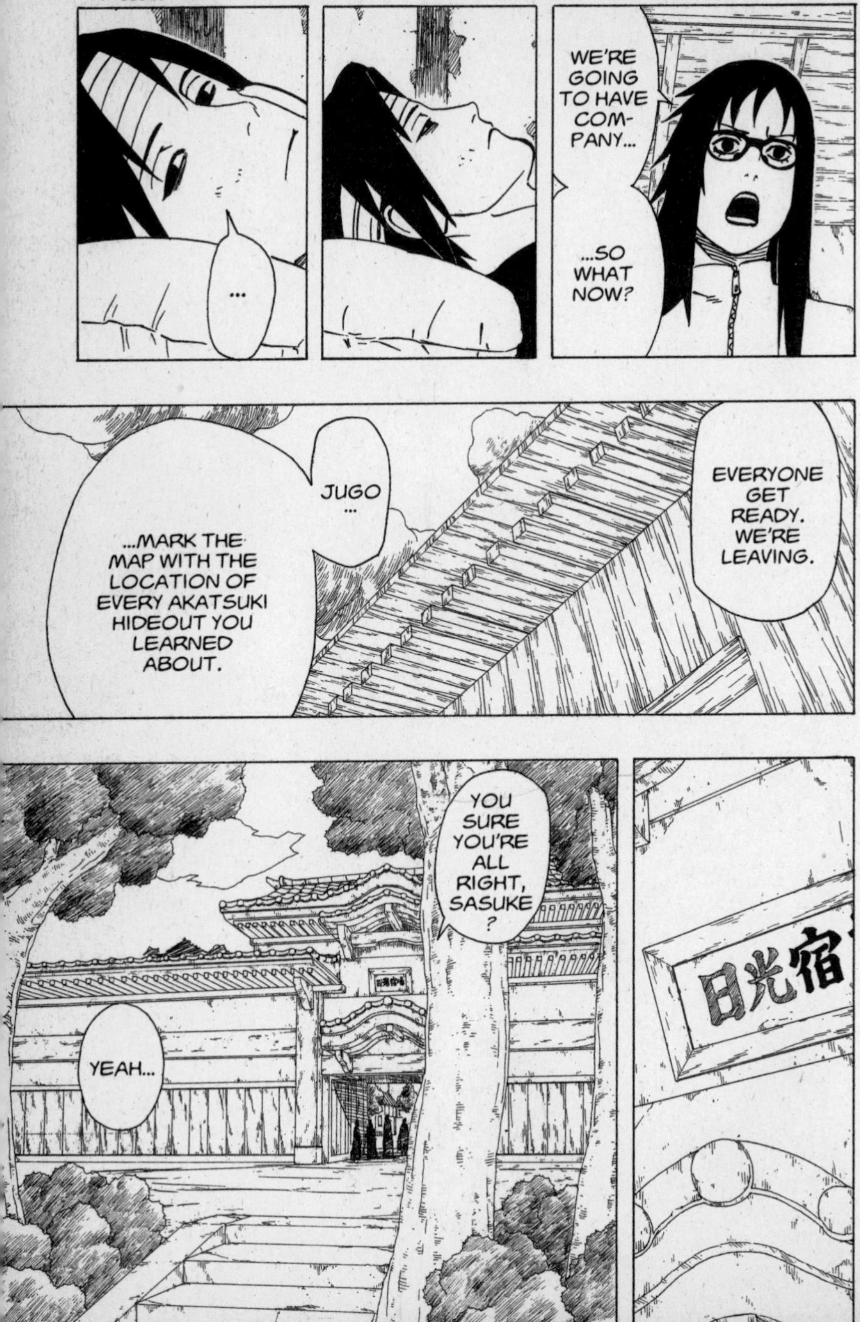
WE'RE GOING TO HAVE COMPANY...
...SO WHAT NOW?
...
EVERYONE GET READY. WE'RE LEAVING.
JUGO ...
...MARK THE MAP WITH THE LOCATION OF EVERY AKATSUKI HIDEOUT YOU LEARNED ABOUT.
日光宿
YOU SURE YOU'RE ALL RIGHT, SASUKE?
YEAH...

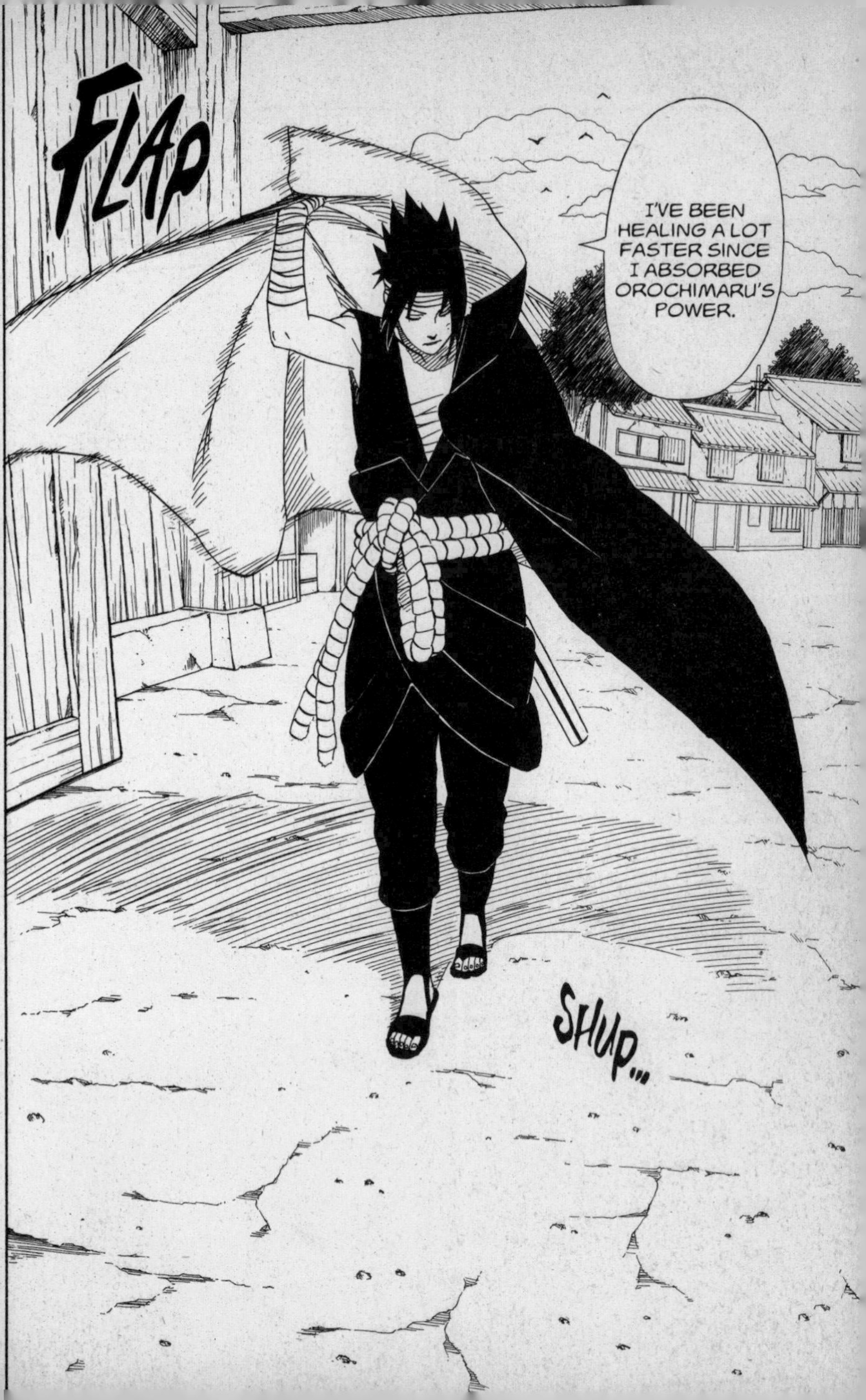
I'VE BEEN HEALING A LOT FASTER SINCE I ABSORBED OROCHIMARU'S POWER.
FLAP
SHUP...

READ THIS WAY

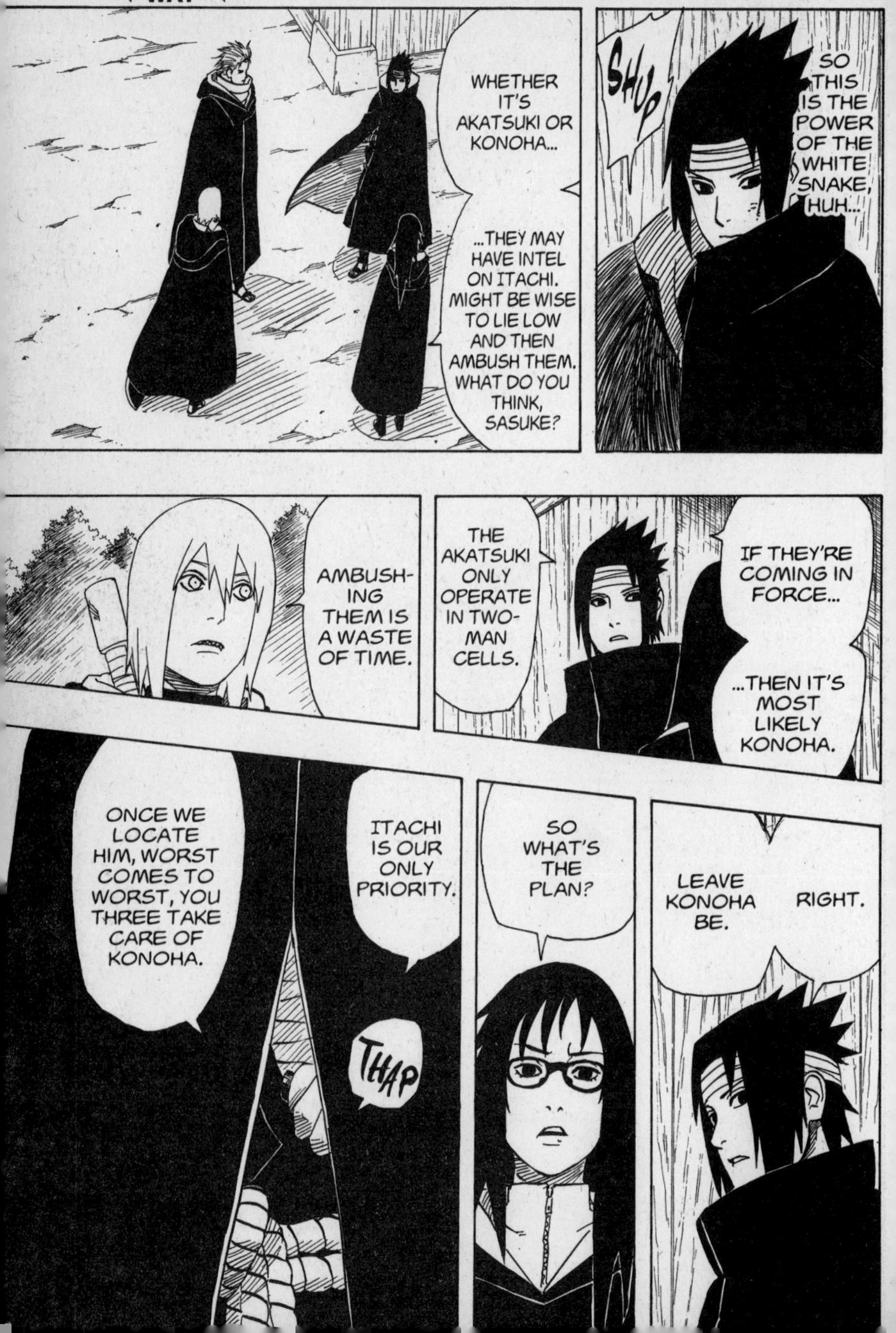
SHUP
SO THIS IS THE POWER OF THE WHITE SNAKE, HUH...
WHETHER IT'S AKATSUKI OR KONOHA...
...THEY MAY HAVE INTEL ON ITACHI. MIGHT BE WISE TO LIE LOW AND THEN AMBUSH THEM. WHAT DO YOU THINK, SASUKE?
IF THEY'RE COMING IN FORCE...
...THEN IT'S MOST LIKELY KONOHA.
THE AKATSUKI ONLY OPERATE IN TWO-MAN CELLS.
AMBUSHING THEM IS A WASTE OF TIME.
RIGHT.
LEAVE KONOHA BE.
SO WHAT'S THE PLAN?
ITACHI IS OUR ONLY PRIORITY.
ONCE WE LOCATE HIM, WORST COMES TO WORST, YOU THREE TAKE CARE OF KONOHA.
THAP

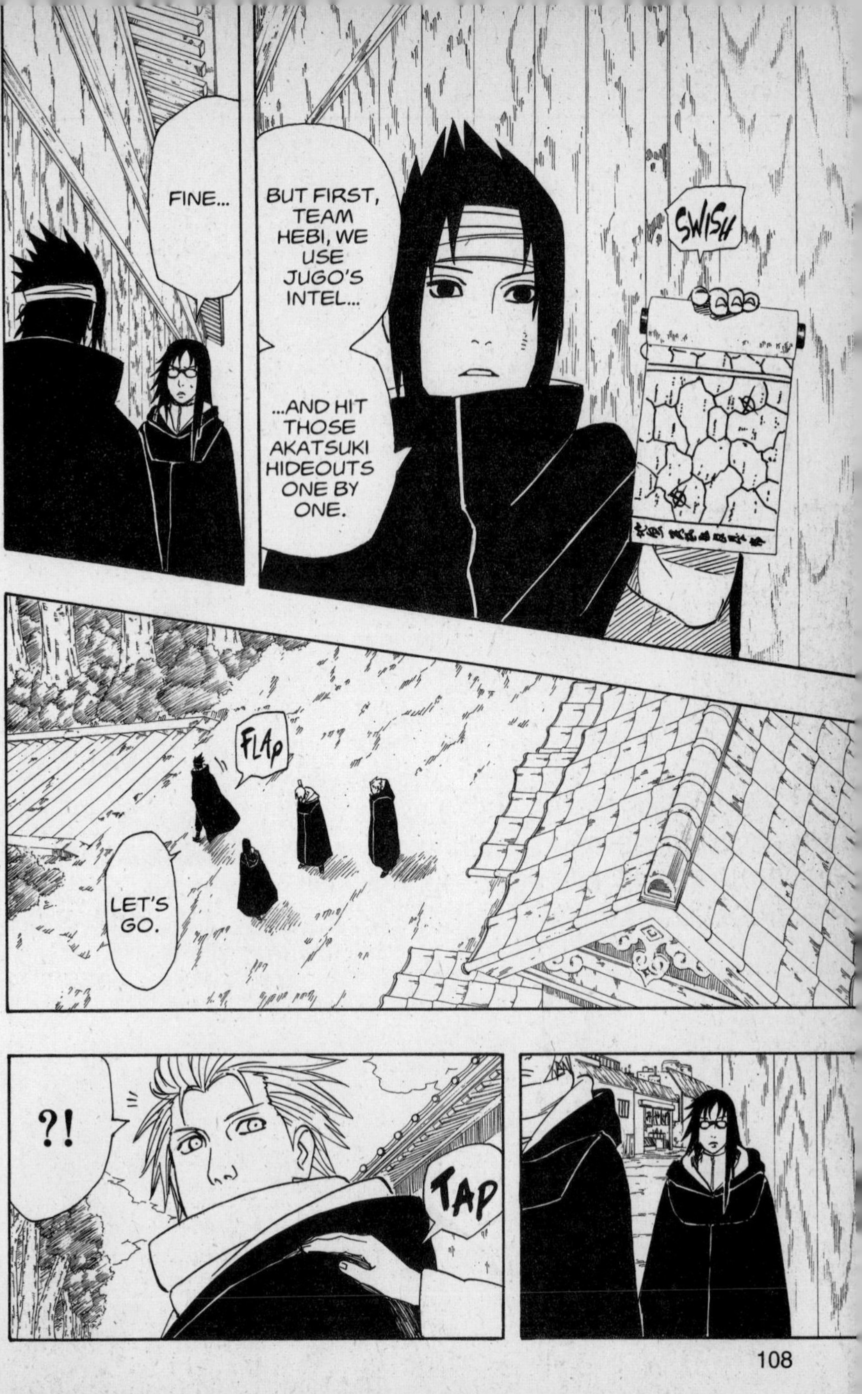
SWISH
BUT FIRST, TEAM HEBI, WE USE JUGO'S INTEL...
...AND HIT THOSE AKATSUKI HIDEOUTS ONE BY ONE.
FINE...
FLAP
LET'S GO.
TAP
?!

READ THIS WAY

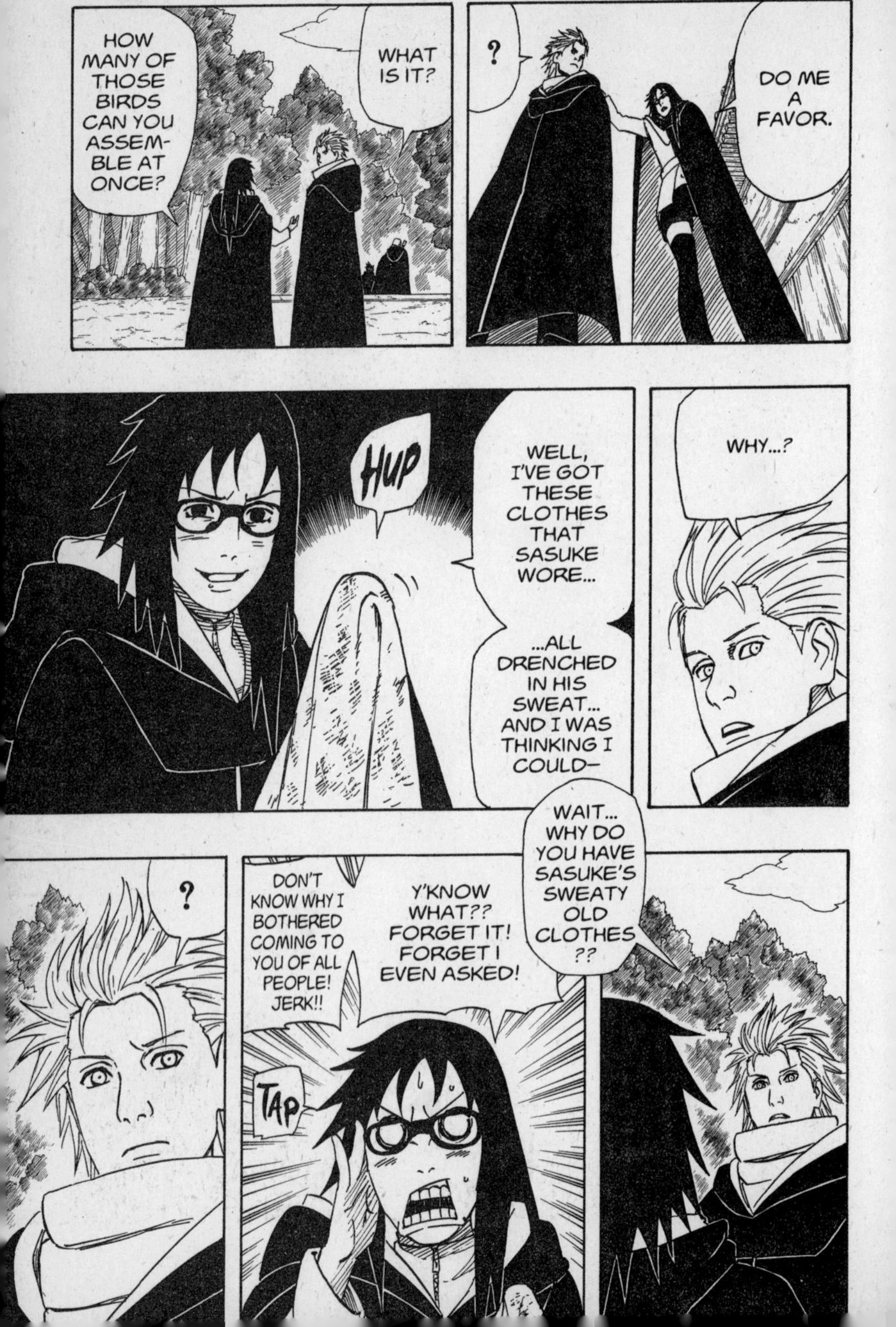
DO ME A FAVOR.
?
WHAT IS IT?
HOW MANY OF THOSE BIRDS CAN YOU ASSEMBLE AT ONCE?
WHY...?
WELL, I'VE GOT THESE CLOTHES THAT SASUKE WORE...
...ALL DRENCHED IN HIS SWEAT... AND I WAS THINKING I COULD—
HUP
WAIT... WHY DO YOU HAVE SASUKE'S SWEATY OLD CLOTHES??
Y'KNOW WHAT?? FORGET IT! FORGET I EVEN ASKED!
DON'T KNOW WHY I BOTHERED COMING TO YOU OF ALL PEOPLE! JERK!!
TAP
?

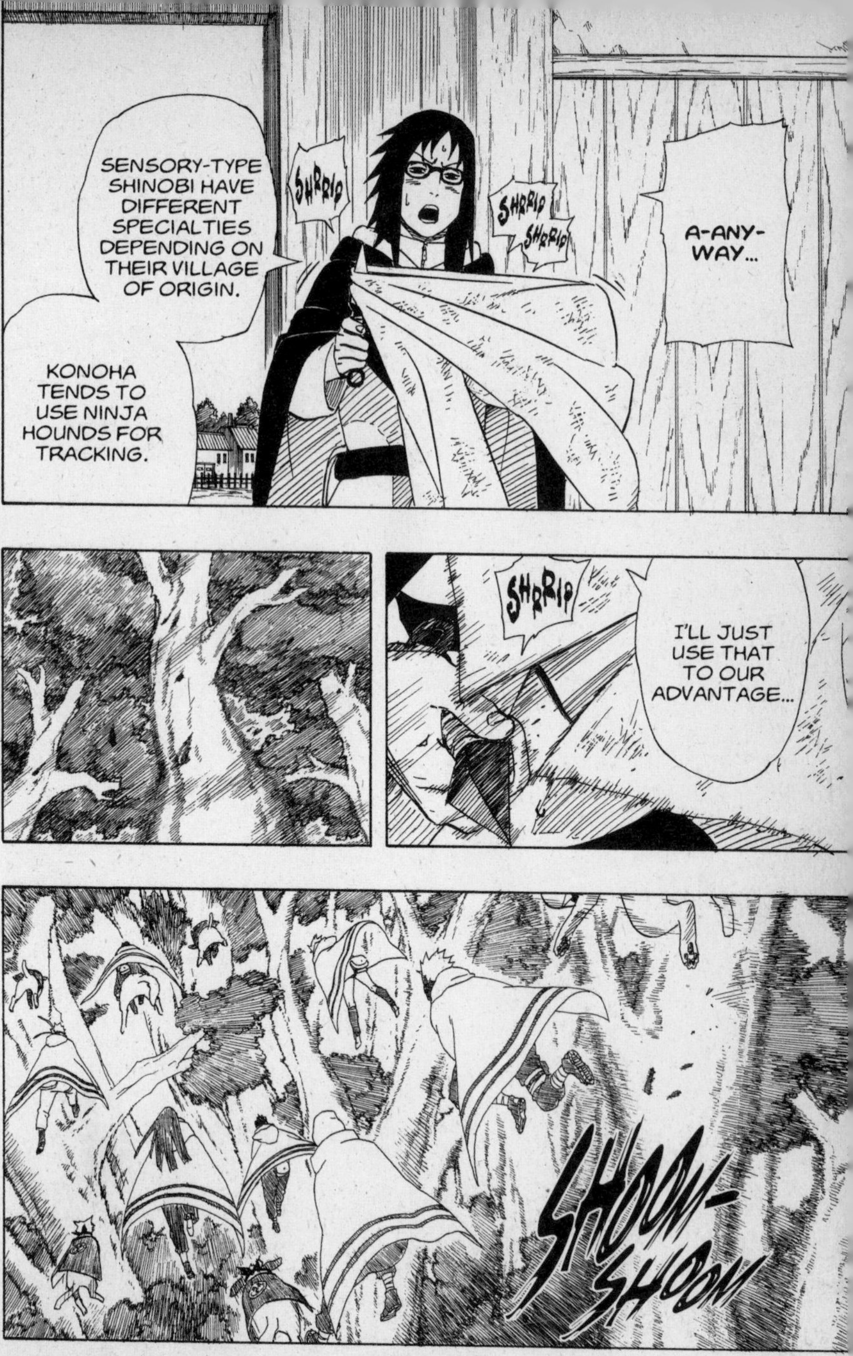
A-ANY-WAY...
SHRRIP
SHRRIP SHRRIP
SHRRIP
SENSORY-TYPE SHINOBI HAVE DIFFERENT SPECIALTIES DEPENDING ON THEIR VILLAGE OF ORIGIN.
KONOHA TENDS TO USE NINJA HOUNDS FOR TRACKING.
SHRRIP
I'LL JUST USE THAT TO OUR ADVANTAGE...
SHOOM-SHOOM

READ THIS WAY

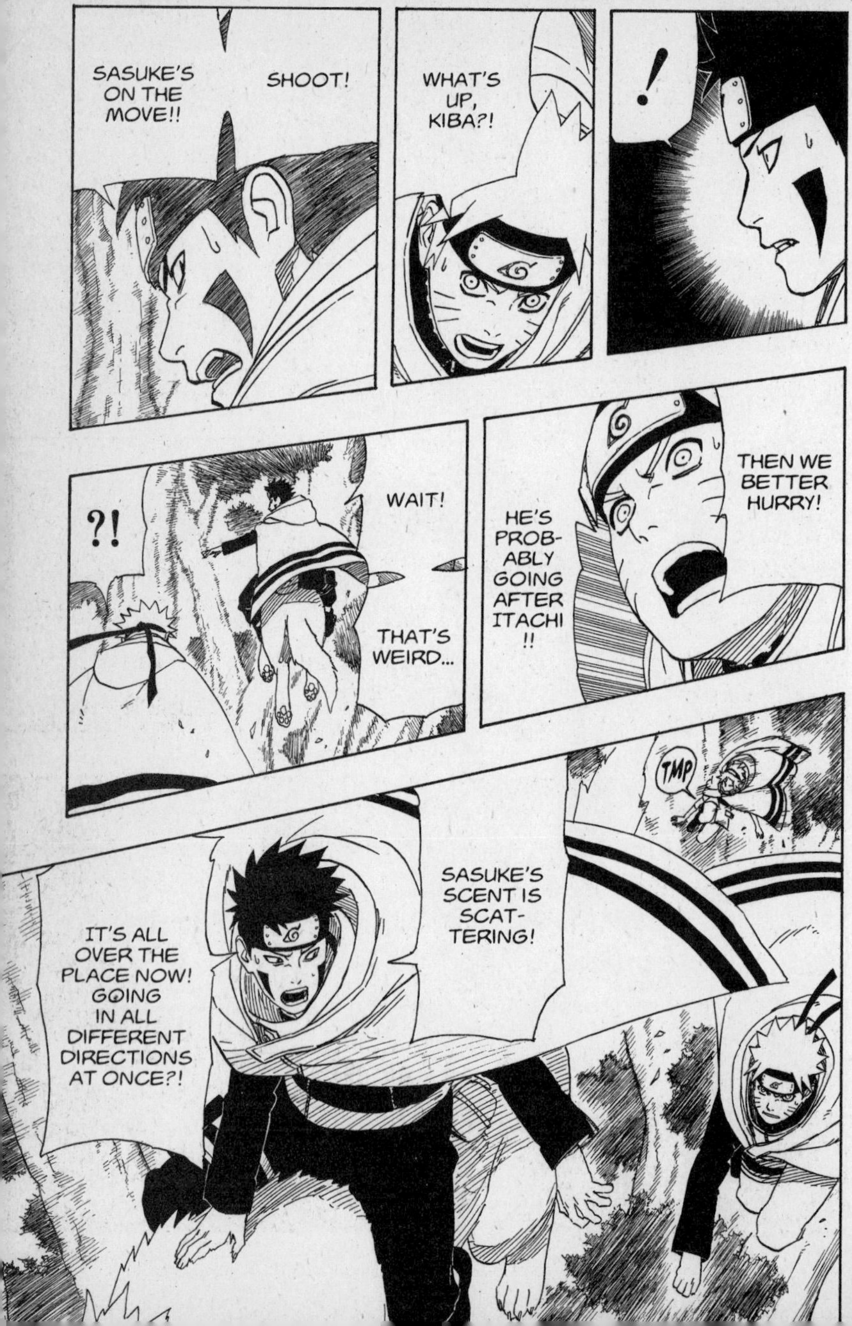
!
WHAT'S UP, KIBA?!
SHOOT!
SASUKE'S ON THE MOVE!!
THEN WE BETTER HURRY!
HE'S PROBABLY GOING AFTER ITACHI!!
WAIT!
THAT'S WEIRD...
?!
TMP
SASUKE'S SCENT IS SCATTERING!
IT'S ALL OVER THE PLACE NOW! GOING IN ALL DIFFERENT DIRECTIONS AT ONCE?!

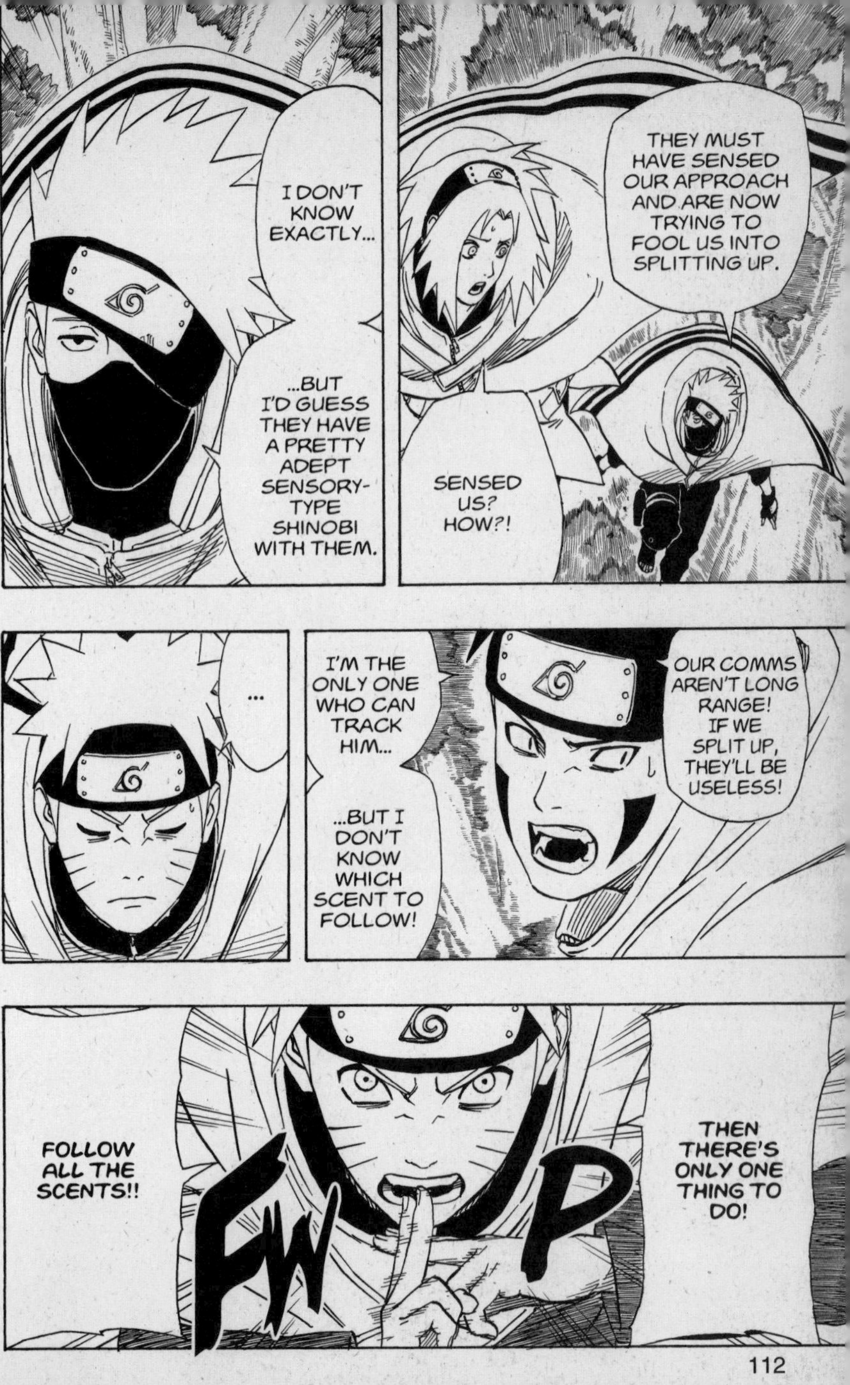
THEY MUST HAVE SENSED OUR APPROACH AND ARE NOW TRYING TO FOOL US INTO SPLITTING UP.
SENSED US? HOW?!
I DON'T KNOW EXACTLY...
...BUT I'D GUESS THEY HAVE A PRETTY ADEPT SENSORY-TYPE SHINOBI WITH THEM.
OUR COMMS AREN'T LONG RANGE! IF WE SPLIT UP, THEY'LL BE USELESS!
I'M THE ONLY ONE WHO CAN TRACK HIM...
...BUT I DON'T KNOW WHICH SCENT TO FOLLOW!
...
THEN THERE'S ONLY ONE THING TO DO!
FWIP
FOLLOW ALL THE SCENTS!!

READ THIS WAY

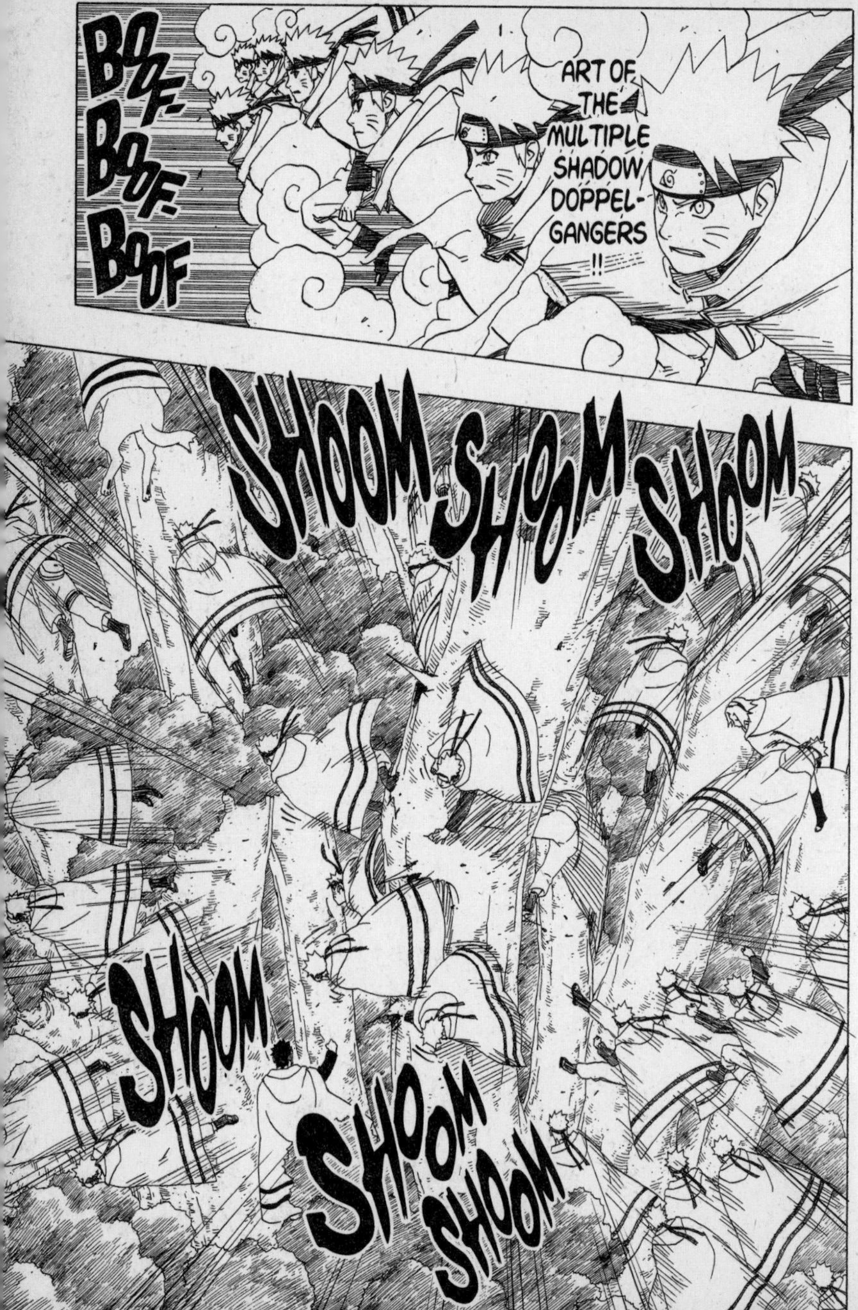
ART OF THE MULTIPLE SHADOW DOPPEL-GANGERS!!
BOOF- BOOF- BOOF
SHOOM SHOOM SHOOM
SHOOM
SHOOM SHOOM SHOOM

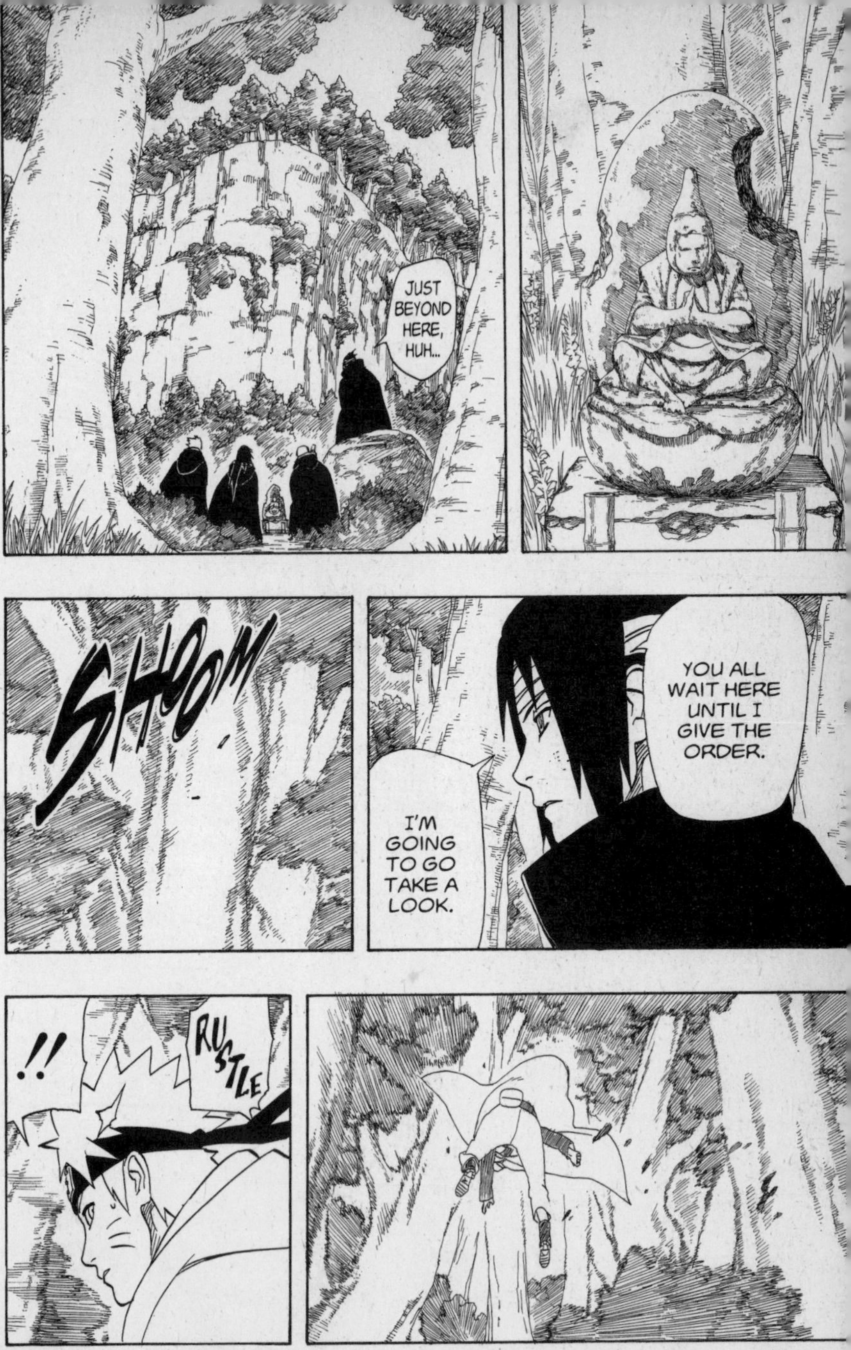
JUST BEYOND HERE, HUH...
YOU ALL WAIT HERE UNTIL I GIVE THE ORDER.
I'M GOING TO GO TAKE A LOOK.
SHOOM
!!
RUSTLE

READ THIS WAY

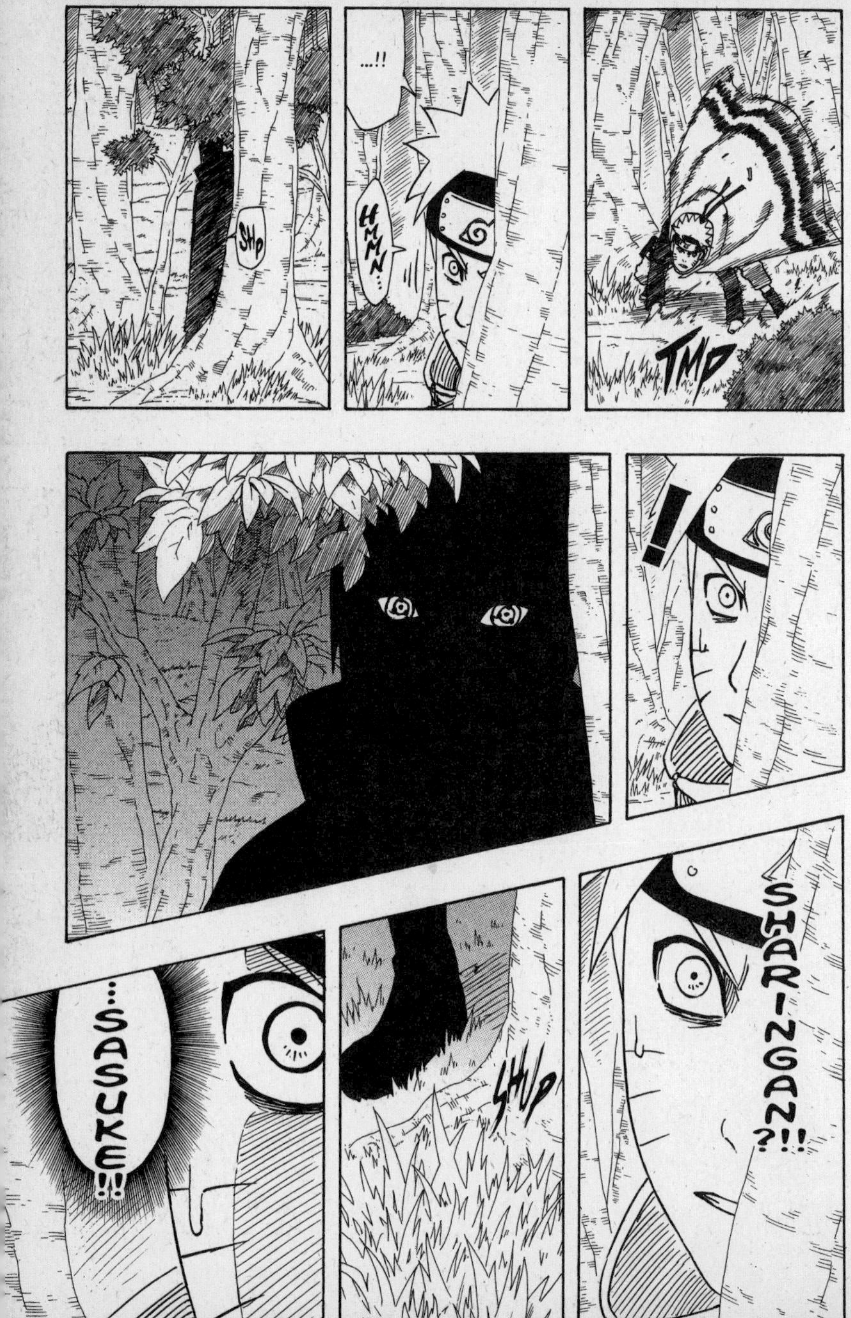
TMP
...!!
HMMN...
SHP
!
SHARINGAN?!!
SHUP
...SASUKE!!

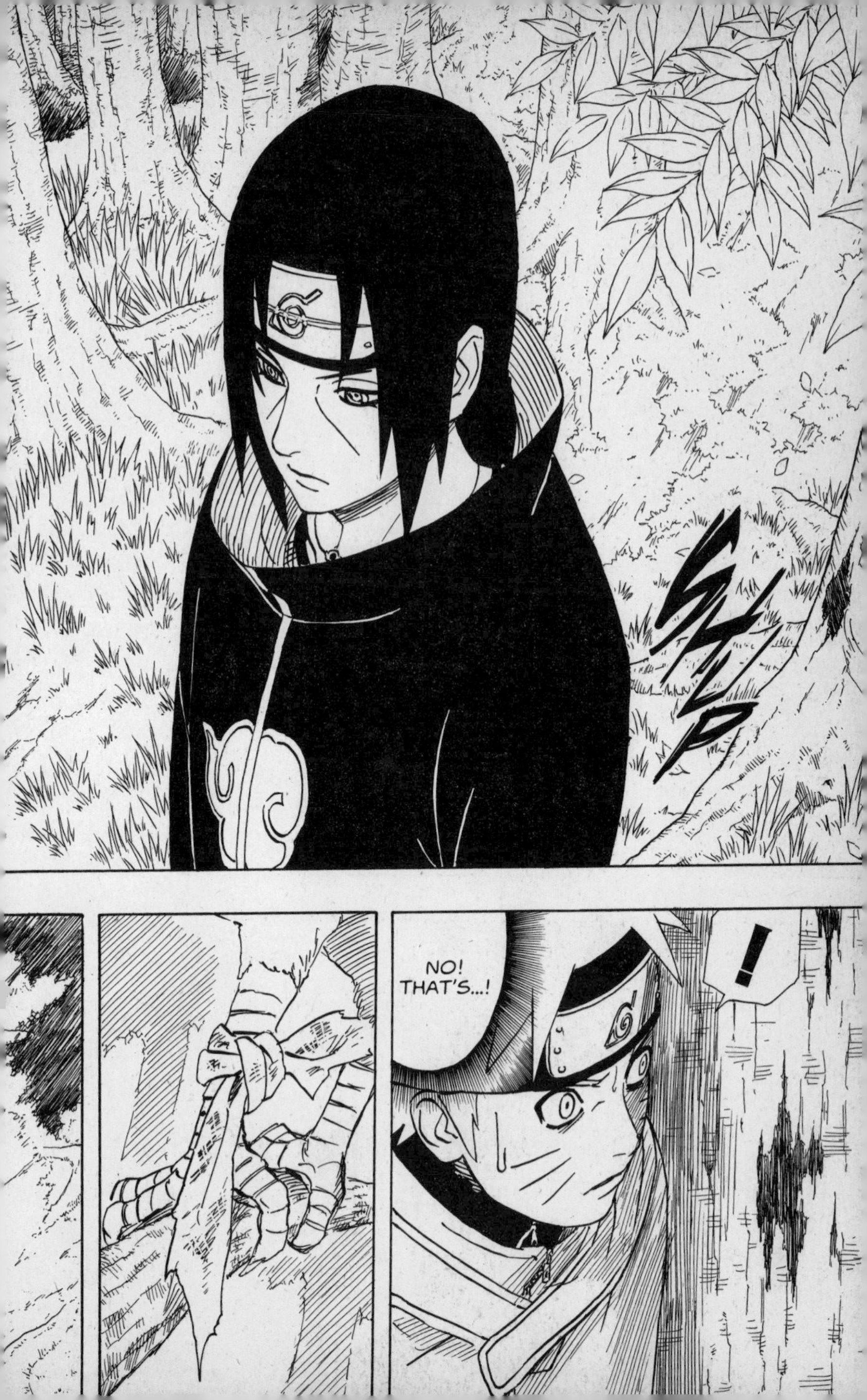
SHIP
!
NO! THAT'S...!

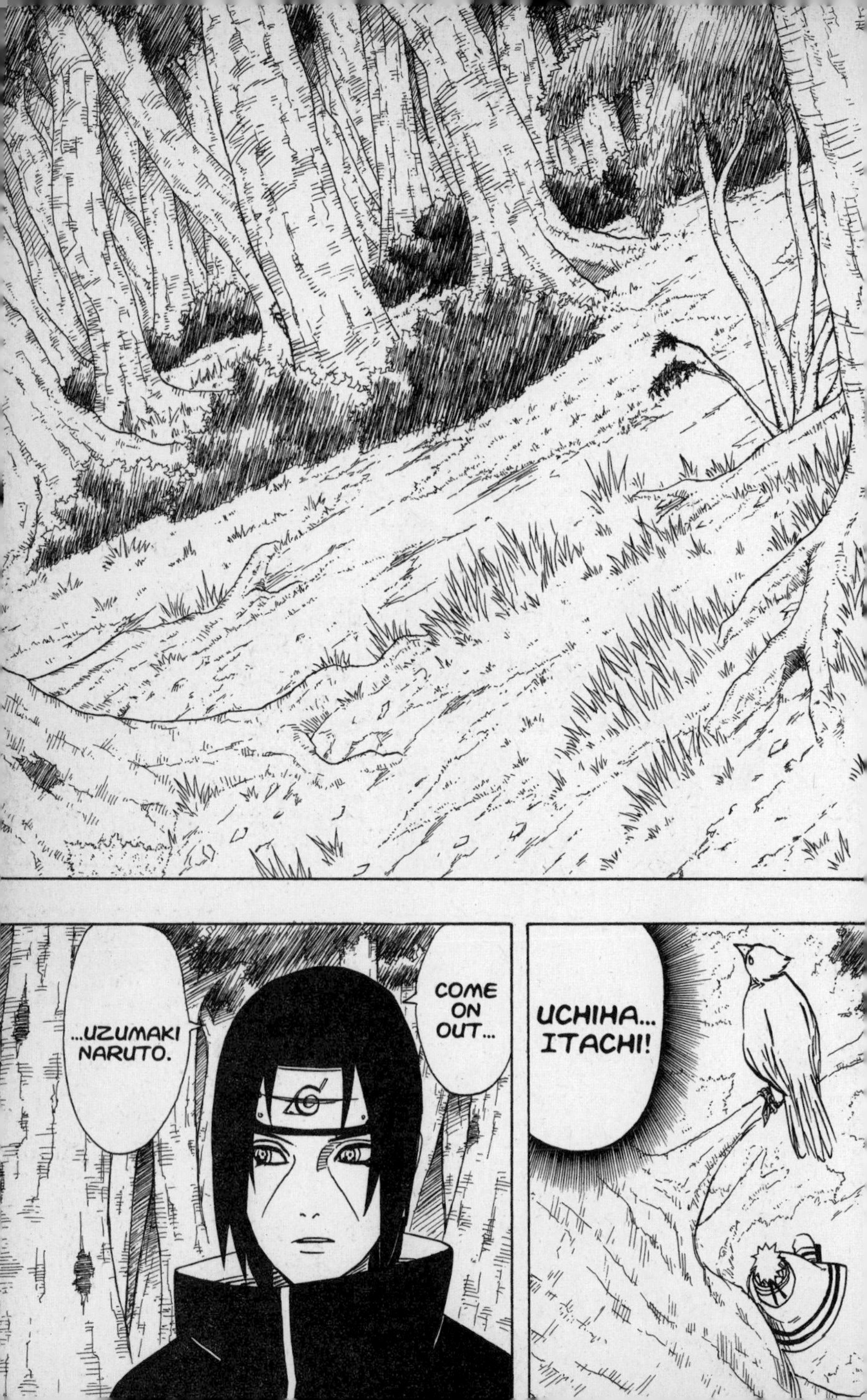
UCHIHA... ITACHI!
COME ON OUT...
...UZUMAKI NARUTO.

NARUTO

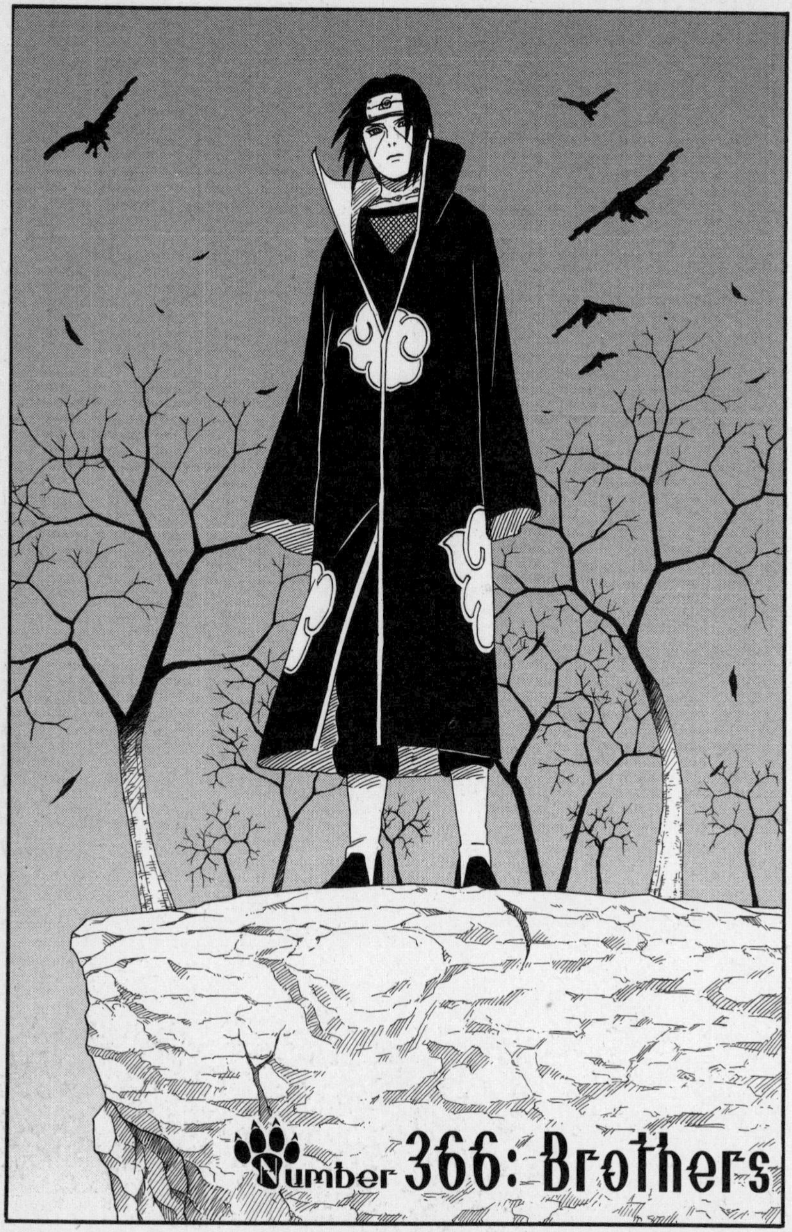
Number 366: Brothers

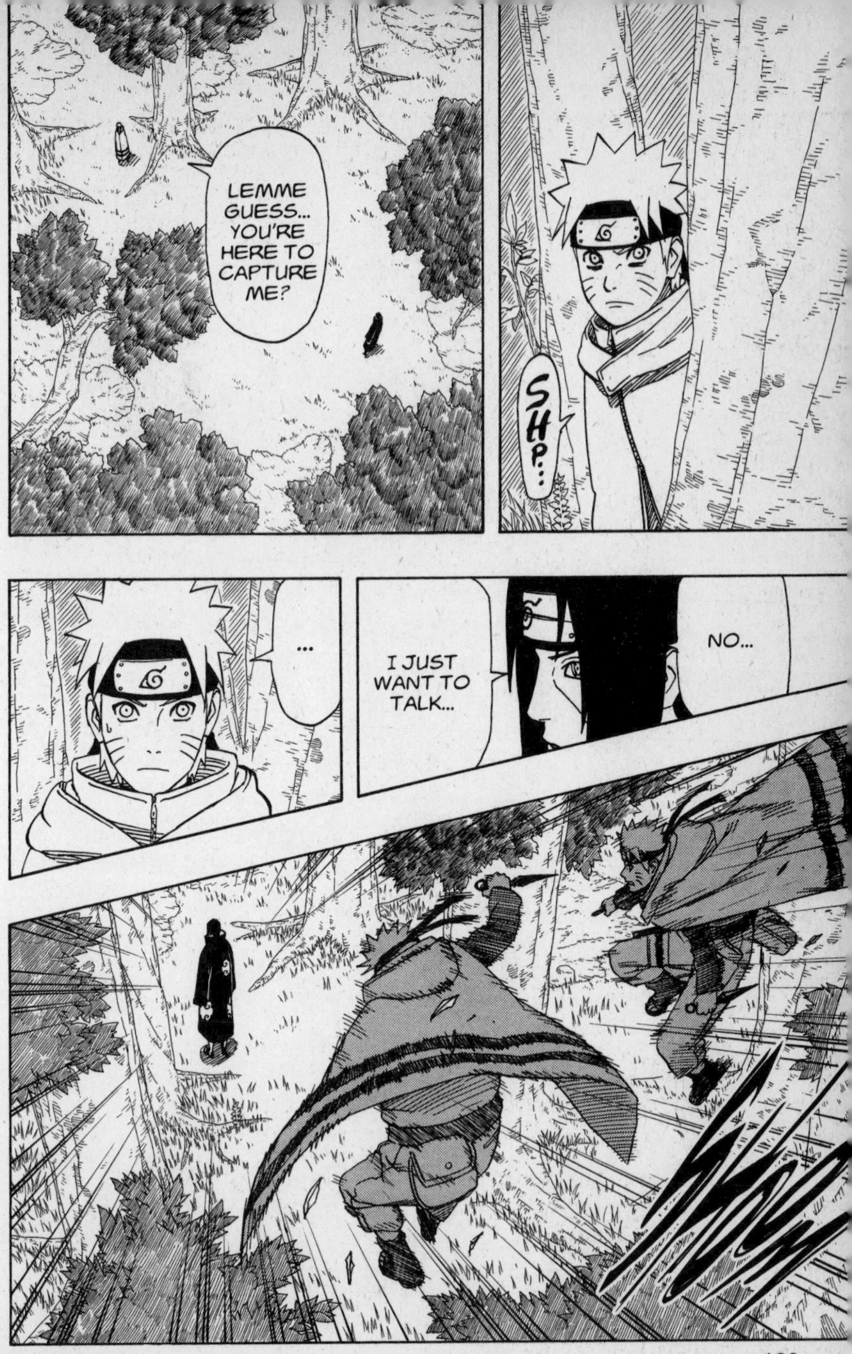
SHP...
LEMME GUESS... YOU'RE HERE TO CAPTURE ME?
NO...
I JUST WANT TO TALK...
...

READ THIS WAY

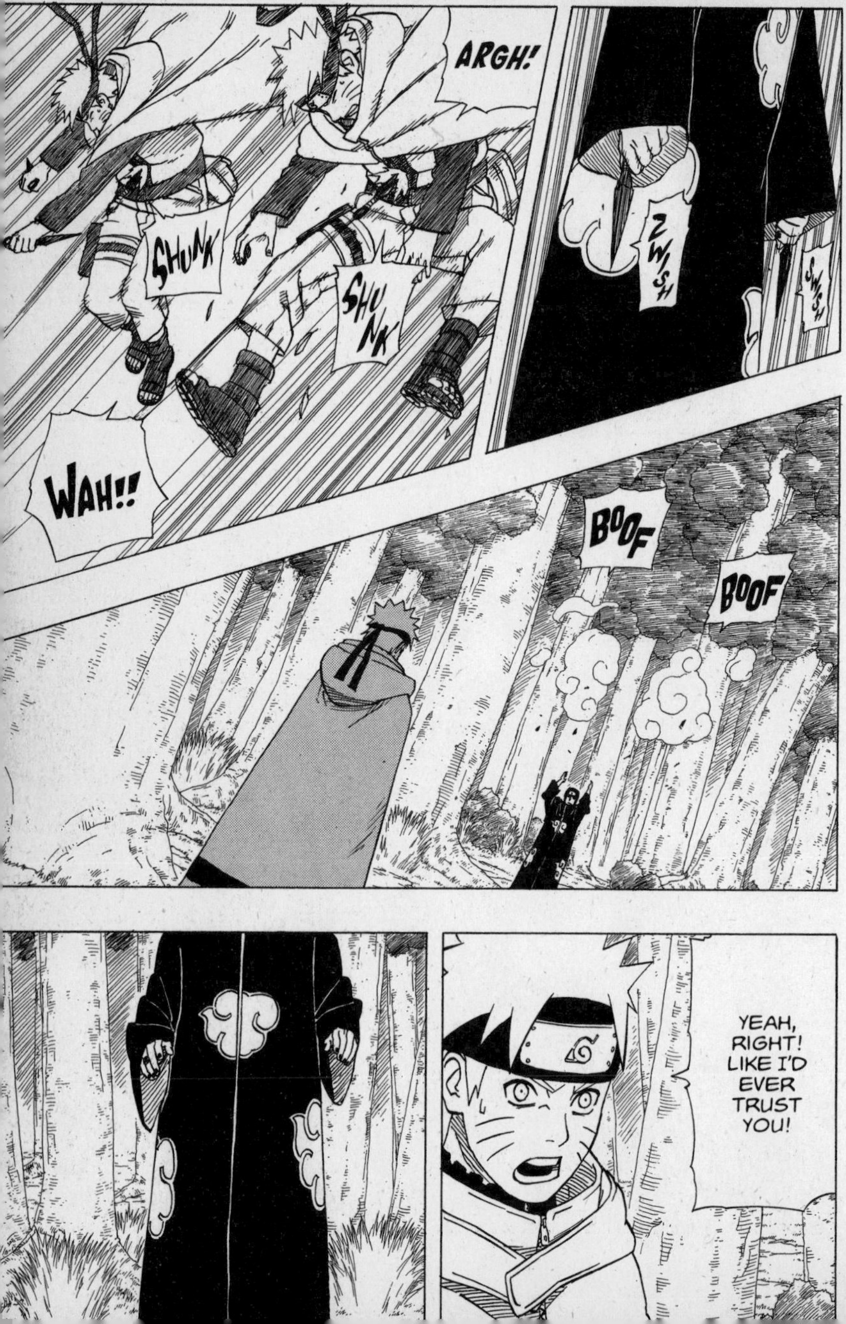
ZWISH
SWISH
ARGH!
SHUNK
SHUNK
WAH!!
BOOF
BOOF
YEAH, RIGHT! LIKE I'D EVER TRUST YOU!

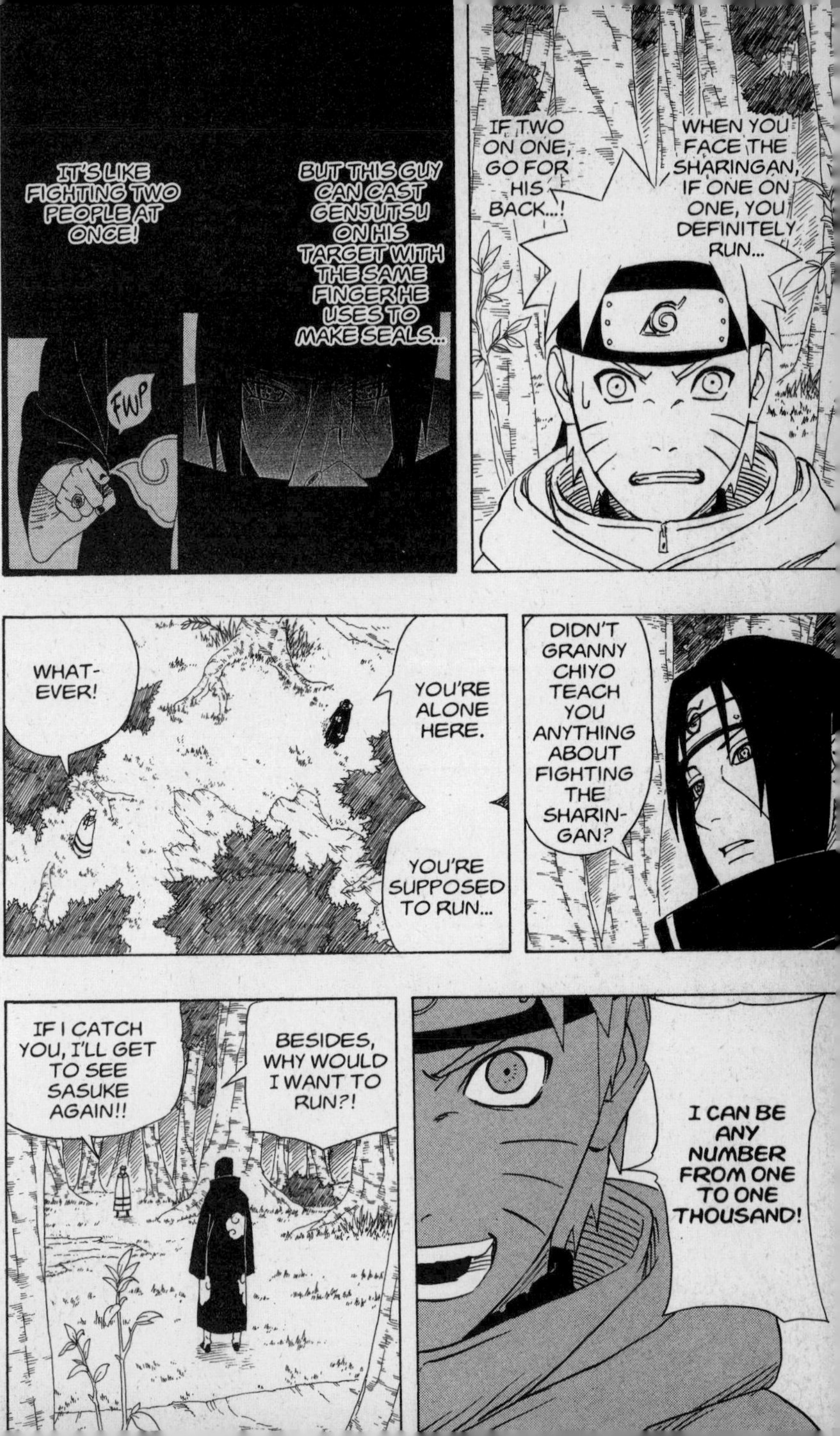
WHEN YOU FACE THE SHARINGAN, IF ONE ON ONE, YOU DEFINITELY RUN...
IF TWO ON ONE, GO FOR HIS BACK...!
BUT THIS GUY CAN CAST GENJUTSU ON HIS TARGET WITH THE SAME FINGER HE USES TO MAKE SEALS...
IT'S LIKE FIGHTING TWO PEOPLE AT ONCE!
FWP
DIDN'T GRANNY CHIYO TEACH YOU ANYTHING ABOUT FIGHTING THE SHARIN-GAN?
YOU'RE ALONE HERE.
YOU'RE SUPPOSED TO RUN...
WHAT-EVER!
I CAN BE ANY NUMBER FROM ONE TO ONE THOUSAND!
BESIDES, WHY WOULD I WANT TO RUN?!
IF I CATCH YOU, I'LL GET TO SEE SASUKE AGAIN!!

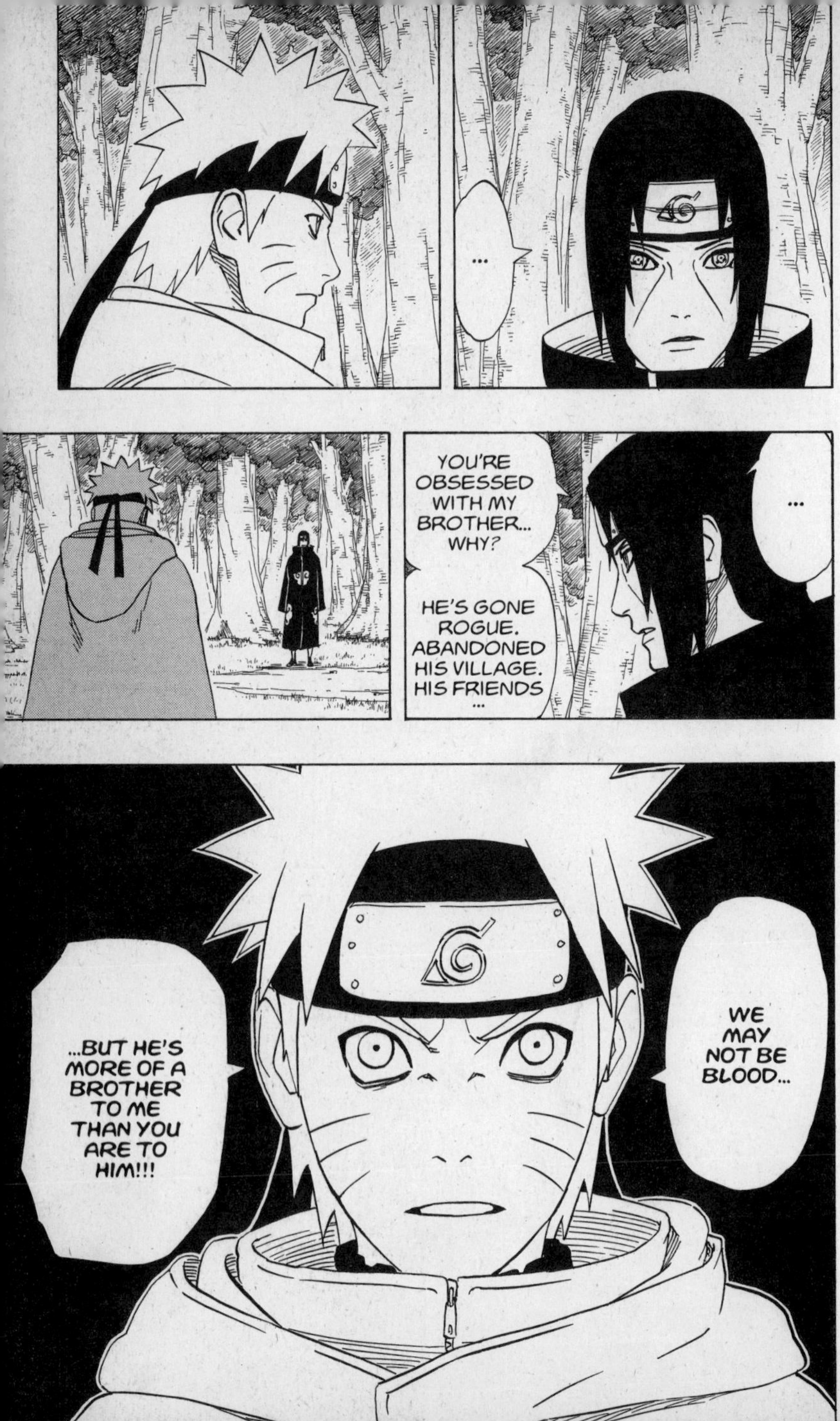
...
...
YOU'RE OBSESSED WITH MY BROTHER... WHY?
HE'S GONE ROGUE. ABANDONED HIS VILLAGE. HIS FRIENDS ...
WE MAY NOT BE BLOOD...
...BUT HE'S MORE OF A BROTHER TO ME THAN YOU ARE TO HIM!!!

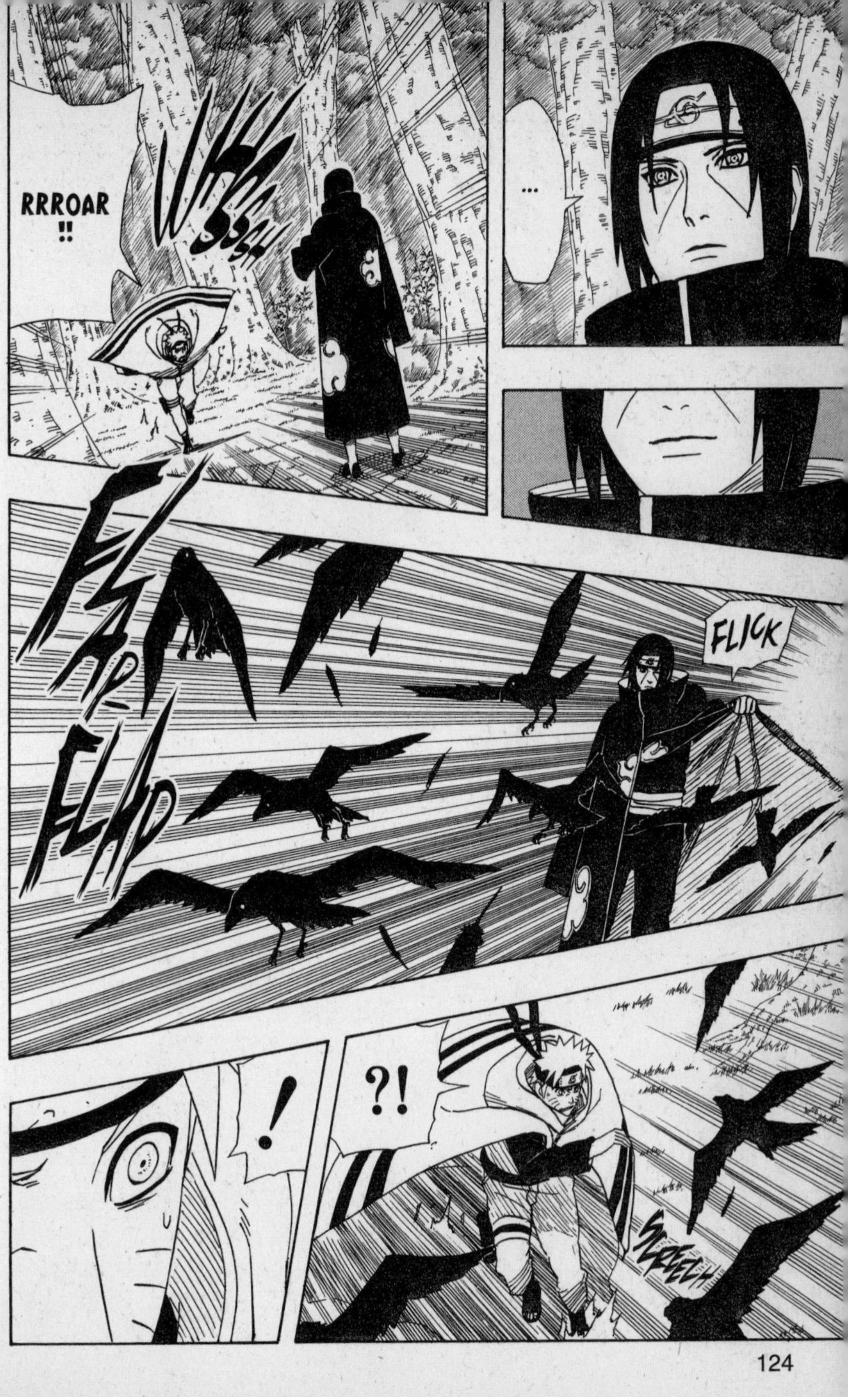

...
RRROAR !!
FLICK
FLAP FLAP
?!
!

READ THIS WAY

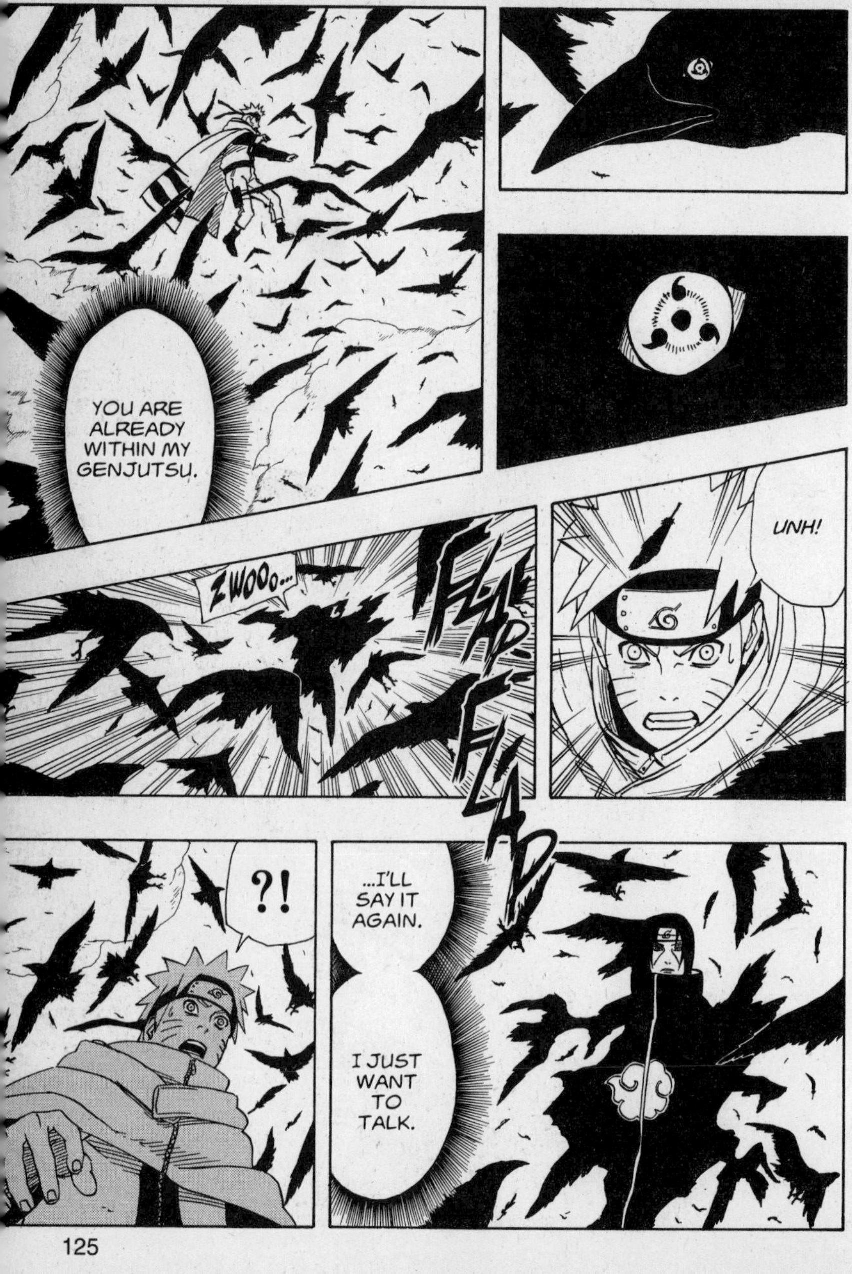

YOU ARE ALREADY WITHIN MY GENJUTSU.
UNH!
ZWOOO...
FLAP FLAP
...I'LL SAY IT AGAIN.
I JUST WANT TO TALK.
?!

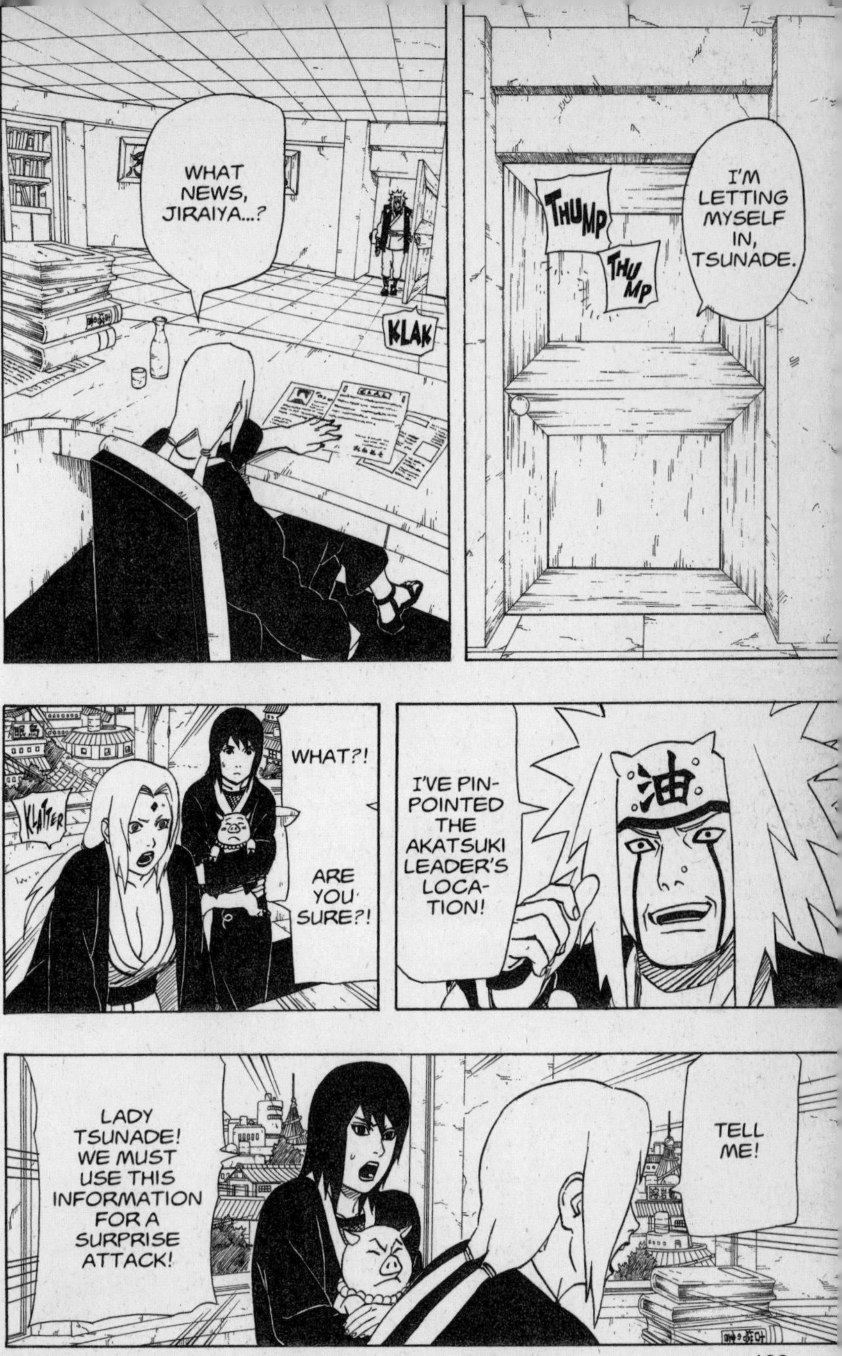
I'M LETTING MYSELF IN, TSUNADE.
THUMP
THUMP
WHAT NEWS, JIRAIYA...?
KLAK
I'VE PIN-POINTED THE AKATSUKI LEADER'S LOCA-TION!
WHAT?!
ARE YOU SURE?!
KLATTER
TELL ME!
LADY TSUNADE! WE MUST USE THIS INFORMATION FOR A SURPRISE ATTACK!

READ THIS WAY

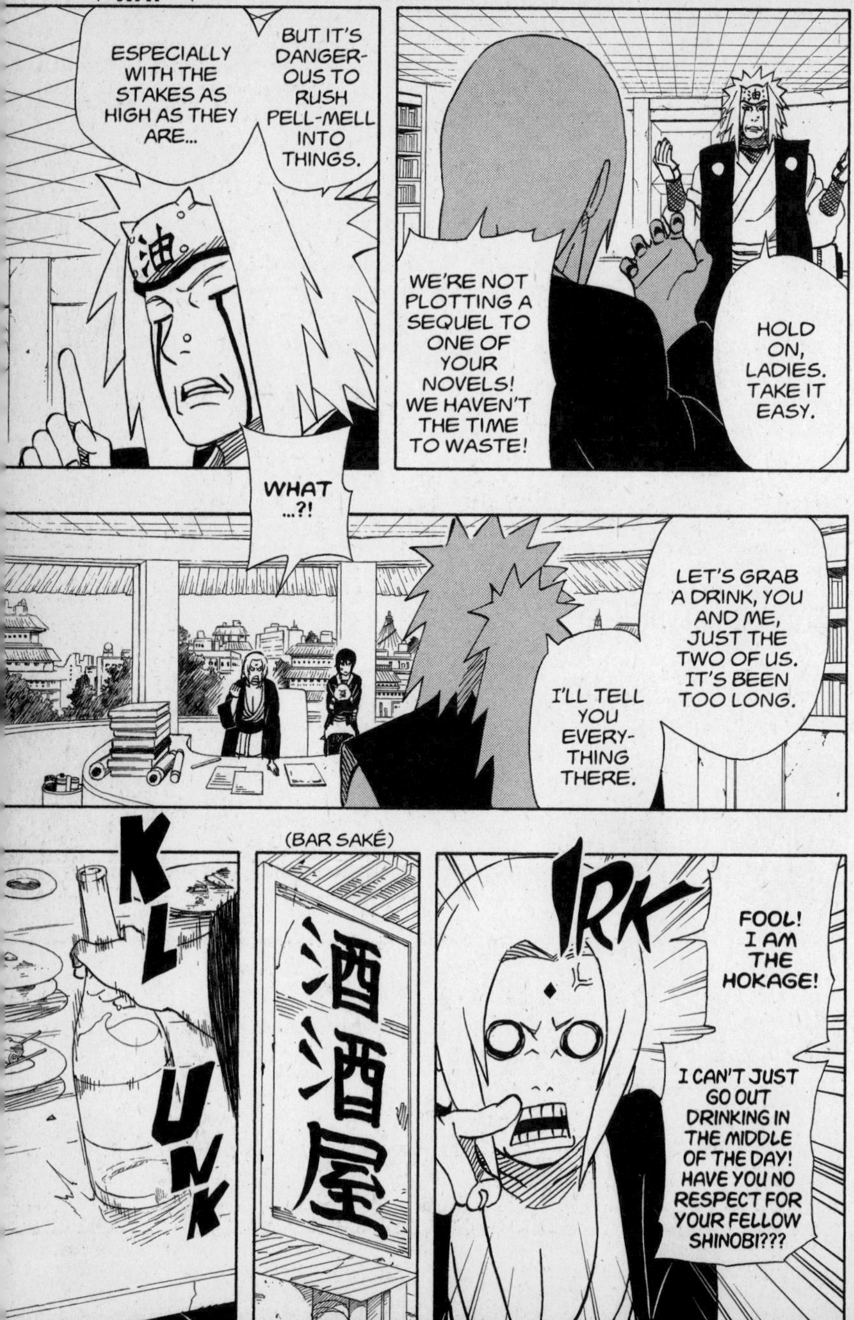
HOLD ON, LADIES. TAKE IT EASY.
WE'RE NOT PLOTTING A SEQUEL TO ONE OF YOUR NOVELS! WE HAVEN'T THE TIME TO WASTE!
BUT IT'S DANGEROUS TO RUSH PELL-MELL INTO THINGS.
ESPECIALLY WITH THE STAKES AS HIGH AS THEY ARE...
WHAT ...?!
LET'S GRAB A DRINK, YOU AND ME, JUST THE TWO OF US. IT'S BEEN TOO LONG.
I'LL TELL YOU EVERYTHING THERE.
IRK
FOOL! I AM THE HOKAGE!
I CAN'T JUST GO OUT DRINKING IN THE MIDDLE OF THE DAY! HAVE YOU NO RESPECT FOR YOUR FELLOW SHINOBI???
(BAR SAKÉ)
酒酒屋
KLUNK

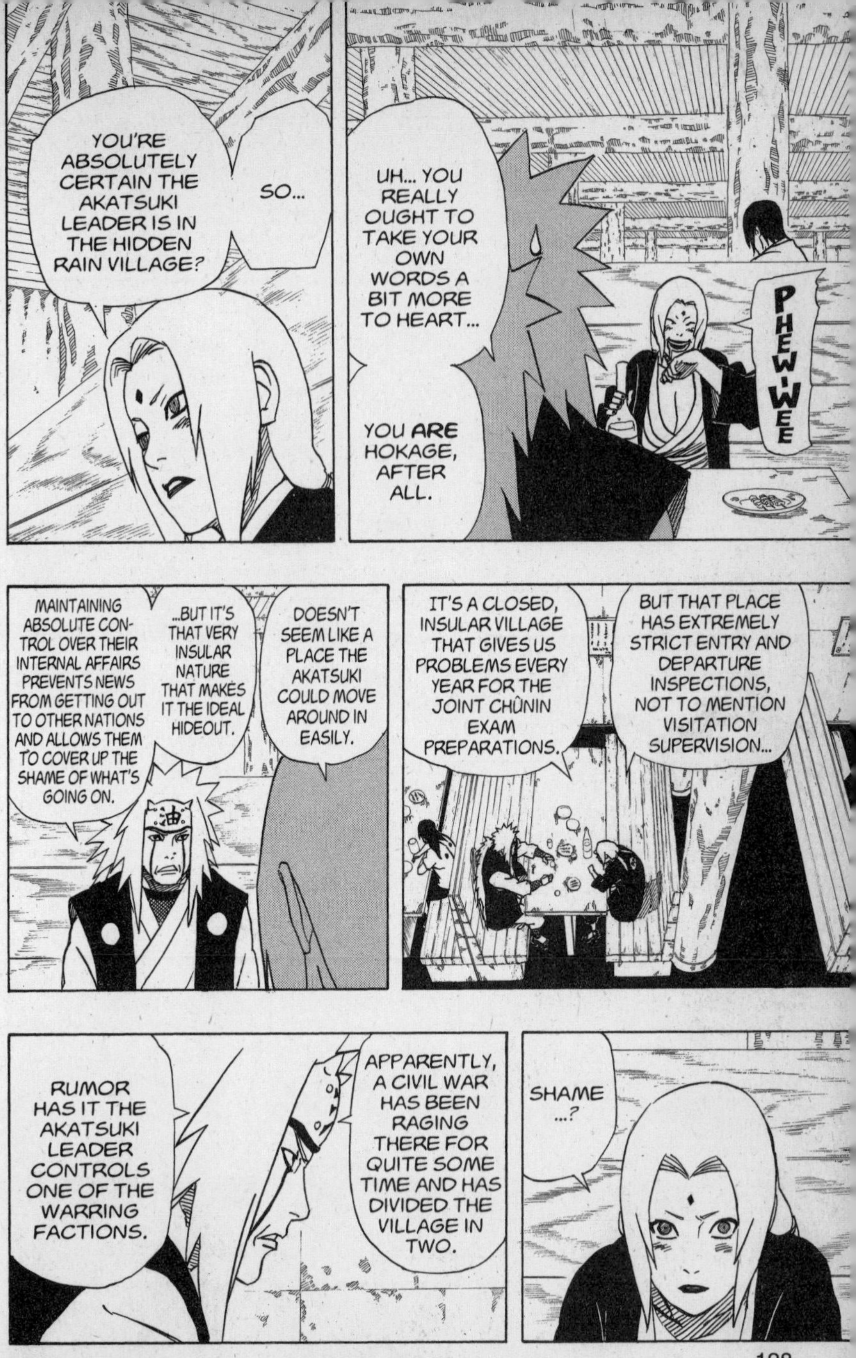
PHEW-WEE
UH... YOU REALLY OUGHT TO TAKE YOUR OWN WORDS A BIT MORE TO HEART...
YOU **ARE** HOKAGE, AFTER ALL.
SO...
YOU'RE ABSOLUTELY CERTAIN THE AKATSUKI LEADER IS IN THE HIDDEN RAIN VILLAGE?
BUT THAT PLACE HAS EXTREMELY STRICT ENTRY AND DEPARTURE INSPECTIONS, NOT TO MENTION VISITATION SUPERVISION...
IT'S A CLOSED, INSULAR VILLAGE THAT GIVES US PROBLEMS EVERY YEAR FOR THE JOINT CHÛNIN EXAM PREPARATIONS.
DOESN'T SEEM LIKE A PLACE THE AKATSUKI COULD MOVE AROUND IN EASILY.
...BUT IT'S THAT VERY INSULAR NATURE THAT MAKES IT THE IDEAL HIDEOUT.
MAINTAINING ABSOLUTE CONTROL OVER THEIR INTERNAL AFFAIRS PREVENTS NEWS FROM GETTING OUT TO OTHER NATIONS AND ALLOWS THEM TO COVER UP THE SHAME OF WHAT'S GOING ON.
SHAME ...?
APPARENTLY, A CIVIL WAR HAS BEEN RAGING THERE FOR QUITE SOME TIME AND HAS DIVIDED THE VILLAGE IN TWO.
RUMOR HAS IT THE AKATSUKI LEADER CONTROLS ONE OF THE WARRING FACTIONS.

READ THIS WAY

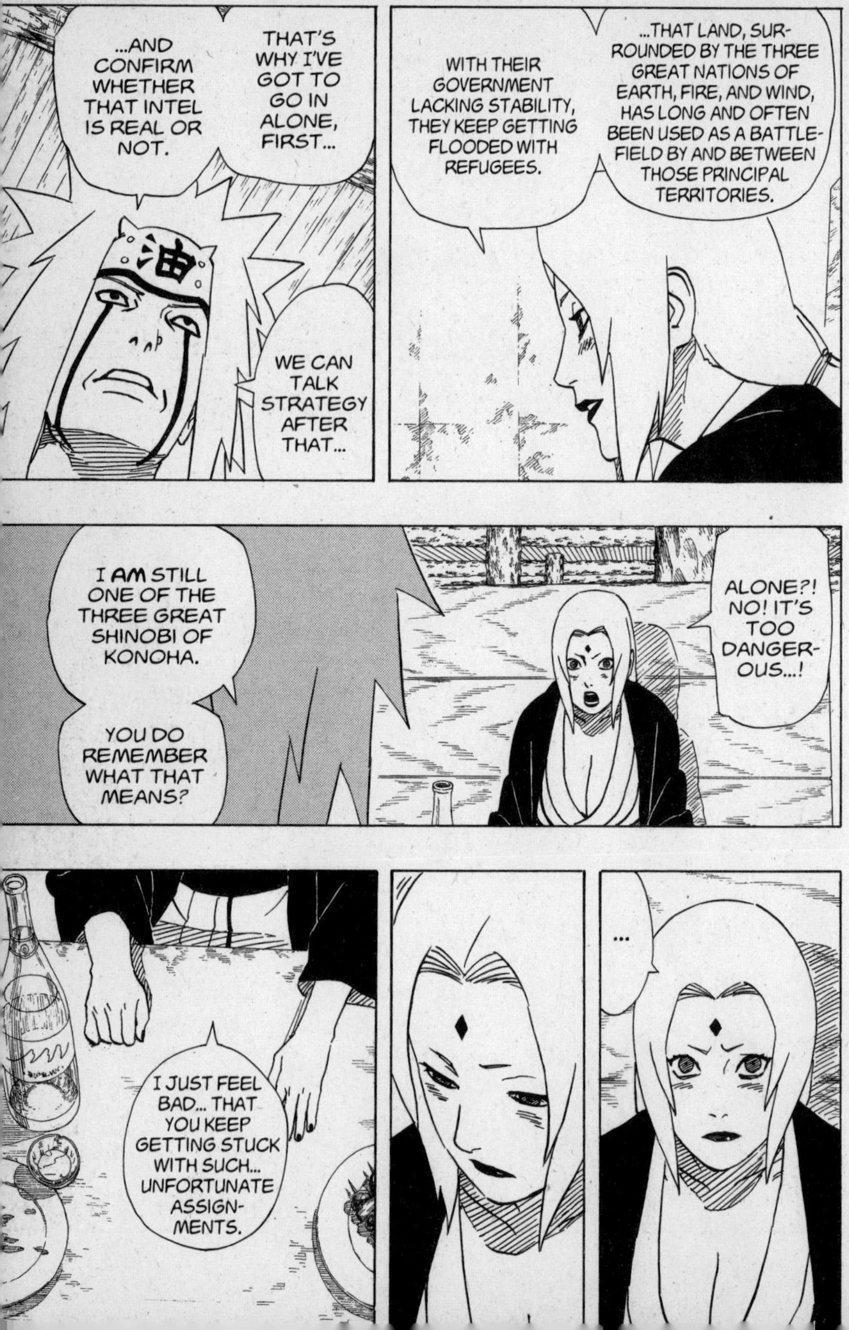
...THAT LAND, SUR-ROUNDED BY THE THREE GREAT NATIONS OF EARTH, FIRE, AND WIND, HAS LONG AND OFTEN BEEN USED AS A BATTLE-FIELD BY AND BETWEEN THOSE PRINCIPAL TERRITORIES.
WITH THEIR GOVERNMENT LACKING STABILITY, THEY KEEP GETTING FLOODED WITH REFUGEES.
THAT'S WHY I'VE GOT TO GO IN ALONE, FIRST...
...AND CONFIRM WHETHER THAT INTEL IS REAL OR NOT.
油
WE CAN TALK STRATEGY AFTER THAT...
ALONE?! NO! IT'S TOO DANGER-OUS...!
I AM STILL ONE OF THE THREE GREAT SHINOBI OF KONOHA.
YOU DO REMEMBER WHAT THAT MEANS?
...
I JUST FEEL BAD... THAT YOU KEEP GETTING STUCK WITH SUCH... UNFORTUNATE ASSIGN-MENTS.

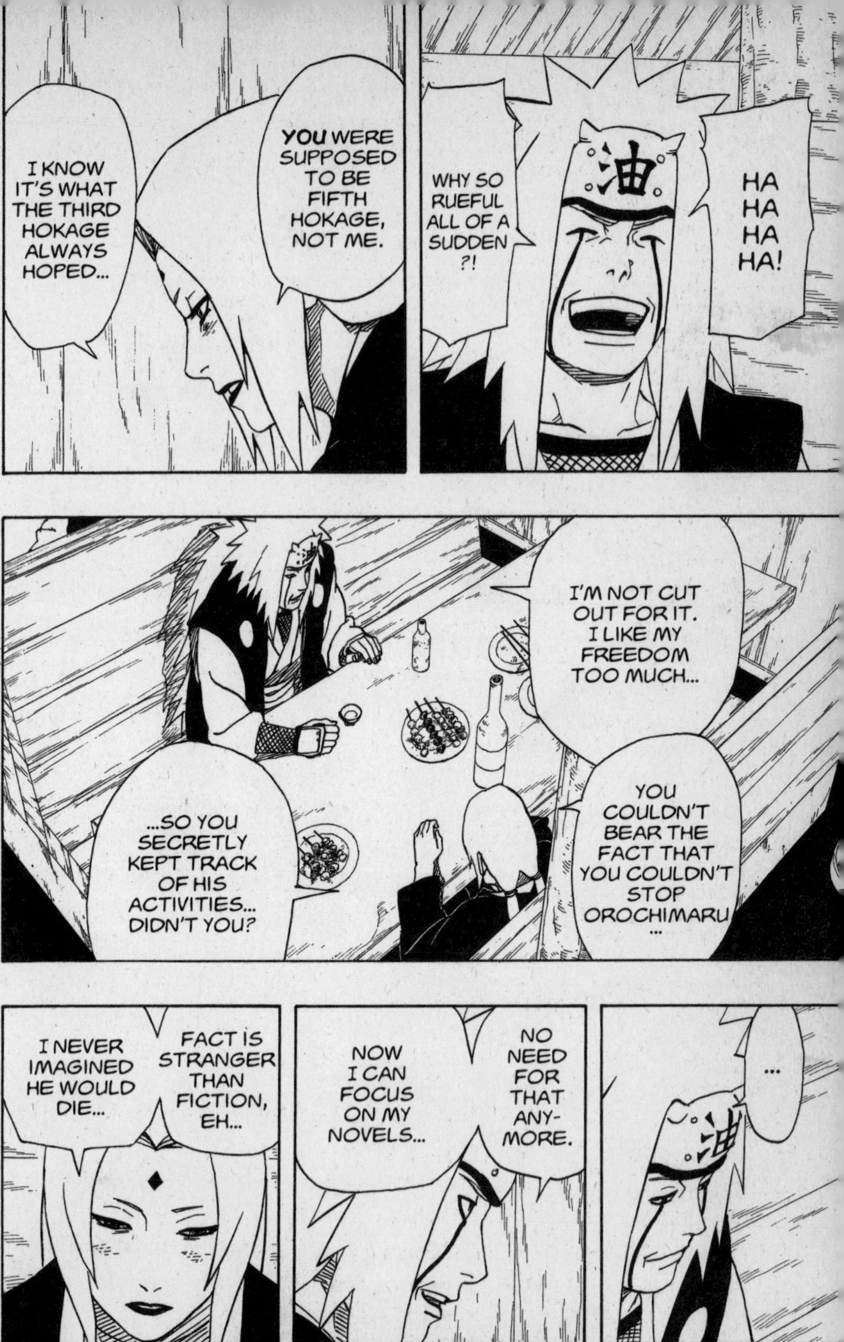
HA HA HA HA!
WHY SO RUEFUL ALL OF A SUDDEN ?!
YOU WERE SUPPOSED TO BE FIFTH HOKAGE, NOT ME.
I KNOW IT'S WHAT THE THIRD HOKAGE ALWAYS HOPED...
I'M NOT CUT OUT FOR IT. I LIKE MY FREEDOM TOO MUCH...
YOU COULDN'T BEAR THE FACT THAT YOU COULDN'T STOP OROCHIMARU...
...SO YOU SECRETLY KEPT TRACK OF HIS ACTIVITIES... DIDN'T YOU?
...
NO NEED FOR THAT ANY-MORE.
NOW I CAN FOCUS ON MY NOVELS...
FACT IS STRANGER THAN FICTION, EH...
I NEVER IMAGINED HE WOULD DIE...

READ THIS WAY

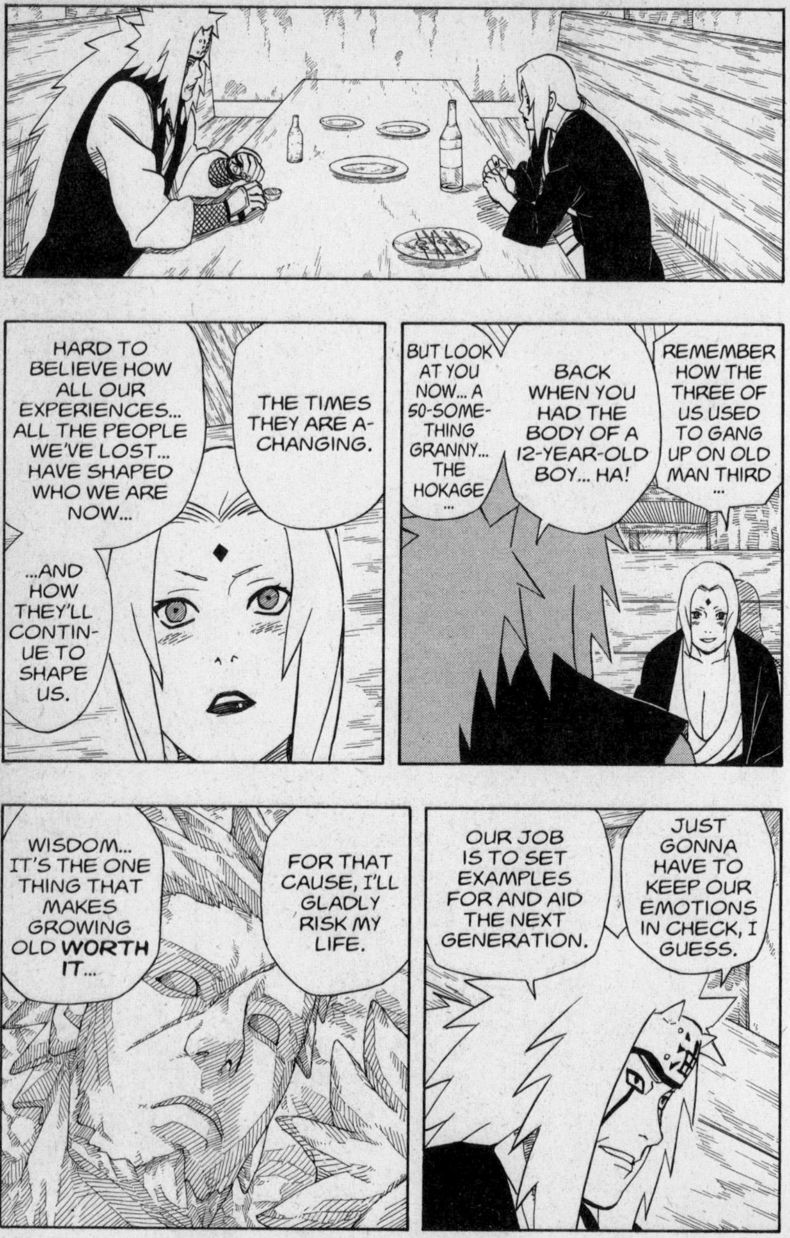

REMEMBER HOW THE THREE OF US USED TO GANG UP ON OLD MAN THIRD...
BACK WHEN YOU HAD THE BODY OF A 12-YEAR-OLD BOY... HA!
BUT LOOK AT YOU NOW... A 50-SOMETHING GRANNY... THE HOKAGE...
THE TIMES THEY ARE A-CHANGING.
HARD TO BELIEVE HOW ALL OUR EXPERIENCES... ALL THE PEOPLE WE'VE LOST... HAVE SHAPED WHO WE ARE NOW...
...AND HOW THEY'LL CONTINUE TO SHAPE US.
JUST GONNA HAVE TO KEEP OUR EMOTIONS IN CHECK, I GUESS.
OUR JOB IS TO SET EXAMPLES FOR AND AID THE NEXT GENERATION.
FOR THAT CAUSE, I'LL GLADLY RISK MY LIFE.
WISDOM... IT'S THE ONE THING THAT MAKES GROWING OLD **WORTH** IT...

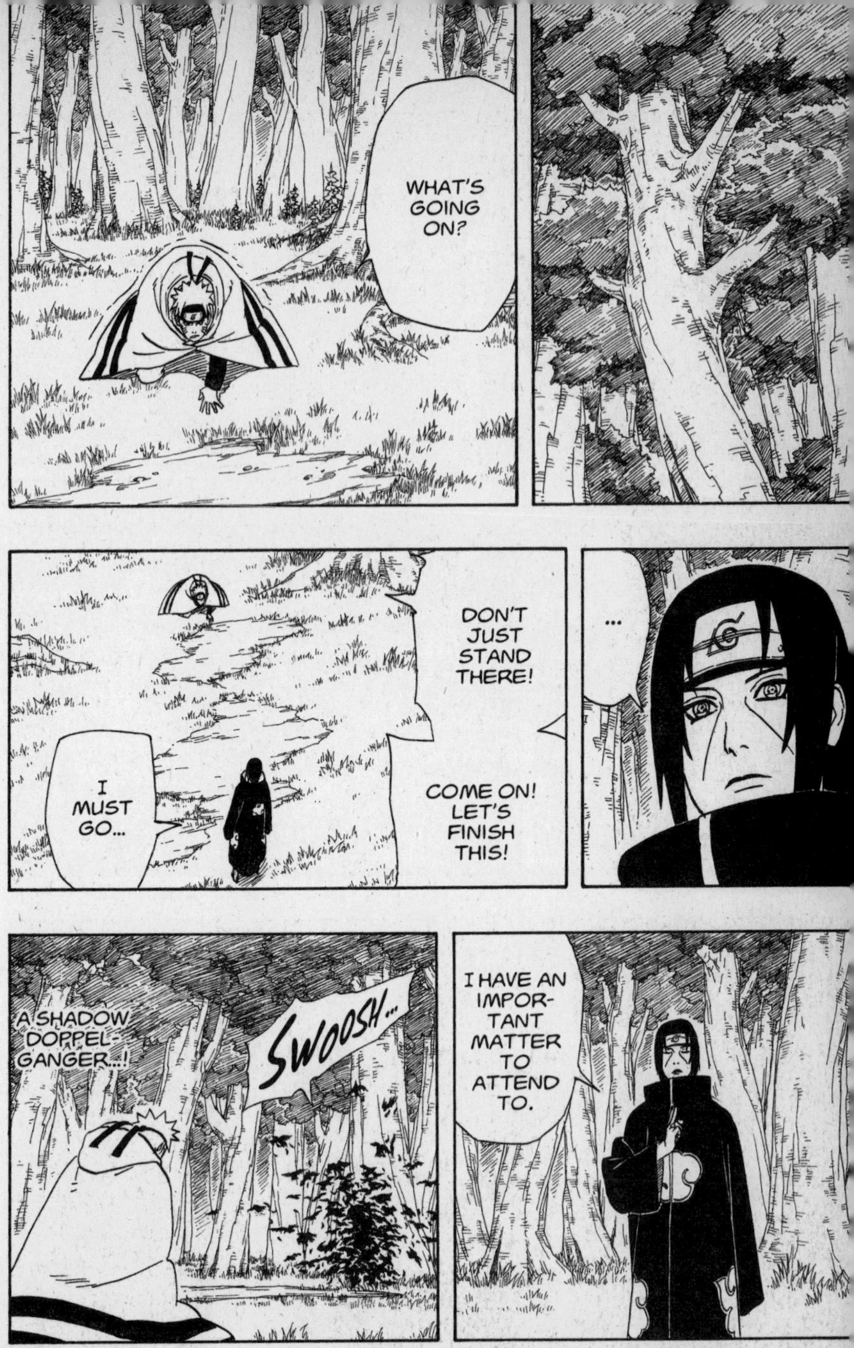
WHAT'S GOING ON?
...
DON'T JUST STAND THERE!
COME ON! LET'S FINISH THIS!
I MUST GO...
I HAVE AN IMPOR-TANT MATTER TO ATTEND TO.
SWOOSH...
A SHADOW DOPPEL-GANGER...!

READ THIS WAY

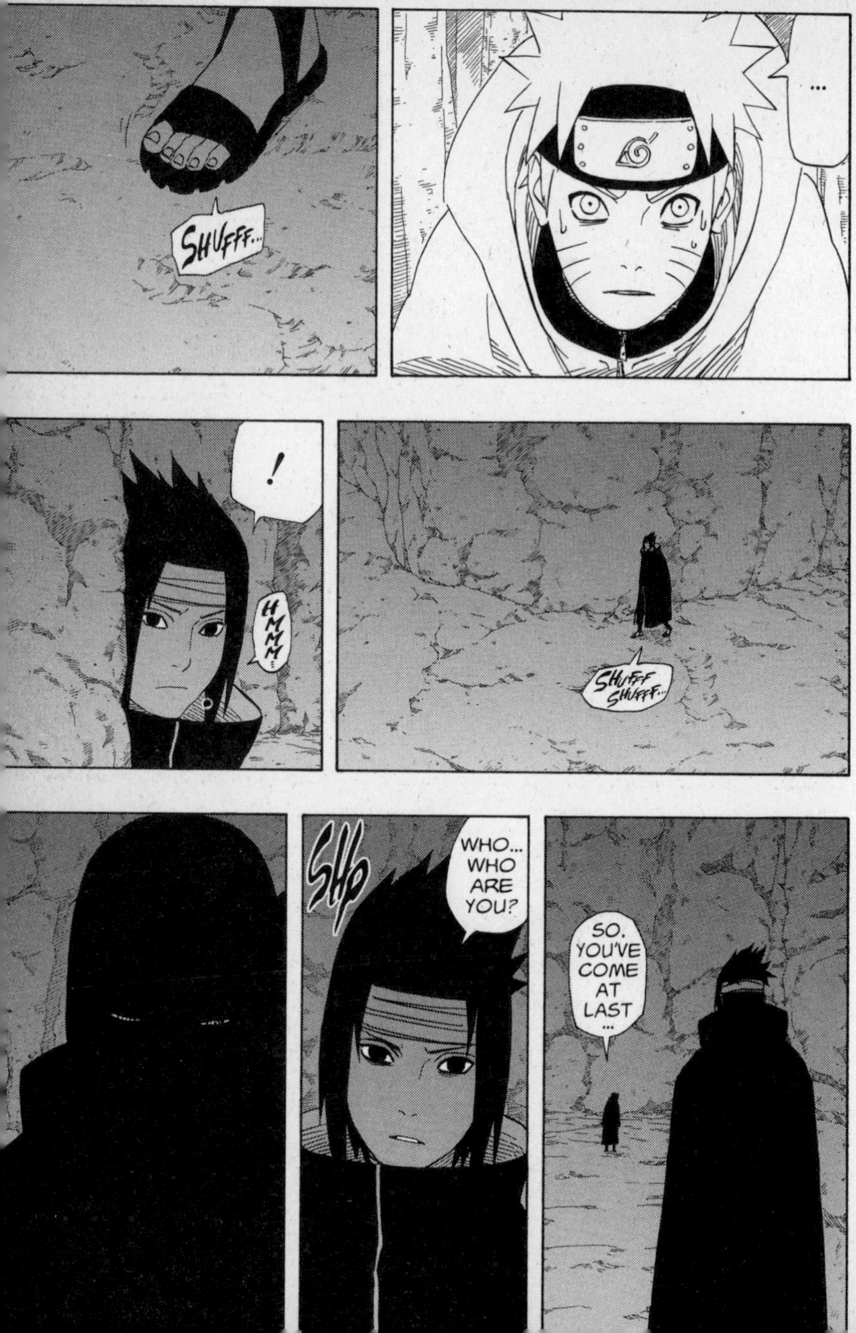
...
SHUFFF...
SHUFFF SHUFFF...
!
HMMM...
SO. YOU'VE COME AT LAST...
SHP
WHO... WHO ARE YOU?

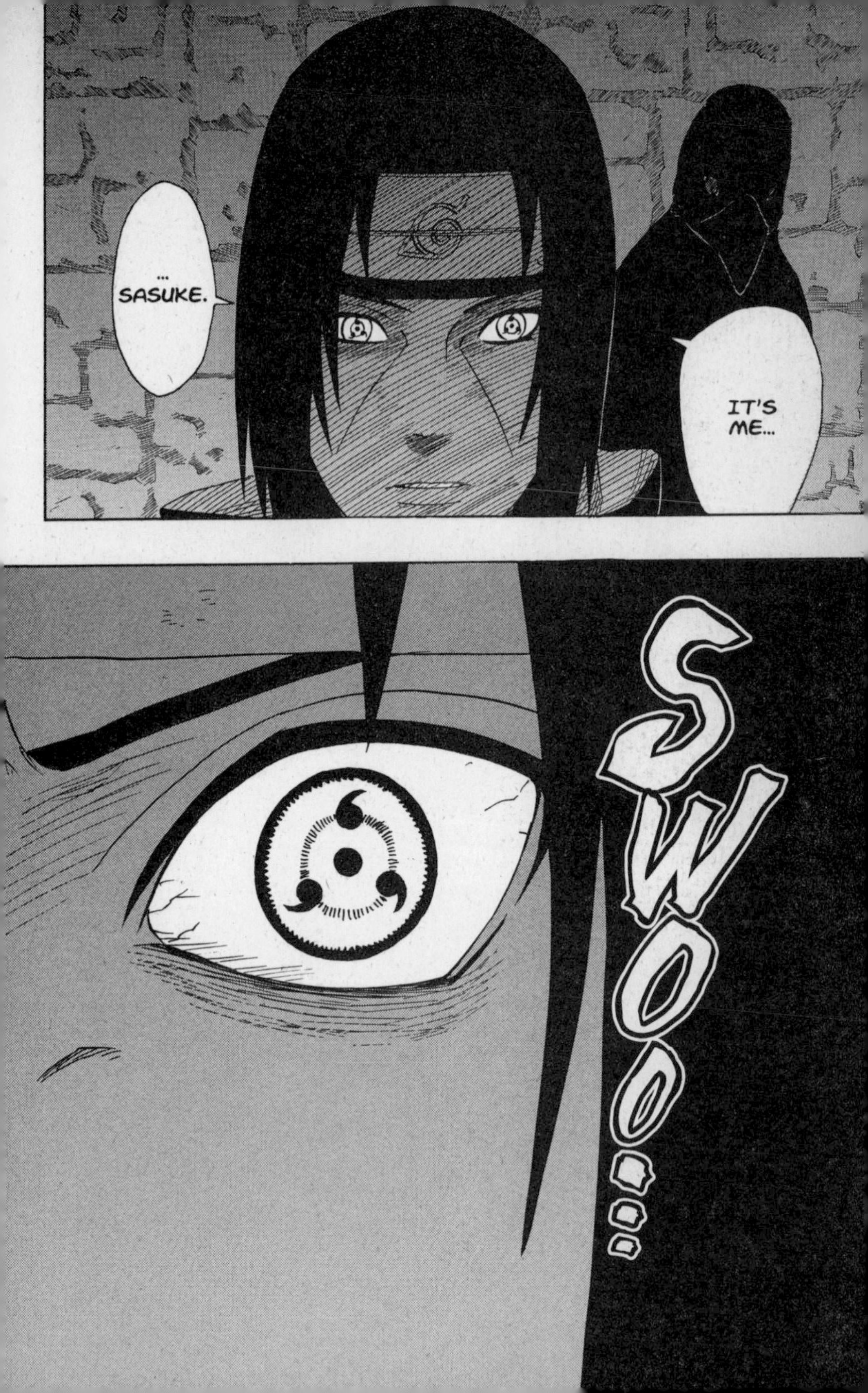
IT'S ME...
...SASUKE.
SWOO...

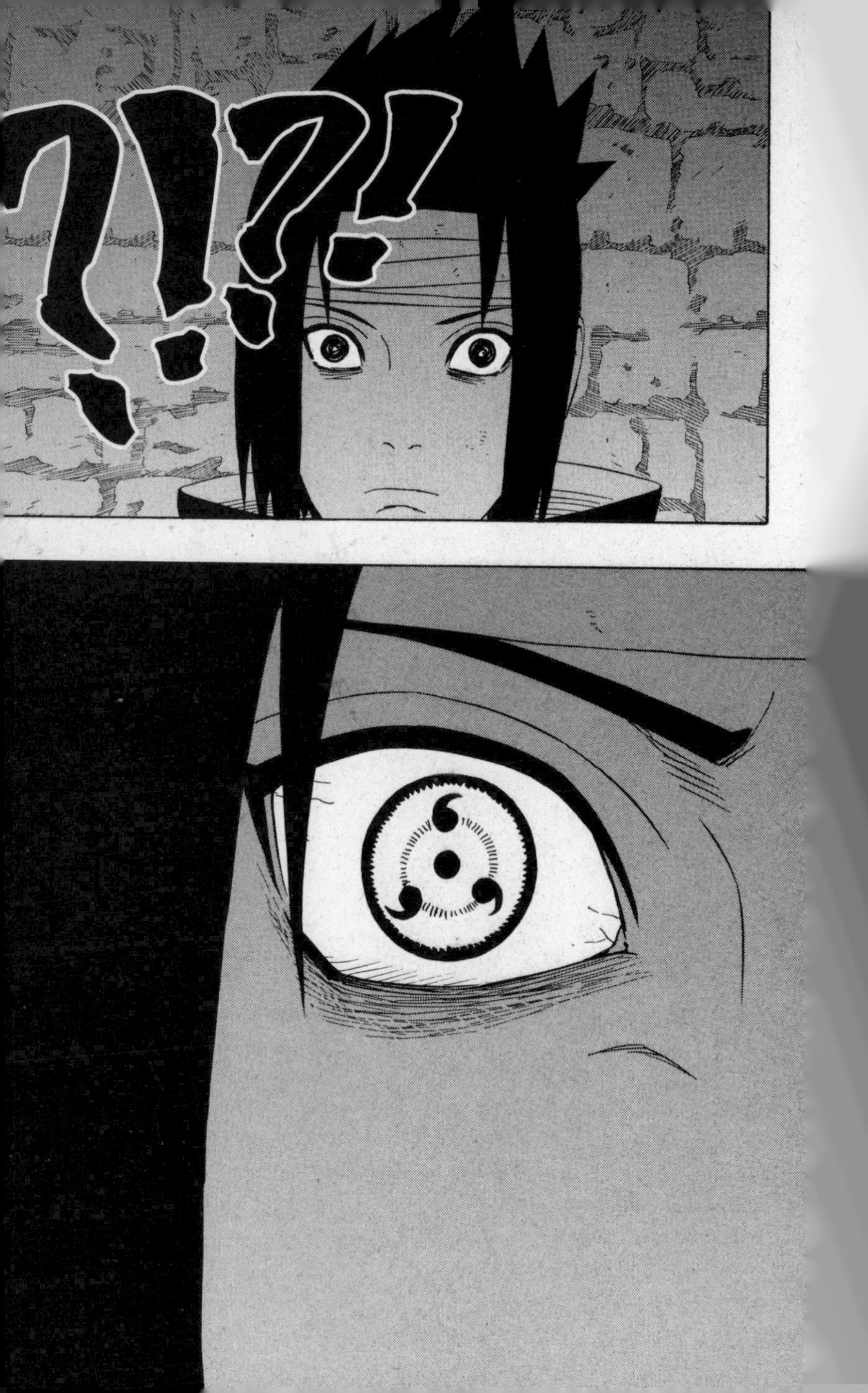
?!?!

NARUTO

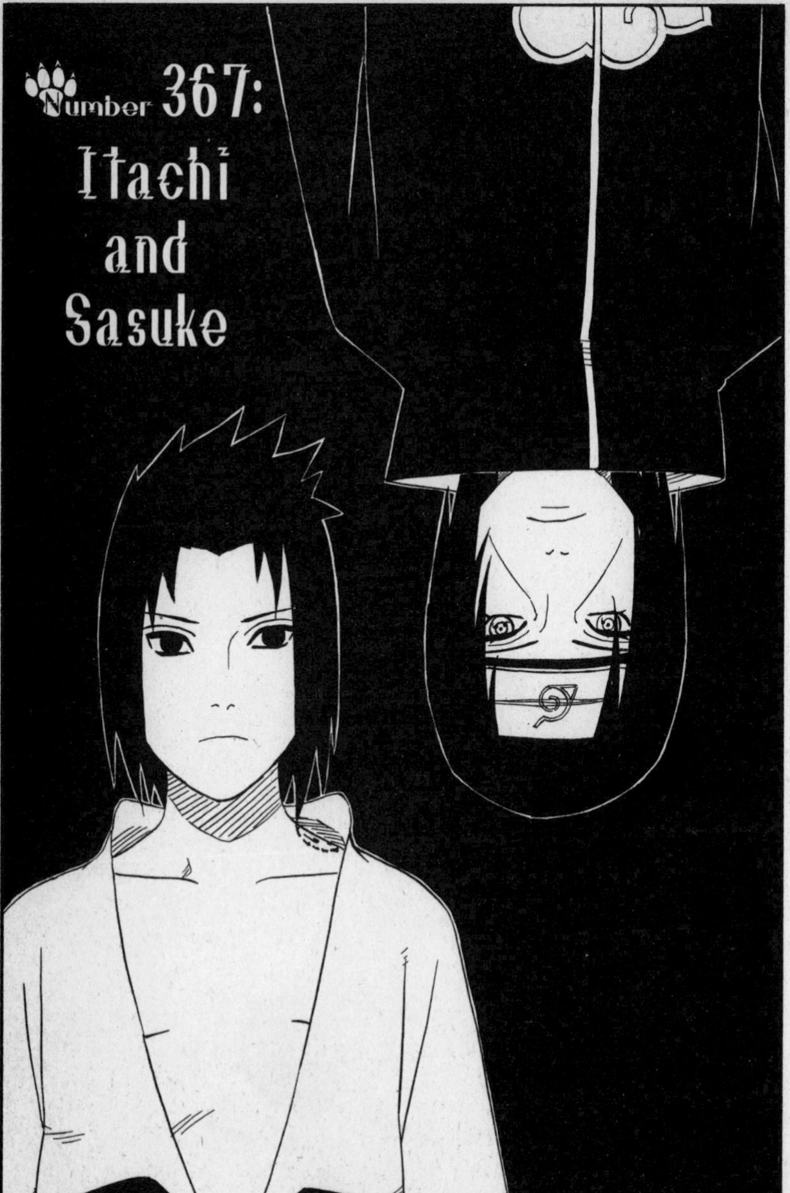
Number 367:
Itachi
and
Sasuke

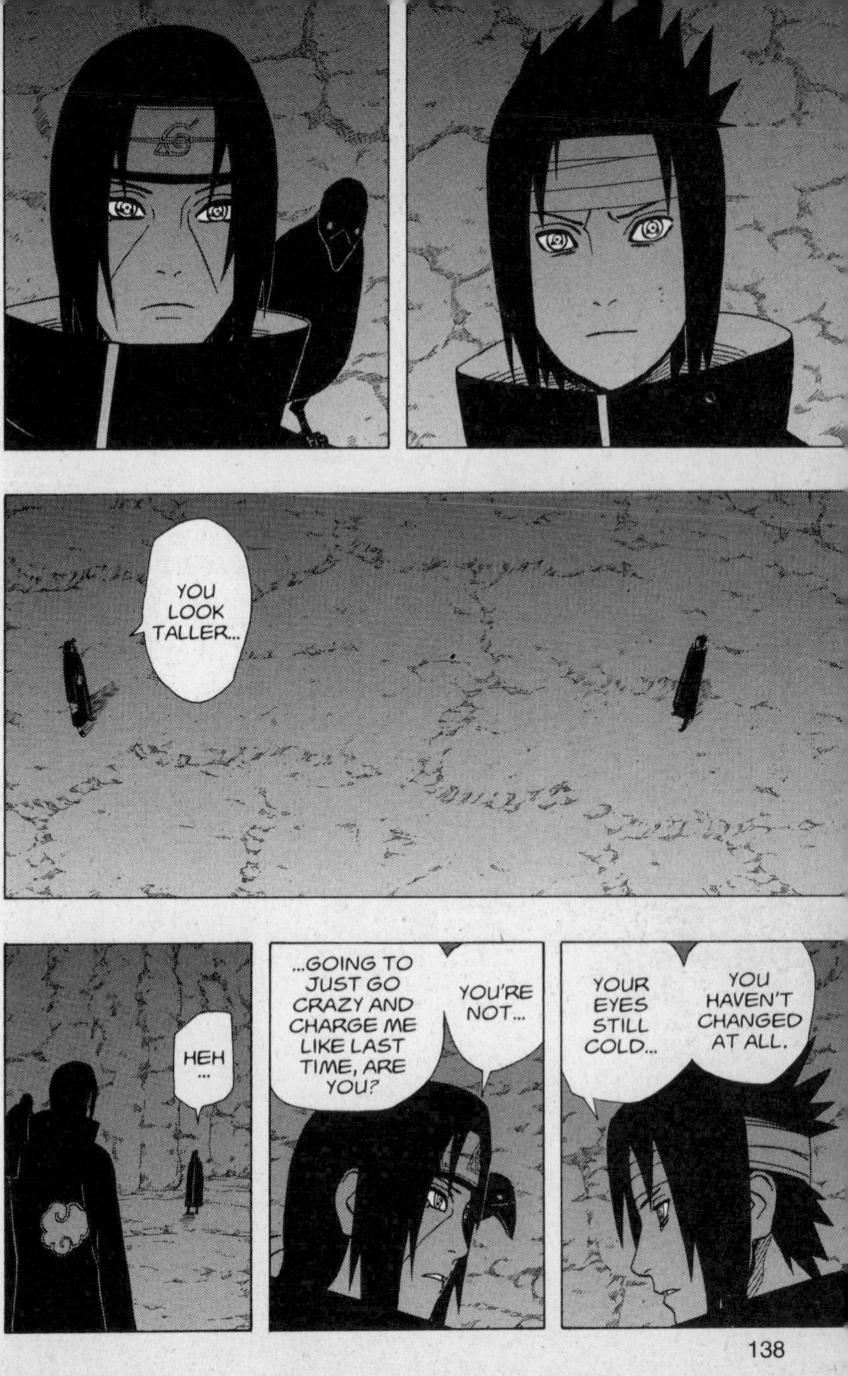
YOU LOOK TALLER...
YOU HAVEN'T CHANGED AT ALL.
YOUR EYES STILL COLD...
YOU'RE NOT...
...GOING TO JUST GO CRAZY AND CHARGE ME LIKE LAST TIME, ARE YOU?
HEH ...

READ THIS WAY

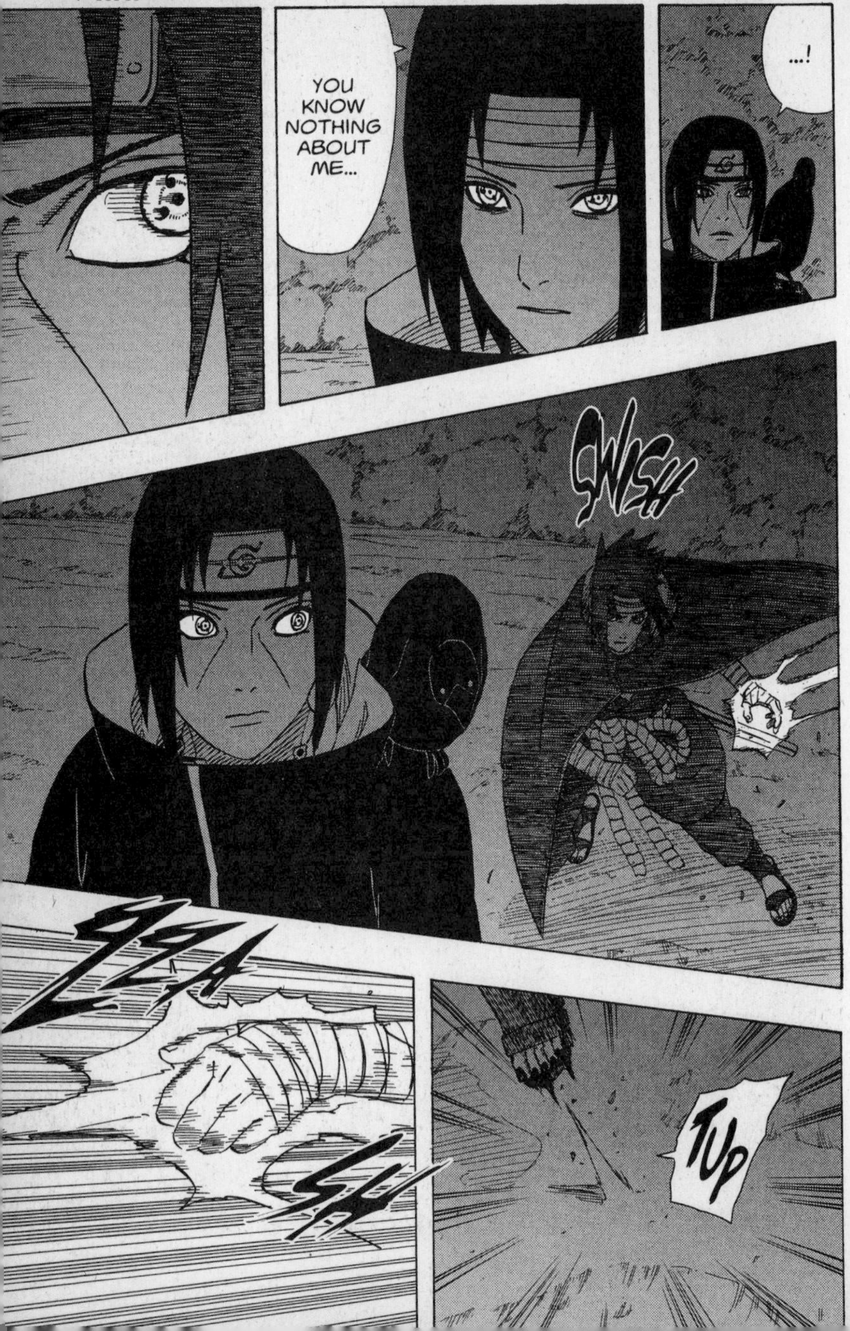
...!
YOU KNOW NOTHING ABOUT ME...
SWISH
TUP
SH

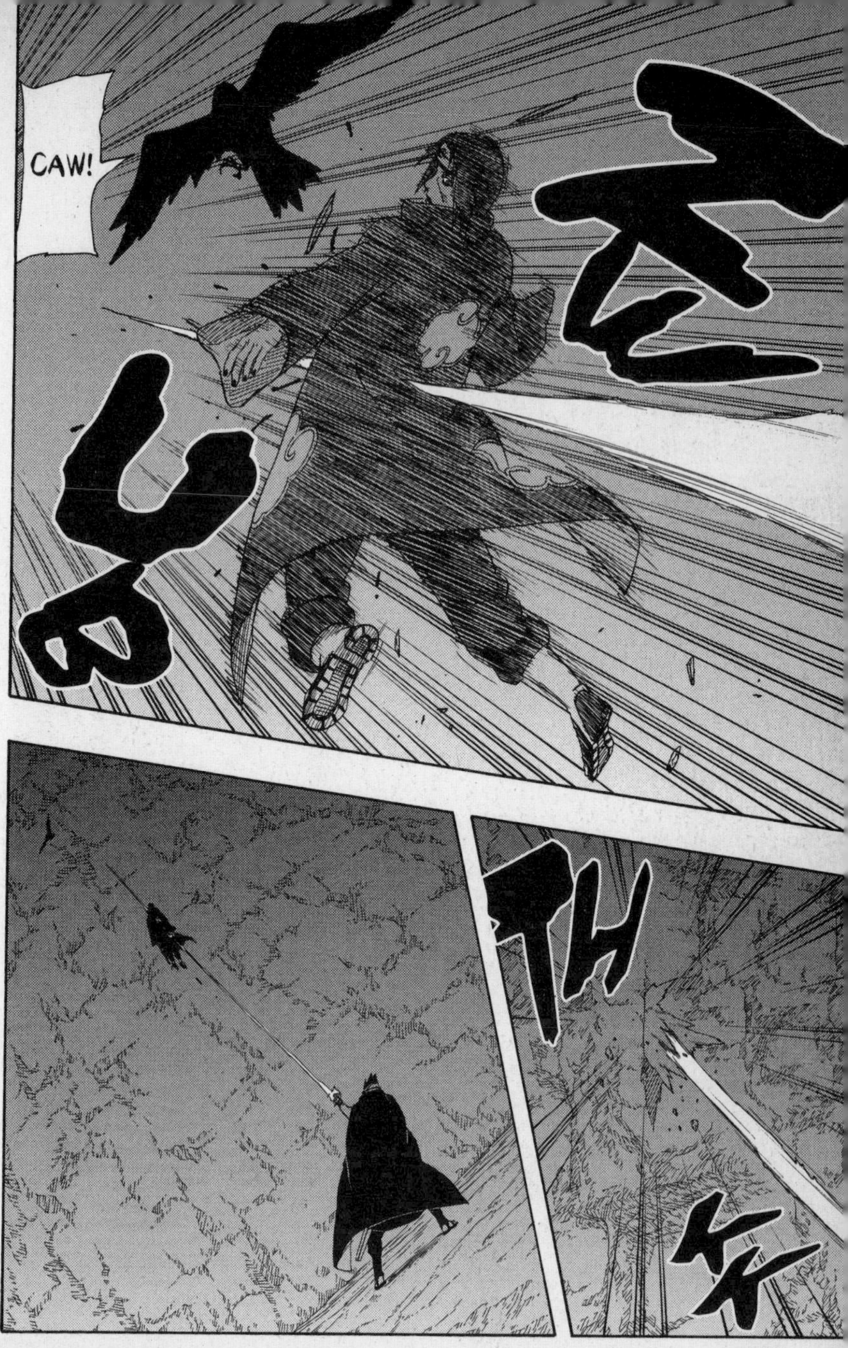
CAW!

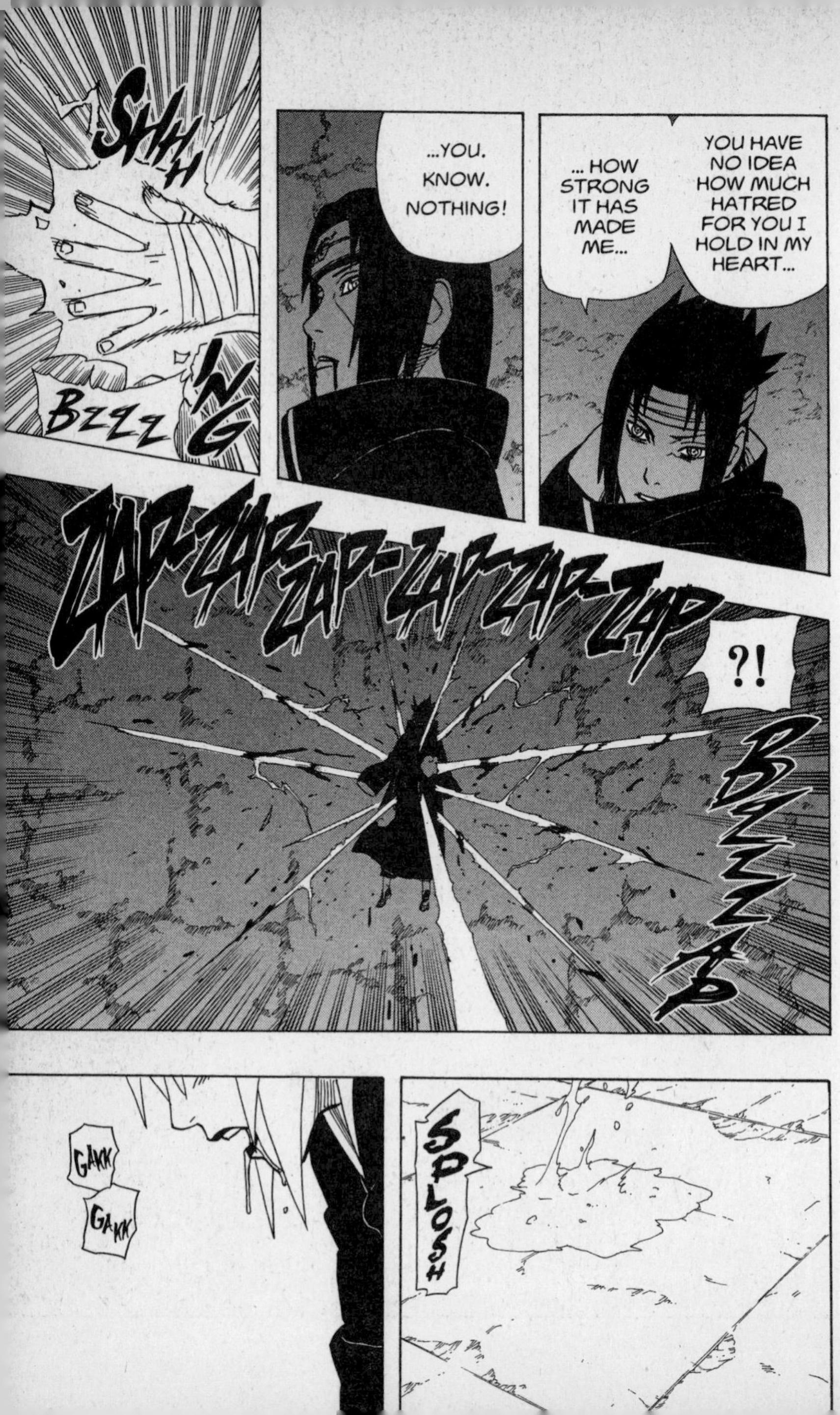
YOU HAVE NO IDEA HOW MUCH HATRED FOR YOU I HOLD IN MY HEART...
... HOW STRONG IT HAS MADE ME...
...YOU. KNOW. NOTHING!
SHHH
ING
BZZZZ
ZAP-ZAP-ZAP-ZAP-ZAP-ZAP
?!
BZZZZAP
SPLOSH
GAKK
GAKK

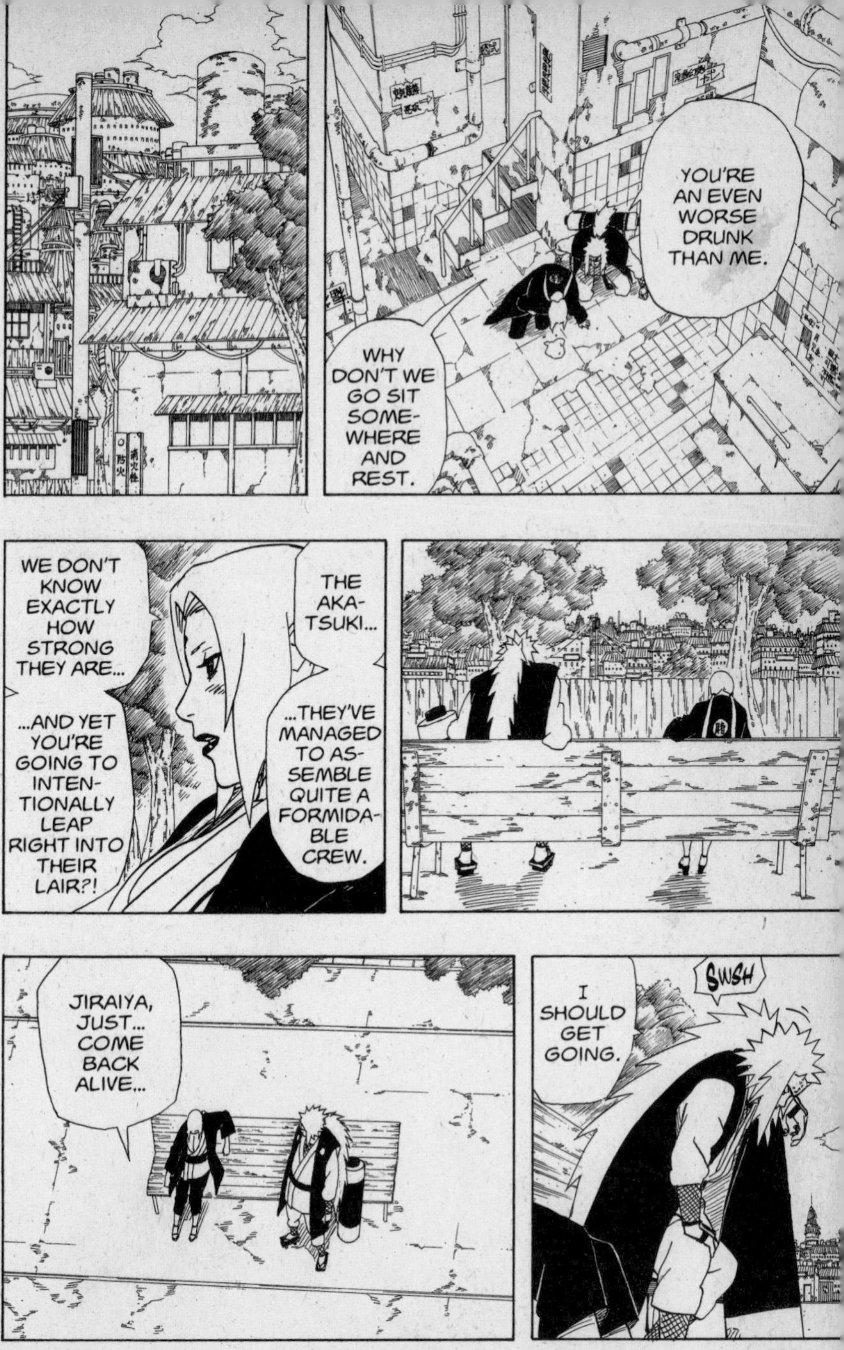

YOU'RE AN EVEN WORSE DRUNK THAN ME.
WHY DON'T WE GO SIT SOME-WHERE AND REST.
THE AKA-TSUKI...
...THEY'VE MANAGED TO AS-SEMBLE QUITE A FORMIDA-BLE CREW.
WE DON'T KNOW EXACTLY HOW STRONG THEY ARE...
...AND YET YOU'RE GOING TO INTEN-TIONALLY LEAP RIGHT INTO THEIR LAIR?!
SWSH
I SHOULD GET GOING.
JIRAIYA, JUST... COME BACK ALIVE...

READ THIS WAY

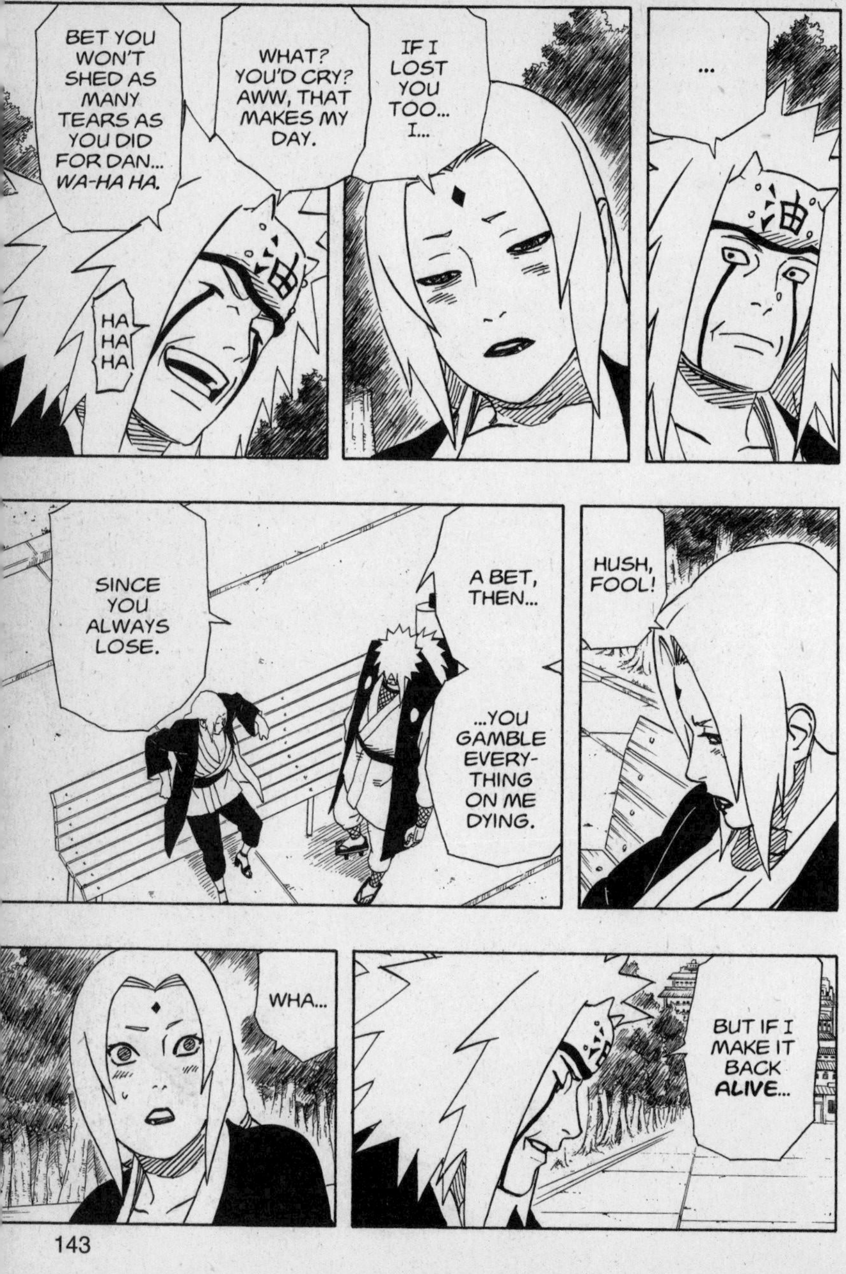
...
IF I LOST YOU TOO... I...
WHAT? YOU'D CRY? AWW, THAT MAKES MY DAY.
BET YOU WON'T SHED AS MANY TEARS AS YOU DID FOR DAN... *WA-HA HA.*
HA HA HA
HUSH, FOOL!
A BET, THEN...
...YOU GAMBLE EVERYTHING ON ME DYING.
SINCE YOU ALWAYS LOSE.
BUT IF I MAKE IT BACK **ALIVE**...
WHA...

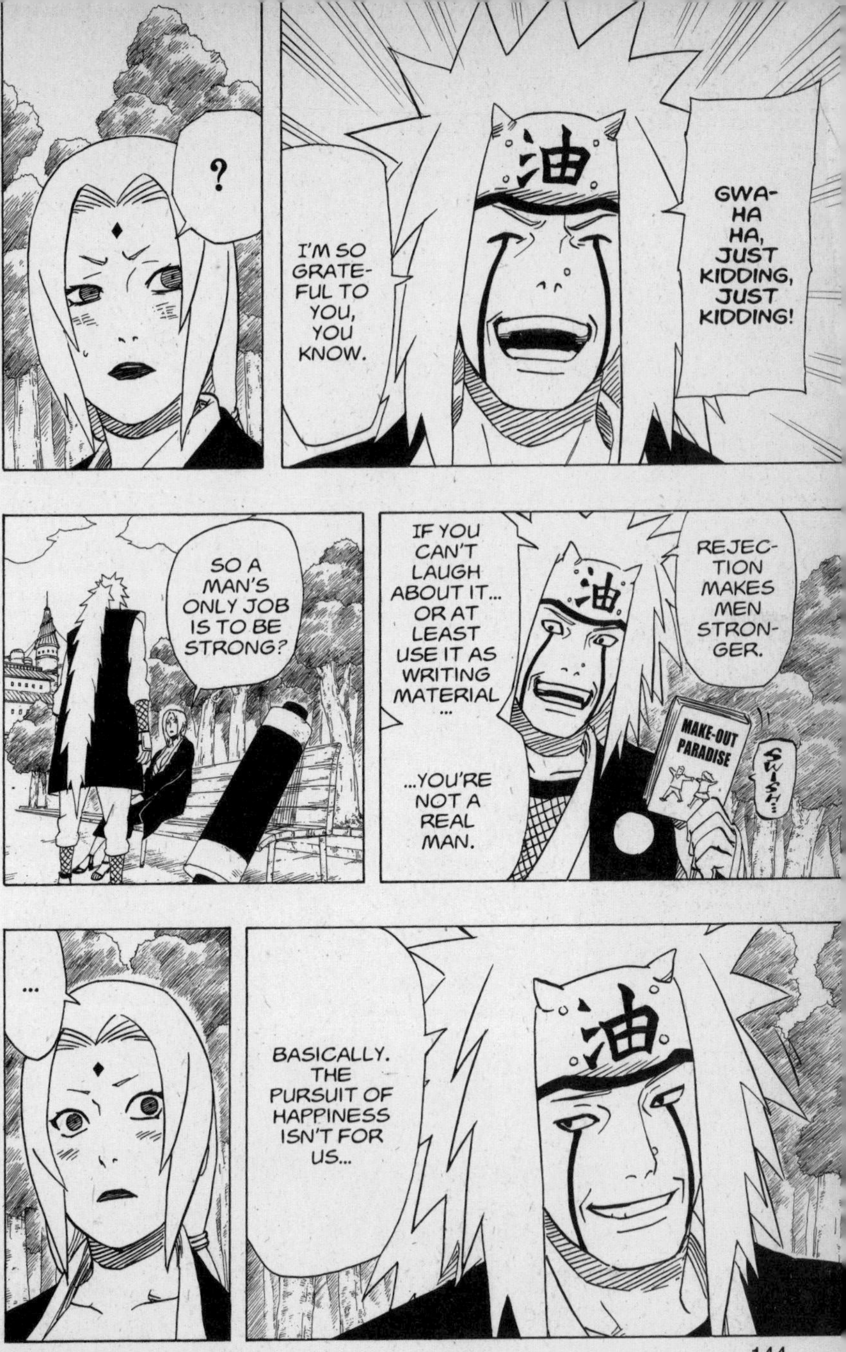
I'M SO GRATEFUL TO YOU, YOU KNOW.
GWA-HA HA, JUST KIDDING, JUST KIDDING!
?
REJECTION MAKES MEN STRONGER.
IF YOU CAN'T LAUGH ABOUT IT... OR AT LEAST USE IT AS WRITING MATERIAL ...
...YOU'RE NOT A REAL MAN.
MAKE-OUT PARADISE
SWISH
SO A MAN'S ONLY JOB IS TO BE STRONG?
BASICALLY. THE PURSUIT OF HAPPINESS ISN'T FOR US...
...

READ THIS WAY

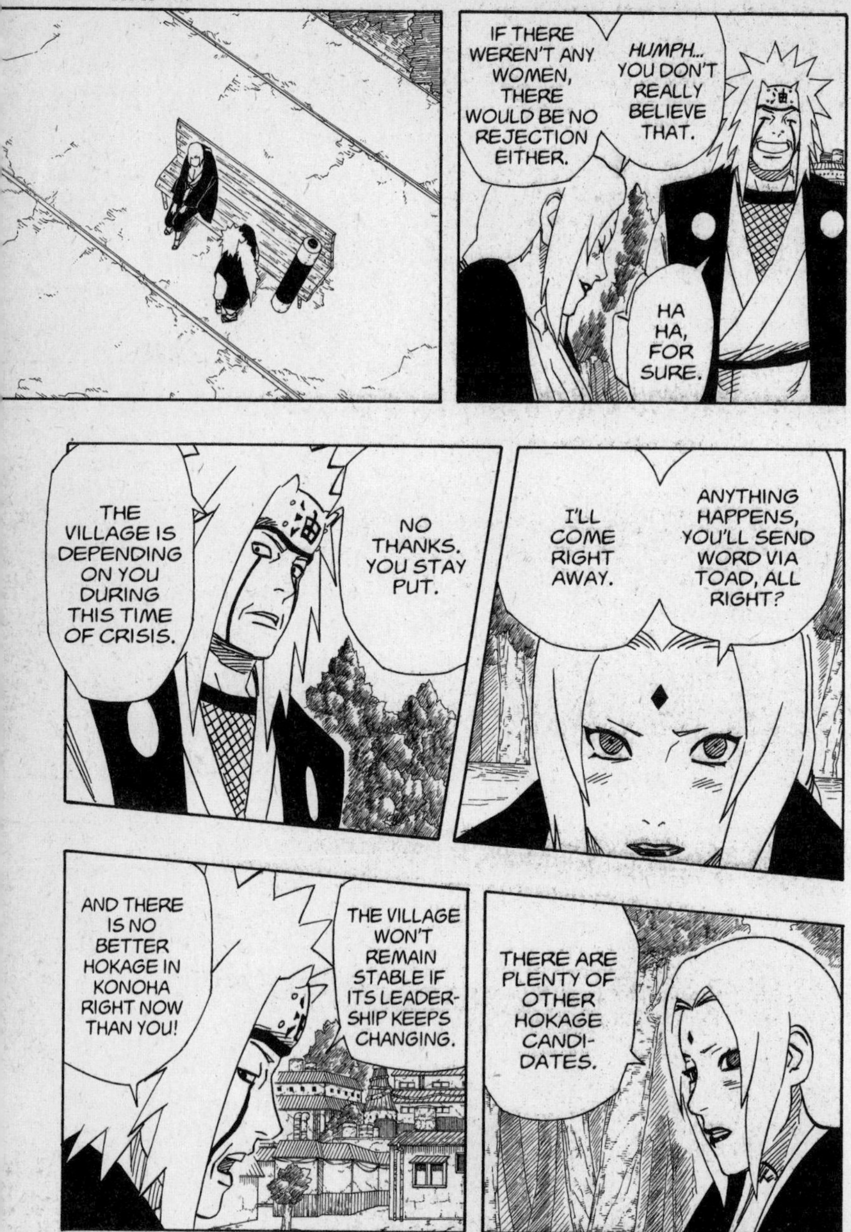
HUMPH... YOU DON'T REALLY BELIEVE THAT.
IF THERE WEREN'T ANY WOMEN, THERE WOULD BE NO REJECTION EITHER.
HA HA, FOR SURE.
ANYTHING HAPPENS, YOU'LL SEND WORD VIA TOAD, ALL RIGHT?
I'LL COME RIGHT AWAY.
NO THANKS. YOU STAY PUT.
THE VILLAGE IS DEPENDING ON YOU DURING THIS TIME OF CRISIS.
THERE ARE PLENTY OF OTHER HOKAGE CANDIDATES.
THE VILLAGE WON'T REMAIN STABLE IF ITS LEADERSHIP KEEPS CHANGING.
AND THERE IS NO BETTER HOKAGE IN KONOHA RIGHT NOW THAN YOU!

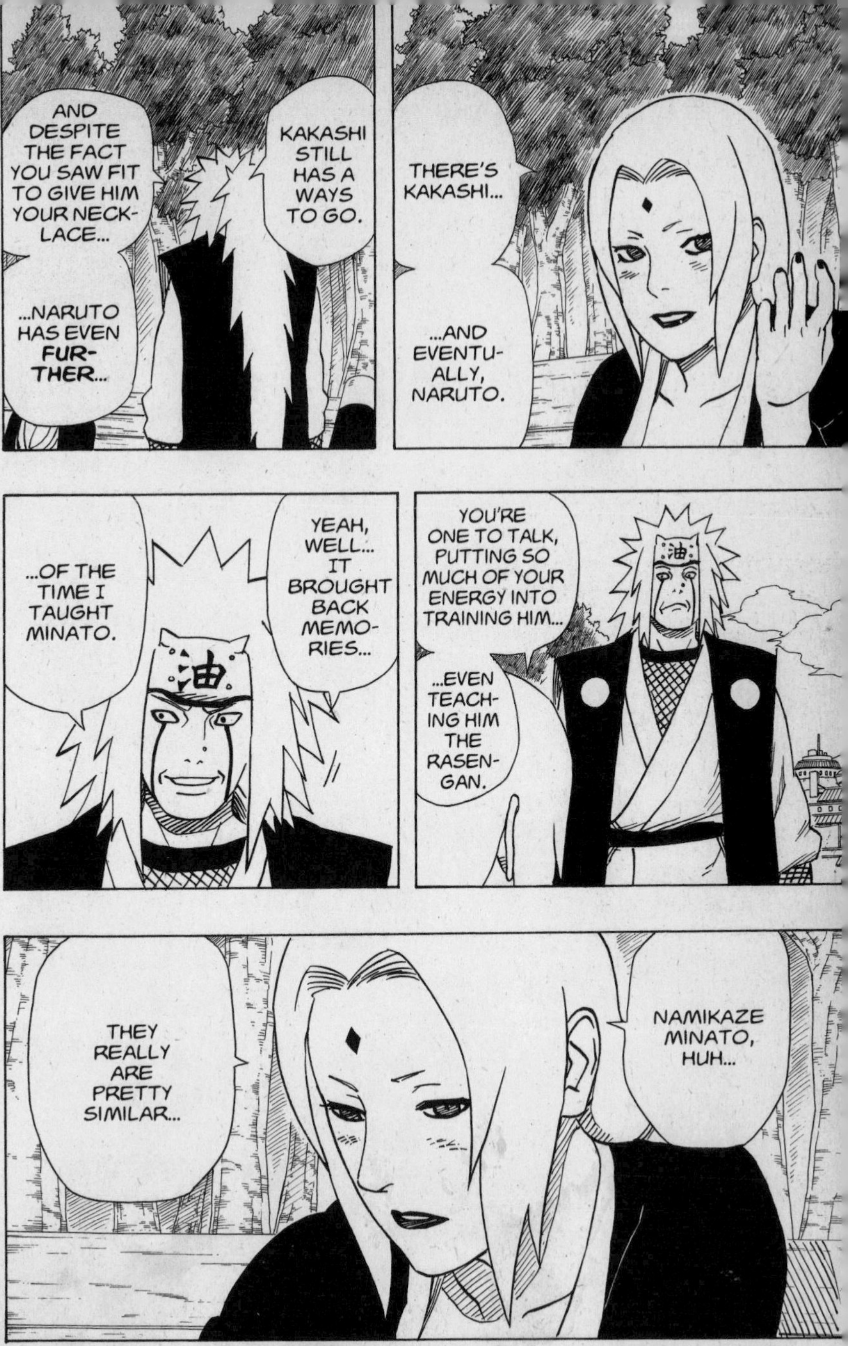
THERE'S KAKASHI...
...AND EVENTUALLY, NARUTO.
KAKASHI STILL HAS A WAYS TO GO.
AND DESPITE THE FACT YOU SAW FIT TO GIVE HIM YOUR NECKLACE...
...NARUTO HAS EVEN **FURTHER**...
YOU'RE ONE TO TALK, PUTTING SO MUCH OF YOUR ENERGY INTO TRAINING HIM...
...EVEN TEACHING HIM THE RASENGAN.
YEAH, WELL... IT BROUGHT BACK MEMORIES...
...OF THE TIME I TAUGHT MINATO.
NAMIKAZE MINATO, HUH...
THEY REALLY ARE PRETTY SIMILAR...

READ THIS WAY

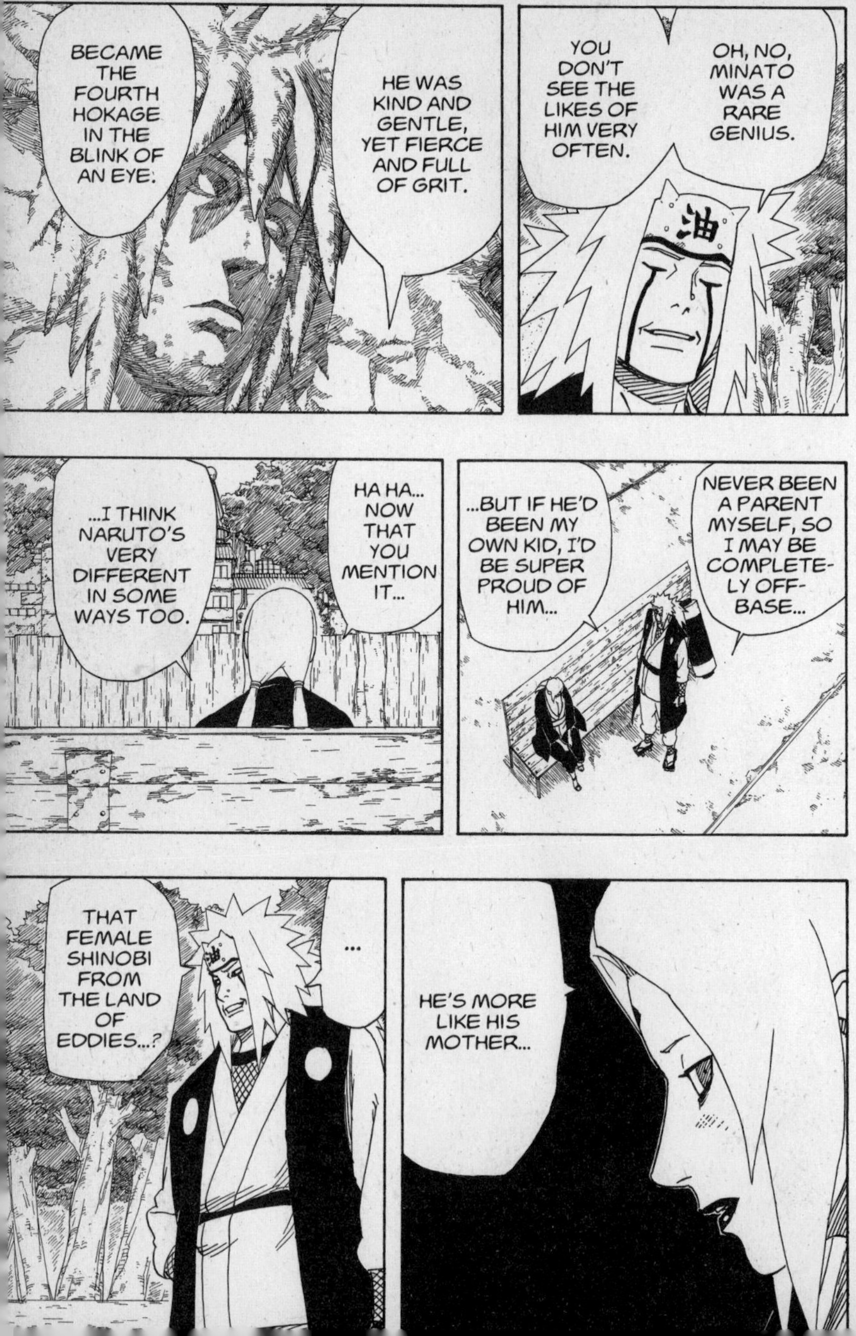
OH, NO, MINATO WAS A RARE GENIUS.
YOU DON'T SEE THE LIKES OF HIM VERY OFTEN.
HE WAS KIND AND GENTLE, YET FIERCE AND FULL OF GRIT.
BECAME THE FOURTH HOKAGE IN THE BLINK OF AN EYE.
NEVER BEEN A PARENT MYSELF, SO I MAY BE COMPLETELY OFF-BASE...
...BUT IF HE'D BEEN MY OWN KID, I'D BE SUPER PROUD OF HIM...
HA HA... NOW THAT YOU MENTION IT...
...I THINK NARUTO'S VERY DIFFERENT IN SOME WAYS TOO.
HE'S MORE LIKE HIS MOTHER...
...
THAT FEMALE SHINOBI FROM THE LAND OF EDDIES...?

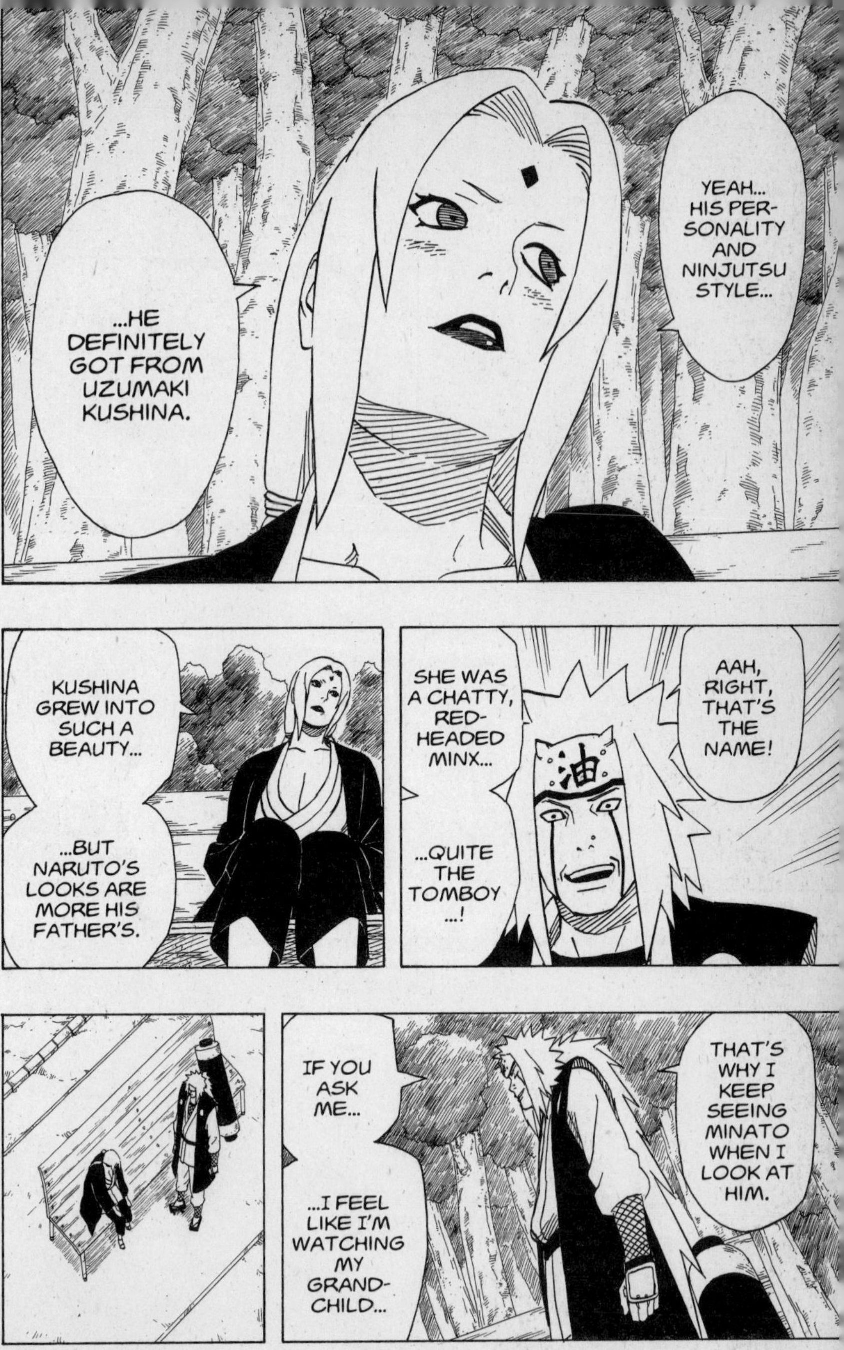
YEAH... HIS PERSONALITY AND NINJUTSU STYLE...
...HE DEFINITELY GOT FROM UZUMAKI KUSHINA.
AAH, RIGHT, THAT'S THE NAME!
SHE WAS A CHATTY, RED-HEADED MINX...
...QUITE THE TOMBOY ...!
KUSHINA GREW INTO SUCH A BEAUTY...
...BUT NARUTO'S LOOKS ARE MORE HIS FATHER'S.
THAT'S WHY I KEEP SEEING MINATO WHEN I LOOK AT HIM.
IF YOU ASK ME...
...I FEEL LIKE I'M WATCHING MY GRANDCHILD...

READ THIS WAY

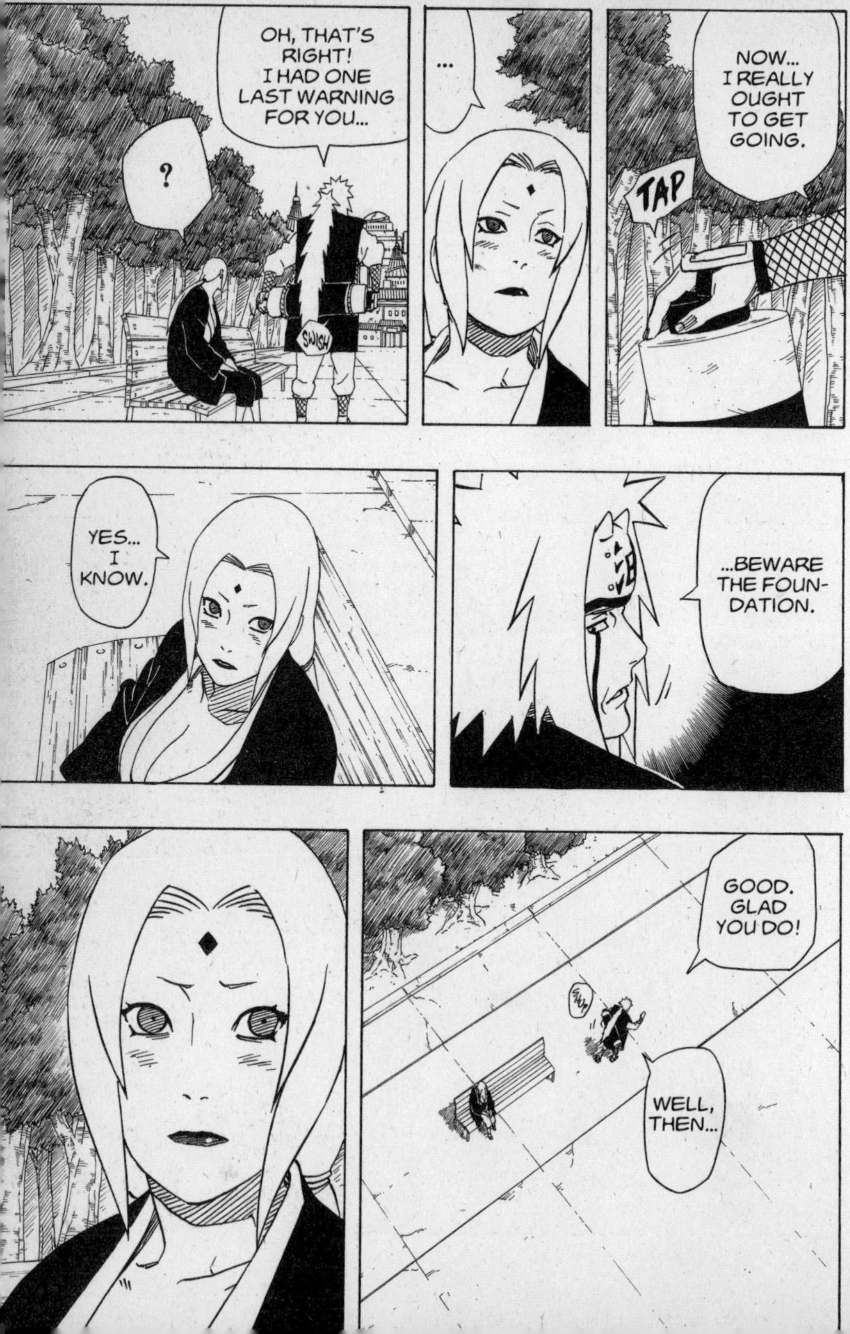
NOW... I REALLY OUGHT TO GET GOING.
TAP
...
OH, THAT'S RIGHT! I HAD ONE LAST WARNING FOR YOU...
?
SWISH
...BEWARE THE FOUNDATION.
YES... I KNOW.
GOOD. GLAD YOU DO!
SHUP
WELL, THEN...

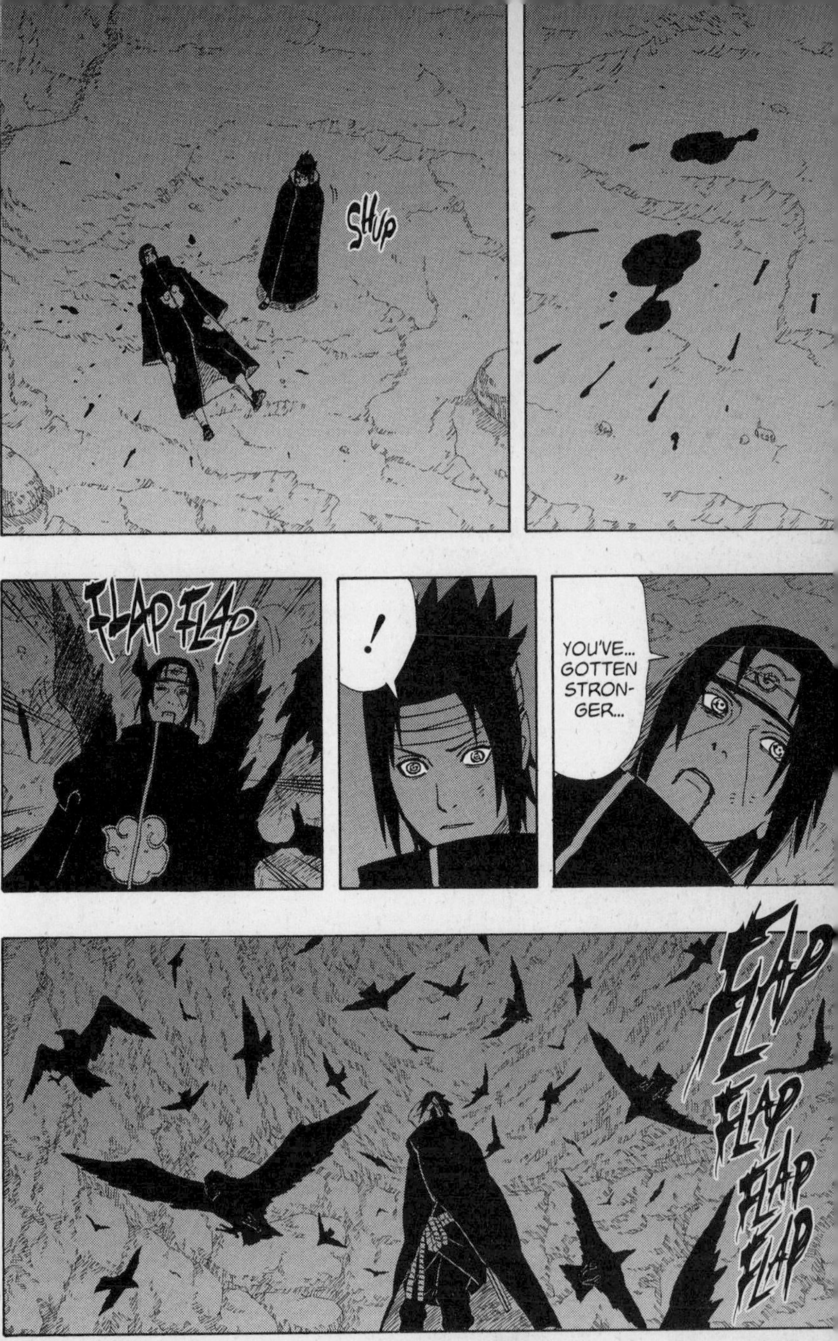
SHUP
YOU'VE... GOTTEN STRONGER...
!
FLAP FLAP
FLAP FLAP FLAP FLAP

READ THIS WAY

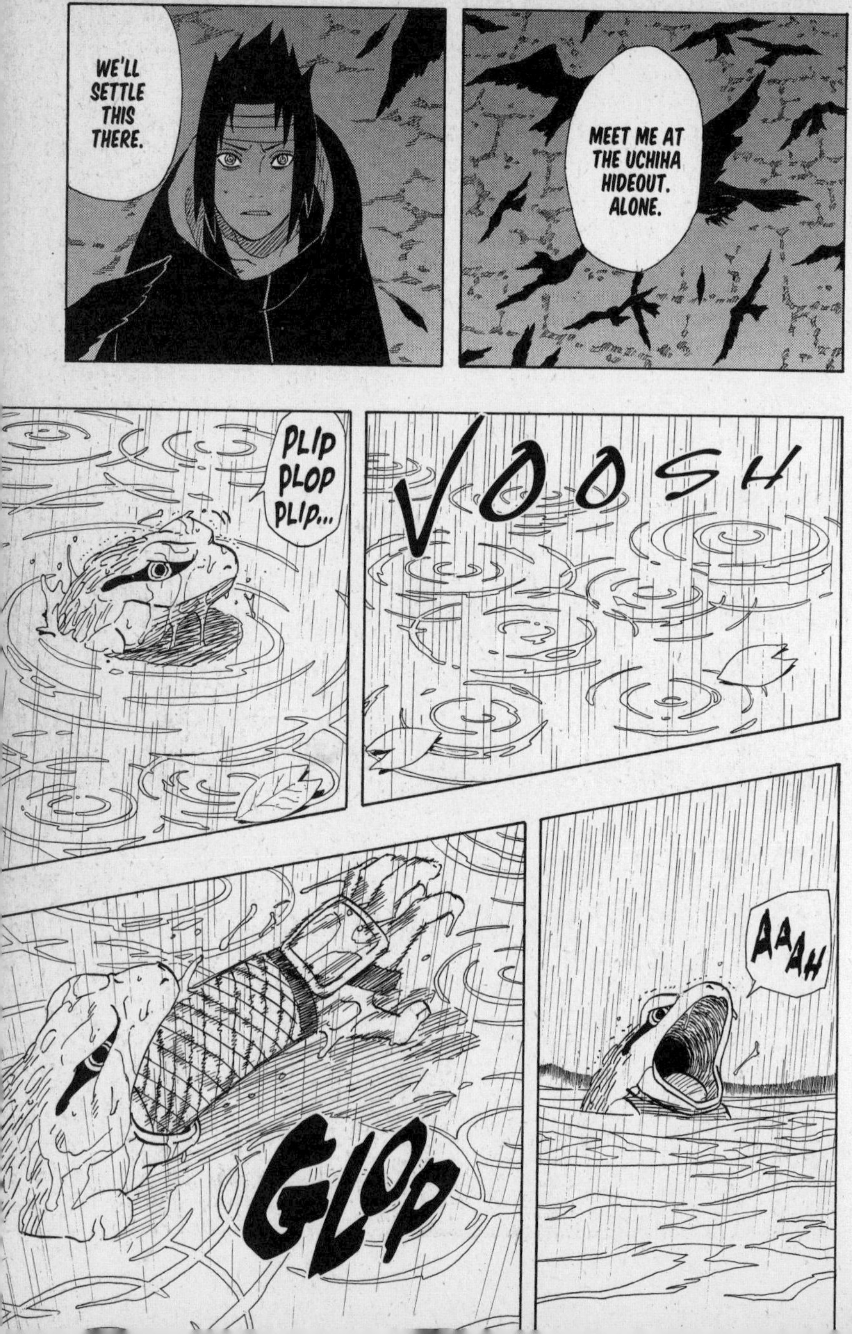
MEET ME AT THE UCHIHA HIDEOUT. ALONE.
WE'LL SETTLE THIS THERE.
VOOSH
PLIP PLOP PLIP...
AAAH
GLOP

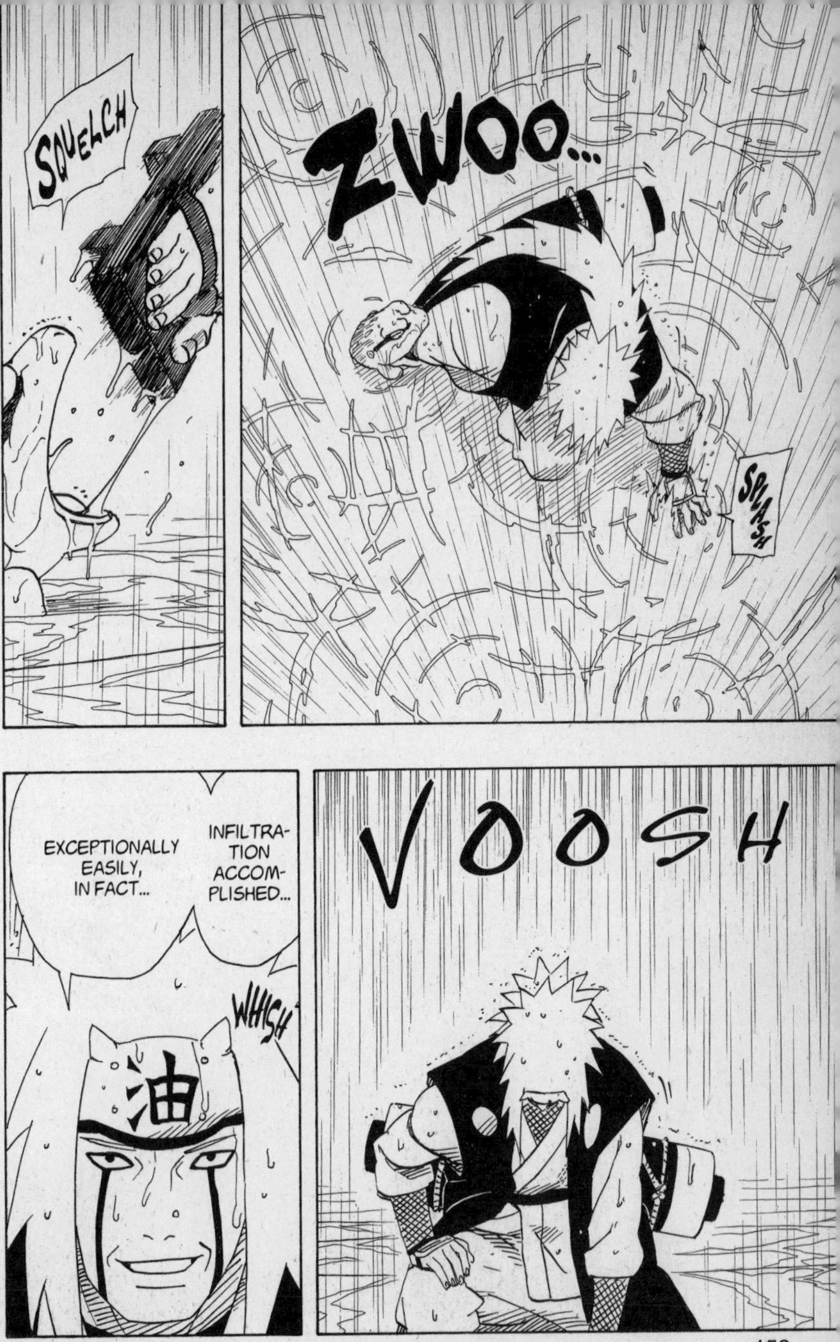
ZWOO...
SPLASH
SQUELCH
VOOSH
INFILTRATION ACCOMPLISHED...
EXCEPTIONALLY EASILY, IN FACT...
WHISH

READ THIS WAY

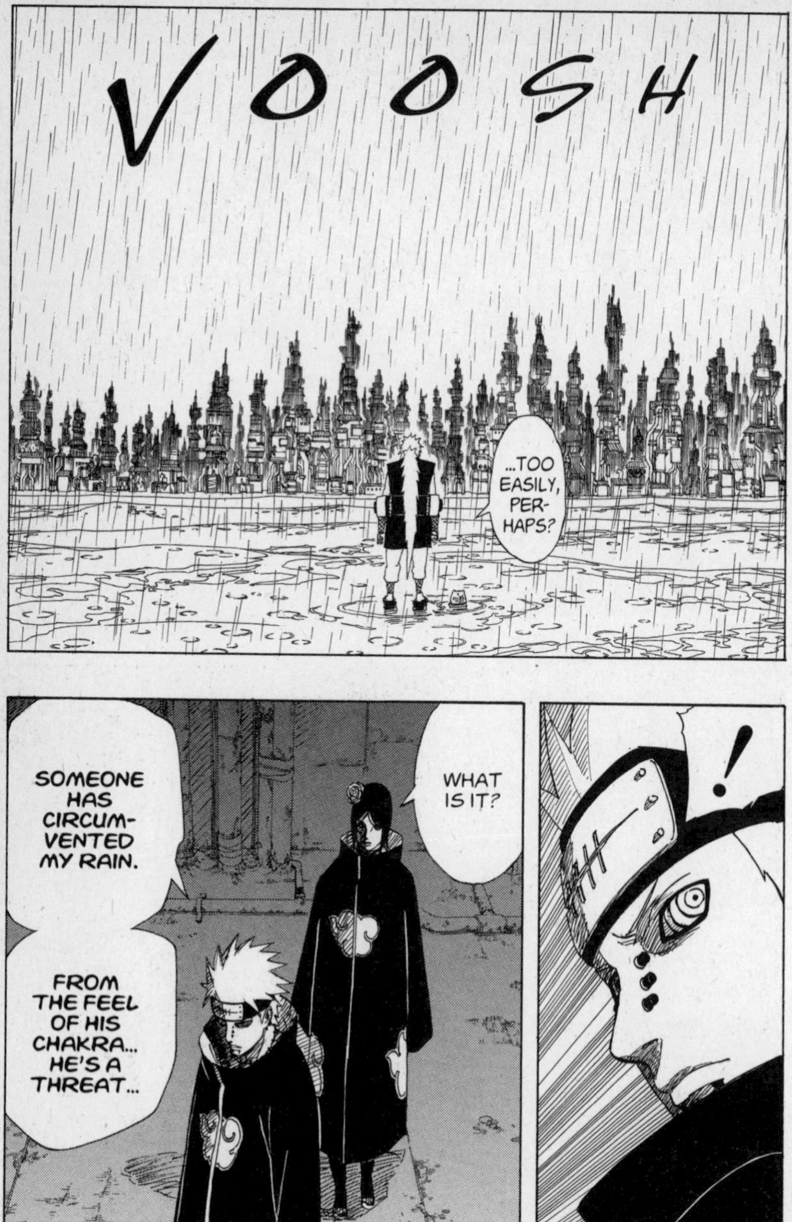
VOOSH
...TOO EASILY, PER-HAPS?
!
WHAT IS IT?
SOMEONE HAS CIRCUM-VENTED MY RAIN.
FROM THE FEEL OF HIS CHAKRA... HE'S A THREAT...

NARUTO

Number 368: Intel

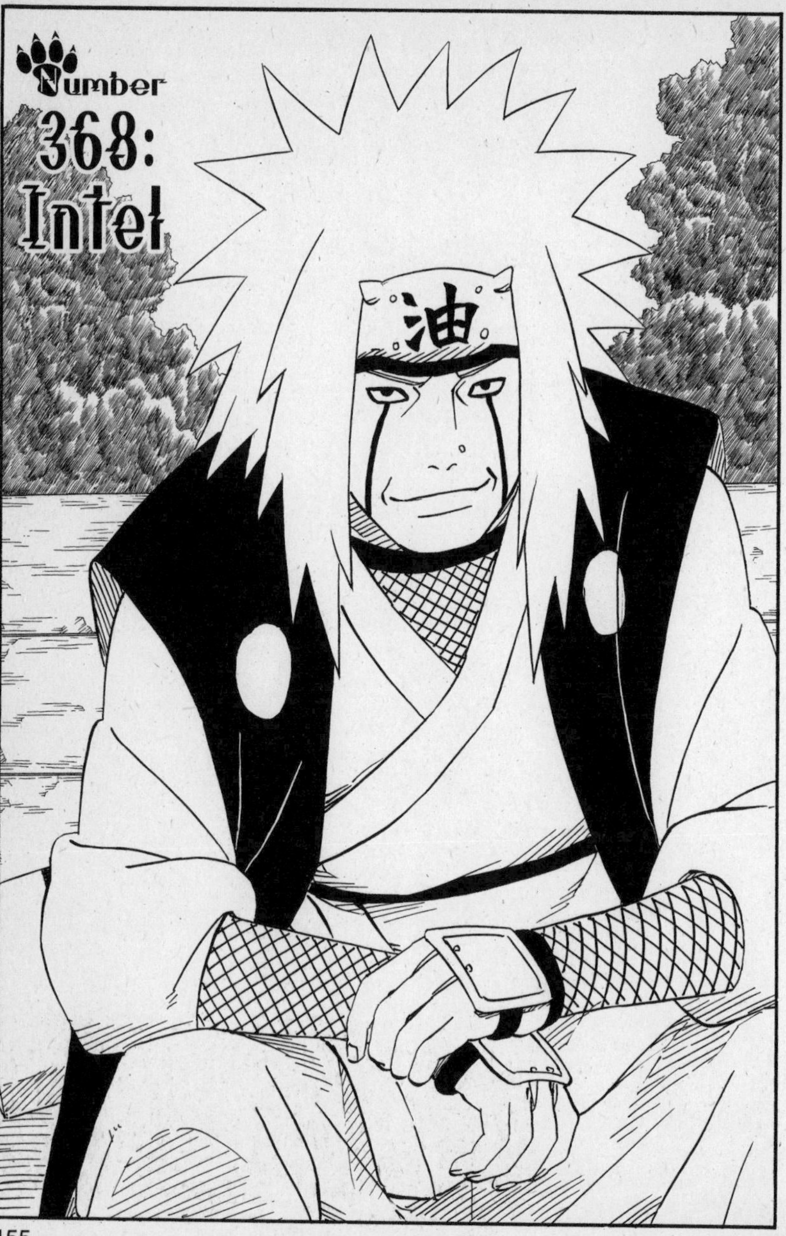
油

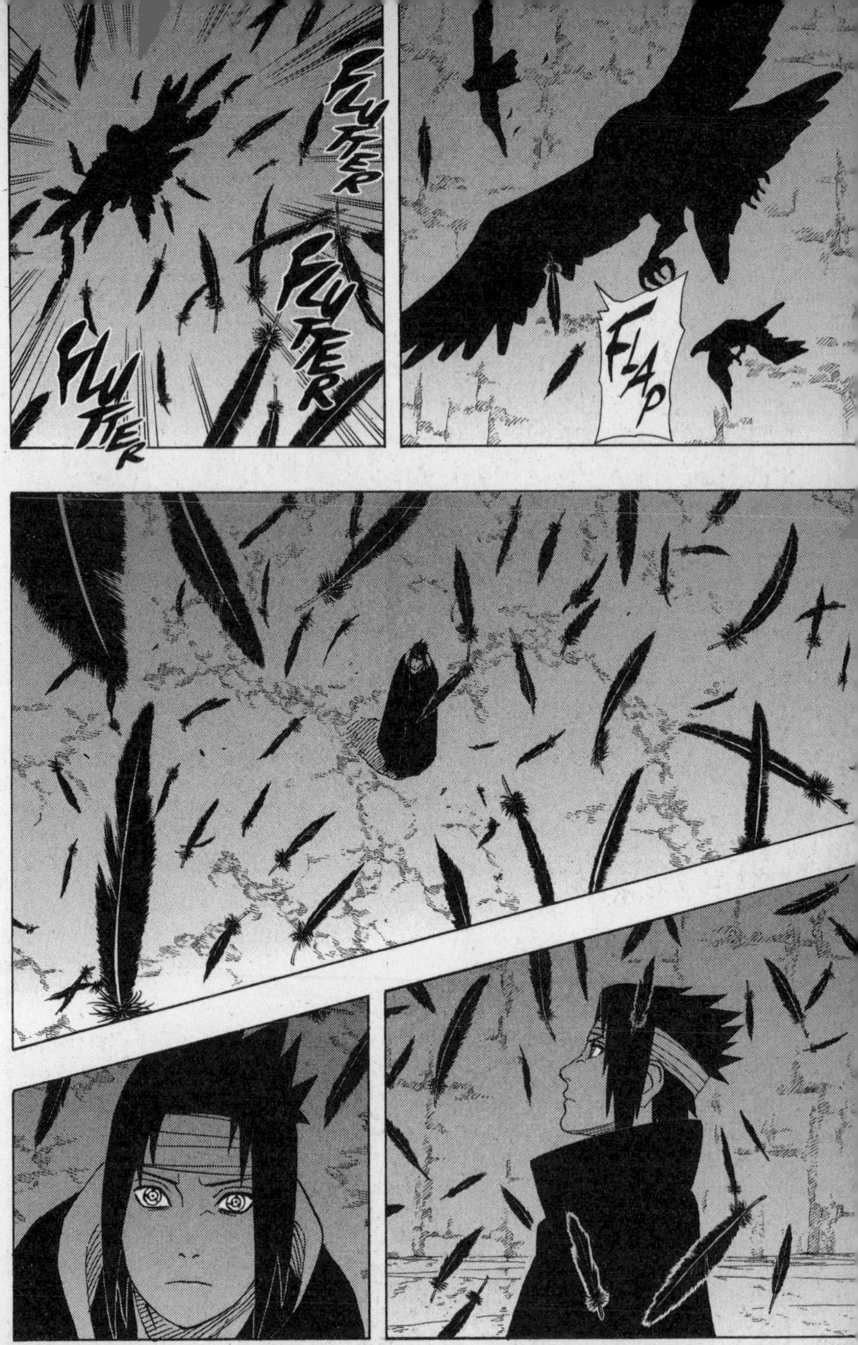
FLAP
FLUTTER
FLUTTER
FLUTTER

READ THIS WAY

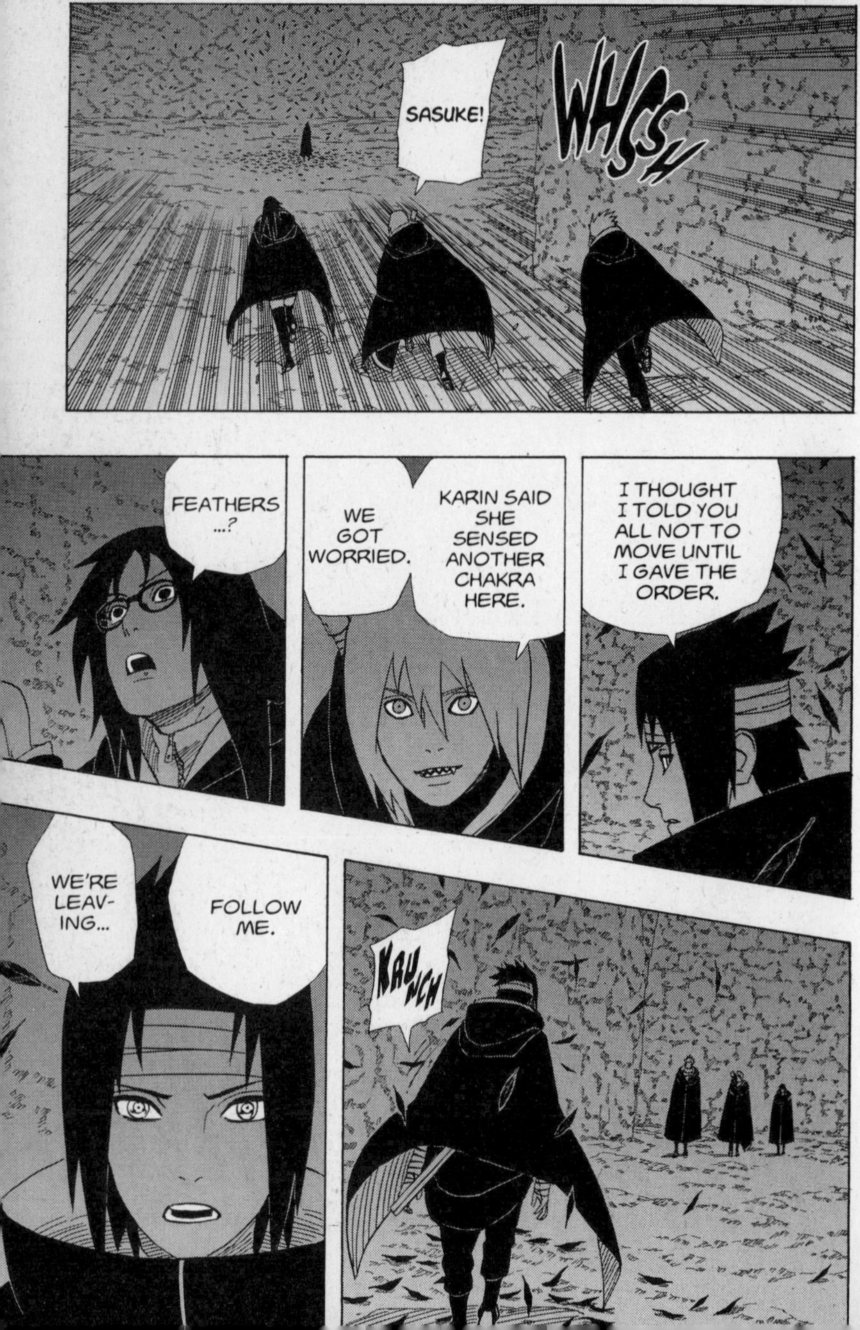
WHSSH
SASUKE!
I THOUGHT I TOLD YOU ALL NOT TO MOVE UNTIL I GAVE THE ORDER.
KARIN SAID SHE SENSED ANOTHER CHAKRA HERE.
WE GOT WORRIED.
FEATHERS ...?
KRAUNCH
FOLLOW ME.
WE'RE LEAV-ING...

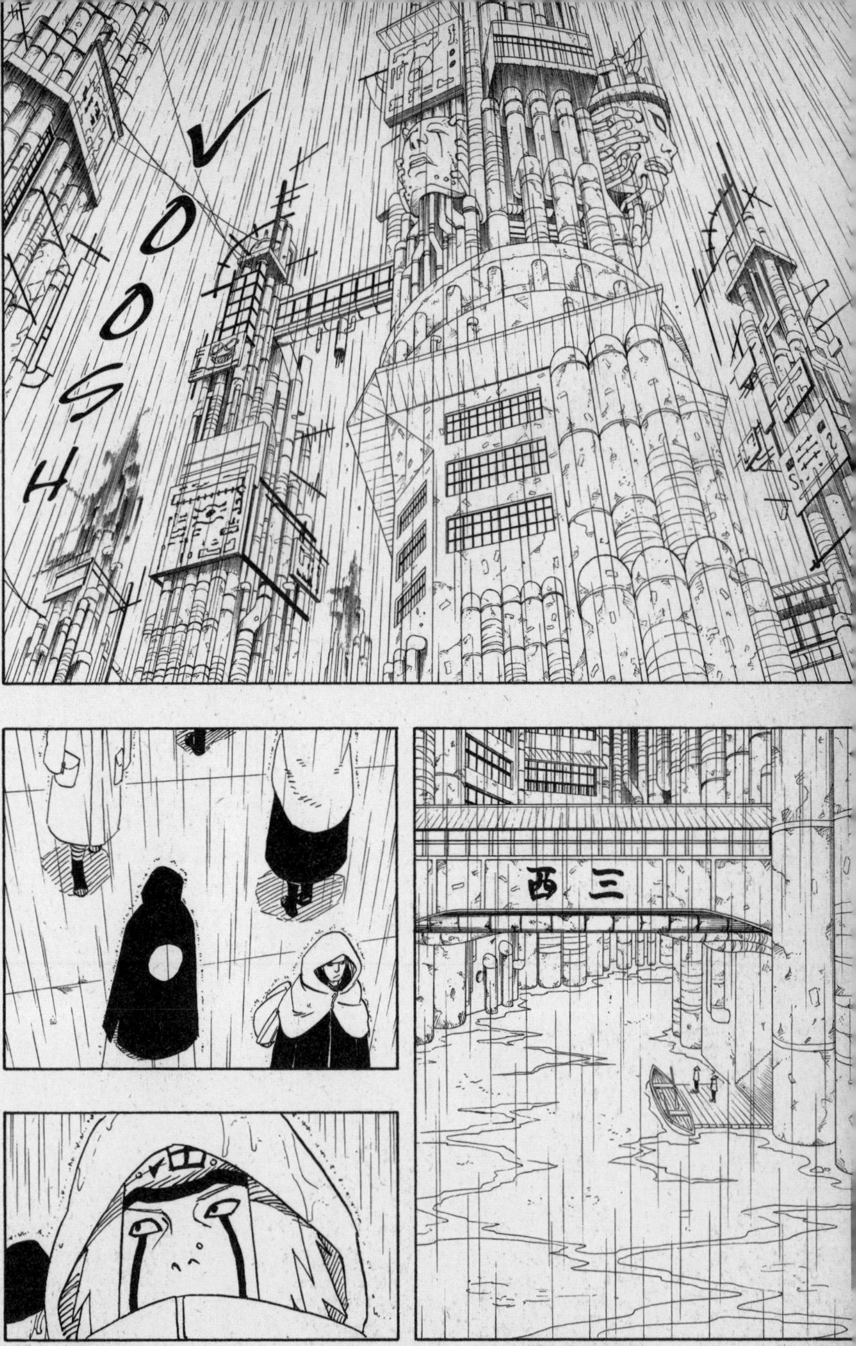
VOOSH
西三

(WEST THREE)

READ THIS WAY

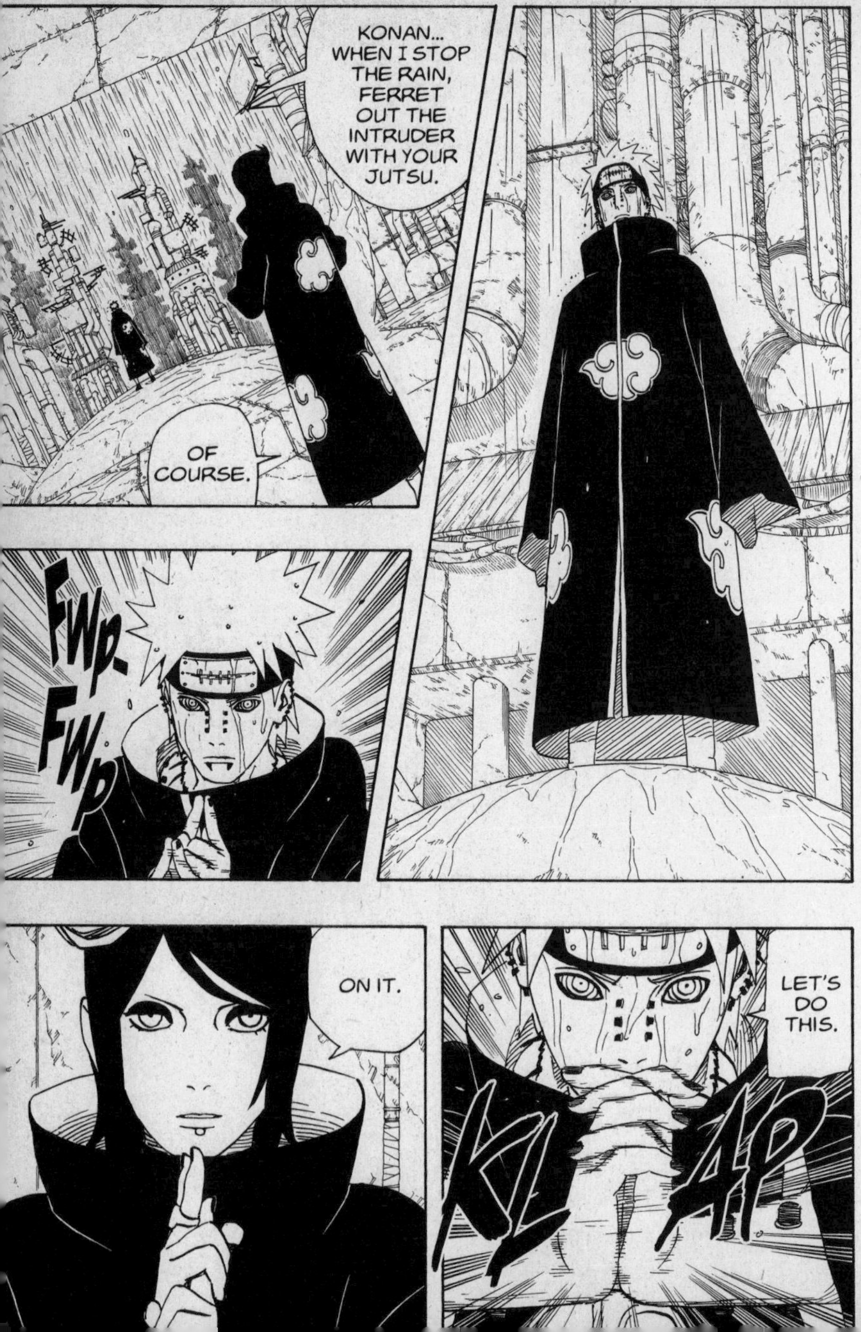
KONAN... WHEN I STOP THE RAIN, FERRET OUT THE INTRUDER WITH YOUR JUTSU.
OF COURSE.
FWP-FWP
LET'S DO THIS.
KLAP
ON IT.

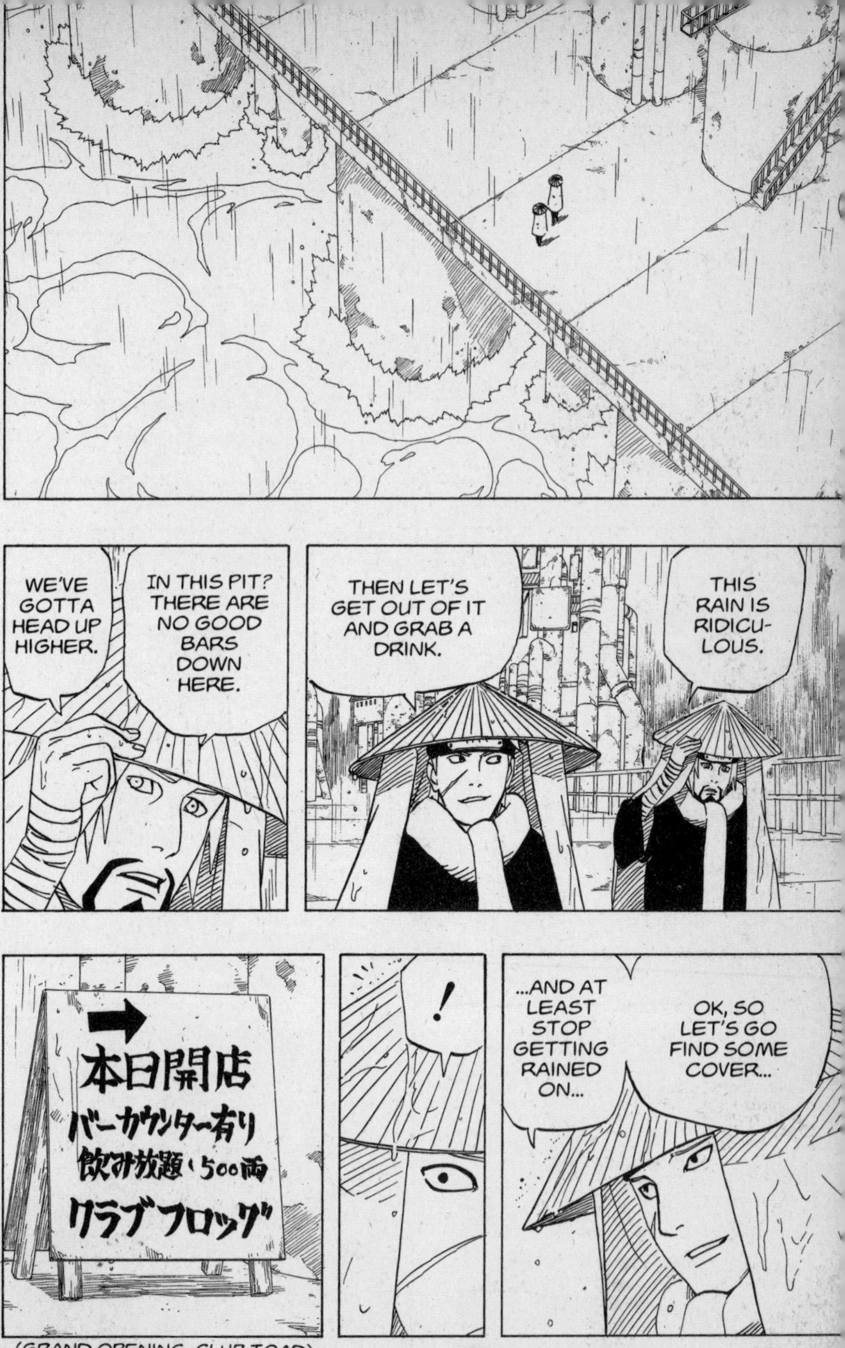
THIS RAIN IS RIDICULOUS.
THEN LET'S GET OUT OF IT AND GRAB A DRINK.
IN THIS PIT? THERE ARE NO GOOD BARS DOWN HERE.
WE'VE GOTTA HEAD UP HIGHER.
OK, SO LET'S GO FIND SOME COVER...
...AND AT LEAST STOP GETTING RAINED ON...
!
本日開店
バーカウンター有り
飲み放題・500両
クラブフロッグ
(GRAND OPENING, CLUB TOAD)

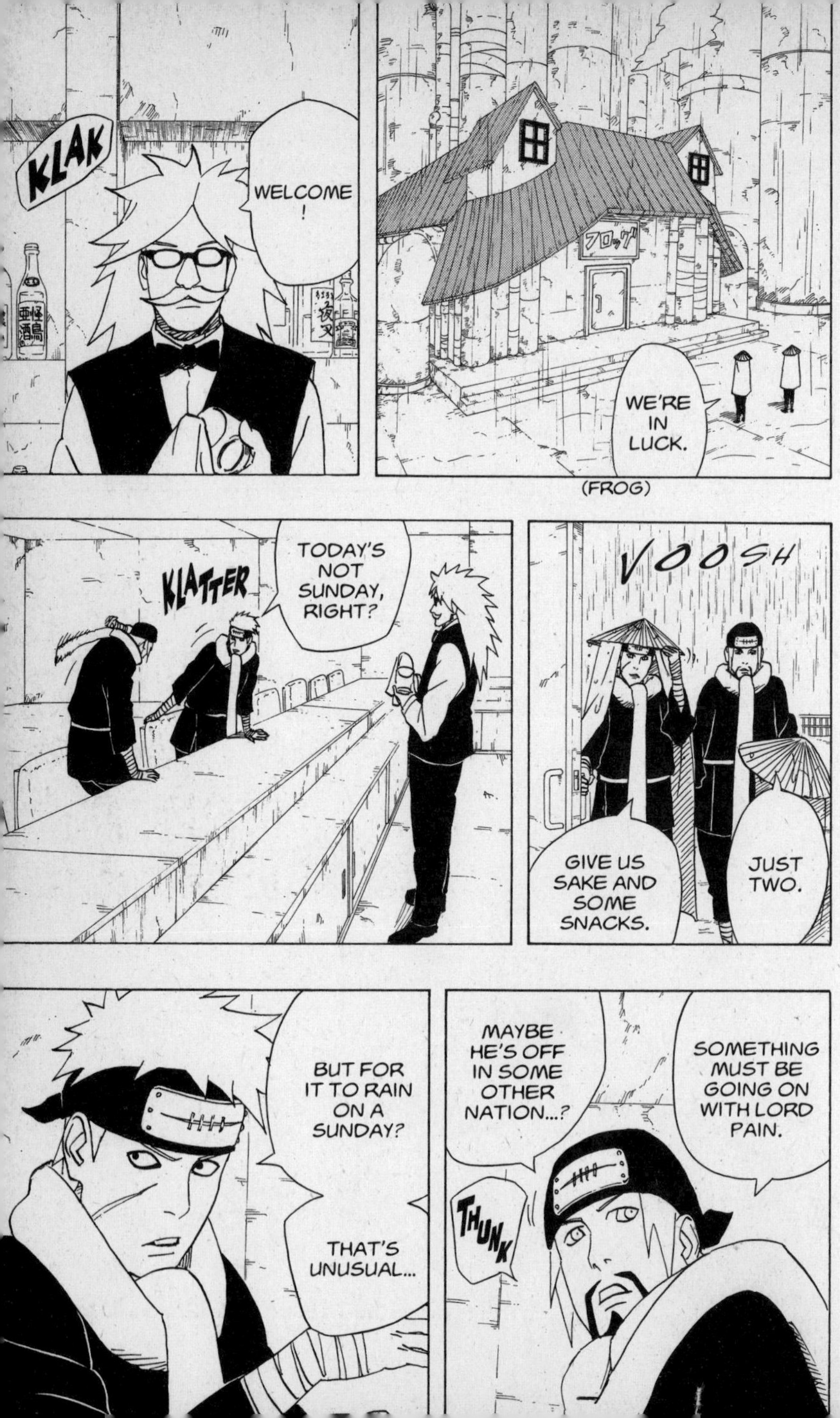

フロッグ
WE'RE IN LUCK.
(FROG)
KLAK
WELCOME!
VOOSH
JUST TWO.
GIVE US SAKE AND SOME SNACKS.
KLATTER
TODAY'S NOT SUNDAY, RIGHT?
SOMETHING MUST BE GOING ON WITH LORD PAIN.
MAYBE HE'S OFF IN SOME OTHER NATION...?
THUNK
BUT FOR IT TO RAIN ON A SUNDAY?
THAT'S UNUSUAL...

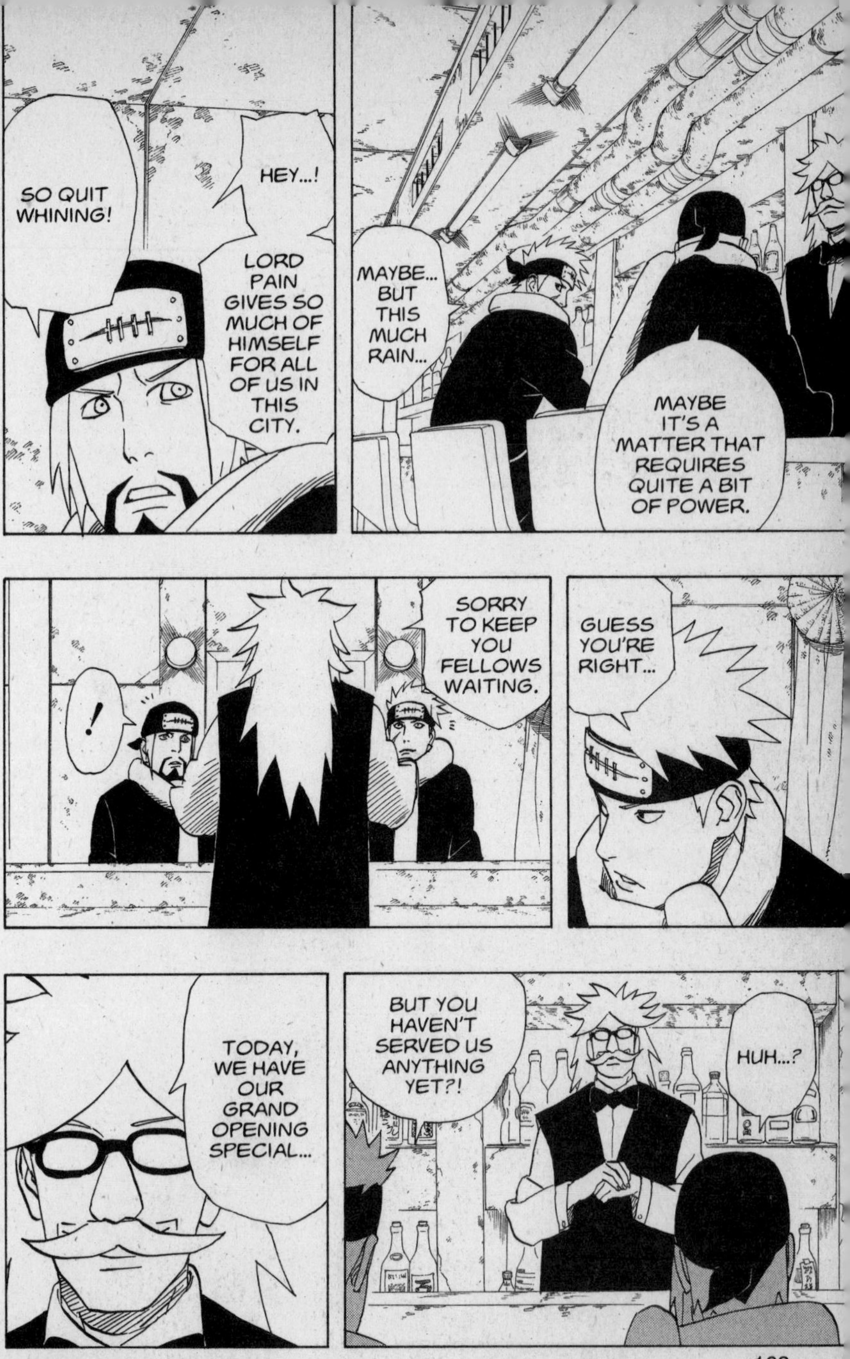
MAYBE... BUT THIS MUCH RAIN...
MAYBE IT'S A MATTER THAT REQUIRES QUITE A BIT OF POWER.
HEY...!
LORD PAIN GIVES SO MUCH OF HIMSELF FOR ALL OF US IN THIS CITY.
SO QUIT WHINING!
GUESS YOU'RE RIGHT...
SORRY TO KEEP YOU FELLOWS WAITING.
!
HUH...?
BUT YOU HAVEN'T SERVED US ANYTHING YET?!
TODAY, WE HAVE OUR GRAND OPENING SPECIAL...

READ THIS WAY

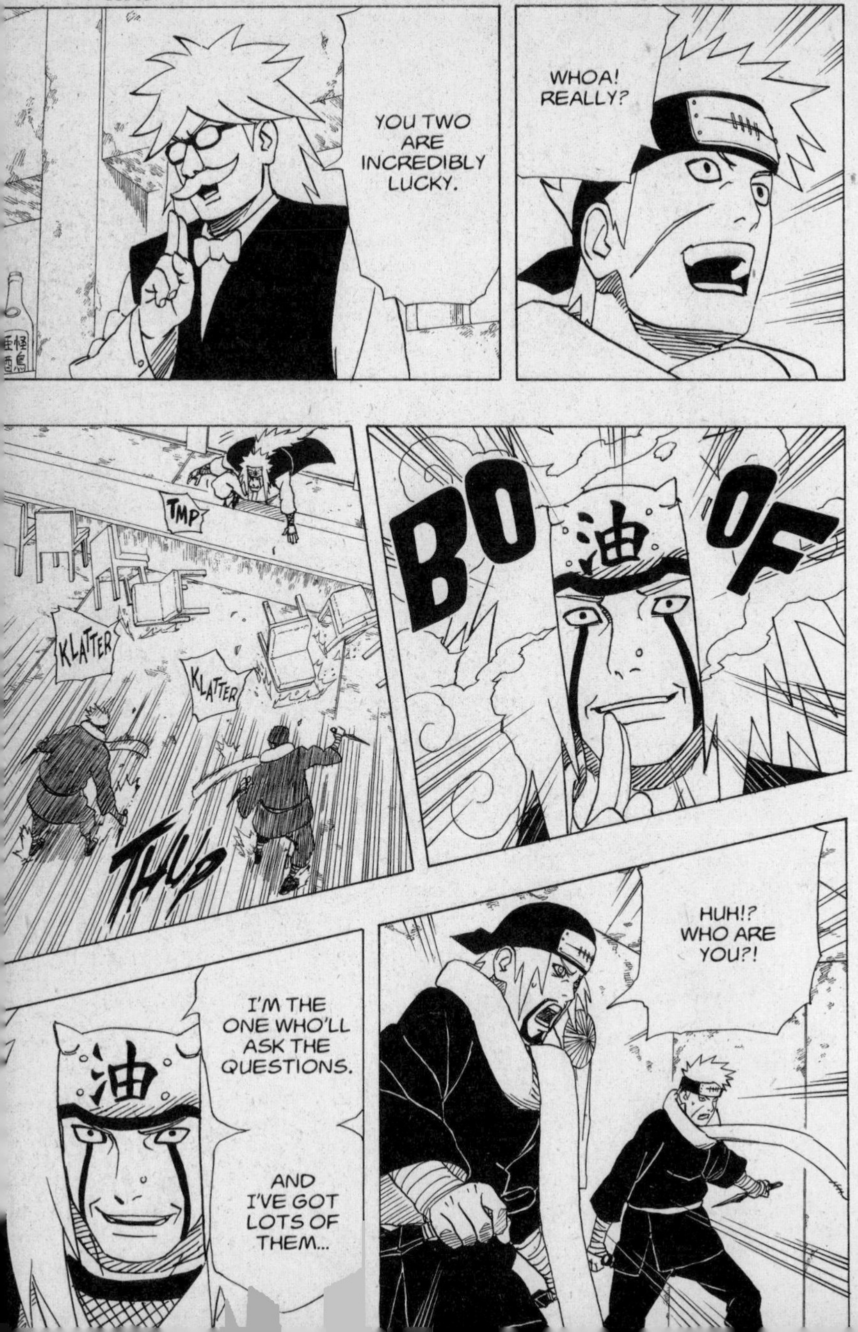

WHOA! REALLY?
YOU TWO ARE INCREDIBLY LUCKY.
BOOF
油
TMP
KLATTER
KLATTER
THUP
HUH!? WHO ARE YOU?!
I'M THE ONE WHO'LL ASK THE QUESTIONS.
AND I'VE GOT LOTS OF THEM...
油

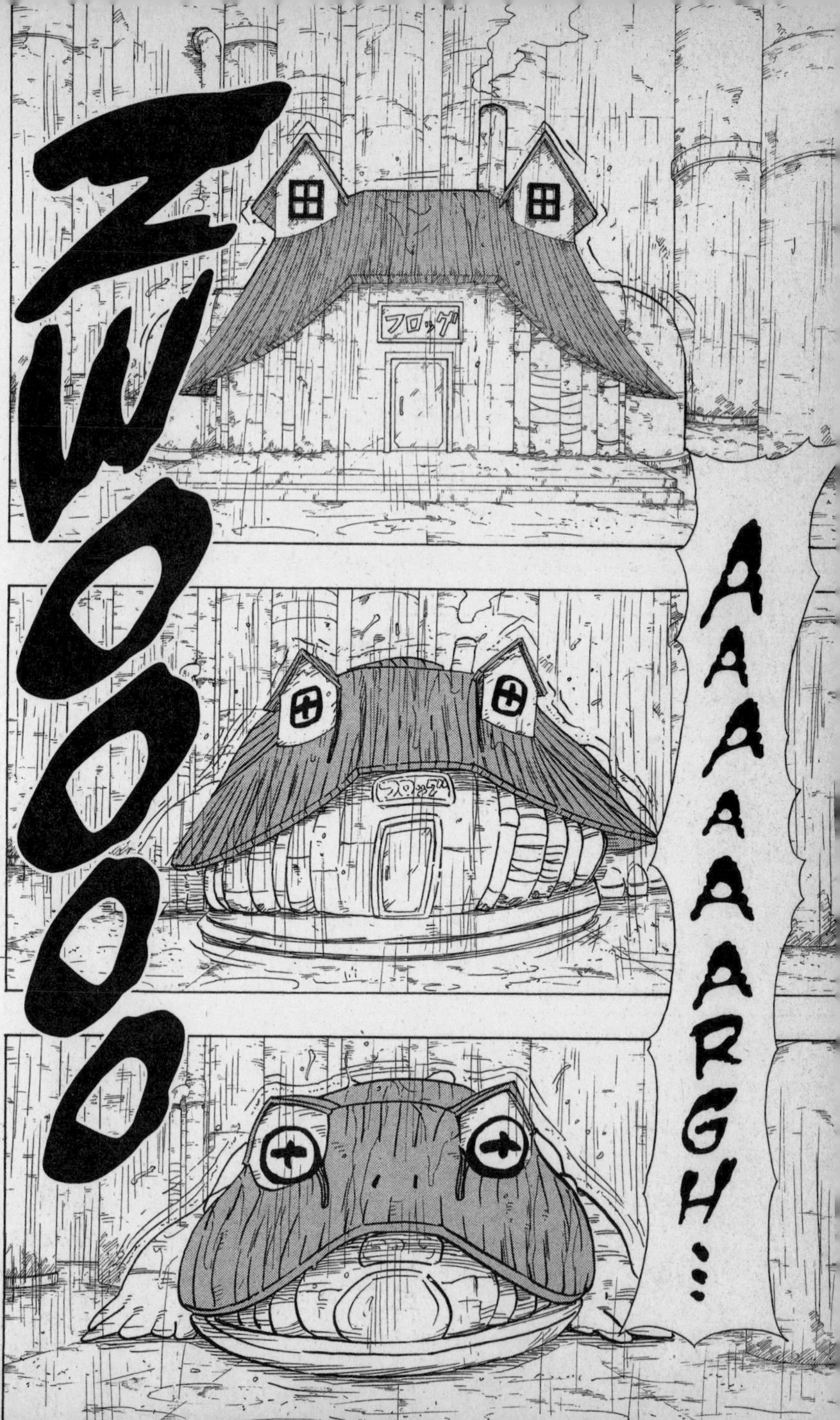
AAAAAARGH...
ZWOOOO
フロッグ

READ THIS WAY

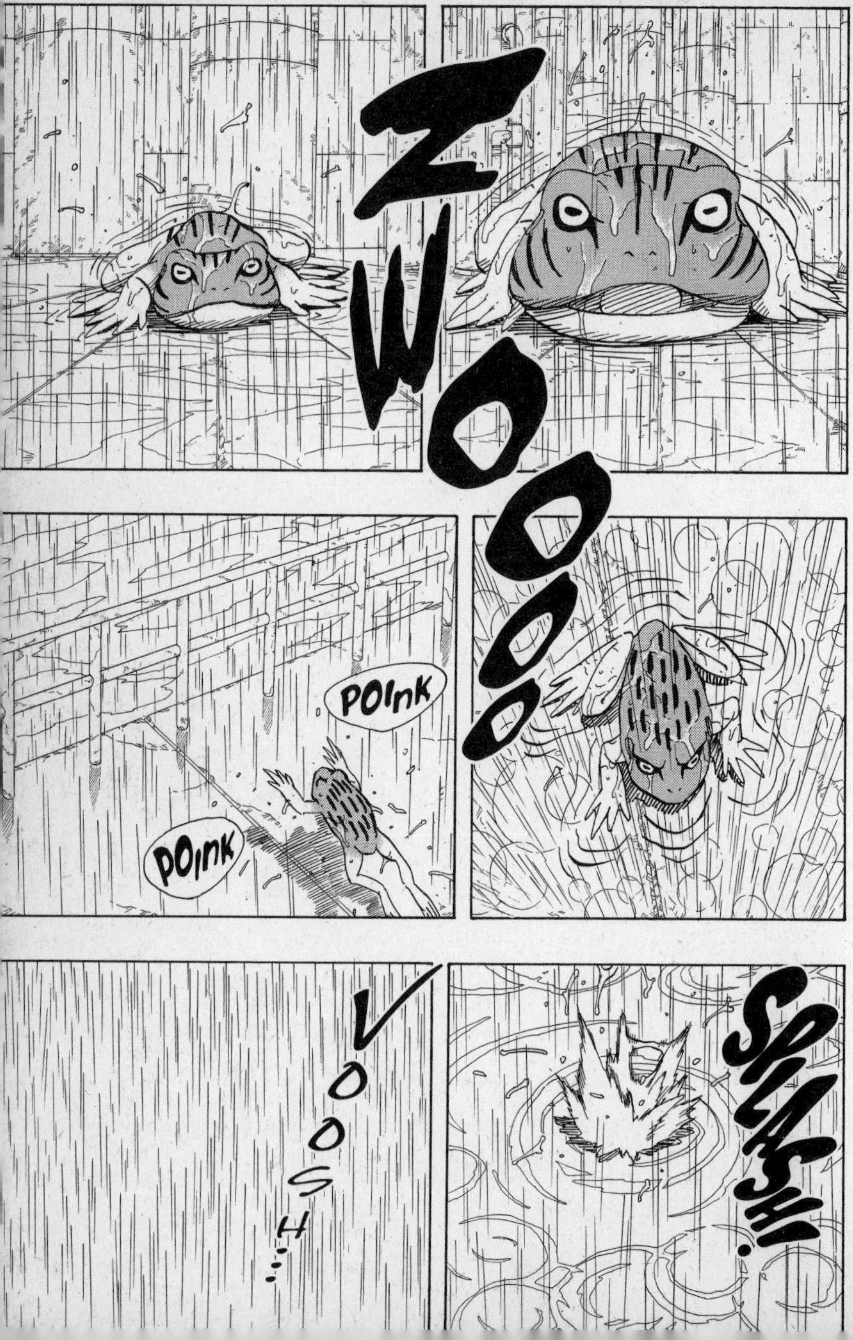

ZWOOOOO
POINK
POINK
SPLASH!
VOOSH...

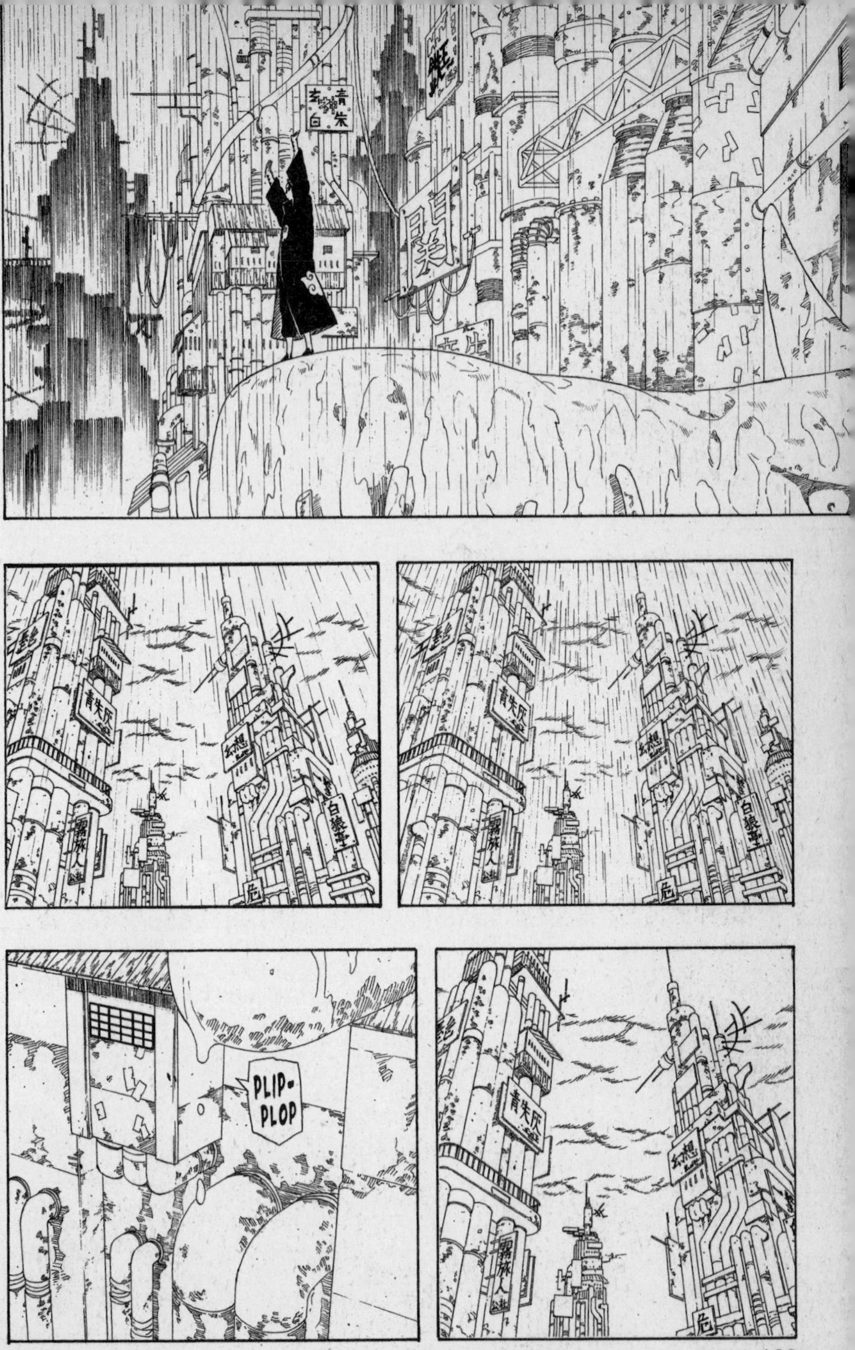
PLIP-PLOP

READ THIS WAY

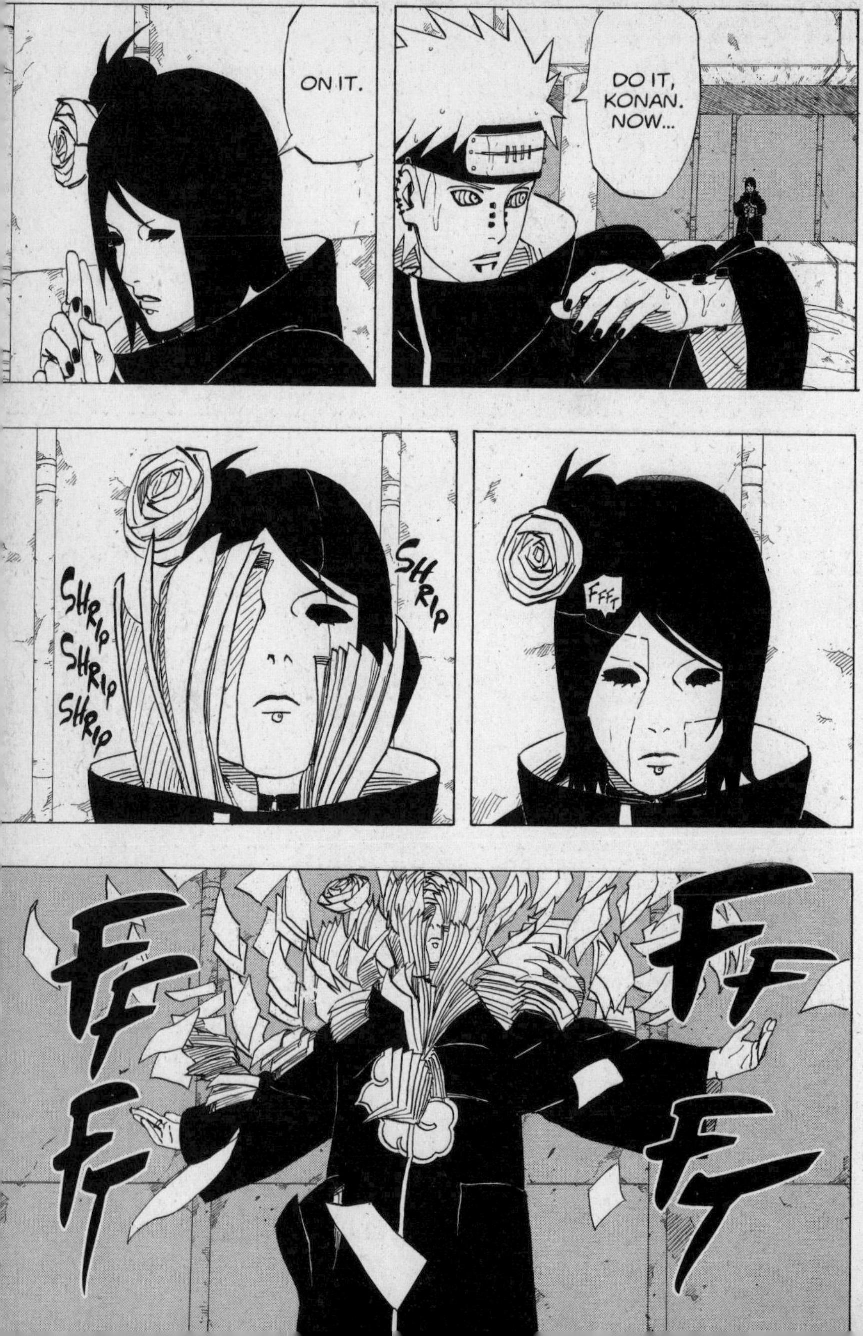
DO IT, KONAN. NOW...
ON IT.
FFFT
SHRIP
SHRIP
SHRIP
SHRIP
FFFT
FFFFT

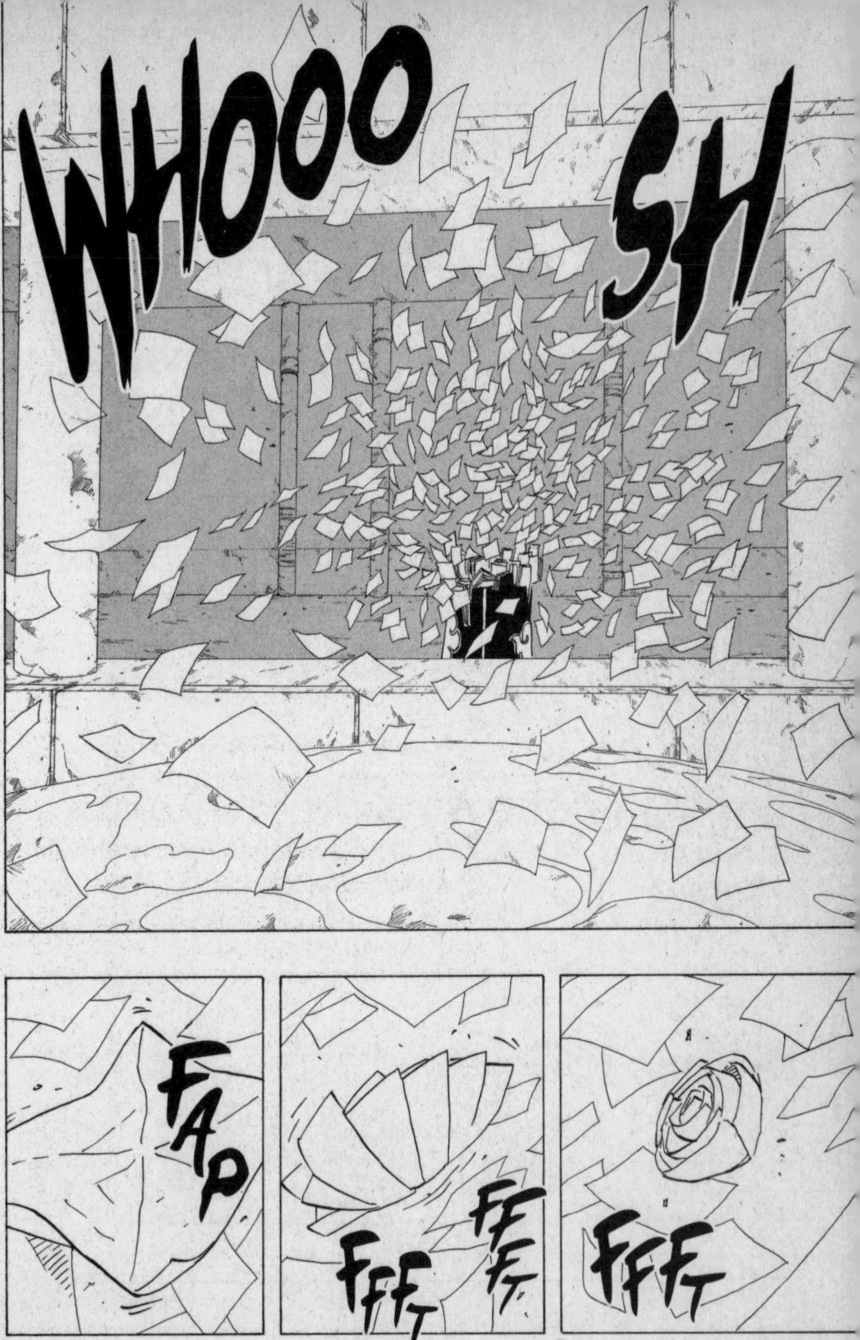
WHOOOSH
FFFT
FFFT
FFFT
FAP

READ THIS WAY

FFFT
FFFT
FFFT
FFFT

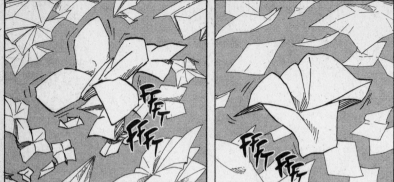

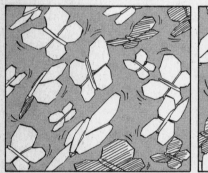

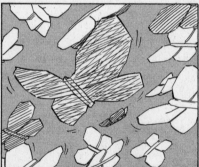

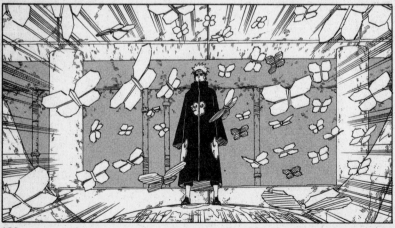

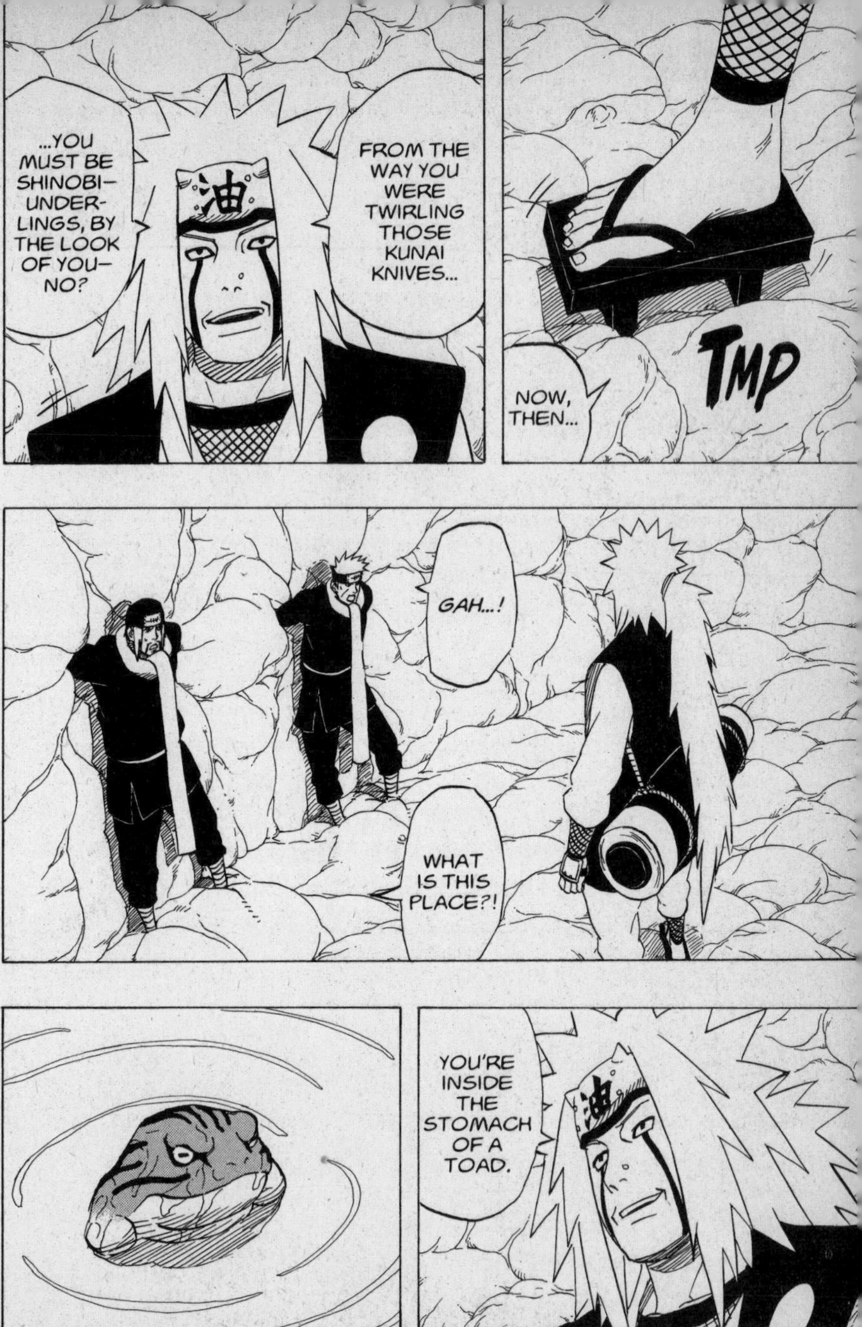
TMP
NOW, THEN...
FROM THE WAY YOU WERE TWIRLING THOSE KUNAI KNIVES...
...YOU MUST BE SHINOBI-UNDERLINGS, BY THE LOOK OF YOU—NO?
GAH...!
WHAT IS THIS PLACE?!
YOU'RE INSIDE THE STOMACH OF A TOAD.

READ THIS WAY

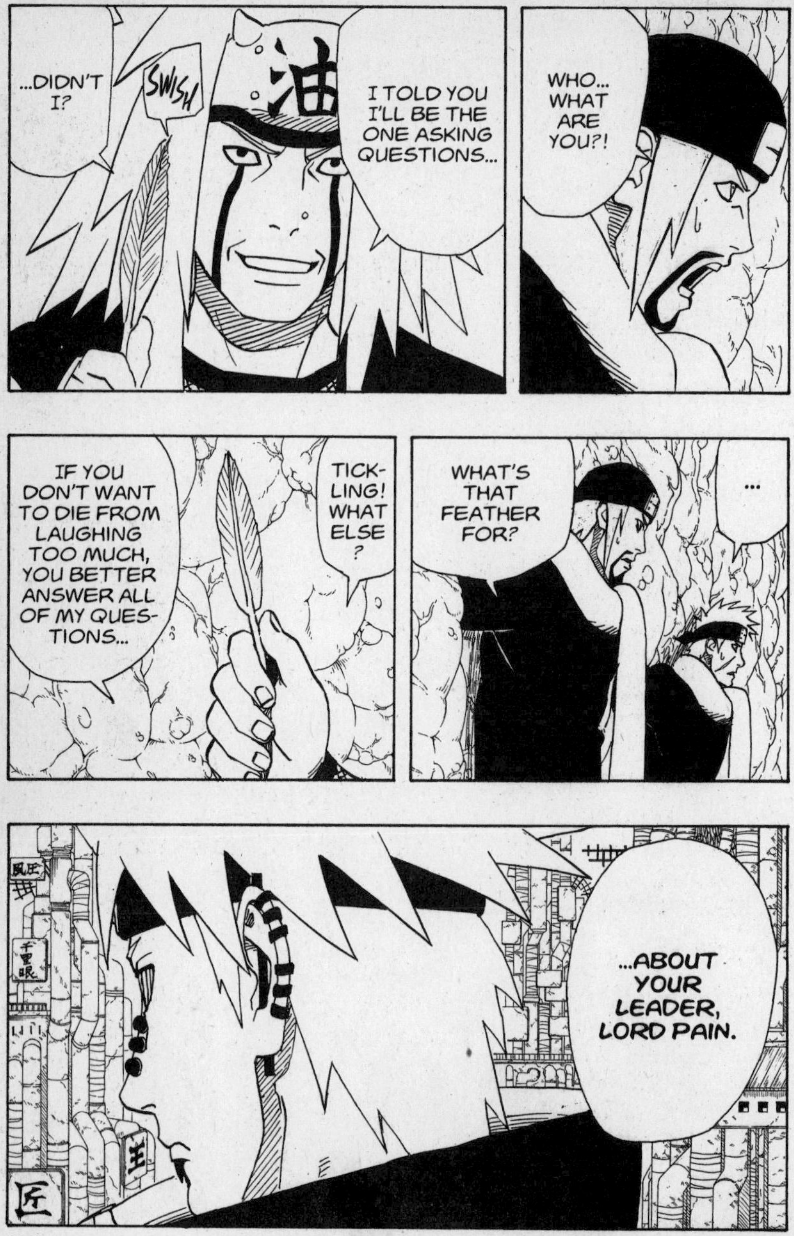
WHO... WHAT ARE YOU?!
I TOLD YOU I'LL BE THE ONE ASKING QUESTIONS...
SWISH
...DIDN'T I?
...
WHAT'S THAT FEATHER FOR?
TICK-LING! WHAT ELSE?
IF YOU DON'T WANT TO DIE FROM LAUGHING TOO MUCH, YOU BETTER ANSWER ALL OF MY QUES-TIONS...
...ABOUT YOUR LEADER, LORD PAIN.

NARUTO

Number 369: Regarding Pain

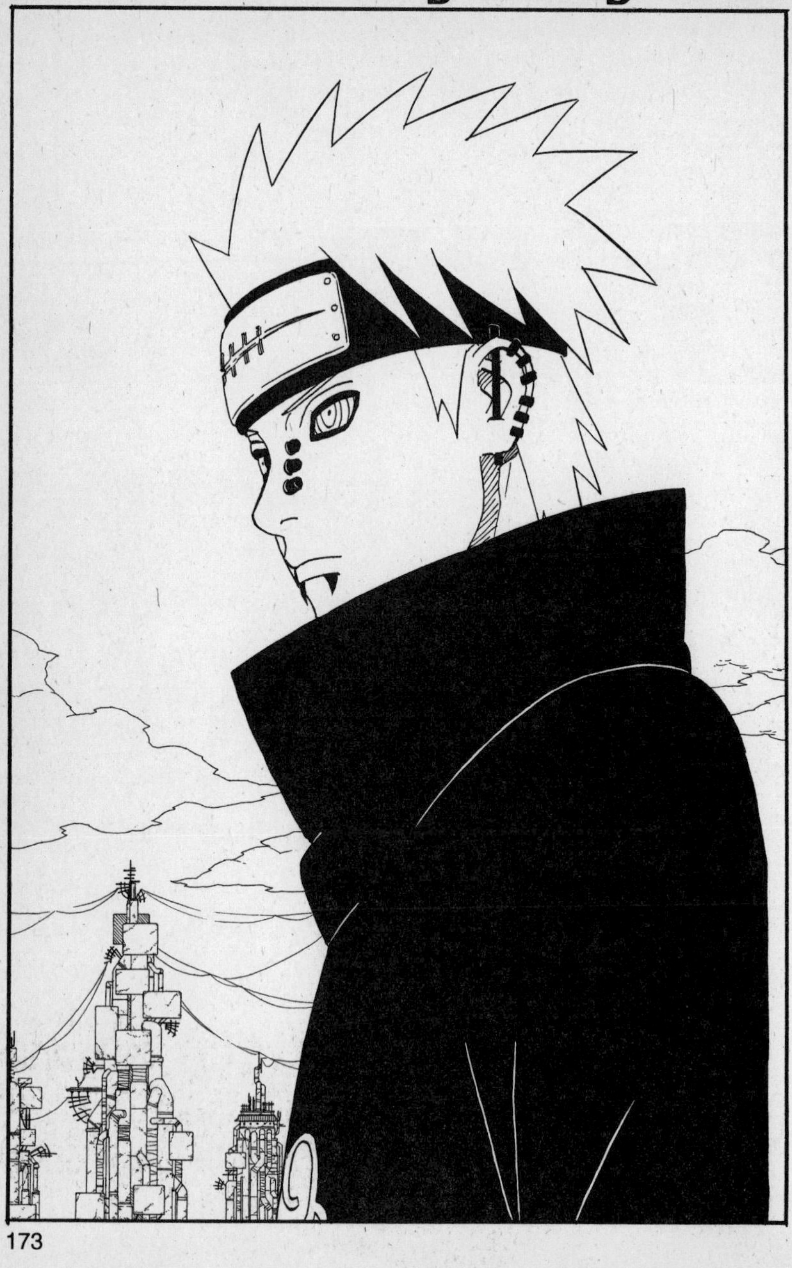

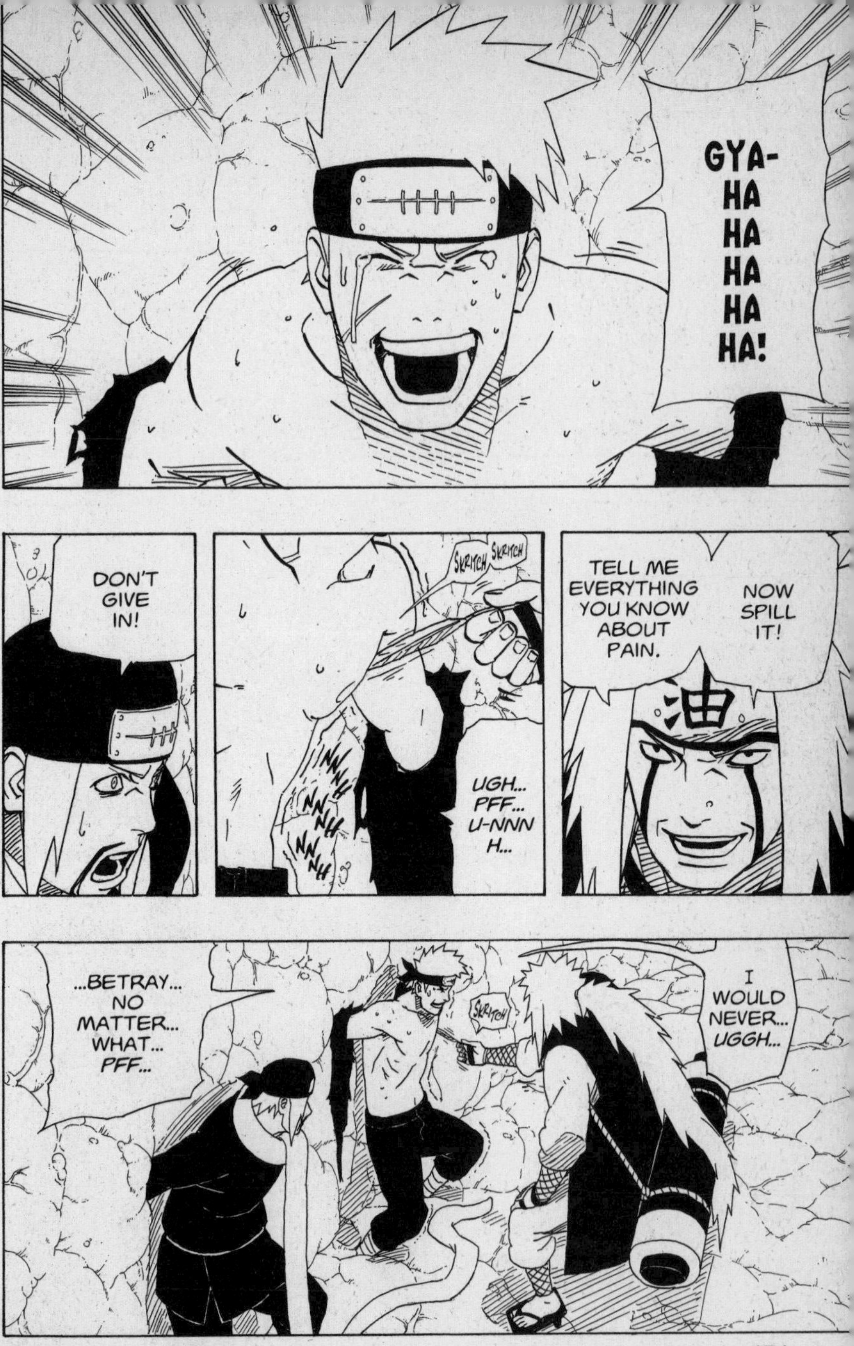
GYA-HA HA HA HA HA!
NOW SPILL IT!
TELL ME EVERYTHING YOU KNOW ABOUT PAIN.
SKRITCH
SKRITCH
UGH... PFF... U-NNNH...
DON'T GIVE IN!
I WOULD NEVER... UGGH...
SKRITCH
...BETRAY... NO MATTER... WHAT... PFF...

READ THIS WAY

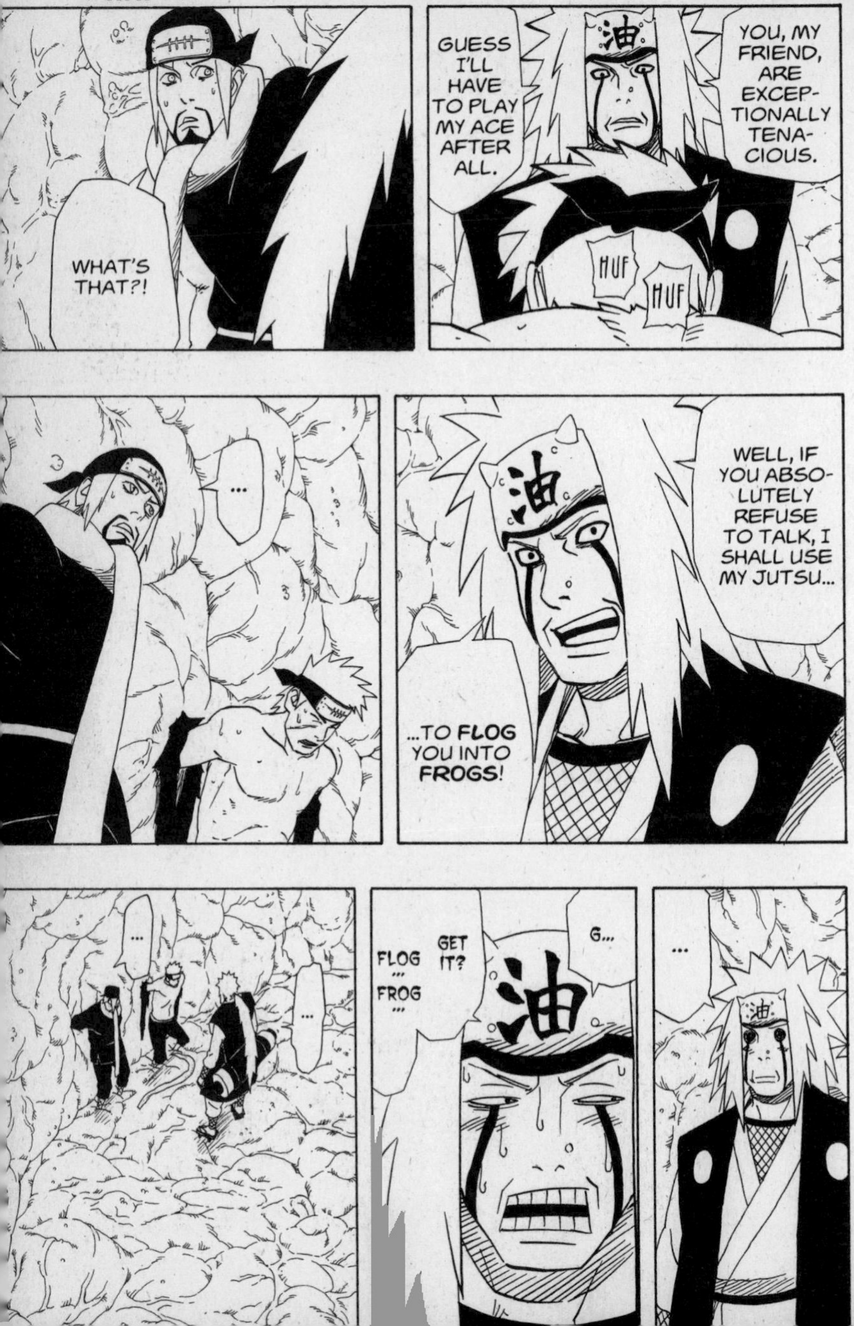

YOU, MY FRIEND, ARE EXCEPTIONALLY TENACIOUS.
GUESS I'LL HAVE TO PLAY MY ACE AFTER ALL.
HUF
HUF
WHAT'S THAT?!
WELL, IF YOU ABSOLUTELY REFUSE TO TALK, I SHALL USE MY JUTSU...
...TO FLOG YOU INTO FROGS!
...
...
G...
GET IT?
FLOG... FROG...
...
...

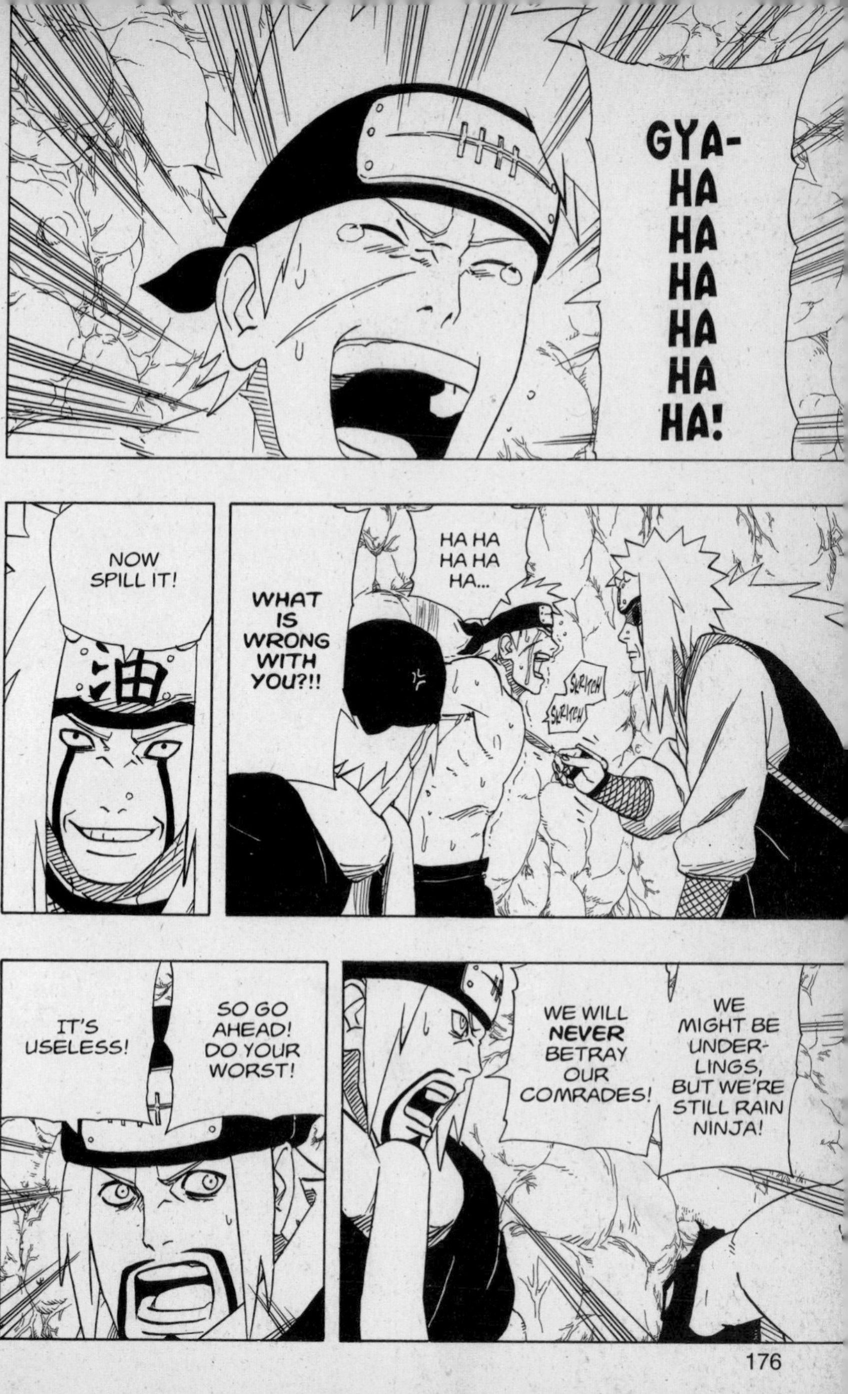
GYA-HA HA HA HA HA HA!
HA HA HA HA HA...
WHAT IS WRONG WITH YOU?!!
SKRITCH
SKRITCH
NOW SPILL IT!
WE MIGHT BE UNDER-LINGS, BUT WE'RE STILL RAIN NINJA!
WE WILL **NEVER** BETRAY OUR COMRADES!
SO GO AHEAD! DO YOUR WORST!
IT'S USELESS!

READ THIS WAY

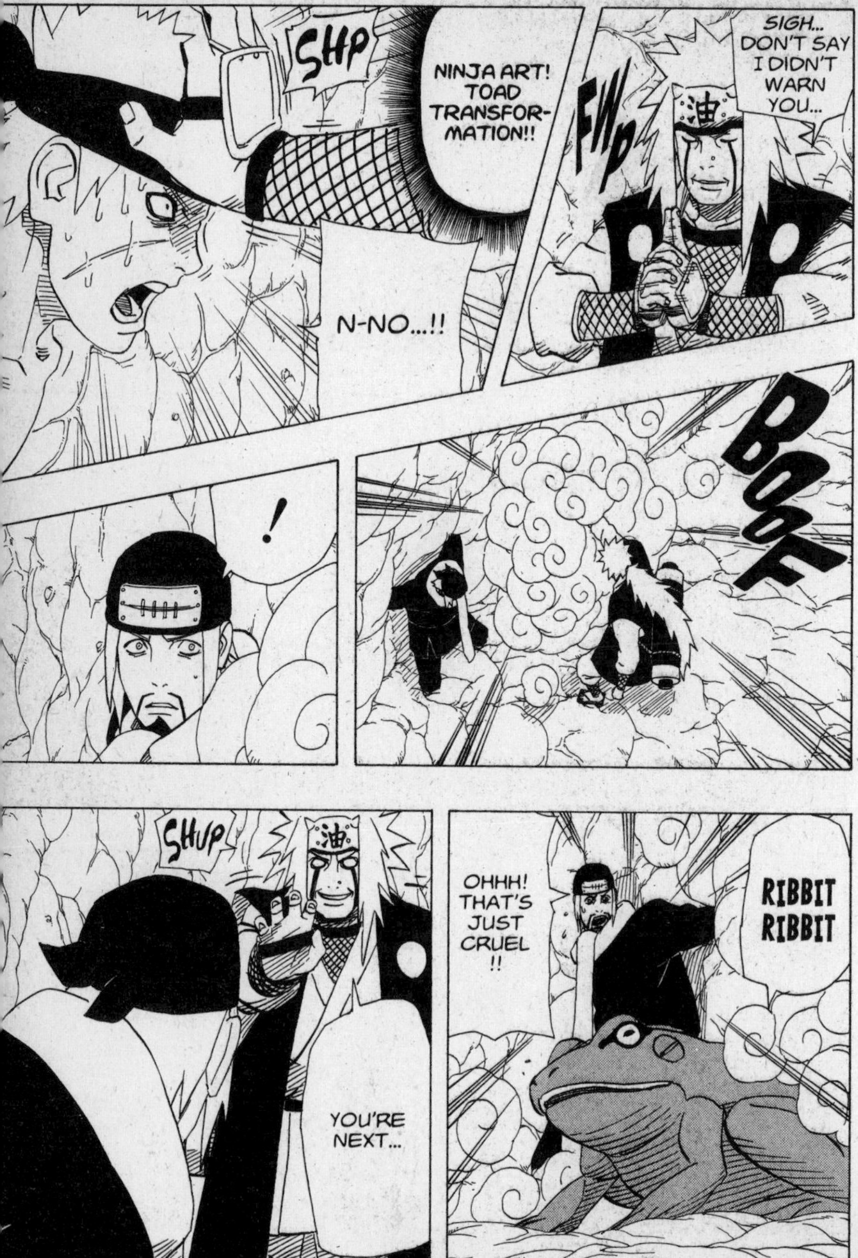
SIGH... DON'T SAY I DIDN'T WARN YOU...
FWP
SHP
NINJA ART! TOAD TRANSFORMATION!!
N-NO...!!
BOOF
!
RIBBIT RIBBIT
OHHH! THAT'S JUST CRUEL !!
SHUP
YOU'RE NEXT...

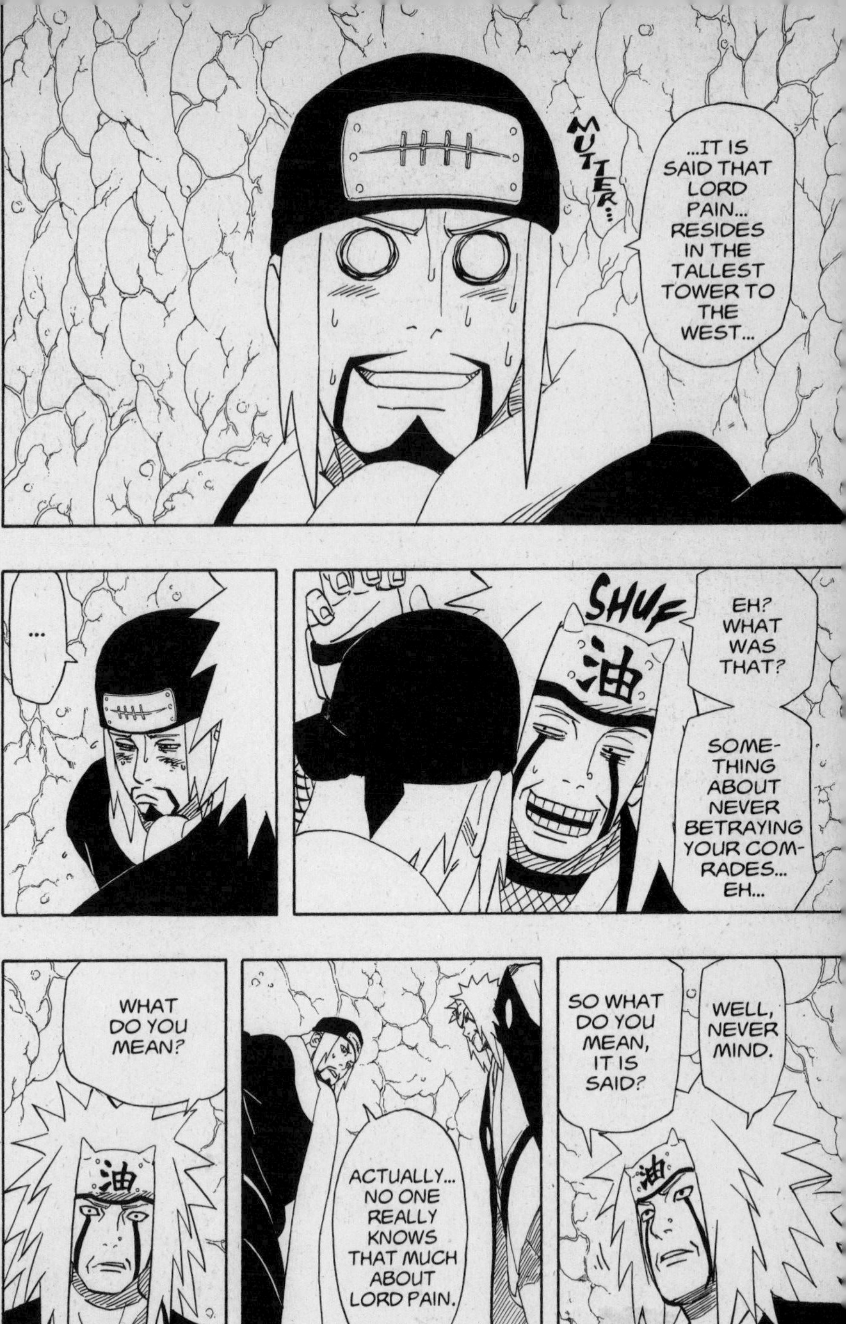
MUTTER...
...IT IS SAID THAT LORD PAIN... RESIDES IN THE TALLEST TOWER TO THE WEST...
SHUF
EH? WHAT WAS THAT?
SOMETHING ABOUT NEVER BETRAYING YOUR COMRADES... EH...
...
WELL, NEVER MIND.
SO WHAT DO YOU MEAN, IT IS SAID?
ACTUALLY... NO ONE REALLY KNOWS THAT MUCH ABOUT LORD PAIN.
WHAT DO YOU MEAN?

READ THIS WAY

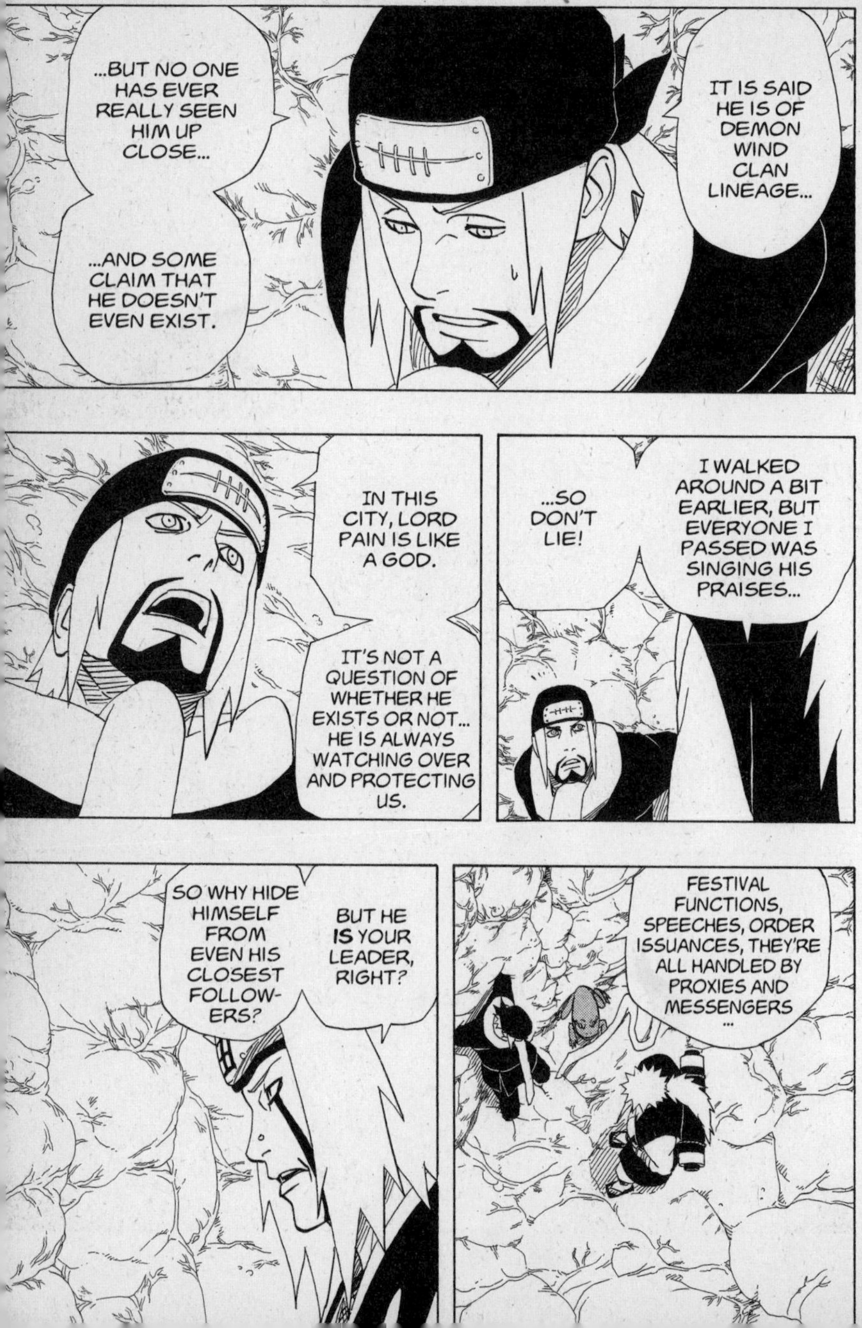

IT IS SAID HE IS OF DEMON WIND CLAN LINEAGE...
...BUT NO ONE HAS EVER REALLY SEEN HIM UP CLOSE...
...AND SOME CLAIM THAT HE DOESN'T EVEN EXIST.
I WALKED AROUND A BIT EARLIER, BUT EVERYONE I PASSED WAS SINGING HIS PRAISES...
...SO DON'T LIE!
IN THIS CITY, LORD PAIN IS LIKE A GOD.
IT'S NOT A QUESTION OF WHETHER HE EXISTS OR NOT... HE IS ALWAYS WATCHING OVER AND PROTECTING US.
FESTIVAL FUNCTIONS, SPEECHES, ORDER ISSUANCES, THEY'RE ALL HANDLED BY PROXIES AND MESSENGERS...
BUT HE **IS** YOUR LEADER, RIGHT?
SO WHY HIDE HIMSELF FROM EVEN HIS CLOSEST FOLLOW-ERS?

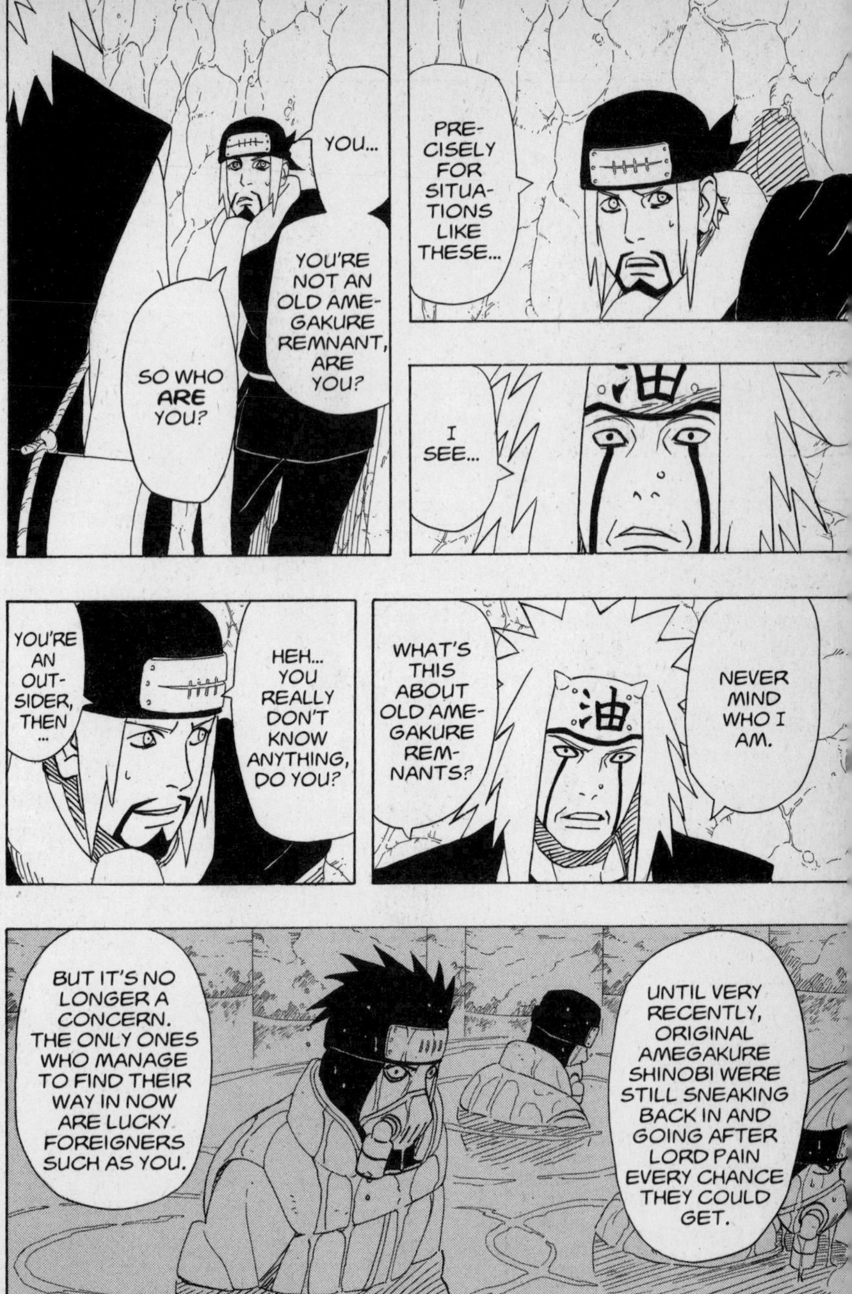
PRECISELY FOR SITUATIONS LIKE THESE...
I SEE...
YOU...
YOU'RE NOT AN OLD AMEGAKURE REMNANT, ARE YOU?
SO WHO ARE YOU?
NEVER MIND WHO I AM.
WHAT'S THIS ABOUT OLD AMEGAKURE REMNANTS?
HEH... YOU REALLY DON'T KNOW ANYTHING, DO YOU?
YOU'RE AN OUTSIDER, THEN...
UNTIL VERY RECENTLY, ORIGINAL AMEGAKURE SHINOBI WERE STILL SNEAKING BACK IN AND GOING AFTER LORD PAIN EVERY CHANCE THEY COULD GET.
BUT IT'S NO LONGER A CONCERN. THE ONLY ONES WHO MANAGE TO FIND THEIR WAY IN NOW ARE LUCKY FOREIGNERS SUCH AS YOU.

READ THIS WAY

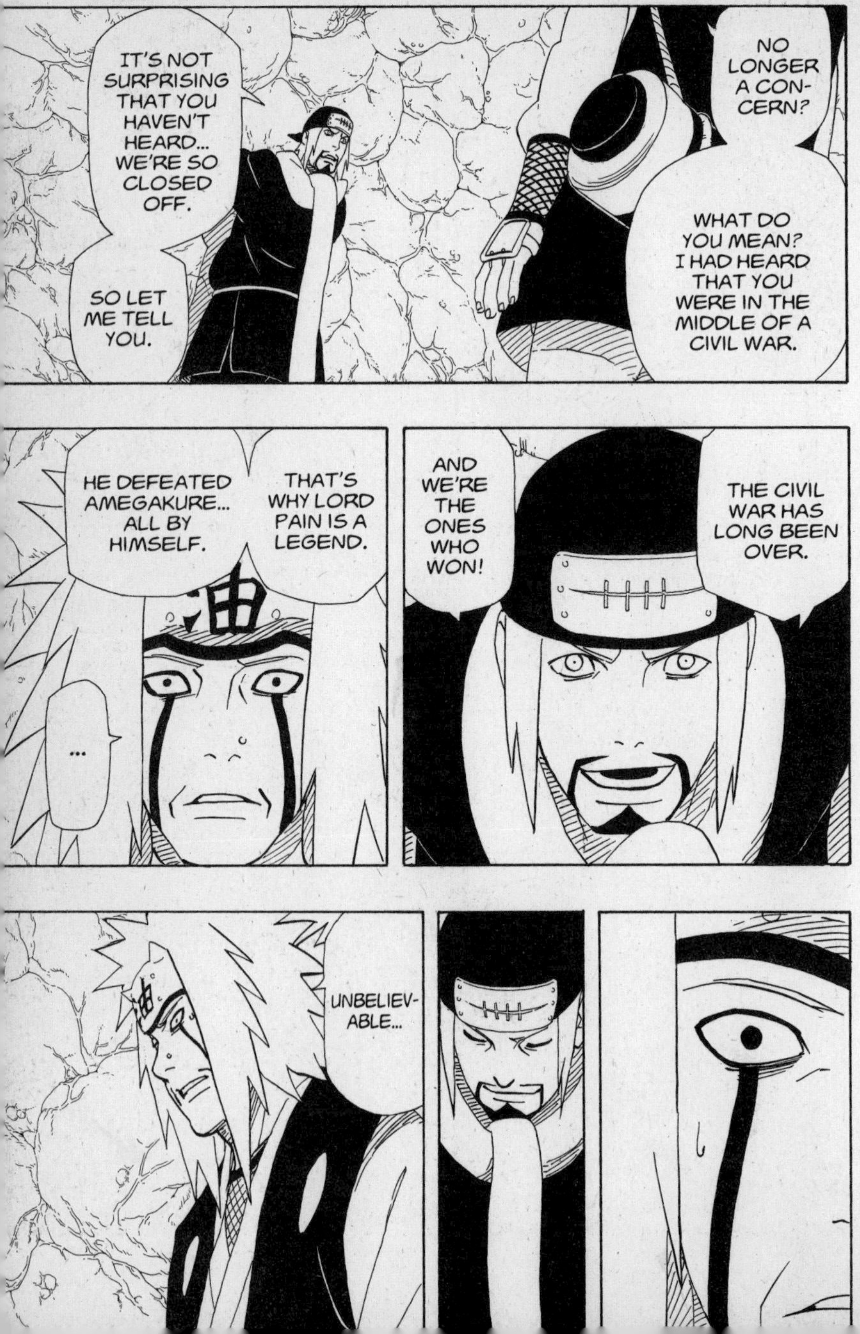

NO LONGER A CONCERN?
WHAT DO YOU MEAN? I HAD HEARD THAT YOU WERE IN THE MIDDLE OF A CIVIL WAR.
IT'S NOT SURPRISING THAT YOU HAVEN'T HEARD... WE'RE SO CLOSED OFF.
SO LET ME TELL YOU.
THE CIVIL WAR HAS LONG BEEN OVER.
AND WE'RE THE ONES WHO WON!
THAT'S WHY LORD PAIN IS A LEGEND.
HE DEFEATED AMEGAKURE... ALL BY HIMSELF.
...
UNBELIEV-ABLE...

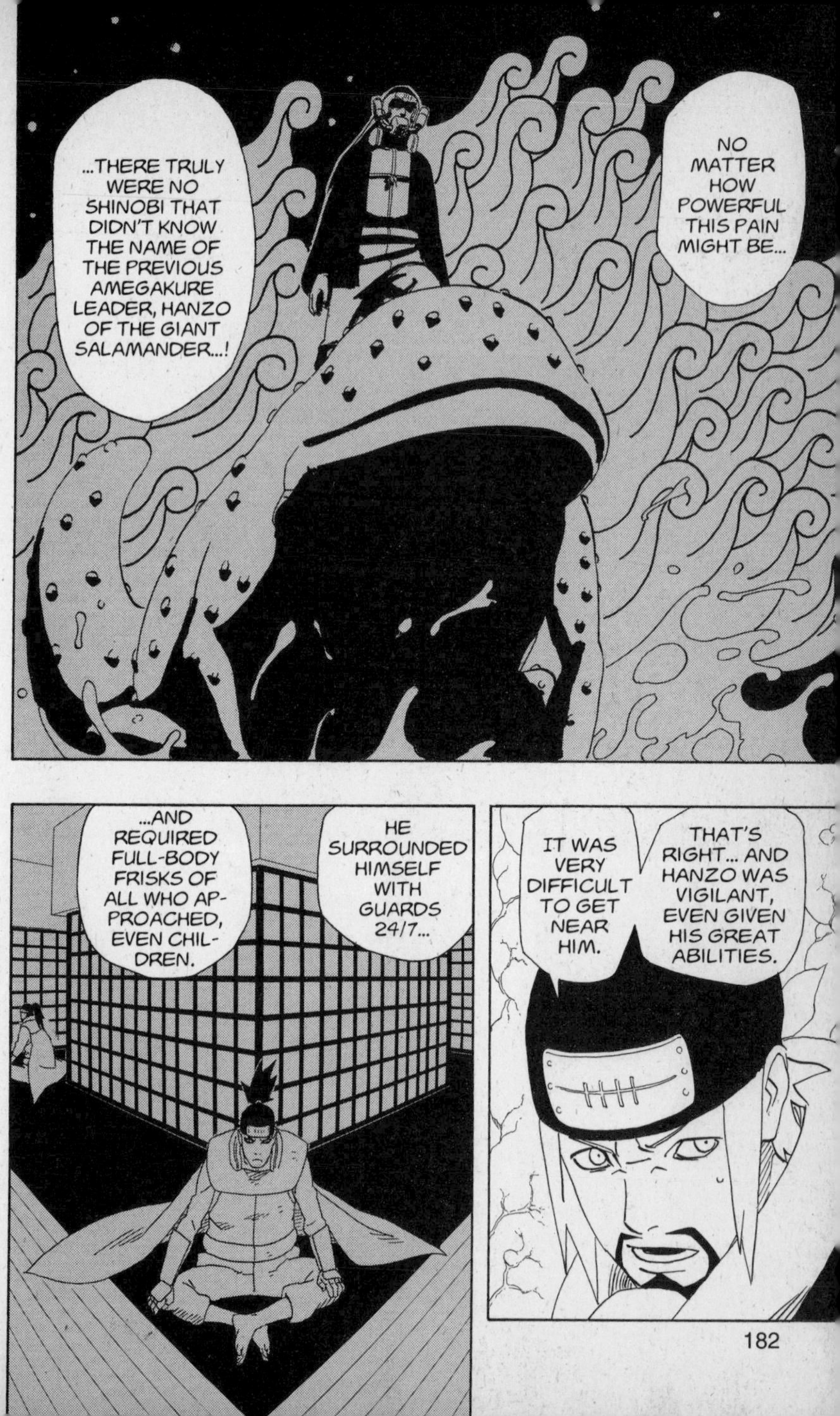
NO MATTER HOW POWERFUL THIS PAIN MIGHT BE...
...THERE TRULY WERE NO SHINOBI THAT DIDN'T KNOW THE NAME OF THE PREVIOUS AMEGAKURE LEADER, HANZO OF THE GIANT SALAMANDER...!
THAT'S RIGHT... AND HANZO WAS VIGILANT, EVEN GIVEN HIS GREAT ABILITIES.
IT WAS VERY DIFFICULT TO GET NEAR HIM.
HE SURROUNDED HIMSELF WITH GUARDS 24/7...
...AND REQUIRED FULL-BODY FRISKS OF ALL WHO APPROACHED, EVEN CHILDREN.

READ THIS WAY

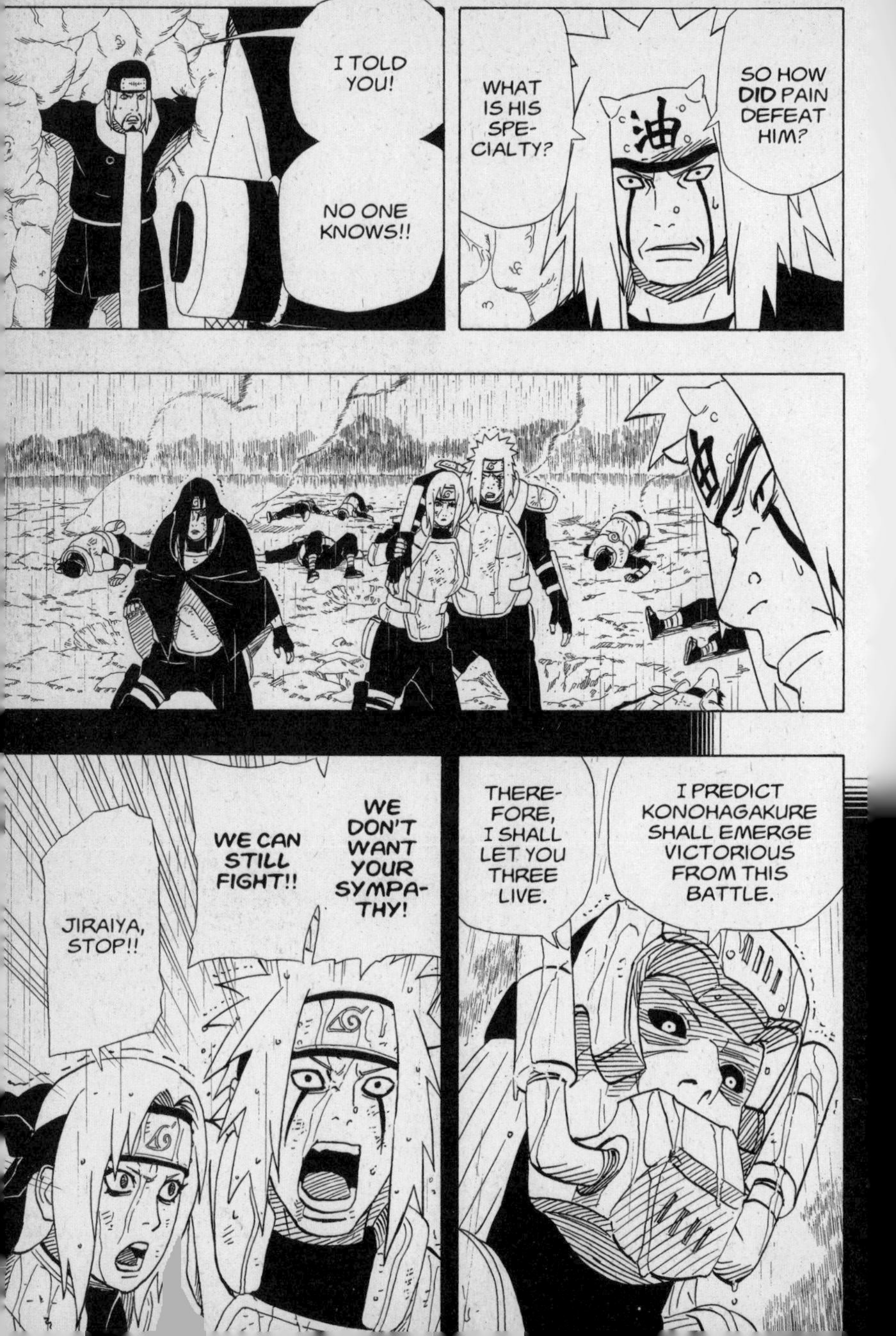

SO HOW DID PAIN DEFEAT HIM?
WHAT IS HIS SPE-CIALTY?
I TOLD YOU!
NO ONE KNOWS!!
I PREDICT KONOHAGAKURE SHALL EMERGE VICTORIOUS FROM THIS BATTLE.
THERE-FORE, I SHALL LET YOU THREE LIVE.
WE DON'T WANT YOUR SYMPA-THY!
WE CAN STILL FIGHT!!
JIRAIYA, STOP!!

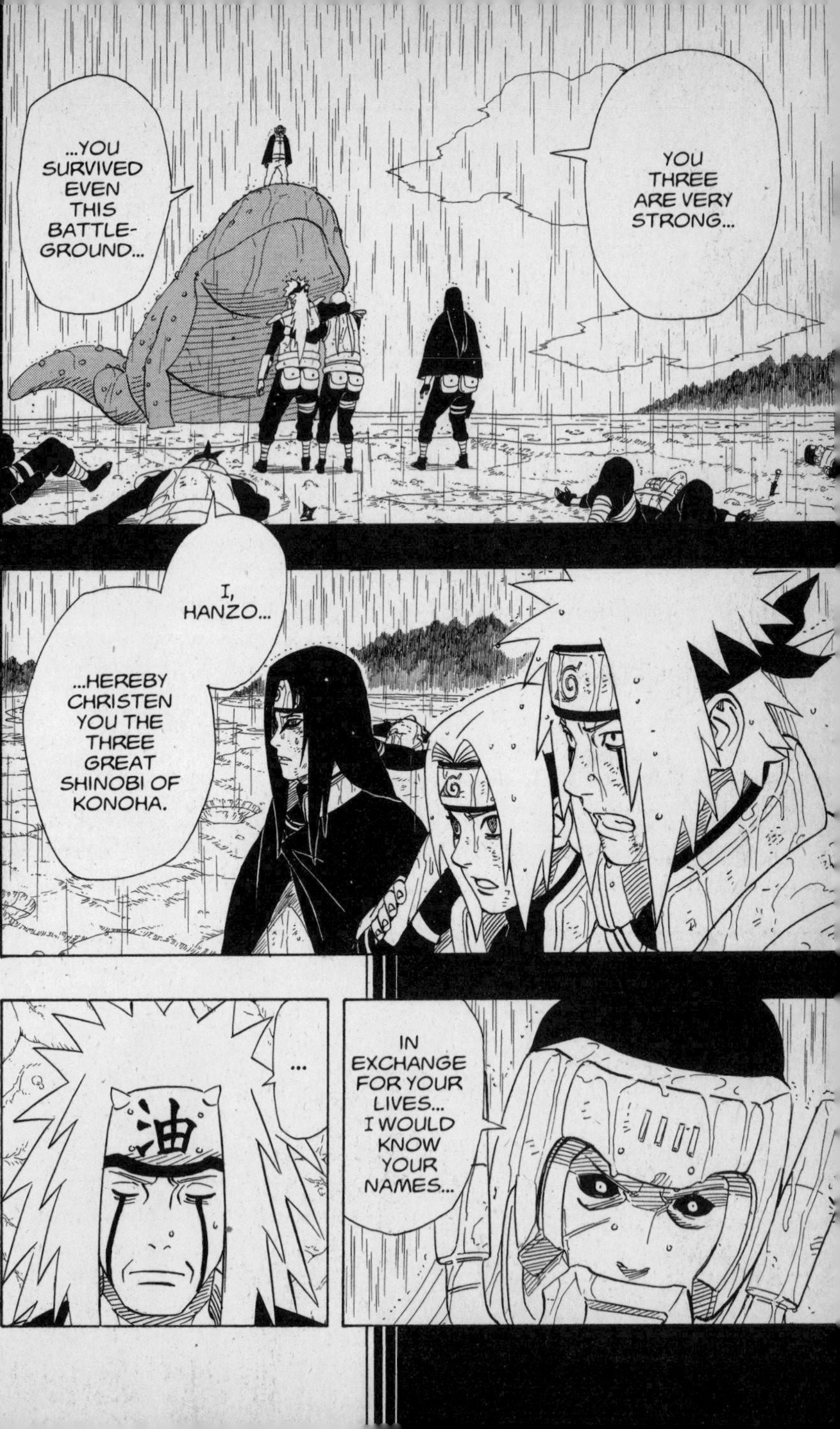
YOU THREE ARE VERY STRONG...
...YOU SURVIVED EVEN THIS BATTLE-GROUND...
I, HANZO...
...HEREBY CHRISTEN YOU THE THREE GREAT SHINOBI OF KONOHA.
IN EXCHANGE FOR YOUR LIVES... I WOULD KNOW YOUR NAMES...
...
油

READ THIS WAY

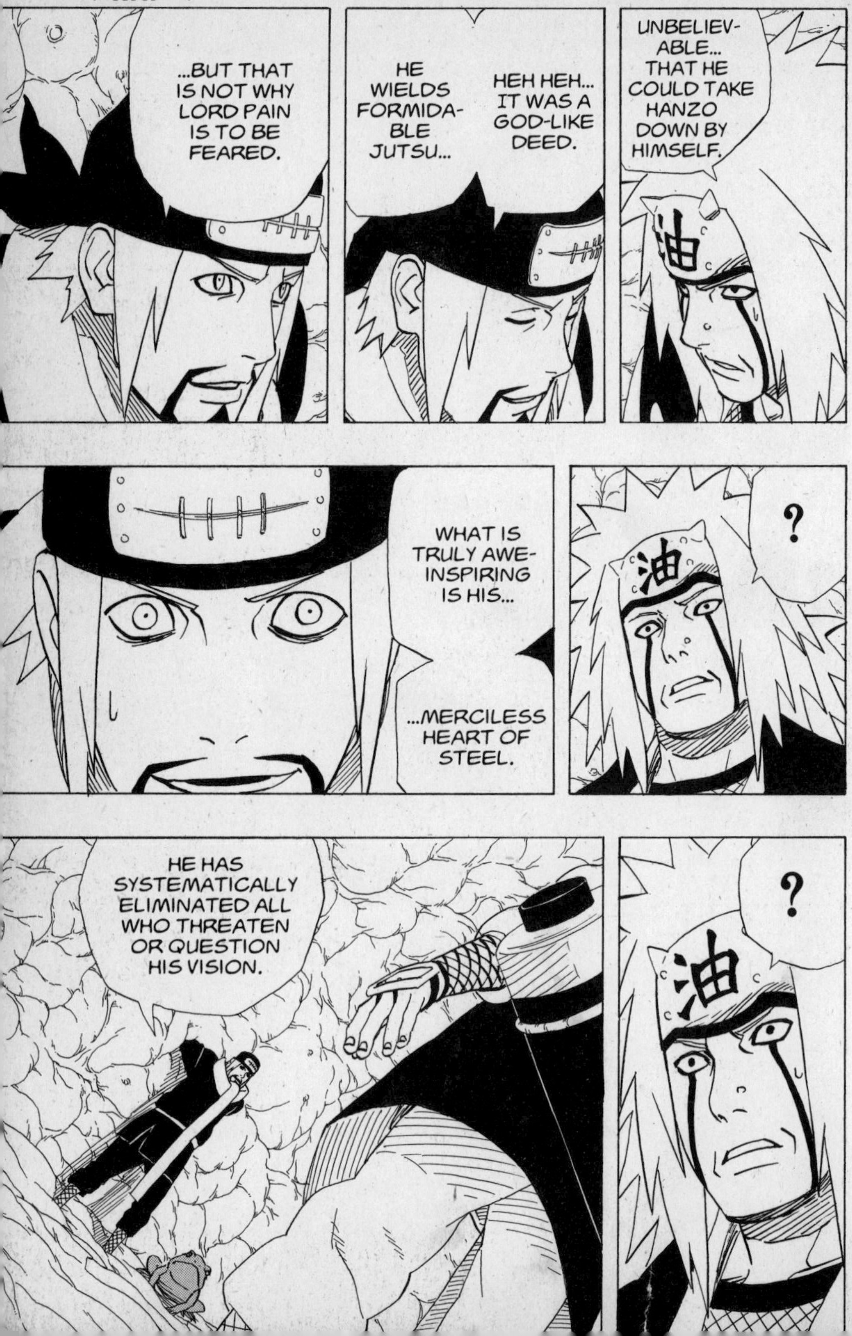
UNBELIEVABLE... THAT HE COULD TAKE HANZO DOWN BY HIMSELF.
HEH HEH... IT WAS A GOD-LIKE DEED.
HE WIELDS FORMIDABLE JUTSU...
...BUT THAT IS NOT WHY LORD PAIN IS TO BE FEARED.
?
WHAT IS TRULY AWE-INSPIRING IS HIS...
...MERCILESS HEART OF STEEL.
?
HE HAS SYSTEMATICALLY ELIMINATED ALL WHO THREATEN OR QUESTION HIS VISION.

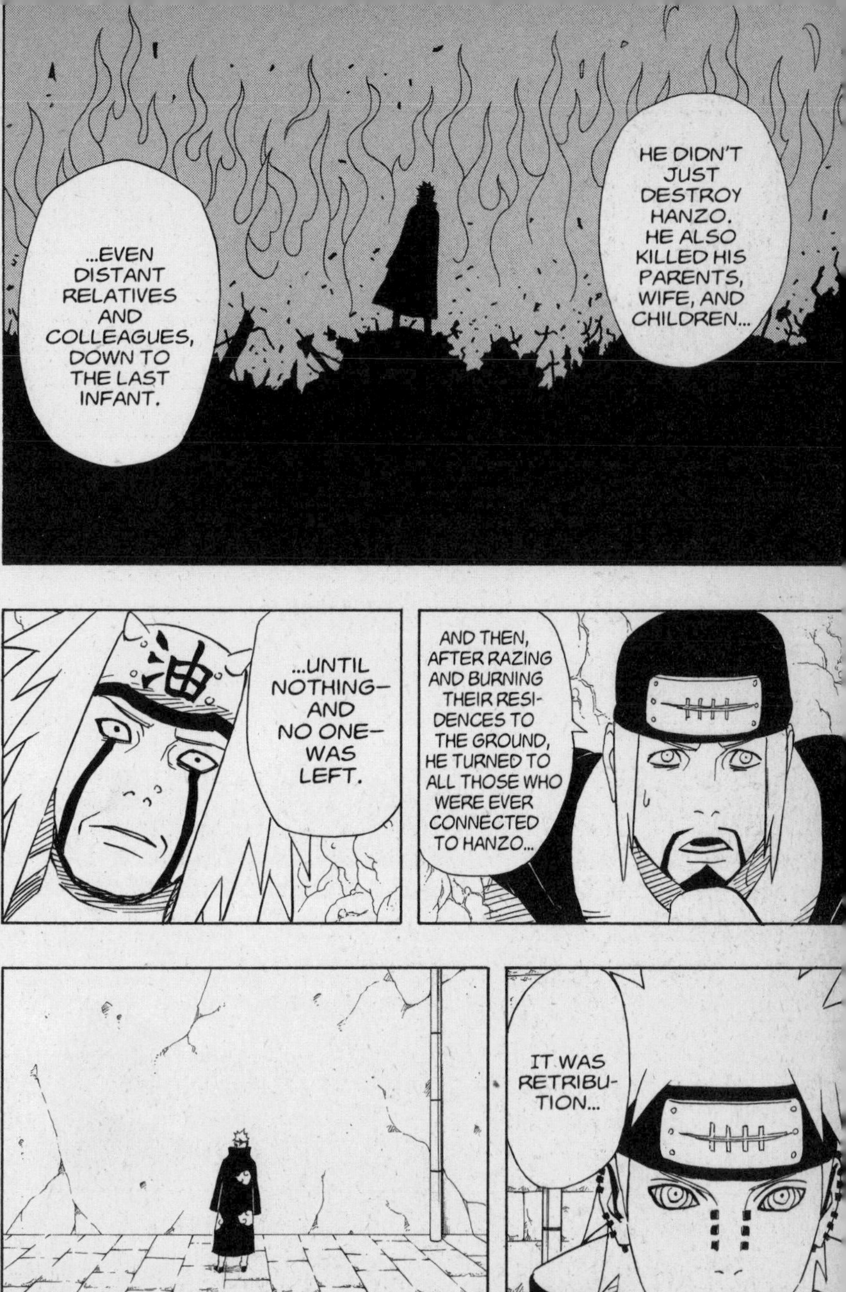
HE DIDN'T JUST DESTROY HANZO. HE ALSO KILLED HIS PARENTS, WIFE, AND CHILDREN...
...EVEN DISTANT RELATIVES AND COLLEAGUES, DOWN TO THE LAST INFANT.
AND THEN, AFTER RAZING AND BURNING THEIR RESI-DENCES TO THE GROUND, HE TURNED TO ALL THOSE WHO WERE EVER CONNECTED TO HANZO...
...UNTIL NOTHING—AND NO ONE—WAS LEFT.
IT WAS RETRIBU-TION...

READ THIS WAY

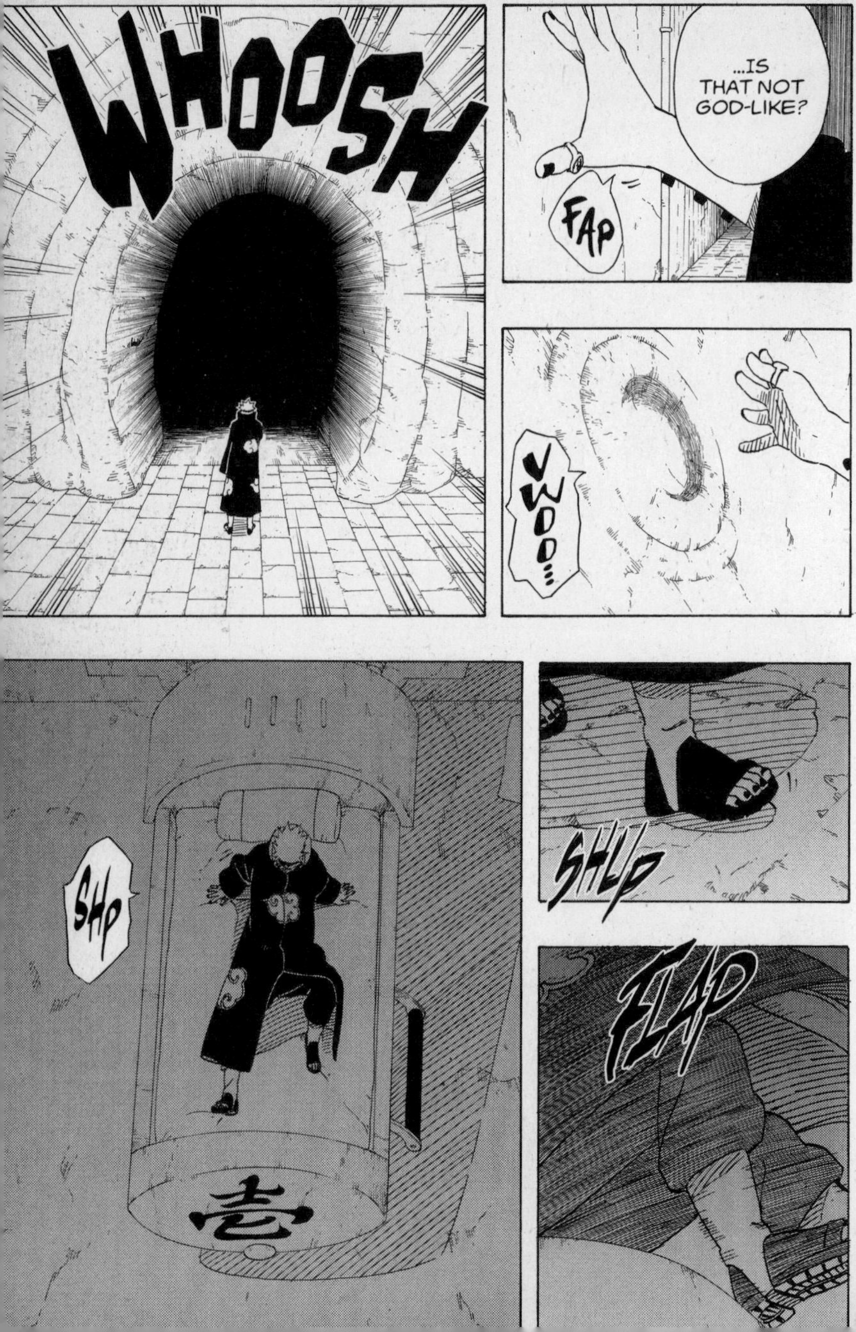

...IS THAT NOT GOD-LIKE?
FAP
VWOO...
WHOOSH
SHLIP
FLAP
SHP

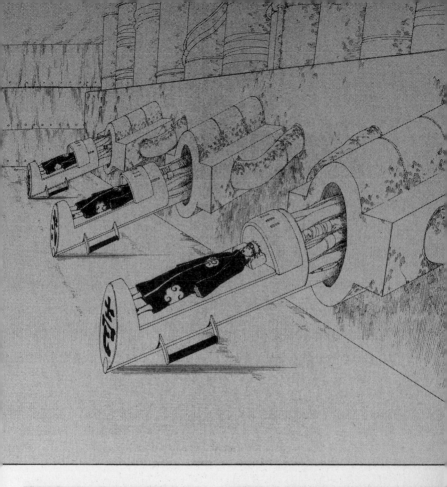

188

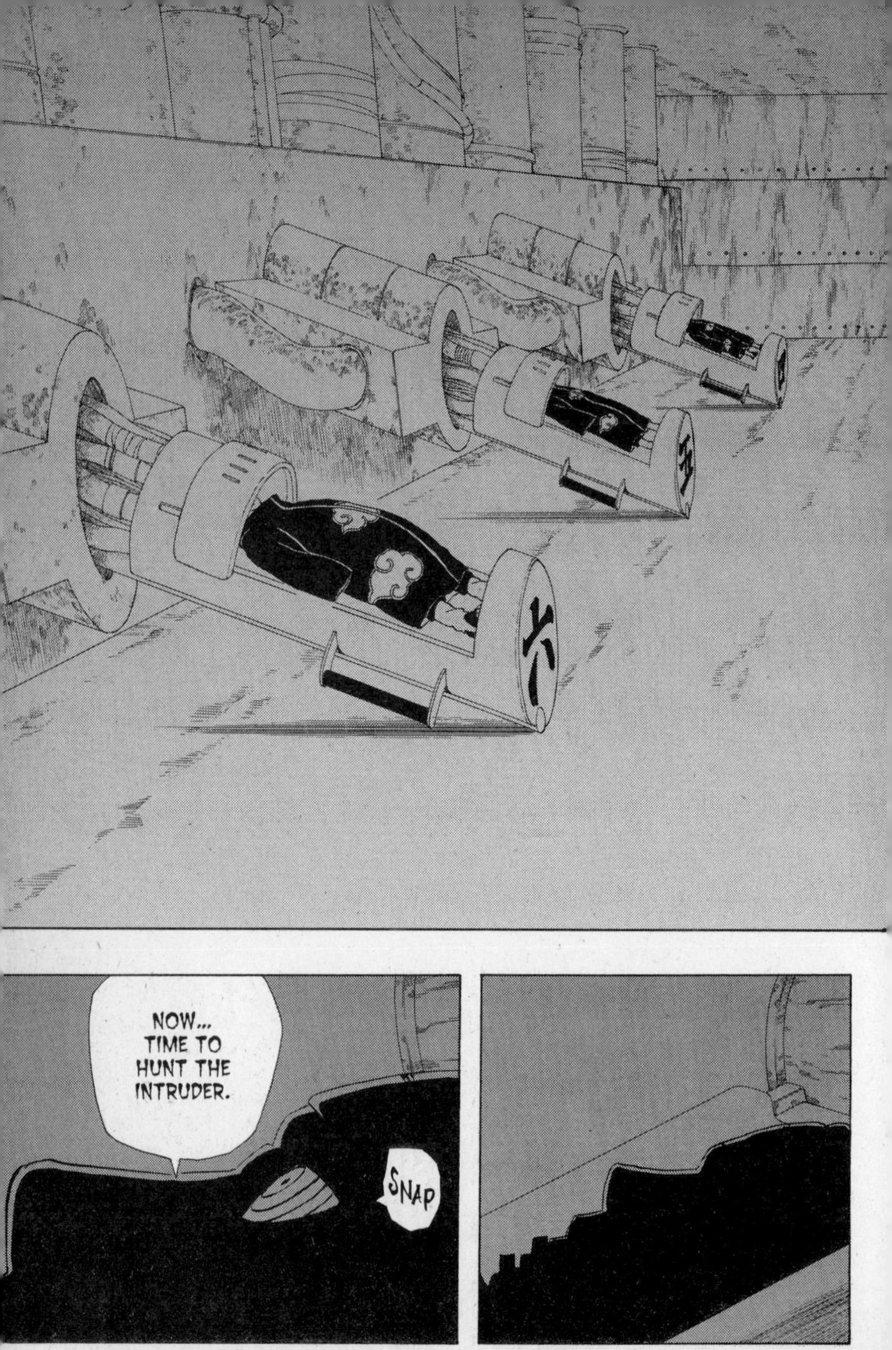
NOW... TIME TO HUNT THE INTRUDER.
SNAP

 TO BE CONTINUED IN *NARUTO* VOLUME 41!

IN THE NEXT VOLUME...

JIRAIYA'S DECISION

Mysteries from Jiraiya's past rise up to confront the Toad Sage.
Could something that the Three Great Shinobi of Konoha legend
did in their youth have deadly consequences now? Find out as
Jiraiya's investigation into the secrets of Pain and the Akatsuki
organization bears shocking fruit!

AVAILABLE NOW!

RELISH MASASHI KISHIMOTO'S ARTWORK IN ALL ITS COLORFUL GLORY

only $19.99

The Art of
NARUTO

Complete your *NARUTO* collection with the hardcover art book, *The Art of NARUTO: Uzumaki*, featuring:

• Over 100 pages of full-color *NARUTO* manga images
• Step-by-step details on creating a *NARUTO* illustration
• Notes about each image
• An extensive interview with creator Masashi Kishimoto

Plus, a beautiful double-sided poster!

UZUMAKI
The Art of
NARUTO

ART OF *SHONEN JUMP*

SHONEN JUMP
THE WORLD'S MOST POPULAR MANGA

ON SALE AT:
www.shonenjump.com
Also available at your local bookstore and comic store.

RATED
T
FOR
TEEN
ratings.viz.com

www.viz.com

SEE INTO THE SOUL
OF *BLEACH*
WITH THE MANGA, PROFILES, AND ART BOOKS

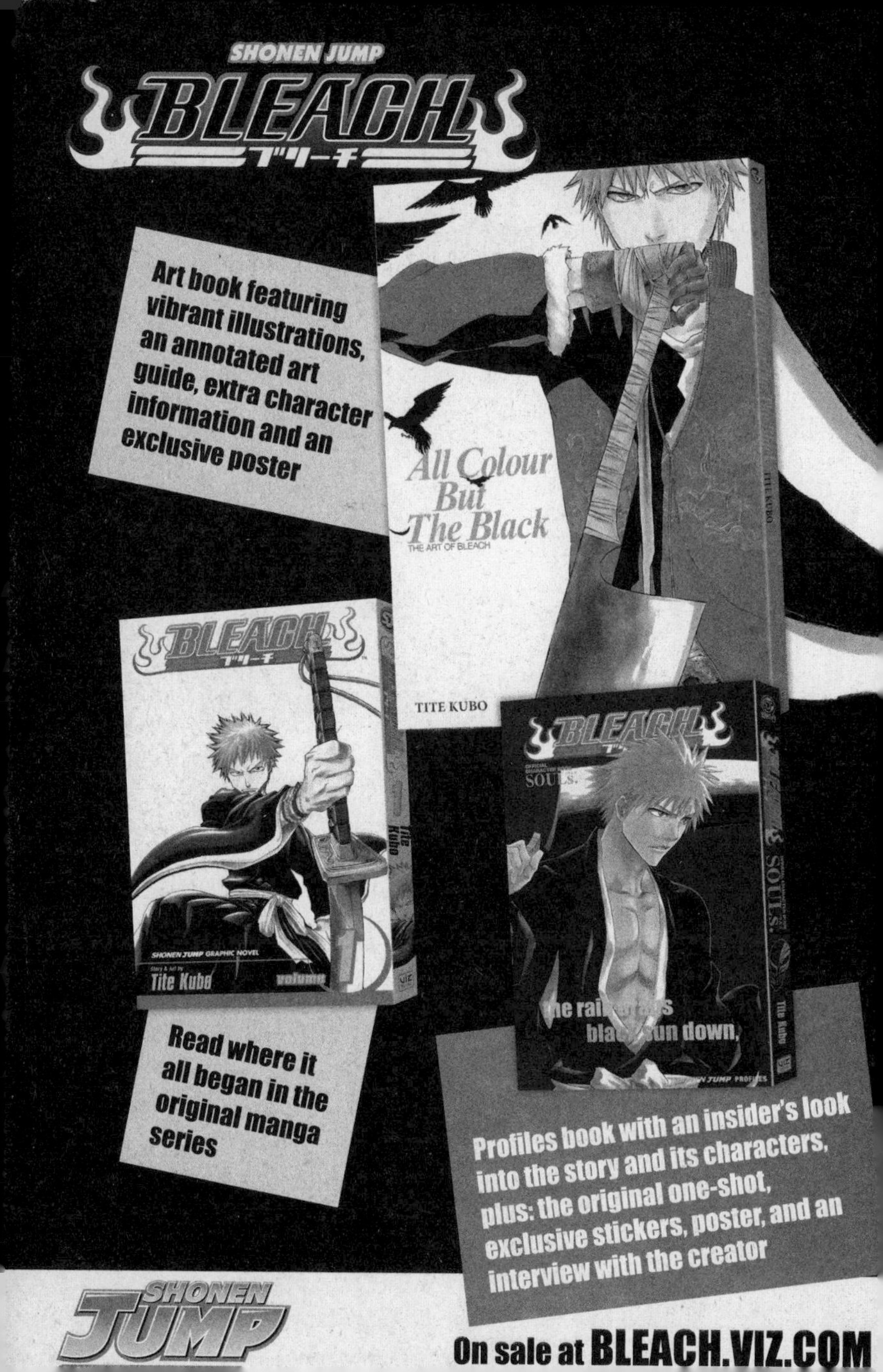
SHONEN JUMP
BLEACH
ブリーチ
Art book featuring vibrant illustrations, an annotated art guide, extra character information and an exclusive poster
All Colour But The Black
THE ART OF BLEACH
TITE KUBO
TITE KUBO
BLEACH
ブリーチ
SHONEN JUMP GRAPHIC NOVEL
Story & Art by
Tite Kubo
volume
Tite Kubo
VIZ
BLEACH
SOULS.
SOULS.
Tite Kubo
Read where it all began in the original manga series
Profiles book with an insider's look into the story and its characters, plus: the original one-shot, exclusive stickers, poster, and an interview with the creator
SHONEN JUMP
On sale at BLEACH.VIZ.COM

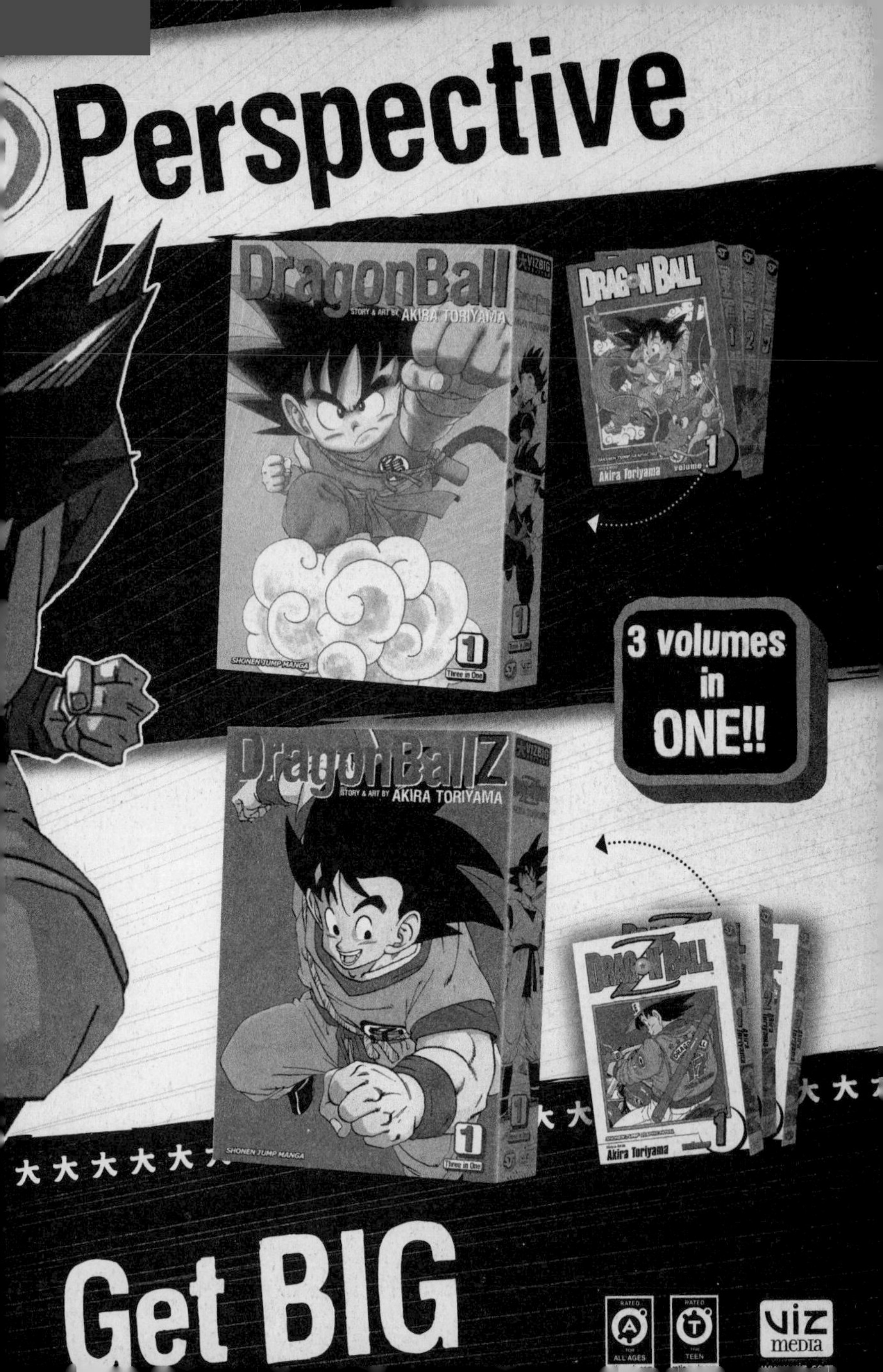

Perspective
DragonBall
STORY & ART BY AKIRA TORIYAMA
SHONEN JUMP MANGA
1
Three in One
DRAGON BALL
Akira Toriyama
volume 1
3 volumes in ONE!!
DragonBall Z
STORY & ART BY AKIRA TORIYAMA
SHONEN JUMP MANGA
1
Three in One
DRAGON BALL Z
Akira Toriyama
Get BIG
RATED A FOR ALL AGES
RATED T FOR TEEN
viz media